WHITE TIGER

A HERO'S COMPULSION

A HERO'S COMPULSION

Writer: Tamora Pierce & Timothy Liebe
Pencils: Phil Briones with Alvaro Rio &
Ronaldo Adriano Silva (Issue #6)
Inks: Don Hillsman
Colors: Chris Sotomayor
Letters: Virtual Calligraphy's Rus Wooton
Cover Art: David Mack
Editor: Ruwan Jayatilleke
Consulting Editor: Ralph Macchio

Special thanks to Jennifer Lee, Olivier Jalabert, Joe Prado,
Jon Hogan, Kristopher Carpenter, Michael Horowitz & James Chan

Collection Editor: Jennifer Grünwald
Assistant Editors: Cory Levine & Michael Short
Associate Editor: Mark D. Beazley
Senior Editor, Special Projects: Jeff Youngquist
Senior Vice President of Sales: David Gabriel
Production: Jerry Kalinowski
Book Designer: Allison Fisher
Vice President of Creative: Tom Marvelli

Editor in Chief: Joe Quesada
Publisher: Dan Buckley

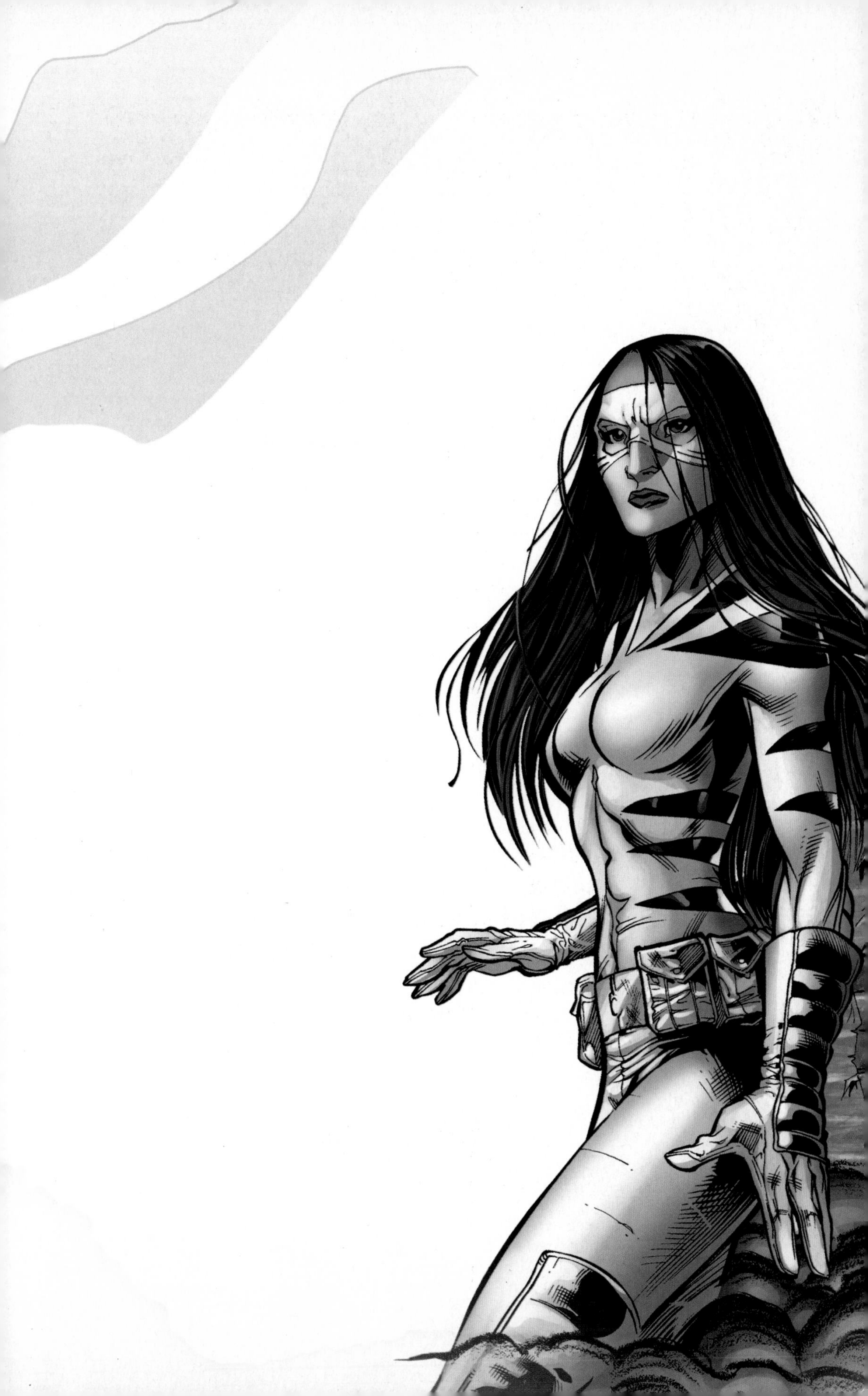

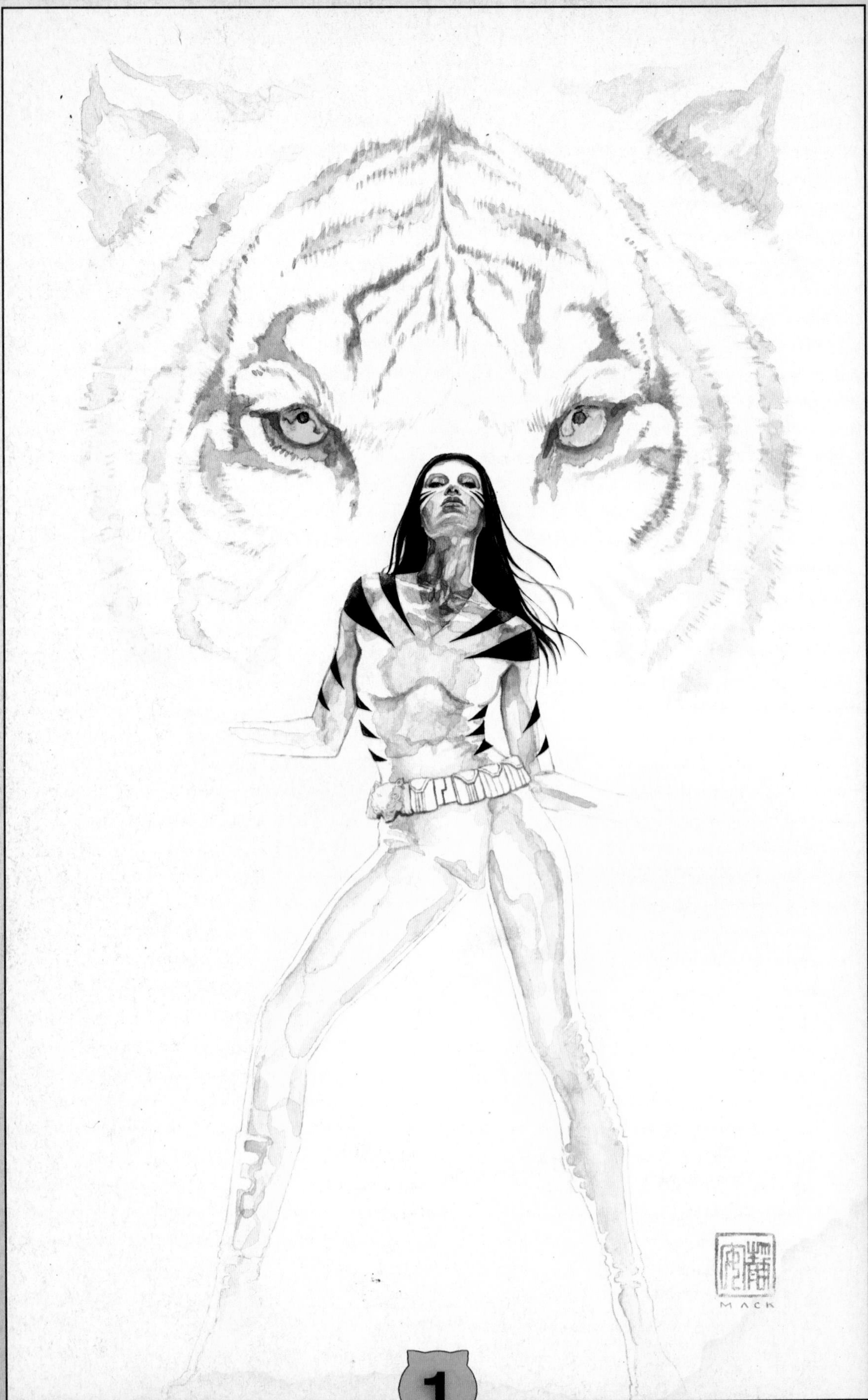
MACK

1

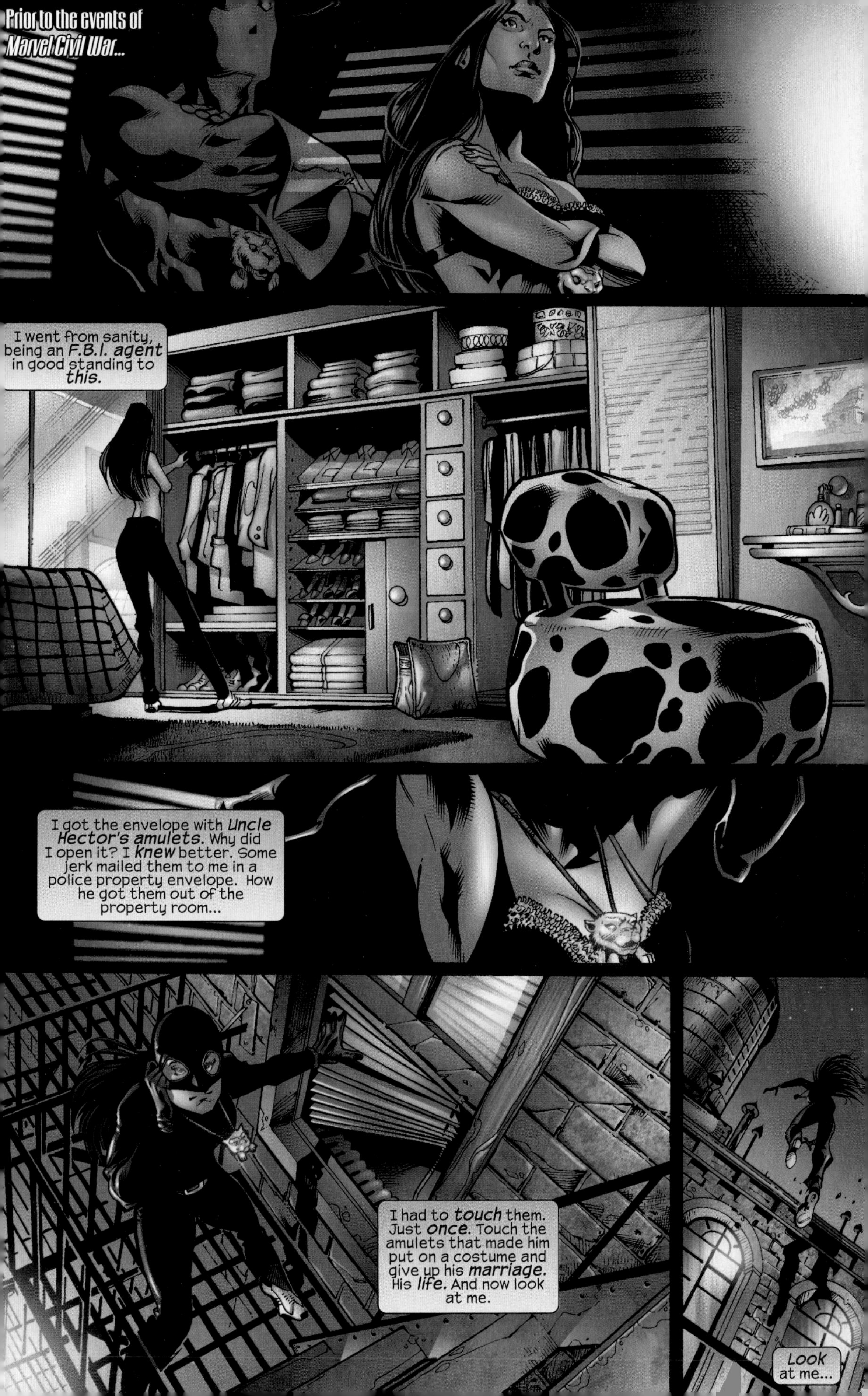
Prior to the events of
Marvel Civil War...
I went from sanity, being an F.B.I. agent in good standing to this.
I got the envelope with Uncle Hector's amulets. Why did I open it? I knew better. Some jerk mailed them to me in a police property envelope. How he got them out of the property room...
I had to touch them. Just once. Touch the amulets that made him put on a costume and give up his marriage. His life. And now look at me.
Look at me...

OBSESSED

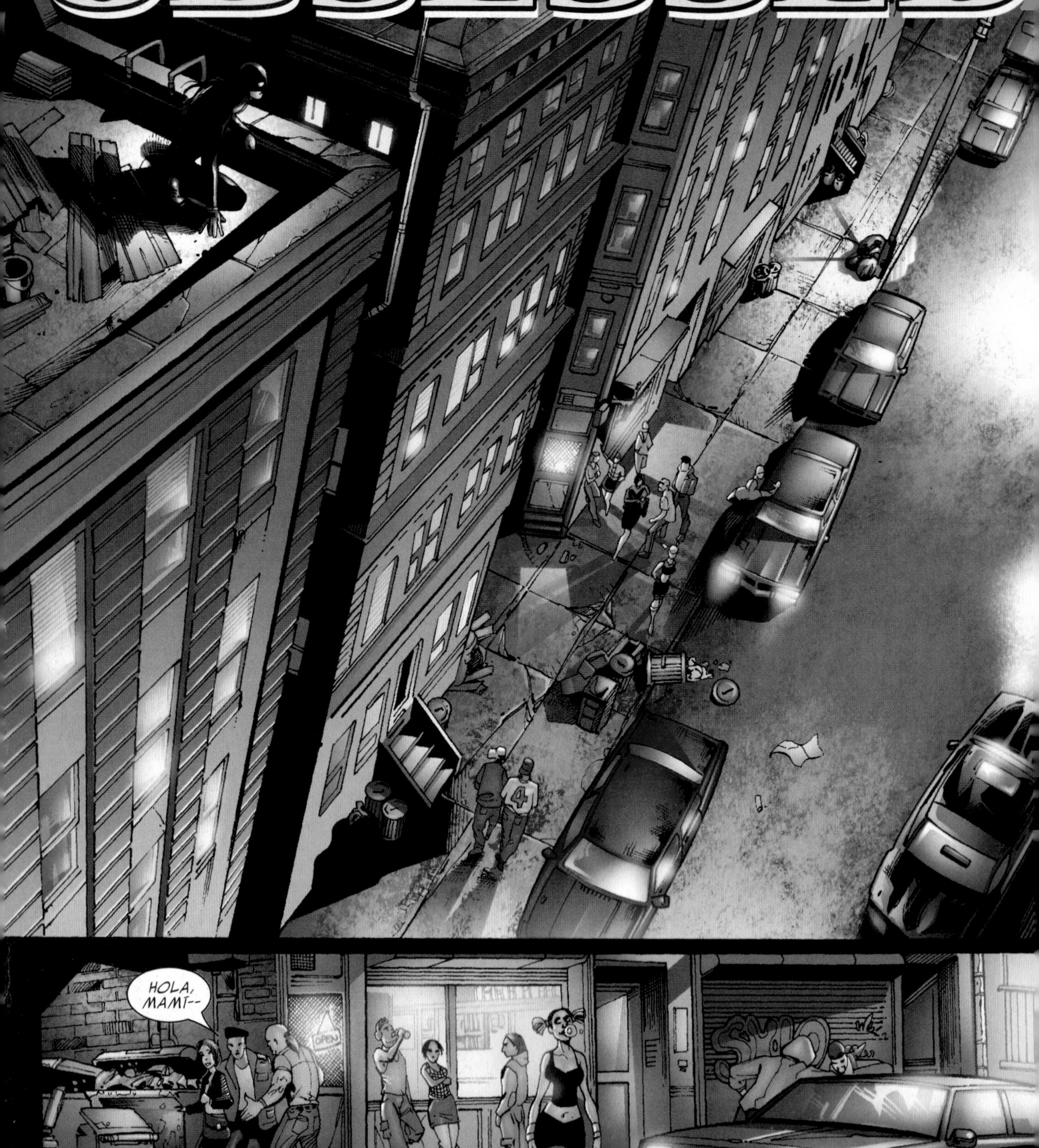

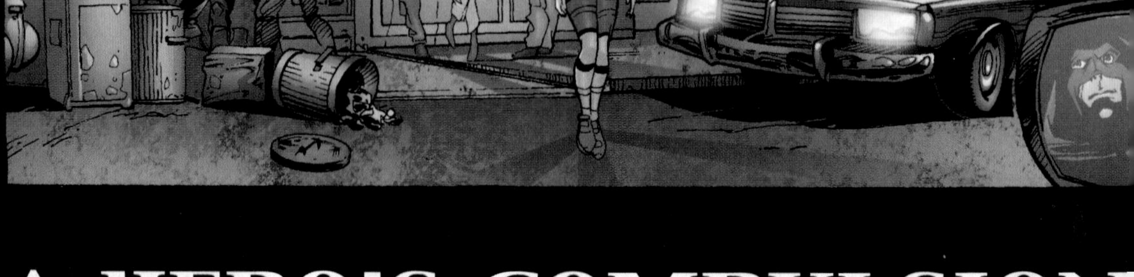
HOLA, MAMI--
OPEN

A HERO'S COMPULSION

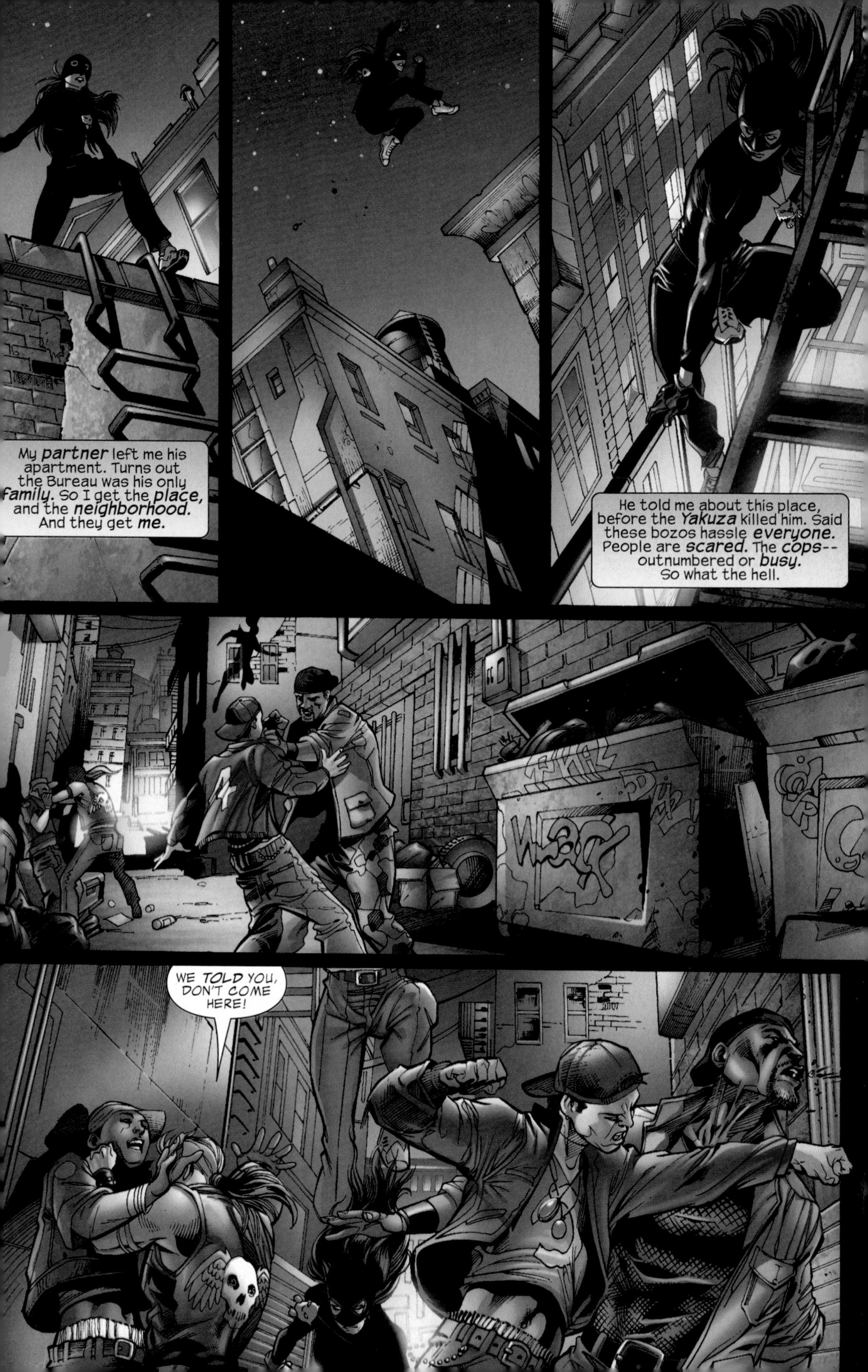

My partner left me his apartment. Turns out the Bureau was his only family. So I get the place, and the neighborhood. And they get me.
He told me about this place, before the Yakuza killed him. Said these bozos hassle everyone. People are scared. The cops-- outnumbered or busy. So what the hell.
WE TOLD YOU, DON'T COME HERE!

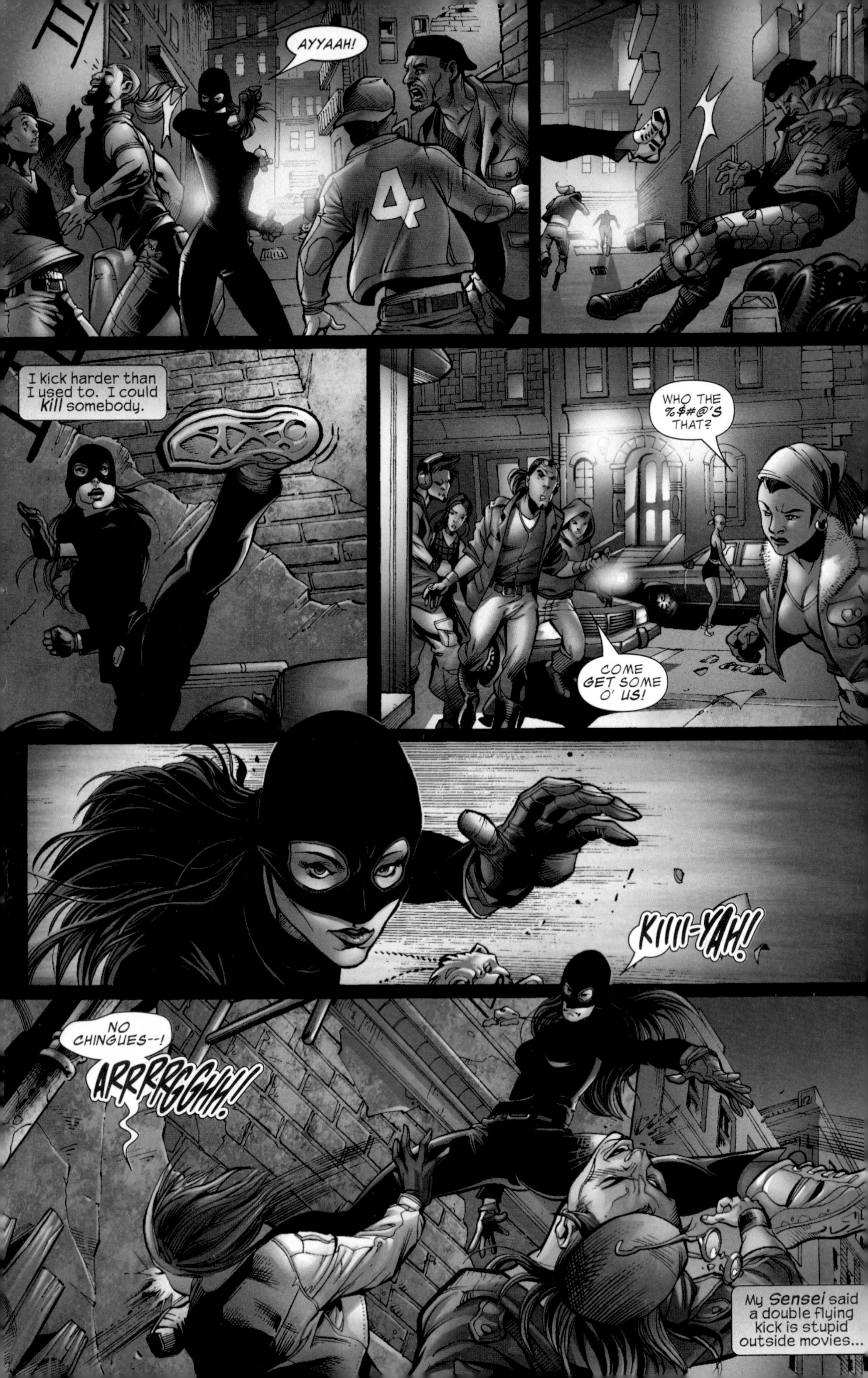
AYYAAH!
I kick harder than I used to. I could *kill* somebody.
WHO THE %$#@'S THAT?
COME GET SOME O' US!
KIIII-YAH!
NO CHINGUES--!
ARRRRGGHH!!
My *Sensei* said a double flying kick is stupid outside movies...

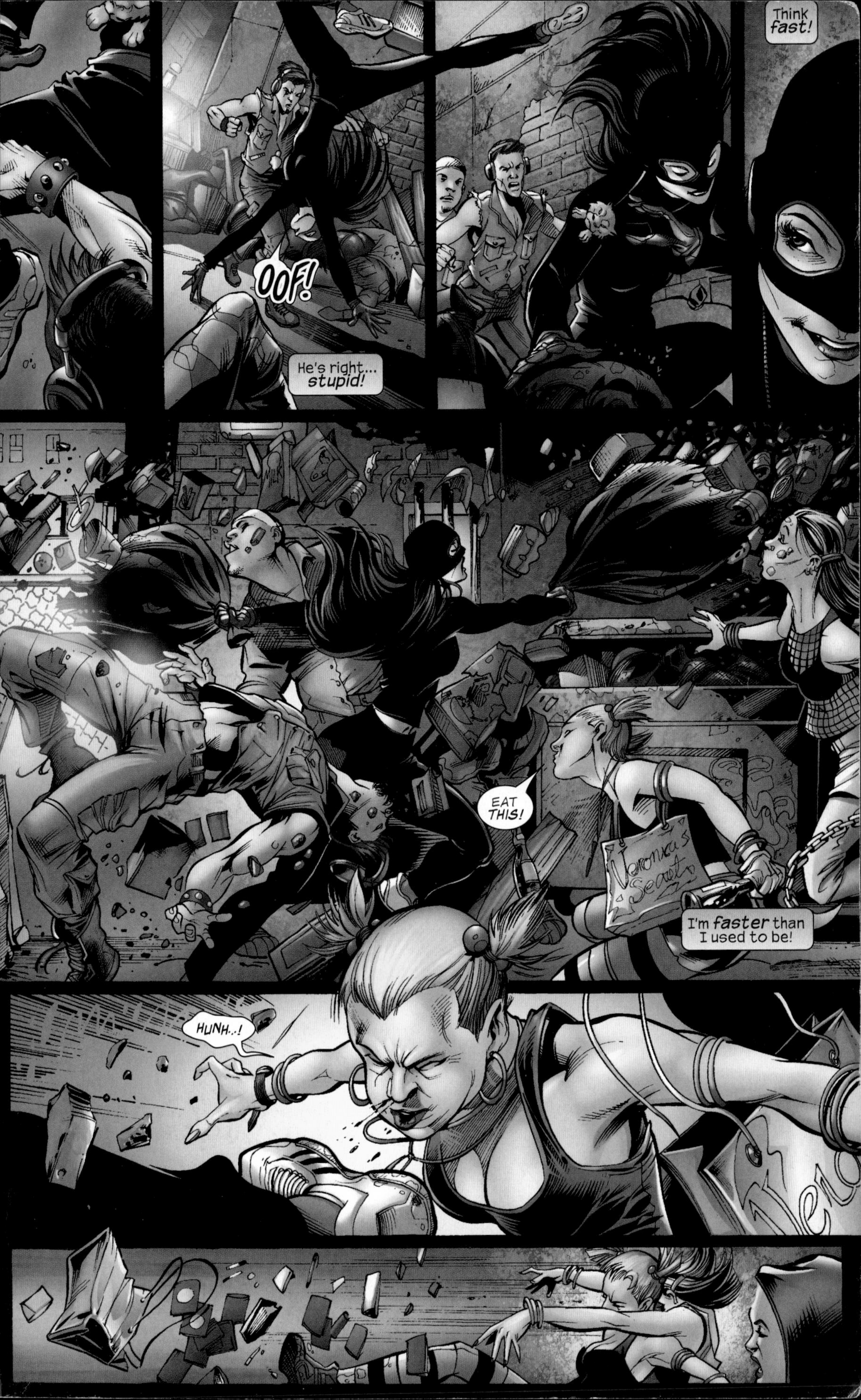
OOF!
He's right... stupid!
Think fast!
EAT THIS!
I'm faster than I used to be!
HUNH..!

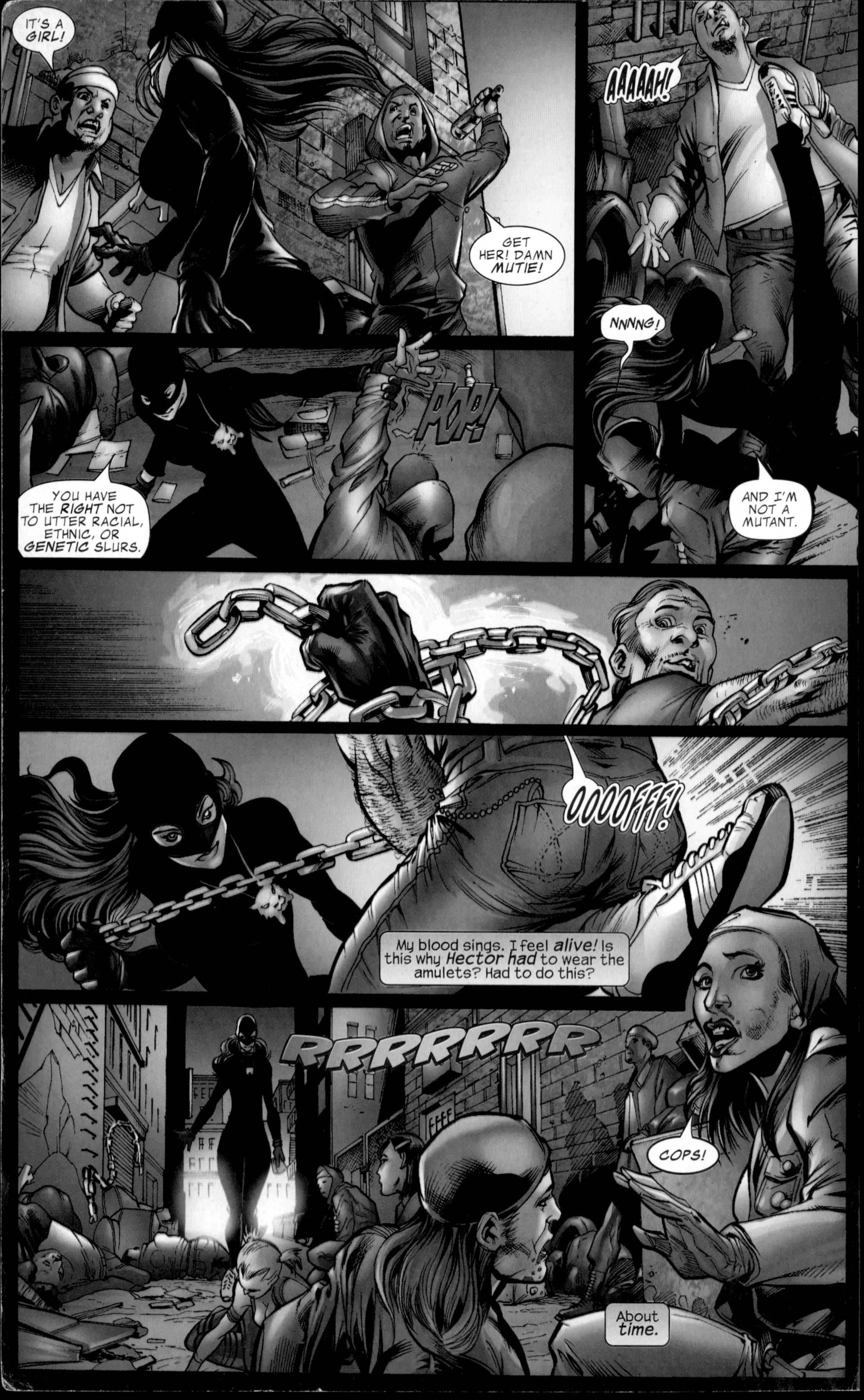
IT'S A GIRL!
GET HER! DAMN MUTIE!
AAAAAH!
NNNNG!
POP!
YOU HAVE THE RIGHT NOT TO UTTER RACIAL, ETHNIC, OR GENETIC SLURS.
AND I'M NOT A MUTANT.
OOOOFFF!
My blood sings. I feel alive! Is this why Hector had to wear the amulets? Had to do this?
RRRRRRR
COPS!
About time.

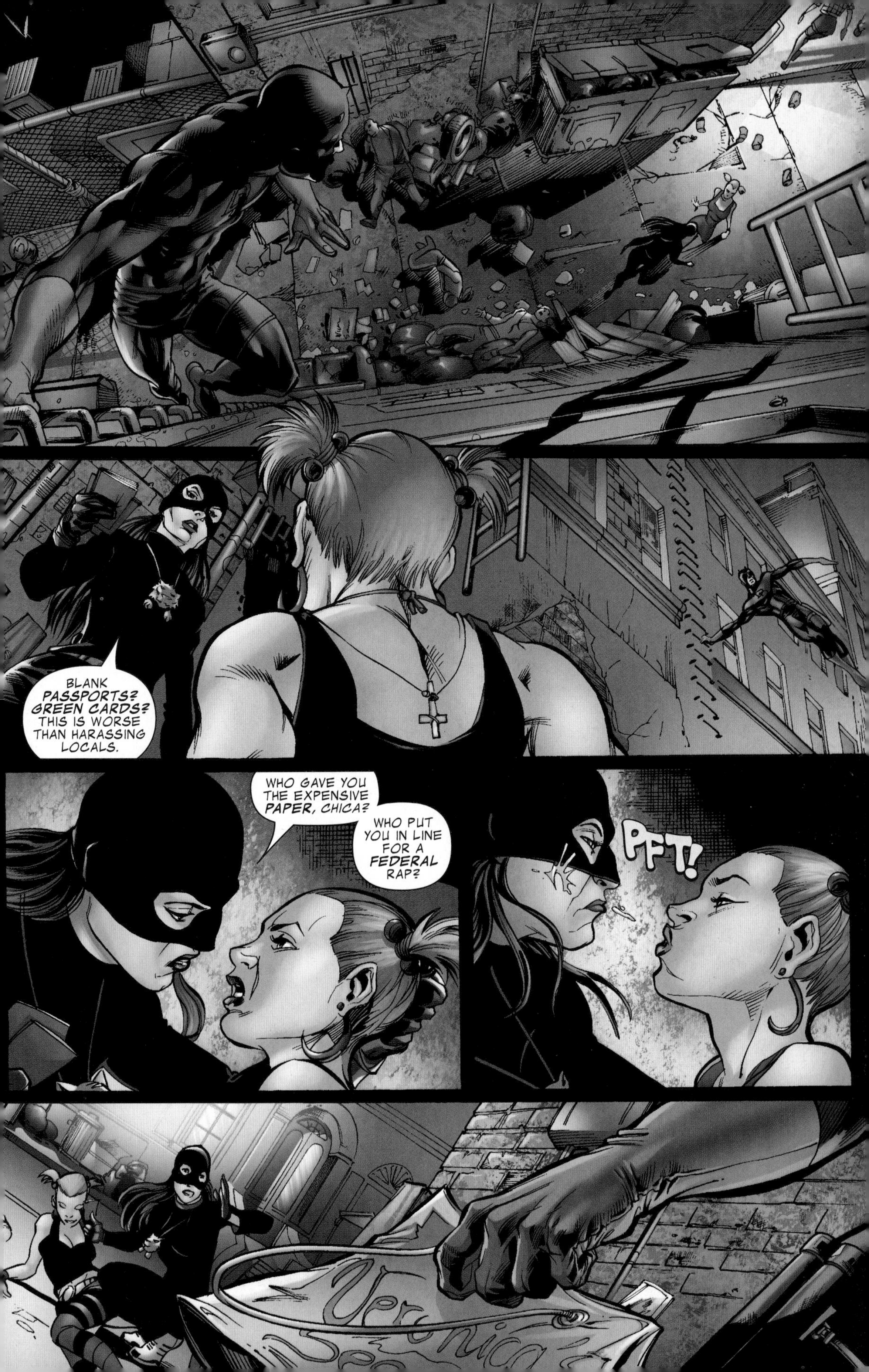
BLANK PASSPORTS? GREEN CARDS? THIS IS WORSE THAN HARASSING LOCALS.
WHO GAVE YOU THE EXPENSIVE PAPER, CHICA?
WHO PUT YOU IN LINE FOR A FEDERAL RAP?
PFT!

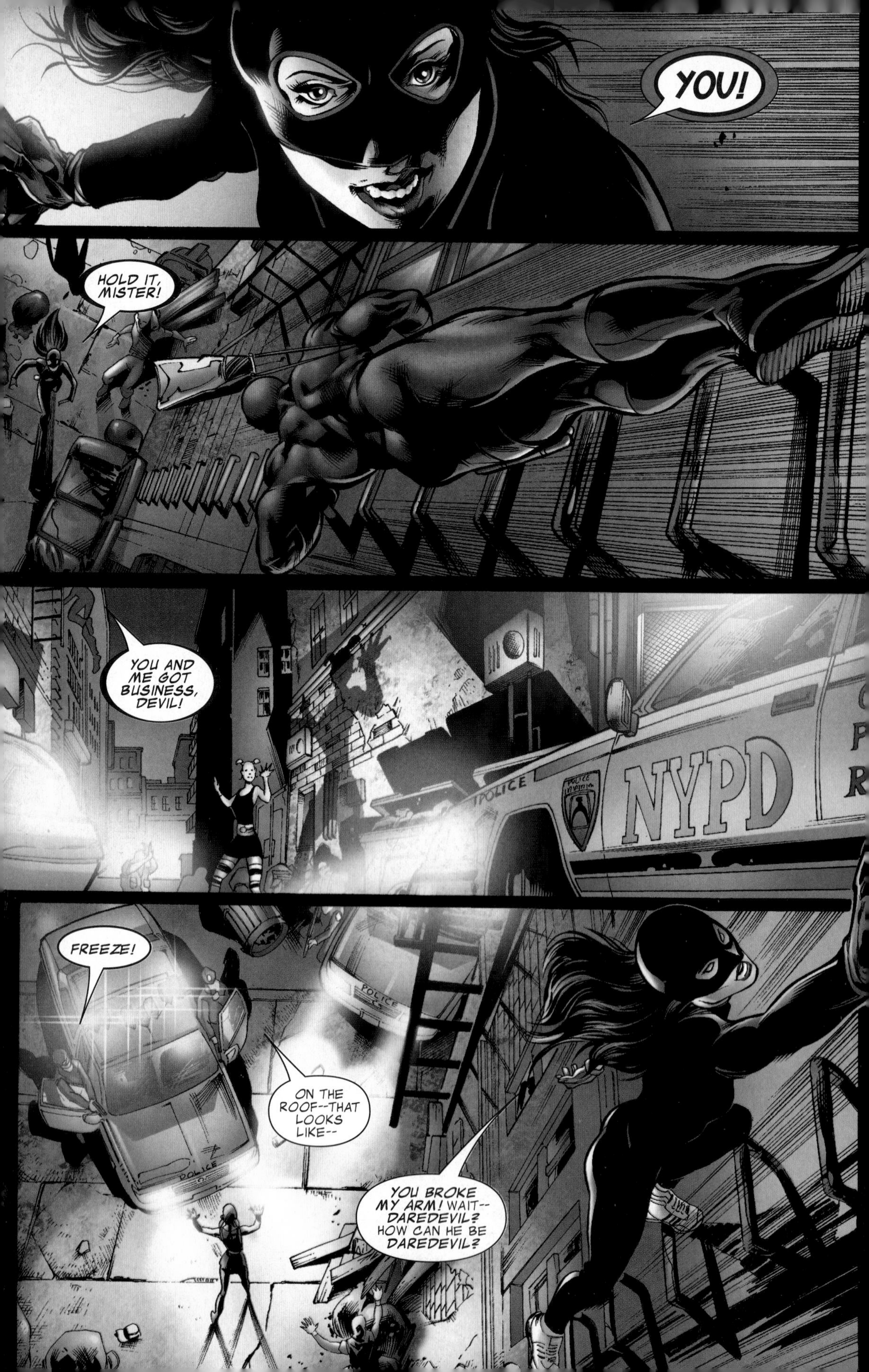
YOU!
HOLD IT, MISTER!
YOU AND ME GOT BUSINESS, DEVIL!
FREEZE!
ON THE ROOF--THAT LOOKS LIKE--
YOU BROKE MY ARM! WAIT-- DAREDEVIL? HOW CAN HE BE DAREDEVIL?
NYPD
POLICE

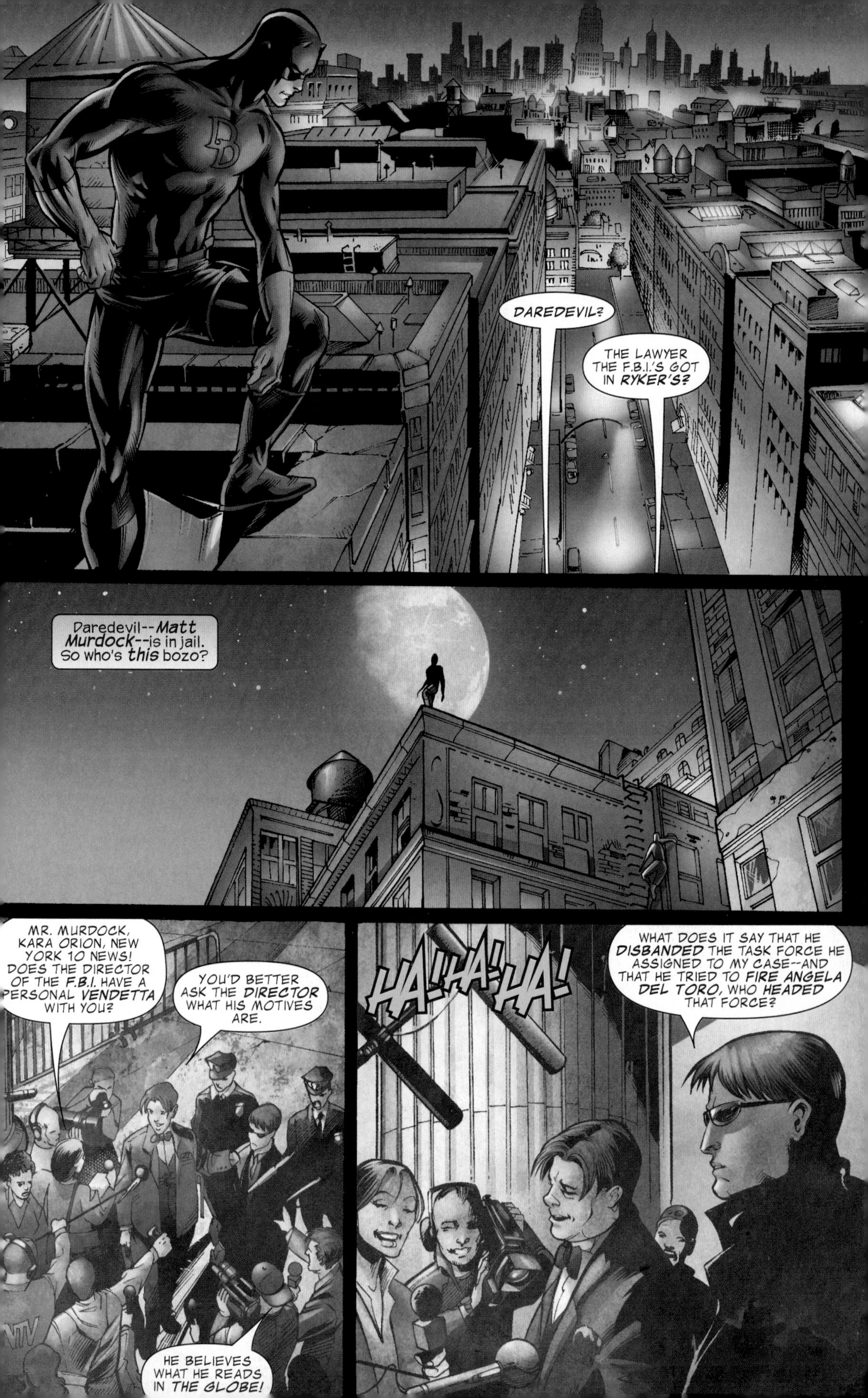
DAREDEVIL?
THE LAWYER THE F.B.I.'S GOT IN RYKER'S?
Daredevil--Matt Murdock--is in jail. So who's this bozo?
MR. MURDOCK, KARA ORION, NEW YORK 10 NEWS! DOES THE DIRECTOR OF THE F.B.I. HAVE A PERSONAL VENDETTA WITH YOU?
YOU'D BETTER ASK THE DIRECTOR WHAT HIS MOTIVES ARE.
HE BELIEVES WHAT HE READS IN THE GLOBE!
HA! HA! HA!
WHAT DOES IT SAY THAT HE DISBANDED THE TASK FORCE HE ASSIGNED TO MY CASE--AND THAT HE TRIED TO FIRE ANGELA DEL TORO, WHO HEADED THAT FORCE?

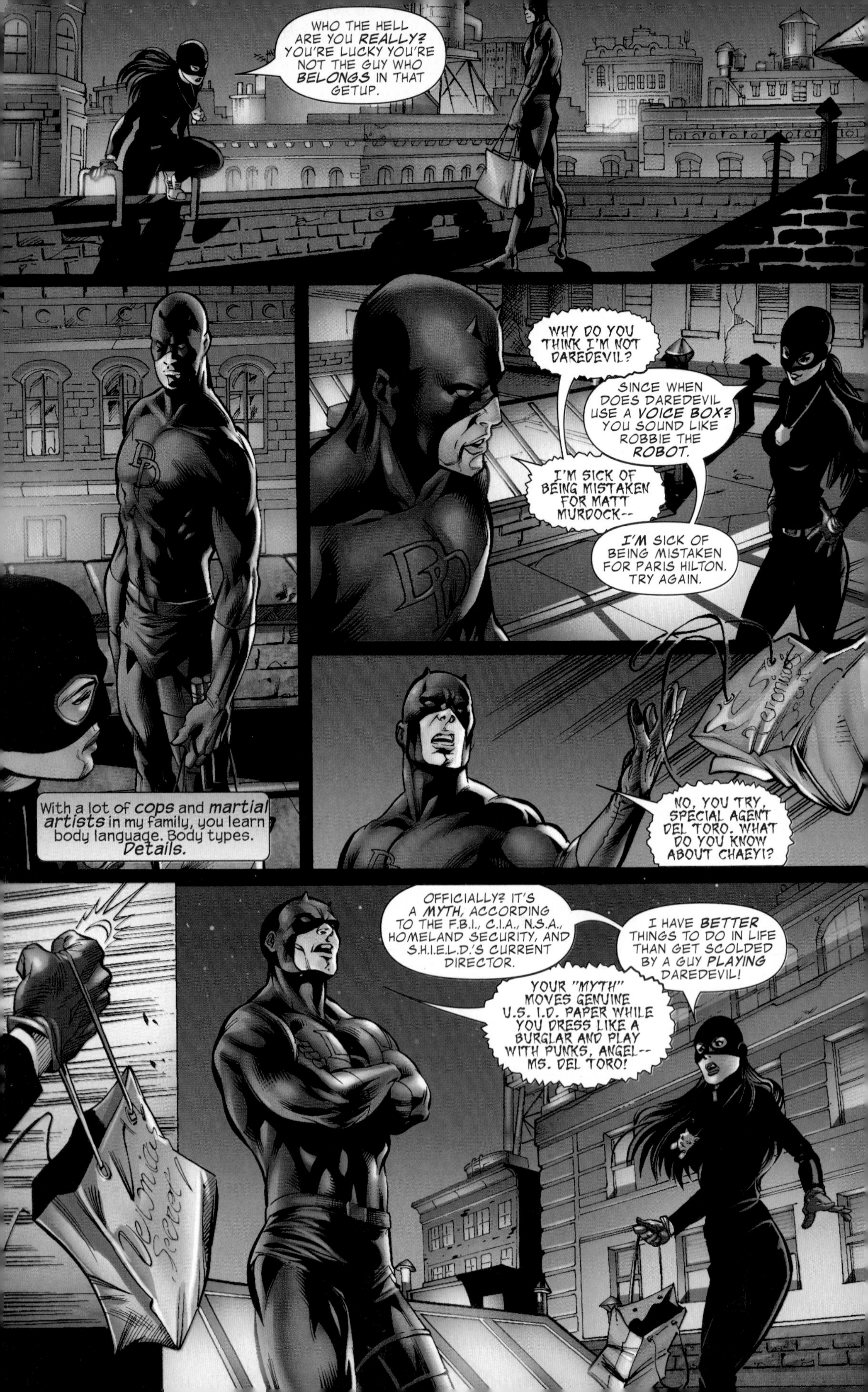

WHO THE HELL ARE YOU REALLY? YOU'RE LUCKY YOU'RE NOT THE GUY WHO BELONGS IN THAT GETUP.
With a lot of cops and martial artists in my family, you learn body language. Body types. Details.
WHY DO YOU THINK I'M NOT DAREDEVIL?
SINCE WHEN DOES DAREDEVIL USE A VOICE BOX? YOU SOUND LIKE ROBBIE THE ROBOT.
I'M SICK OF BEING MISTAKEN FOR MATT MURDOCK--
I'M SICK OF BEING MISTAKEN FOR PARIS HILTON. TRY AGAIN.
NO, YOU TRY, SPECIAL AGENT DEL TORO. WHAT DO YOU KNOW ABOUT CHAEYI?
OFFICIALLY? IT'S A MYTH, ACCORDING TO THE F.B.I., C.I.A., N.S.A., HOMELAND SECURITY, AND S.H.I.E.L.D.'S CURRENT DIRECTOR.
I HAVE BETTER THINGS TO DO IN LIFE THAN GET SCOLDED BY A GUY PLAYING DAREDEVIL!
YOUR "MYTH" MOVES GENUINE U.S. I.D. PAPER WHILE YOU DRESS LIKE A BURGLAR AND PLAY WITH PUNKS, ANGEL-- MS. DEL TORO!

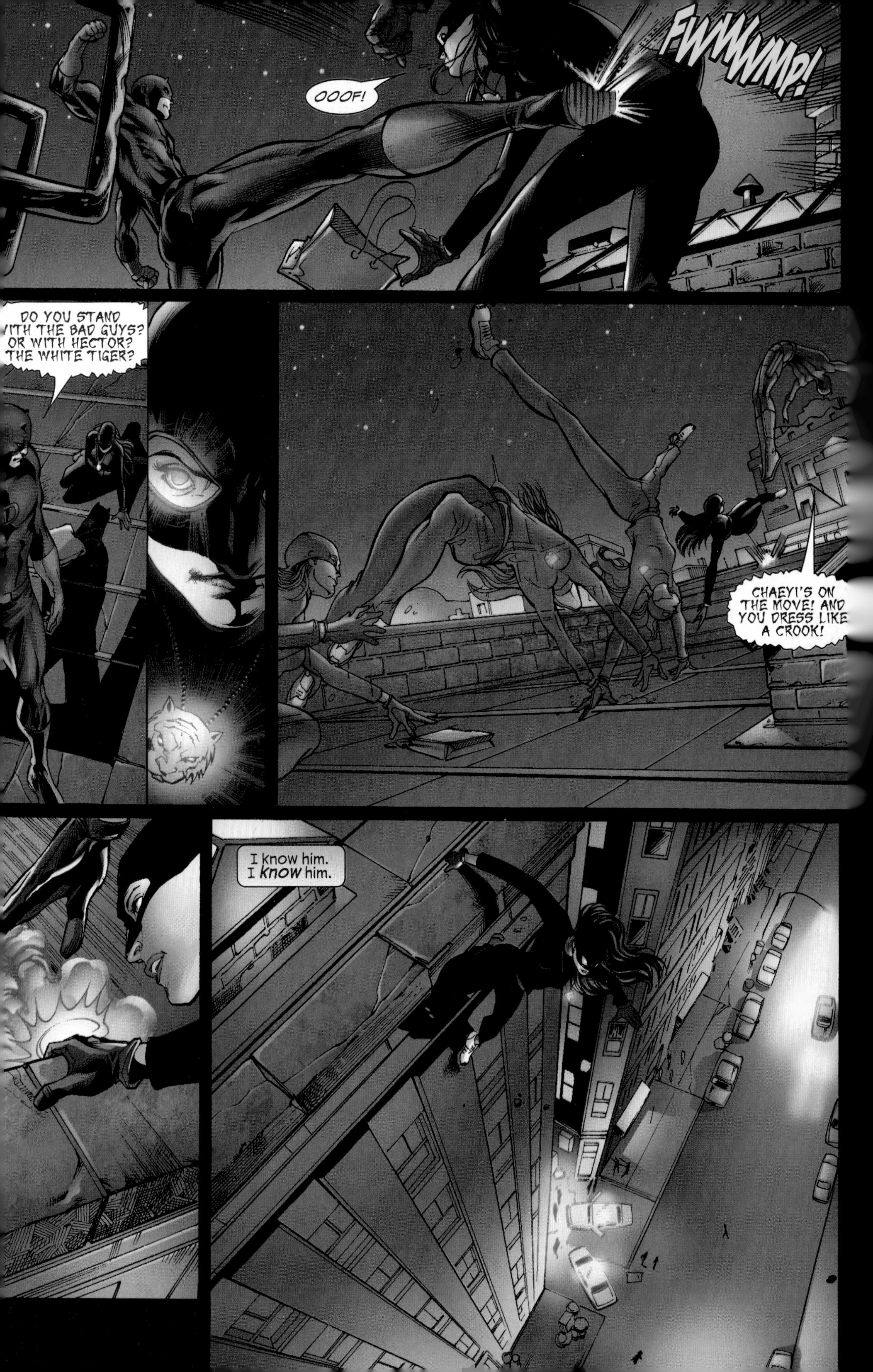
FWMMMP!
OOOF!
DO YOU STAND WITH THE BAD GUYS? OR WITH HECTOR? THE WHITE TIGER?
CHAEYI'S ON THE MOVE! AND YOU DRESS LIKE A CROOK!
I know him. I *know* him.

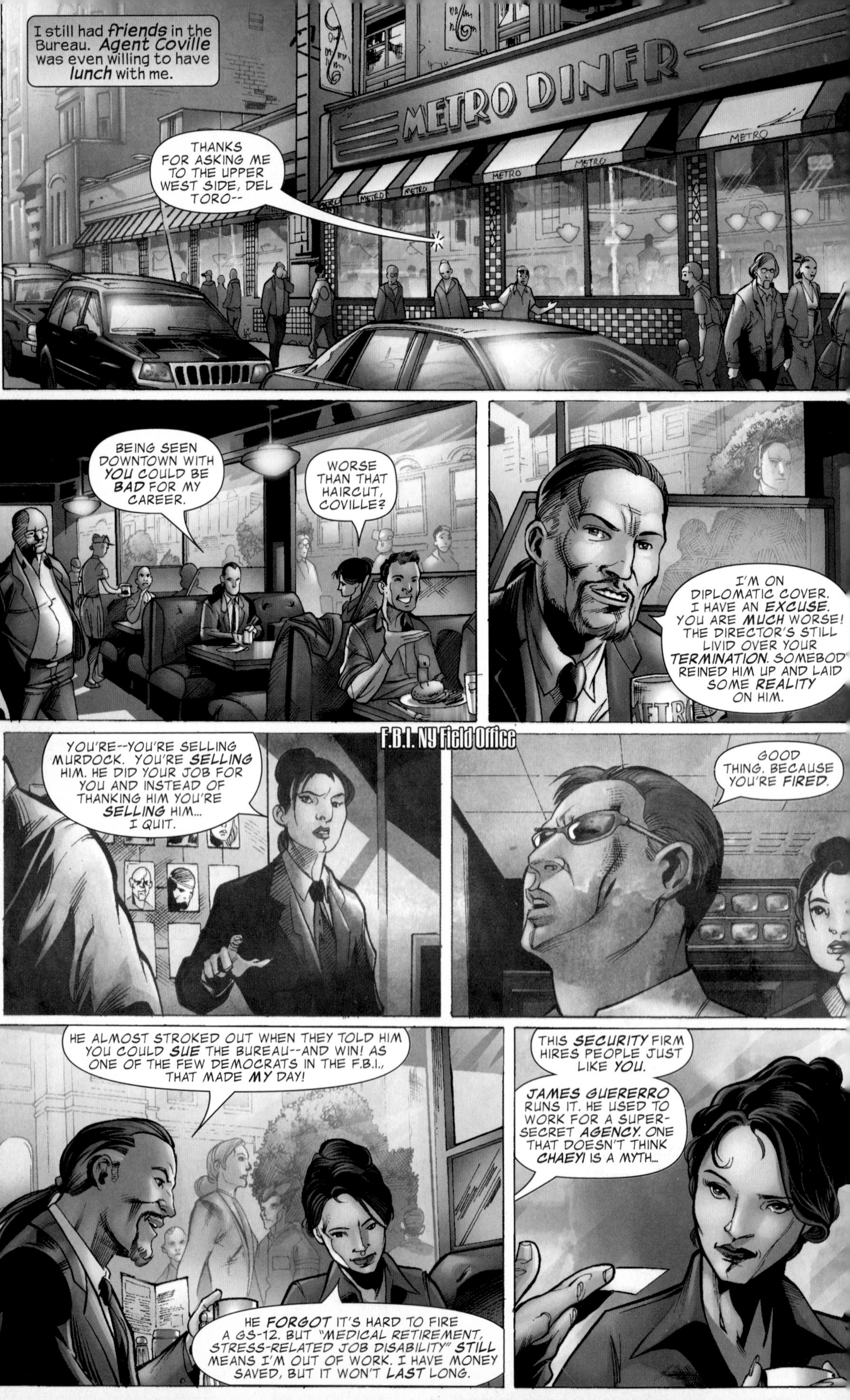
I still had *friends* in the Bureau. *Agent Coville* was even willing to have *lunch* with me.
METRO DINER
THANKS FOR ASKING ME TO THE UPPER WEST SIDE, DEL TORO--
BEING SEEN DOWNTOWN WITH *YOU* COULD BE *BAD* FOR MY CAREER.
WORSE THAN THAT HAIRCUT, COVILLE?
I'M ON DIPLOMATIC COVER. I HAVE AN *EXCUSE*. YOU ARE *MUCH* WORSE! THE DIRECTOR'S STILL LIVID OVER YOUR *TERMINATION*. SOMEBOD REINED HIM UP AND LAID SOME *REALITY* ON HIM.
F.B.I. NY Field Office
YOU'RE--YOU'RE SELLING MURDOCK. YOU'RE *SELLING* HIM. HE DID YOUR JOB FOR YOU AND INSTEAD OF THANKING HIM YOU'RE *SELLING* HIM... I QUIT.
GOOD THING. BECAUSE YOU'RE *FIRED*.
HE ALMOST STROKED OUT WHEN THEY TOLD HIM YOU COULD *SUE* THE BUREAU--AND WIN! AS ONE OF THE FEW DEMOCRATS IN THE F.B.I., THAT MADE *MY* DAY!
HE *FORGOT* IT'S HARD TO FIRE A GS-12. BUT "MEDICAL RETIREMENT, STRESS-RELATED JOB DISABILITY" *STILL* MEANS I'M OUT OF WORK. I HAVE MONEY SAVED, BUT IT WON'T *LAST* LONG.
THIS *SECURITY* FIRM HIRES PEOPLE JUST LIKE *YOU*.
JAMES GUERERRO RUNS IT. HE USED TO WORK FOR A SUPER-SECRET *AGENCY*. ONE THAT DOESN'T THINK *CHAEYI* IS A MYTH...

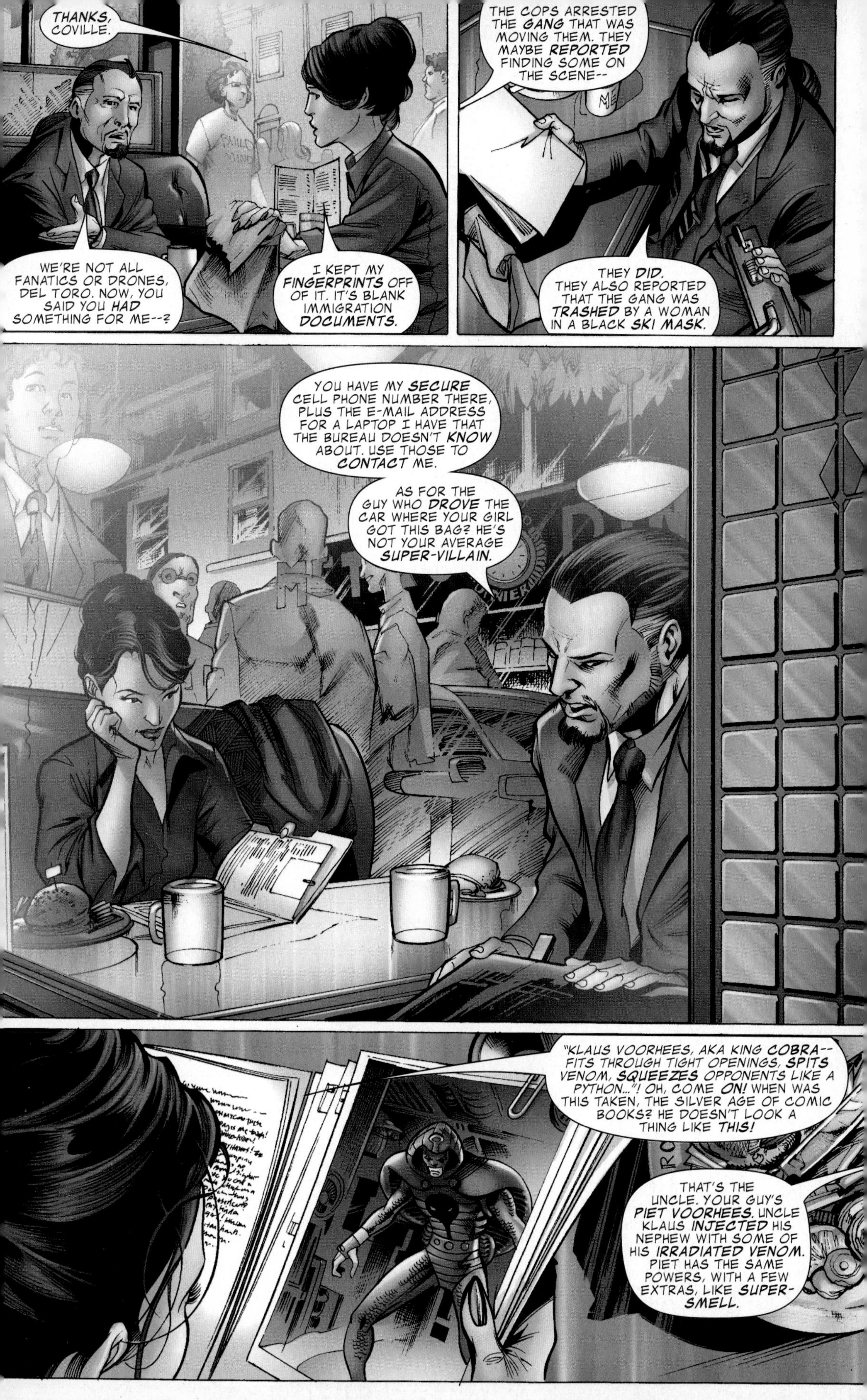
THANKS, COVILLE.
WE'RE NOT ALL FANATICS OR DRONES, DEL TORO. NOW, YOU SAID YOU HAD SOMETHING FOR ME--?
I KEPT MY FINGERPRINTS OFF OF IT. IT'S BLANK IMMIGRATION DOCUMENTS.
THE COPS ARRESTED THE GANG THAT WAS MOVING THEM. THEY MAYBE REPORTED FINDING SOME ON THE SCENE--
THEY DID. THEY ALSO REPORTED THAT THE GANG WAS TRASHED BY A WOMAN IN A BLACK SKI MASK.
YOU HAVE MY SECURE CELL PHONE NUMBER THERE, PLUS THE E-MAIL ADDRESS FOR A LAPTOP I HAVE THAT THE BUREAU DOESN'T KNOW ABOUT. USE THOSE TO CONTACT ME.
AS FOR THE GUY WHO DROVE THE CAR WHERE YOUR GIRL GOT THIS BAG? HE'S NOT YOUR AVERAGE SUPER-VILLAIN.
"KLAUS VOORHEES, AKA KING COBRA-- FITS THROUGH TIGHT OPENINGS, SPITS VENOM, SQUEEZES OPPONENTS LIKE A PYTHON..."! OH, COME ON! WHEN WAS THIS TAKEN, THE SILVER AGE OF COMIC BOOKS? HE DOESN'T LOOK A THING LIKE THIS!
THAT'S THE UNCLE. YOUR GUY'S PIET VOORHEES. UNCLE KLAUS INJECTED HIS NEPHEW WITH SOME OF HIS IRRADIATED VENOM. PIET HAS THE SAME POWERS, WITH A FEW EXTRAS, LIKE SUPER-SMELL.

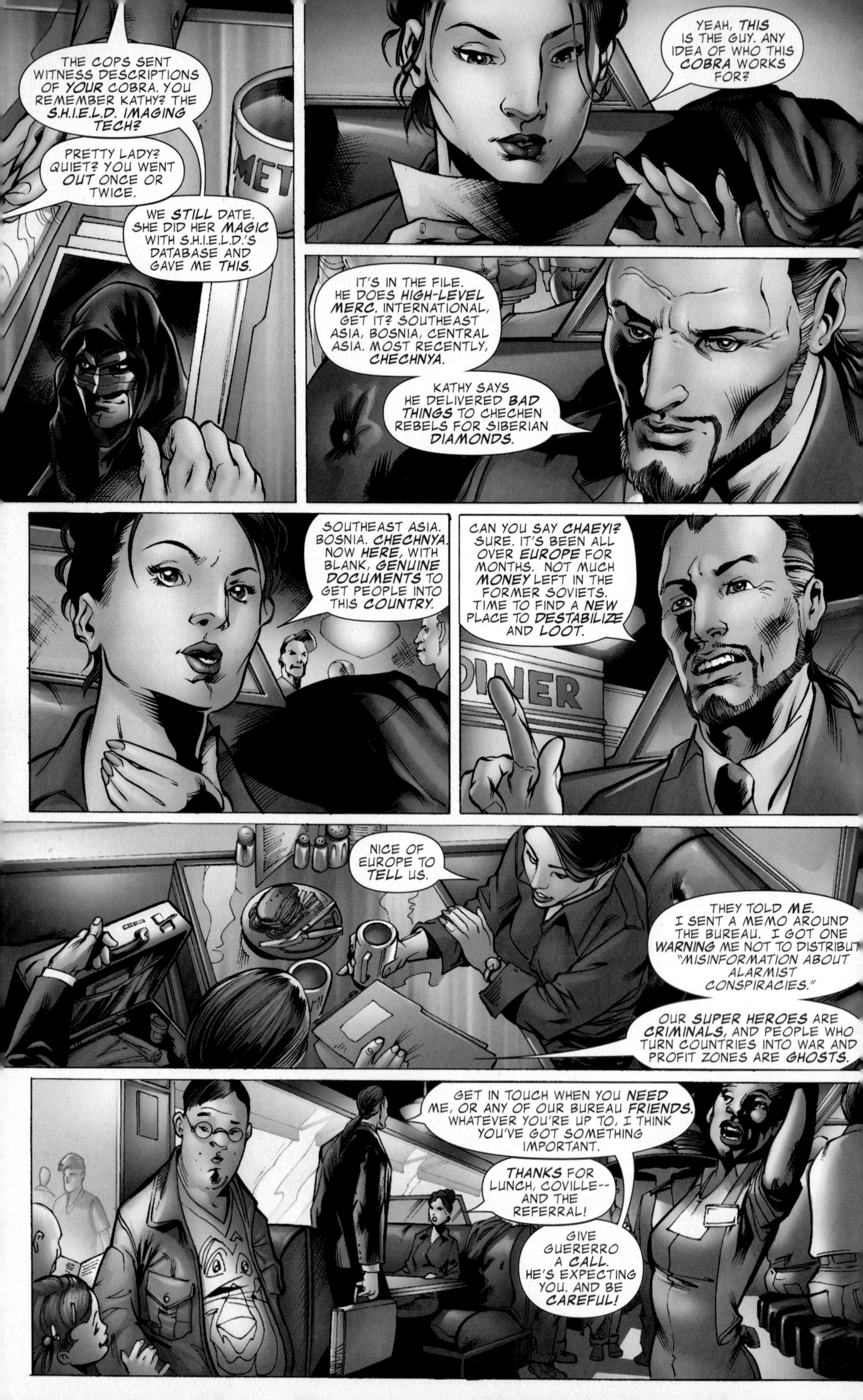
THE COPS SENT WITNESS DESCRIPTIONS OF YOUR COBRA. YOU REMEMBER KATHY? THE S.H.I.E.L.D. IMAGING TECH?
PRETTY LADY? QUIET? YOU WENT OUT ONCE OR TWICE.
WE STILL DATE. SHE DID HER MAGIC WITH S.H.I.E.L.D.'S DATABASE AND GAVE ME THIS.
MET
YEAH, THIS IS THE GUY. ANY IDEA OF WHO THIS COBRA WORKS FOR?
IT'S IN THE FILE. HE DOES HIGH-LEVEL MERC. INTERNATIONAL, GET IT? SOUTHEAST ASIA, BOSNIA, CENTRAL ASIA. MOST RECENTLY, CHECHNYA.
KATHY SAYS HE DELIVERED BAD THINGS TO CHECHEN REBELS FOR SIBERIAN DIAMONDS.
SOUTHEAST ASIA. BOSNIA. CHECHNYA. NOW HERE, WITH BLANK, GENUINE DOCUMENTS TO GET PEOPLE INTO THIS COUNTRY.
CAN YOU SAY CHAEYI? SURE. IT'S BEEN ALL OVER EUROPE FOR MONTHS. NOT MUCH MONEY LEFT IN THE FORMER SOVIETS. TIME TO FIND A NEW PLACE TO DESTABILIZE AND LOOT.
DINER
NICE OF EUROPE TO TELL US.
THEY TOLD ME. I SENT A MEMO AROUND THE BUREAU. I GOT ONE WARNING ME NOT TO DISTRIBUT "MISINFORMATION ABOUT ALARMIST CONSPIRACIES."
OUR SUPER HEROES ARE CRIMINALS, AND PEOPLE WHO TURN COUNTRIES INTO WAR AND PROFIT ZONES ARE GHOSTS.
GET IN TOUCH WHEN YOU NEED ME, OR ANY OF OUR BUREAU FRIENDS. WHATEVER YOU'RE UP TO, I THINK YOU'VE GOT SOMETHING IMPORTANT.
THANKS FOR LUNCH, COVILLE-- AND THE REFERRAL!
GIVE GUERERRO A CALL. HE'S EXPECTING YOU. AND BE CAREFUL!

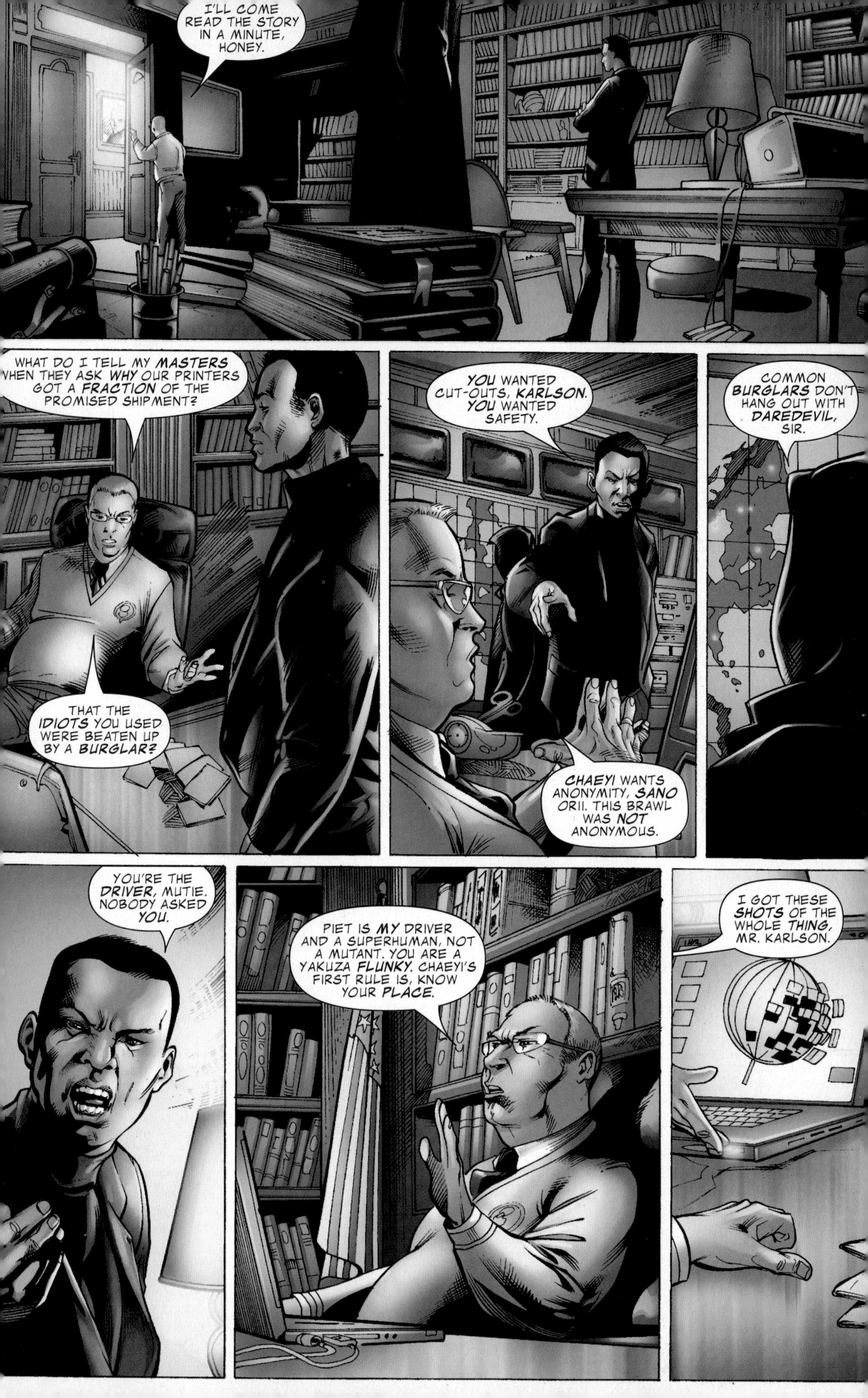
I'LL COME READ THE STORY IN A MINUTE, HONEY.
WHAT DO I TELL MY MASTERS WHEN THEY ASK WHY OUR PRINTERS GOT A FRACTION OF THE PROMISED SHIPMENT?
THAT THE IDIOTS YOU USED WERE BEATEN UP BY A BURGLAR?
YOU WANTED CUT-OUTS, KARLSON. YOU WANTED SAFETY.
CHAEYI WANTS ANONYMITY, SANO ORII. THIS BRAWL WAS NOT ANONYMOUS.
COMMON BURGLARS DON'T HANG OUT WITH DAREDEVIL, SIR.
YOU'RE THE DRIVER, MUTIE. NOBODY ASKED YOU.
PIET IS MY DRIVER AND A SUPERHUMAN, NOT A MUTANT. YOU ARE A YAKUZA FLUNKY. CHAEYI'S FIRST RULE IS, KNOW YOUR PLACE.
I GOT THESE SHOTS OF THE WHOLE THING, MR. KARLSON.

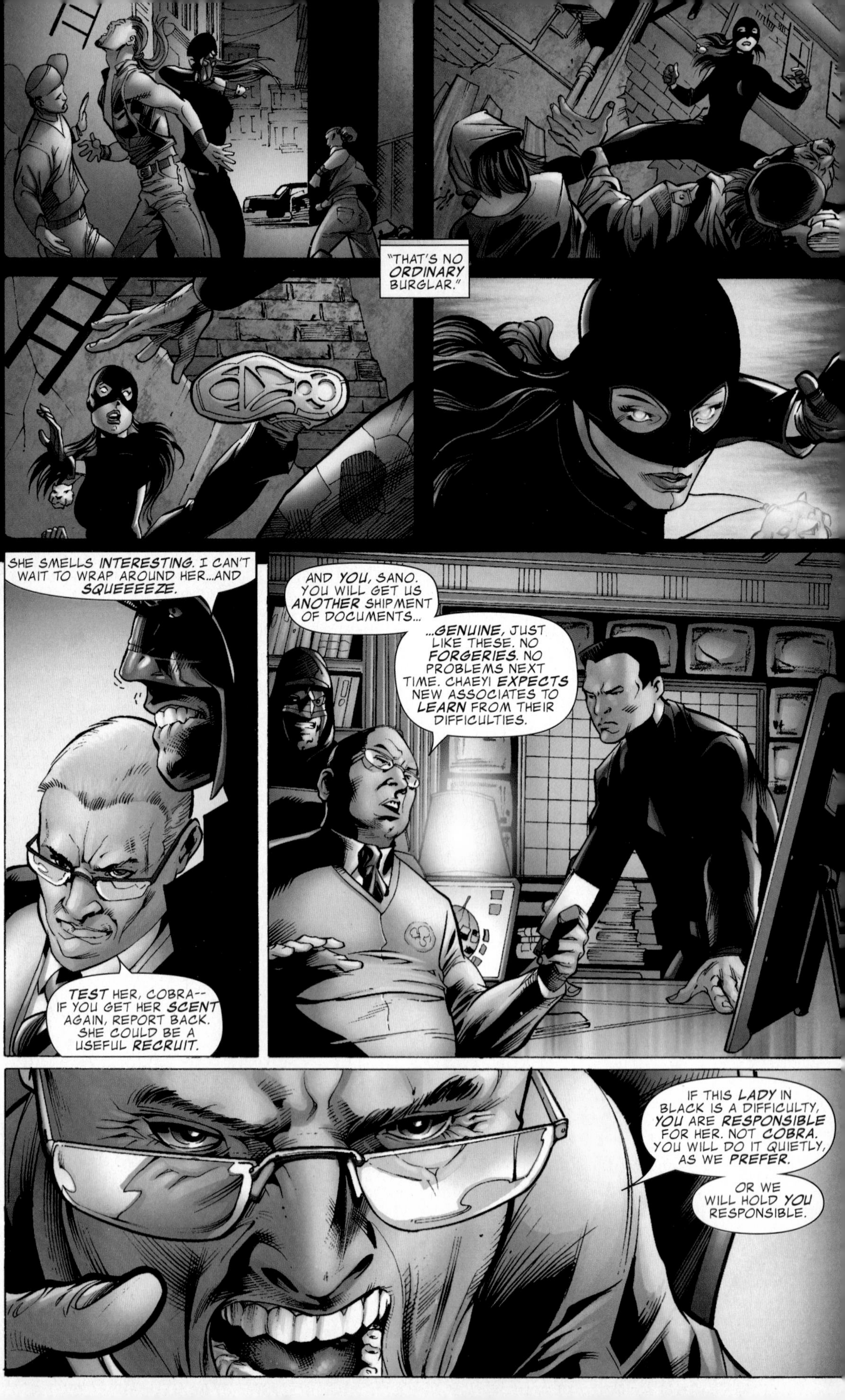
"THAT'S NO ORDINARY BURGLAR."
SHE SMELLS INTERESTING. I CAN'T WAIT TO WRAP AROUND HER...AND SQUEEEEZE.
TEST HER, COBRA--IF YOU GET HER SCENT AGAIN, REPORT BACK. SHE COULD BE A USEFUL RECRUIT.
AND YOU, SANO. YOU WILL GET US ANOTHER SHIPMENT OF DOCUMENTS...
...GENUINE, JUST LIKE THESE. NO FORGERIES. NO PROBLEMS NEXT TIME. CHAEYI EXPECTS NEW ASSOCIATES TO LEARN FROM THEIR DIFFICULTIES.
IF THIS LADY IN BLACK IS A DIFFICULTY, YOU ARE RESPONSIBLE FOR HER. NOT COBRA. YOU WILL DO IT QUIETLY, AS WE PREFER.
OR WE WILL HOLD YOU RESPONSIBLE.

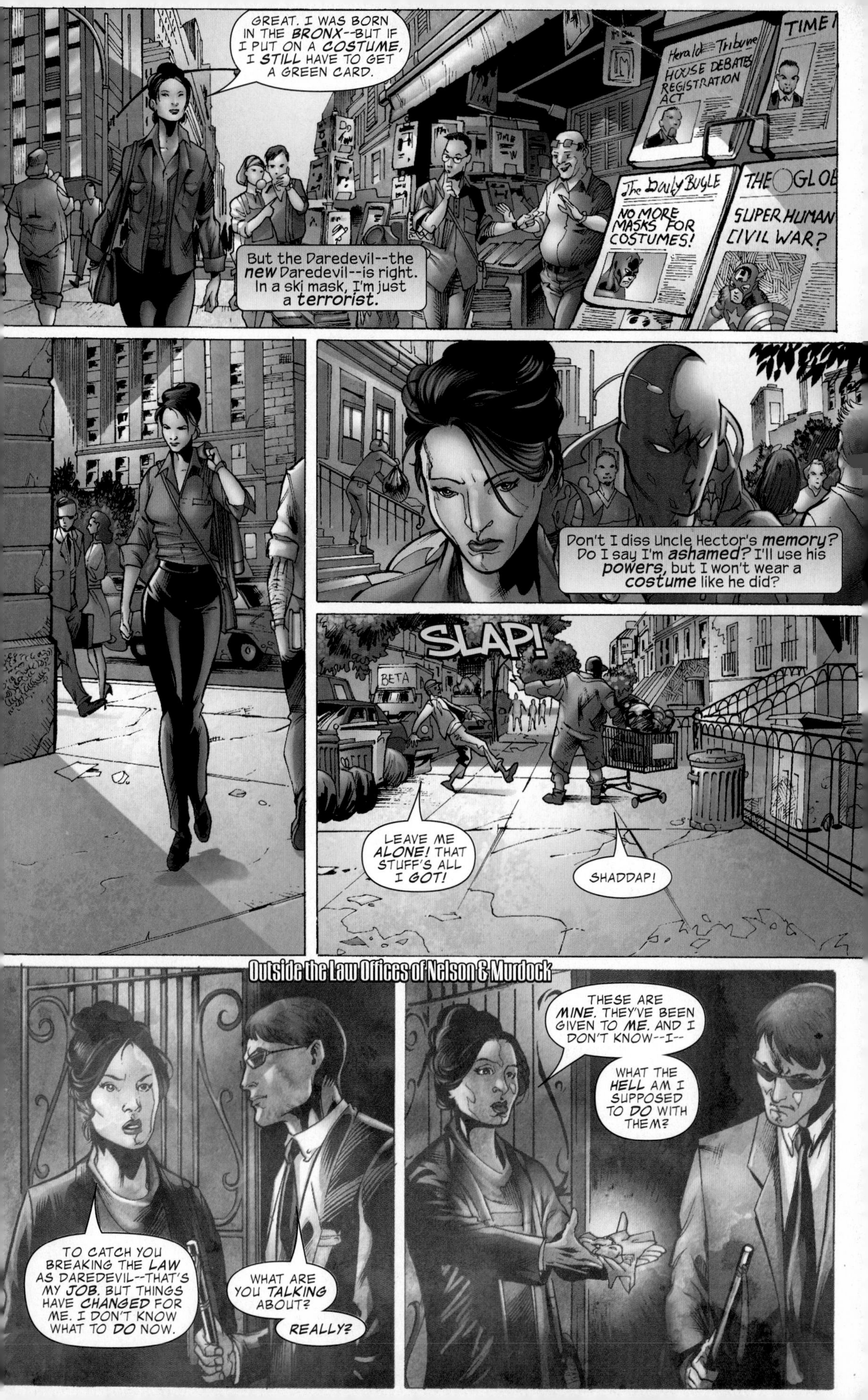

GREAT. I WAS BORN IN THE BRONX--BUT IF I PUT ON A COSTUME, I STILL HAVE TO GET A GREEN CARD.
TIME
Herald Tribune
HOUSE DEBATES REGISTRATION ACT
The Daily Bugle
NO MORE MASKS FOR COSTUMES!
THE GLOB
SUPER HUMAN CIVIL WAR?
But the Daredevil--the new Daredevil--is right. In a ski mask, I'm just a terrorist.
Don't I diss Uncle Hector's memory? Do I say I'm ashamed? I'll use his powers, but I won't wear a costume like he did?
SLAP!
BETA
LEAVE ME ALONE! THAT STUFF'S ALL I GOT!
SHADDAP!
Outside the Law Offices of Nelson & Murdock
TO CATCH YOU BREAKING THE LAW AS DAREDEVIL--THAT'S MY JOB. BUT THINGS HAVE CHANGED FOR ME. I DON'T KNOW WHAT TO DO NOW.
WHAT ARE YOU TALKING ABOUT?
REALLY?
THESE ARE MINE. THEY'VE BEEN GIVEN TO ME. AND I DON'T KNOW--I--
WHAT THE HELL AM I SUPPOSED TO DO WITH THEM?

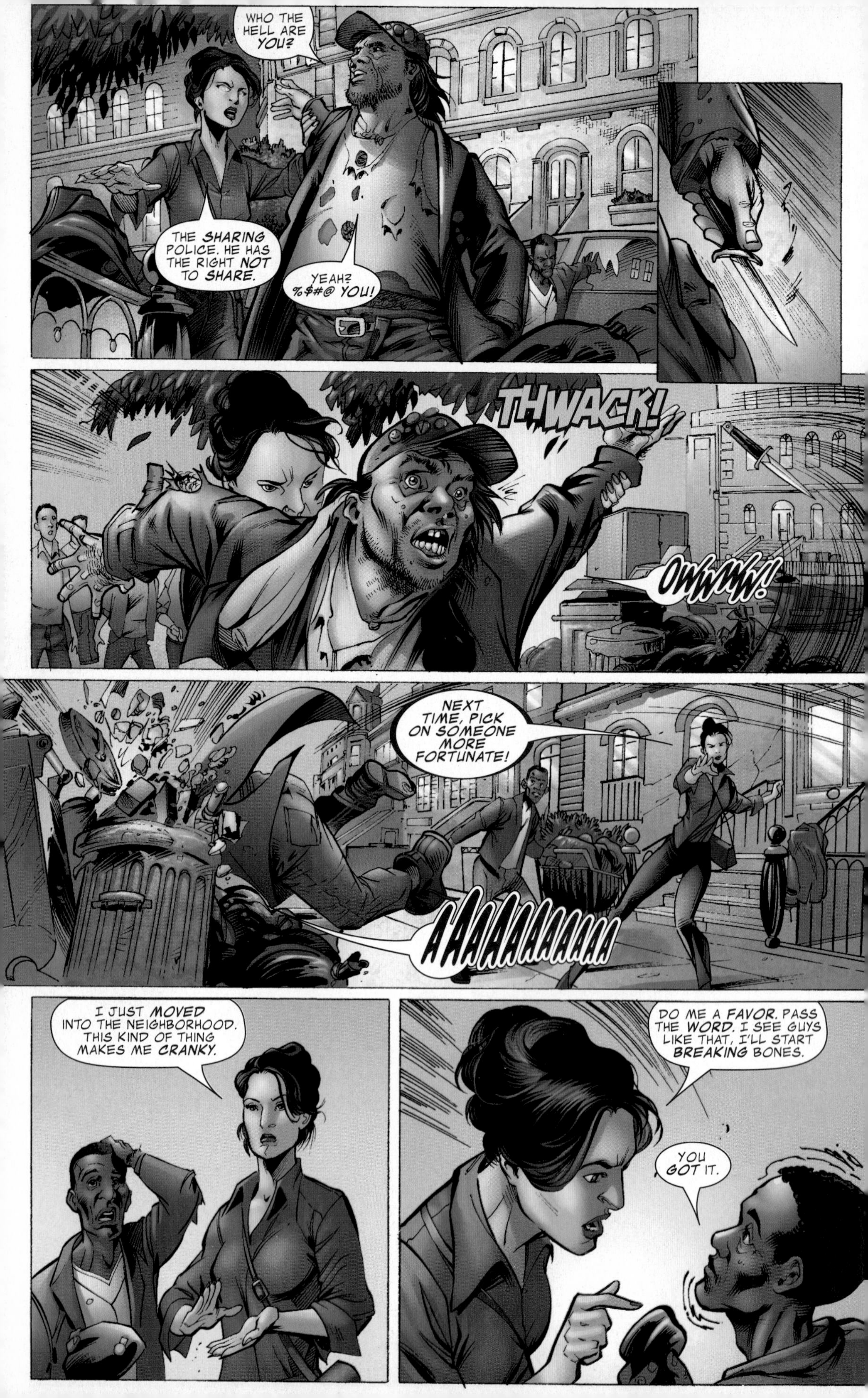
WHO THE HELL ARE YOU?
THE SHARING POLICE. HE HAS THE RIGHT NOT TO SHARE.
YEAH? %$#@ YOU!
THWACK!
OWWWW!
NEXT TIME, PICK ON SOMEONE MORE FORTUNATE!
AAAAAAAAAAAA
I JUST MOVED INTO THE NEIGHBORHOOD. THIS KIND OF THING MAKES ME CRANKY.
DO ME A FAVOR. PASS THE WORD. I SEE GUYS LIKE THAT, I'LL START BREAKING BONES.
YOU GOT IT.

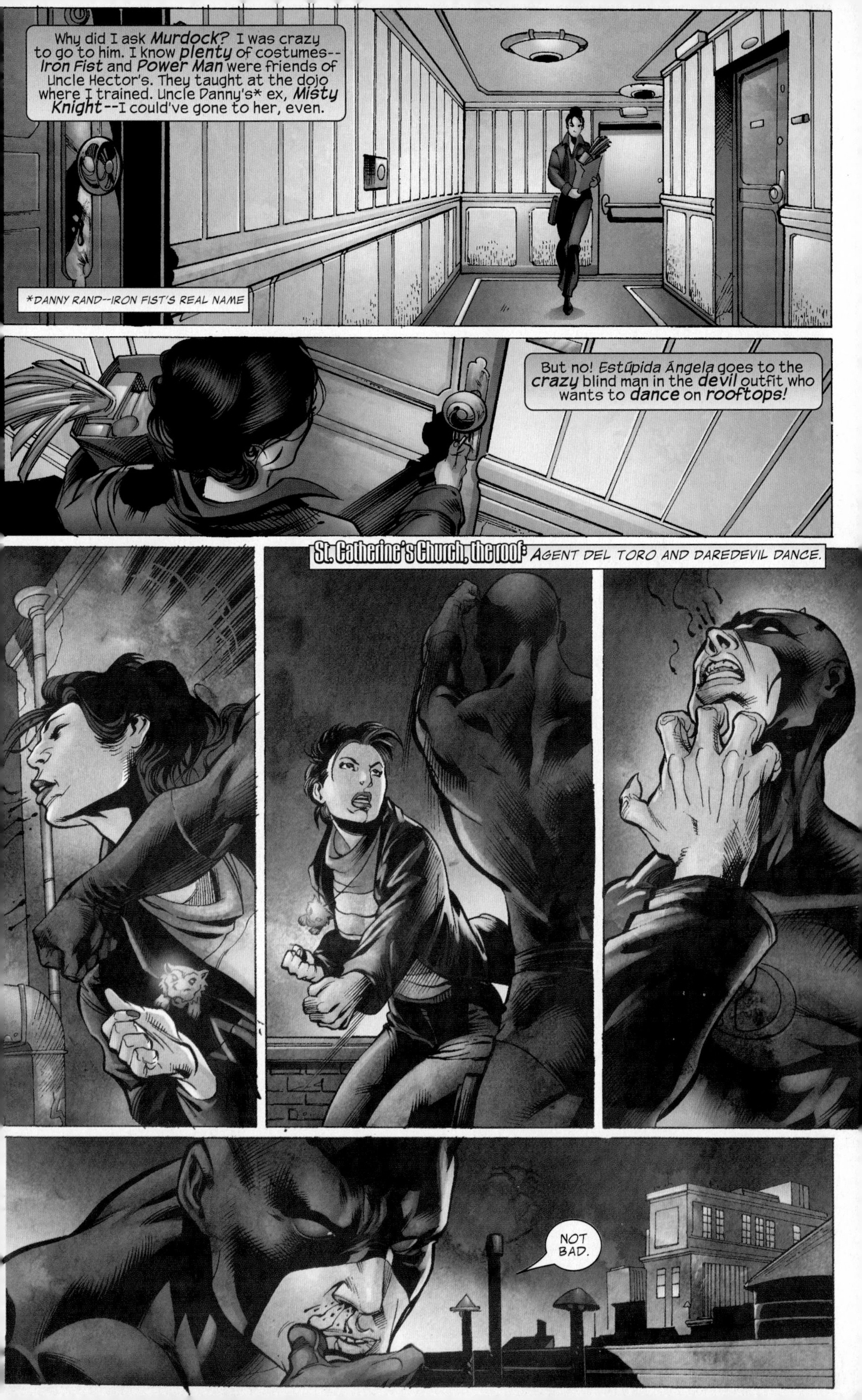
Why did I ask Murdock? I was crazy to go to him. I know plenty of costumes--Iron Fist and Power Man were friends of Uncle Hector's. They taught at the dojo where I trained. Uncle Danny's* ex, Misty Knight--I could've gone to her, even.
*DANNY RAND--IRON FIST'S REAL NAME
But no! Estúpida Ángela goes to the crazy blind man in the devil outfit who wants to dance on rooftops!
St. Catherine's Church, the roof: AGENT DEL TORO AND DAREDEVIL DANCE.
NOT BAD.

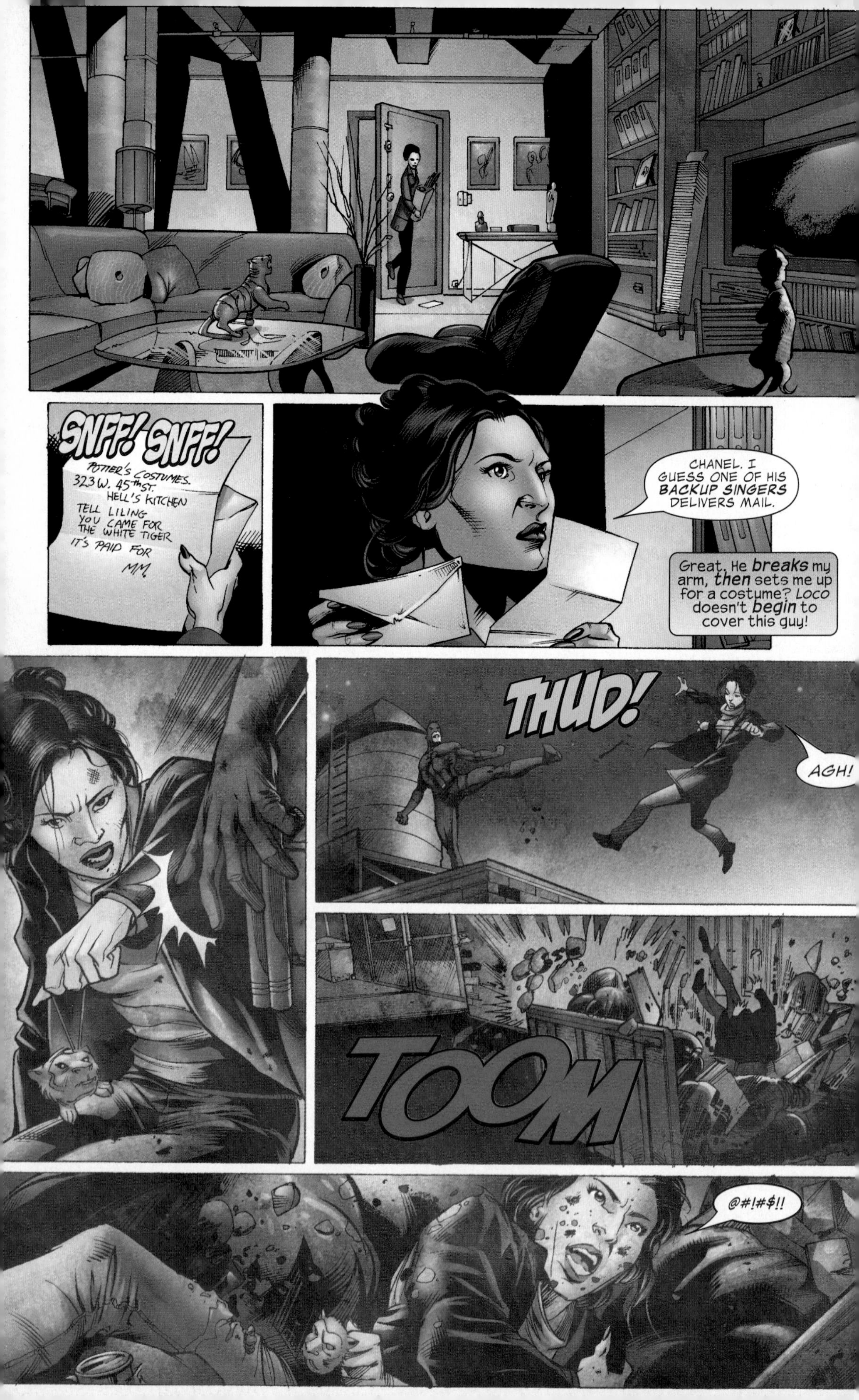

SNFF! SNFF!
POTTER'S COSTUMES.
323 W. 45th ST.
HELL'S KITCHEN
TELL LILING
YOU CAME FOR
THE WHITE TIGER
IT'S PAID FOR
MM.
CHANEL. I GUESS ONE OF HIS BACKUP SINGERS DELIVERS MAIL.
Great. He breaks my arm, then sets me up for a costume? Loco doesn't begin to cover this guy!
THUD!
AGH!
TOOM
@#!#$!!

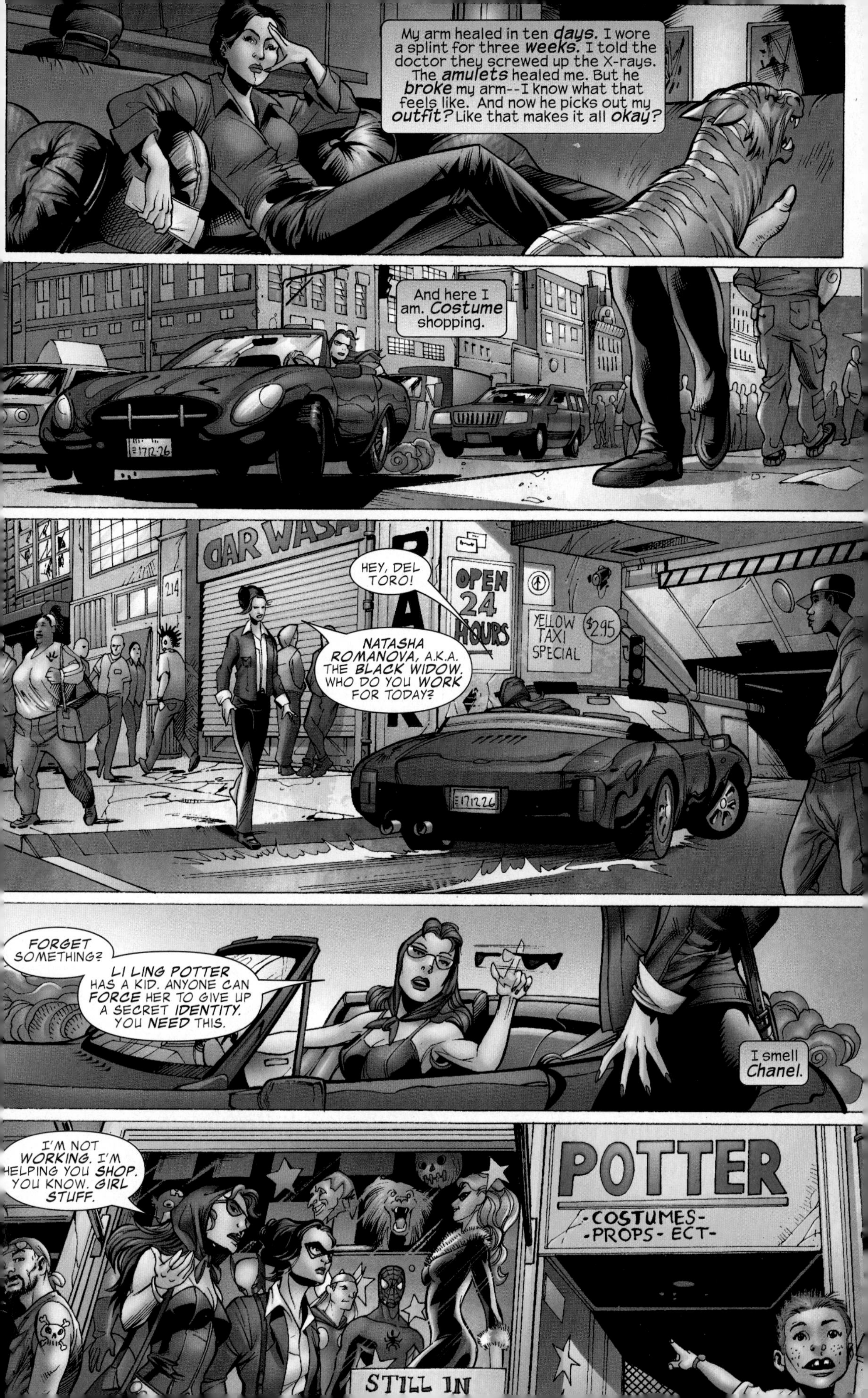
My arm healed in ten days. I wore a splint for three weeks. I told the doctor they screwed up the X-rays. The amulets healed me. But he broke my arm--I know what that feels like. And now he picks out my outfit? Like that makes it all okay?
And here I am. Costume shopping.
CAR WASH
214
OPEN 24 HOURS
YELLOW TAXI SPECIAL
$2.95
HEY, DEL TORO!
NATASHA ROMANOVA, A.K.A. THE BLACK WIDOW. WHO DO YOU WORK FOR TODAY?
FORGET SOMETHING?
LI LING POTTER HAS A KID. ANYONE CAN FORCE HER TO GIVE UP A SECRET IDENTITY. YOU NEED THIS.
I smell Chanel.
I'M NOT WORKING. I'M HELPING YOU SHOP. YOU KNOW. GIRL STUFF.
POTTER
-COSTUMES-
-PROPS- ECT-
STILL IN

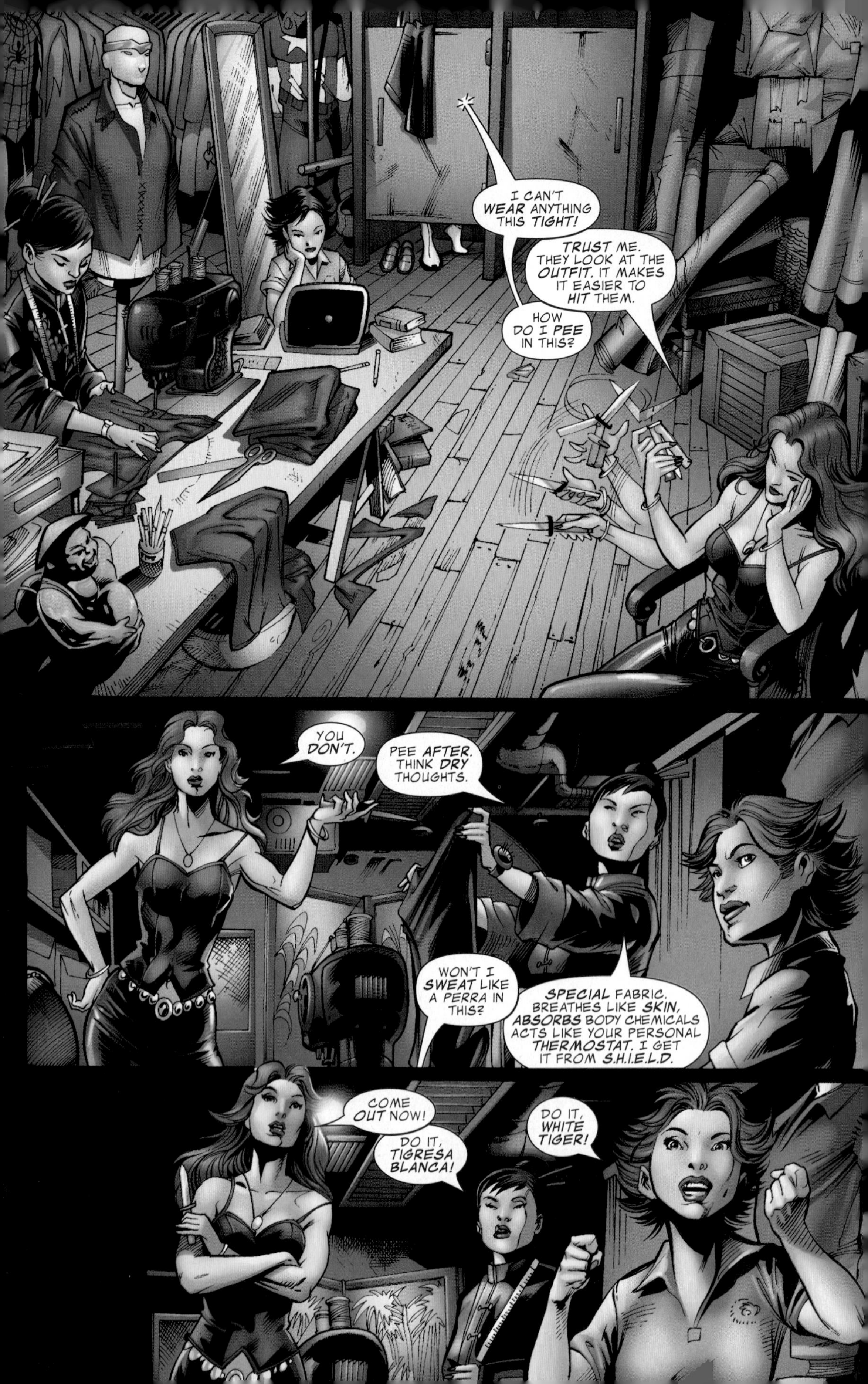
I CAN'T WEAR ANYTHING THIS TIGHT!
TRUST ME. THEY LOOK AT THE OUTFIT. IT MAKES IT EASIER TO HIT THEM.
HOW DO I PEE IN THIS?
YOU DON'T.
PEE AFTER. THINK DRY THOUGHTS.
WON'T I SWEAT LIKE A PERRA IN THIS?
SPECIAL FABRIC. BREATHES LIKE SKIN, ABSORBS BODY CHEMICALS ACTS LIKE YOUR PERSONAL THERMOSTAT. I GET IT FROM S.H.I.E.L.D.
COME OUT NOW!
DO IT, TIGRESA BLANCA!
DO IT, WHITE TIGER!

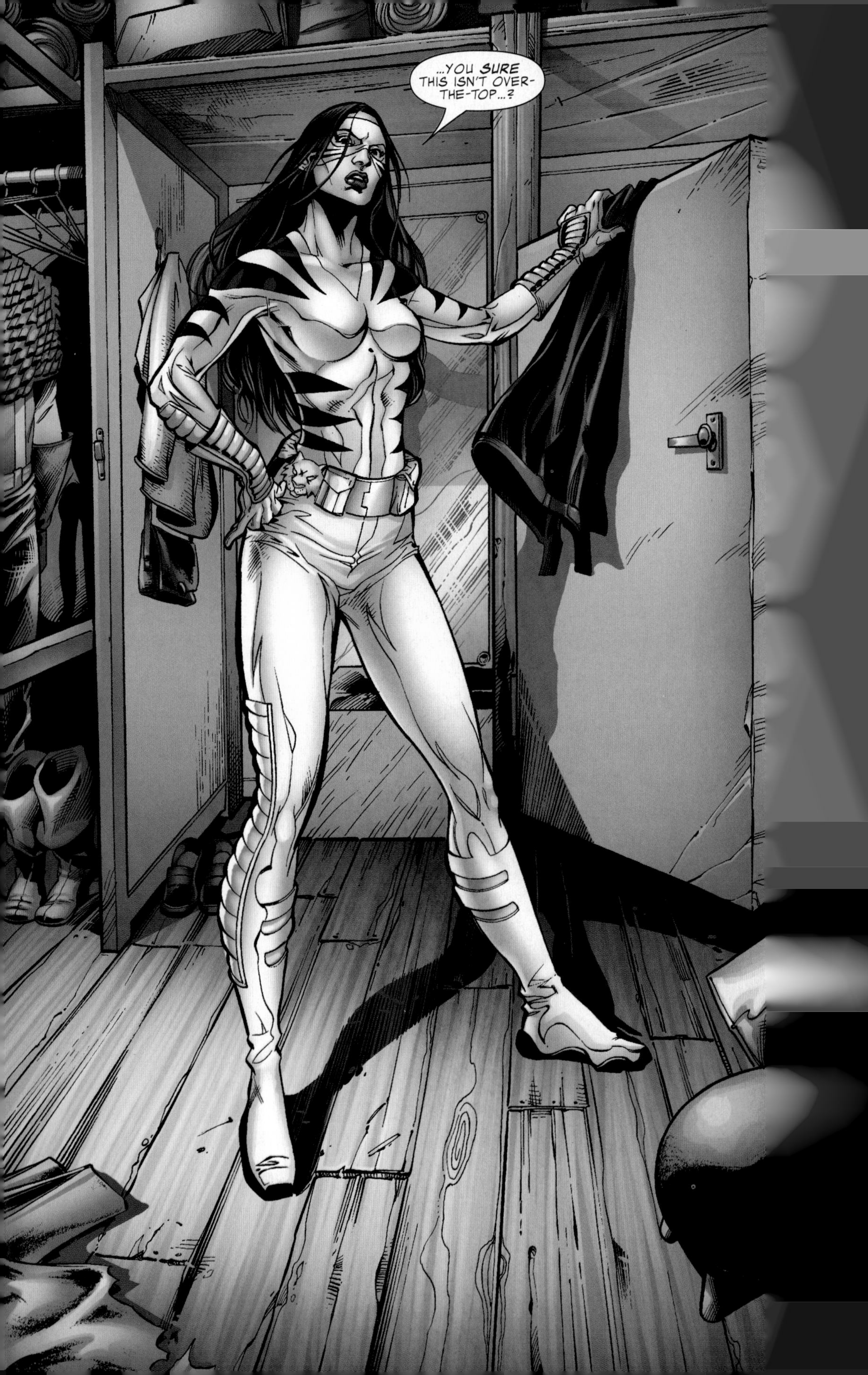
...YOU SURE THIS ISN'T OVER-THE-TOP...?

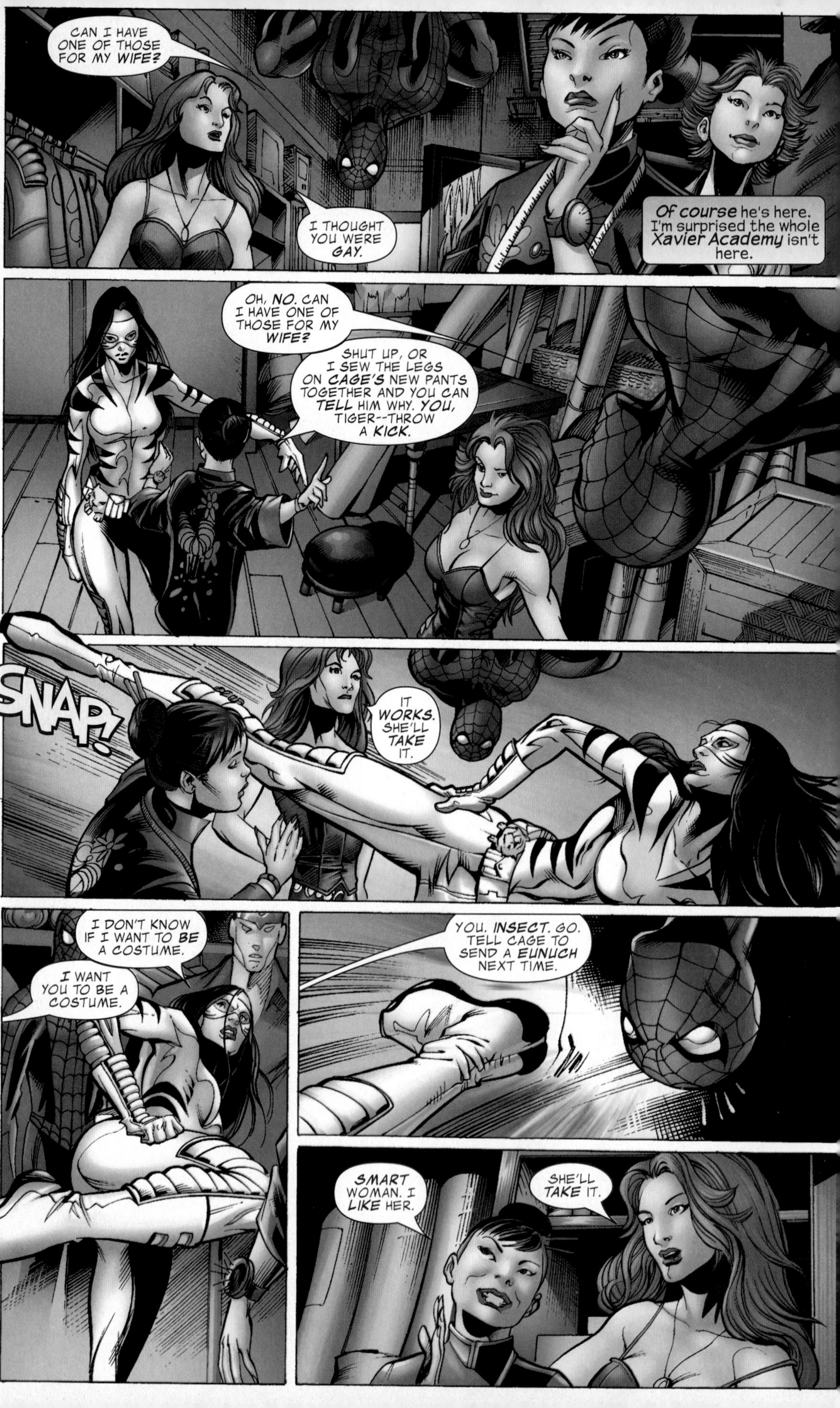
CAN I HAVE ONE OF THOSE FOR MY WIFE?
I THOUGHT YOU WERE GAY.
Of course he's here. I'm surprised the whole Xavier Academy isn't here.
OH, NO. CAN I HAVE ONE OF THOSE FOR MY WIFE?
SHUT UP, OR I SEW THE LEGS ON CAGE'S NEW PANTS TOGETHER AND YOU CAN TELL HIM WHY. YOU, TIGER--THROW A KICK.
SNAP!
IT WORKS. SHE'LL TAKE IT.
I DON'T KNOW IF I WANT TO BE A COSTUME.
I WANT YOU TO BE A COSTUME.
YOU. INSECT. GO. TELL CAGE TO SEND A EUNUCH NEXT TIME.
SMART WOMAN. I LIKE HER.
SHE'LL TAKE IT.

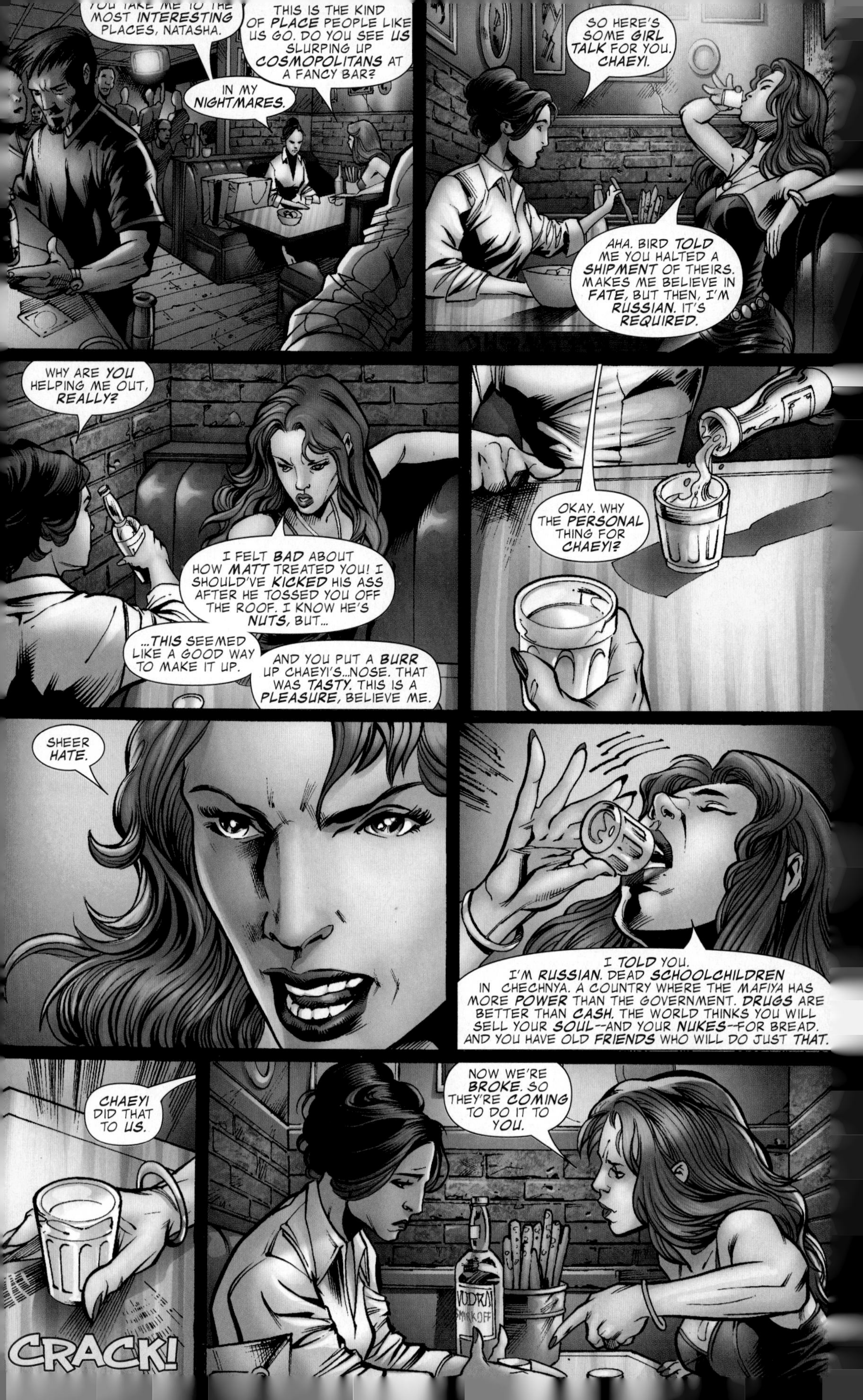
YOU TAKE ME TO THE MOST INTERESTING PLACES, NATASHA.
THIS IS THE KIND OF PLACE PEOPLE LIKE US GO. DO YOU SEE US SLURPING UP COSMOPOLITANS AT A FANCY BAR?
IN MY NIGHTMARES.
SO HERE'S SOME GIRL TALK FOR YOU. CHAEYI.
AHA. BIRD TOLD ME YOU HALTED A SHIPMENT OF THEIRS. MAKES ME BELIEVE IN FATE, BUT THEN, I'M RUSSIAN. IT'S REQUIRED.
WHY ARE YOU HELPING ME OUT, REALLY?
I FELT BAD ABOUT HOW MATT TREATED YOU! I SHOULD'VE KICKED HIS ASS AFTER HE TOSSED YOU OFF THE ROOF. I KNOW HE'S NUTS, BUT...
...THIS SEEMED LIKE A GOOD WAY TO MAKE IT UP.
AND YOU PUT A BURR UP CHAEYI'S...NOSE. THAT WAS TASTY. THIS IS A PLEASURE, BELIEVE ME.
OKAY. WHY THE PERSONAL THING FOR CHAEYI?
SHEER HATE.
I TOLD YOU. I'M RUSSIAN. DEAD SCHOOLCHILDREN IN CHECHNYA. A COUNTRY WHERE THE MAFIYA HAS MORE POWER THAN THE GOVERNMENT. DRUGS ARE BETTER THAN CASH. THE WORLD THINKS YOU WILL SELL YOUR SOUL--AND YOUR NUKES--FOR BREAD. AND YOU HAVE OLD FRIENDS WHO WILL DO JUST THAT.
CHAEYI DID THAT TO US.
CRACK!
NOW WE'RE BROKE. SO THEY'RE COMING TO DO IT TO YOU.

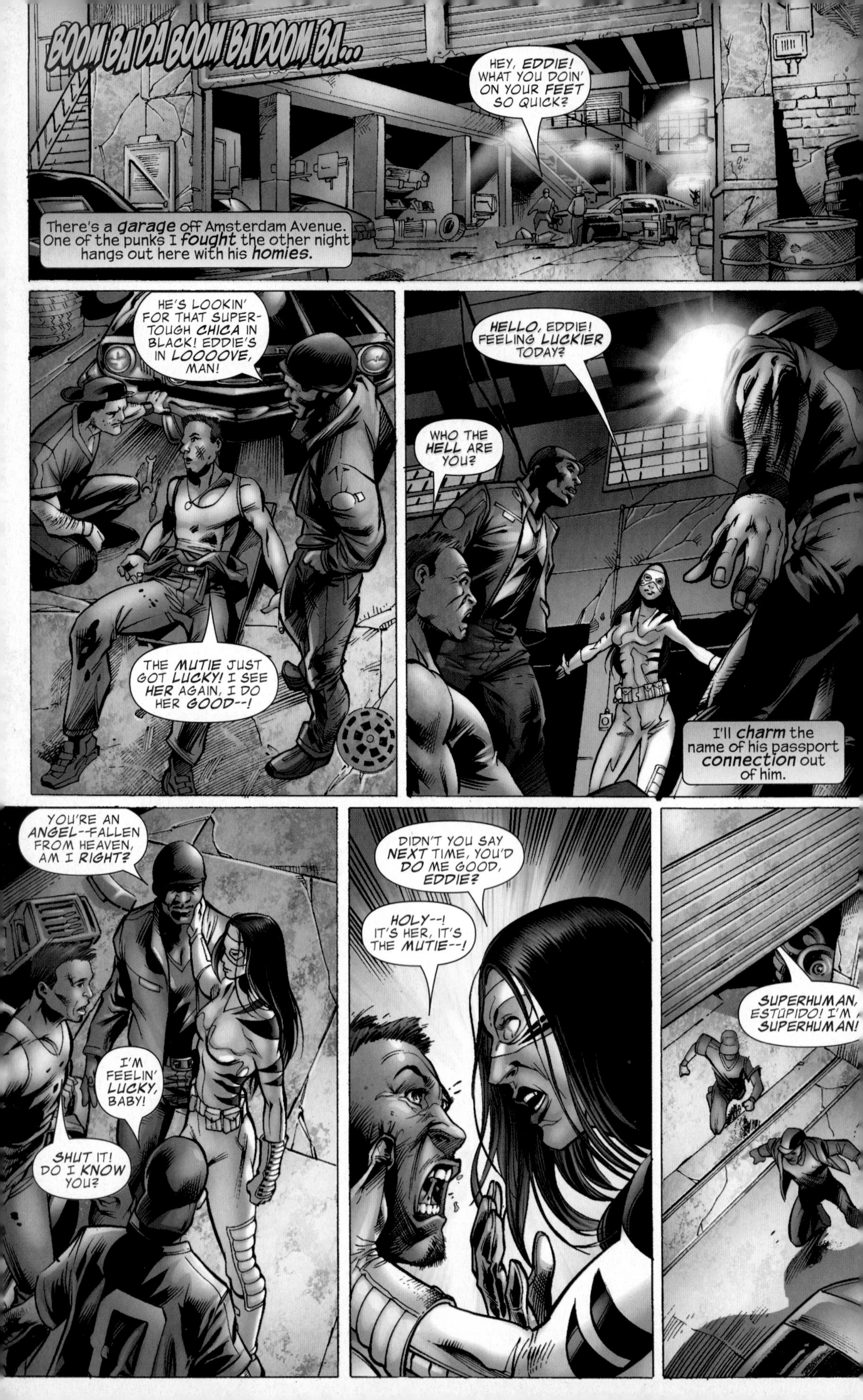

BOOM BA DA BOOM BA DOOM BA...
HEY, EDDIE! WHAT YOU DOIN' ON YOUR FEET SO QUICK?
There's a garage off Amsterdam Avenue. One of the punks I fought the other night hangs out here with his homies.
HE'S LOOKIN' FOR THAT SUPER-TOUGH CHICA IN BLACK! EDDIE'S IN LOOOOVE, MAN!
THE MUTIE JUST GOT LUCKY! I SEE HER AGAIN, I DO HER GOOD--!
HELLO, EDDIE! FEELING LUCKIER TODAY?
WHO THE HELL ARE YOU?
I'll charm the name of his passport connection out of him.
YOU'RE AN ANGEL--FALLEN FROM HEAVEN, AM I RIGHT?
I'M FEELIN' LUCKY, BABY!
SHUT IT! DO I KNOW YOU?
DIDN'T YOU SAY NEXT TIME, YOU'D DO ME GOOD, EDDIE?
HOLY--! IT'S HER, IT'S THE MUTIE--!
SUPERHUMAN, ESTÚPIDO! I'M SUPERHUMAN!

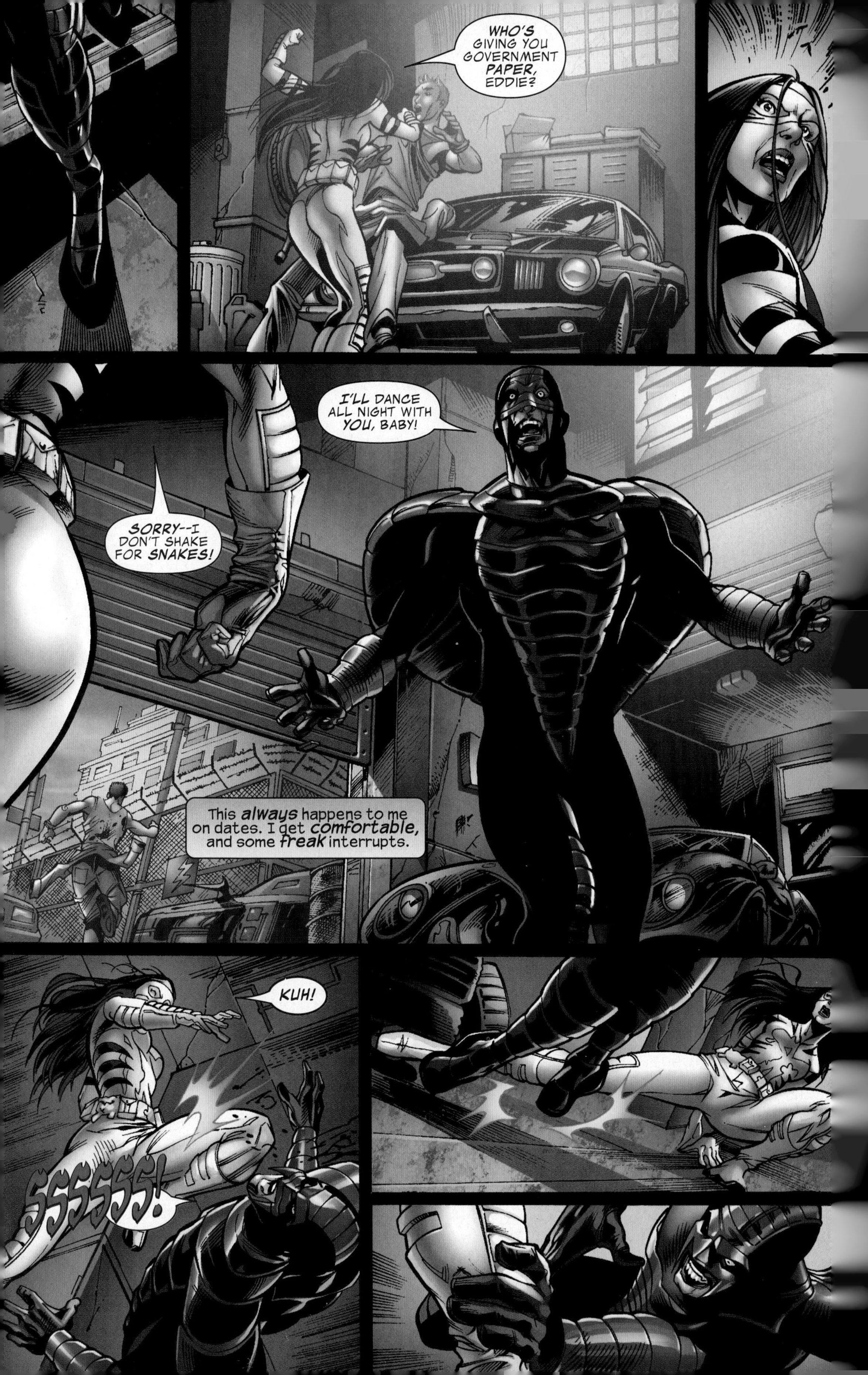
WHO'S GIVING YOU GOVERNMENT PAPER, EDDIE?
I'LL DANCE ALL NIGHT WITH YOU, BABY!
SORRY--I DON'T SHAKE FOR SNAKES!
This always happens to me on dates. I get comfortable, and some freak interrupts.
KUH!
SSSSSS!

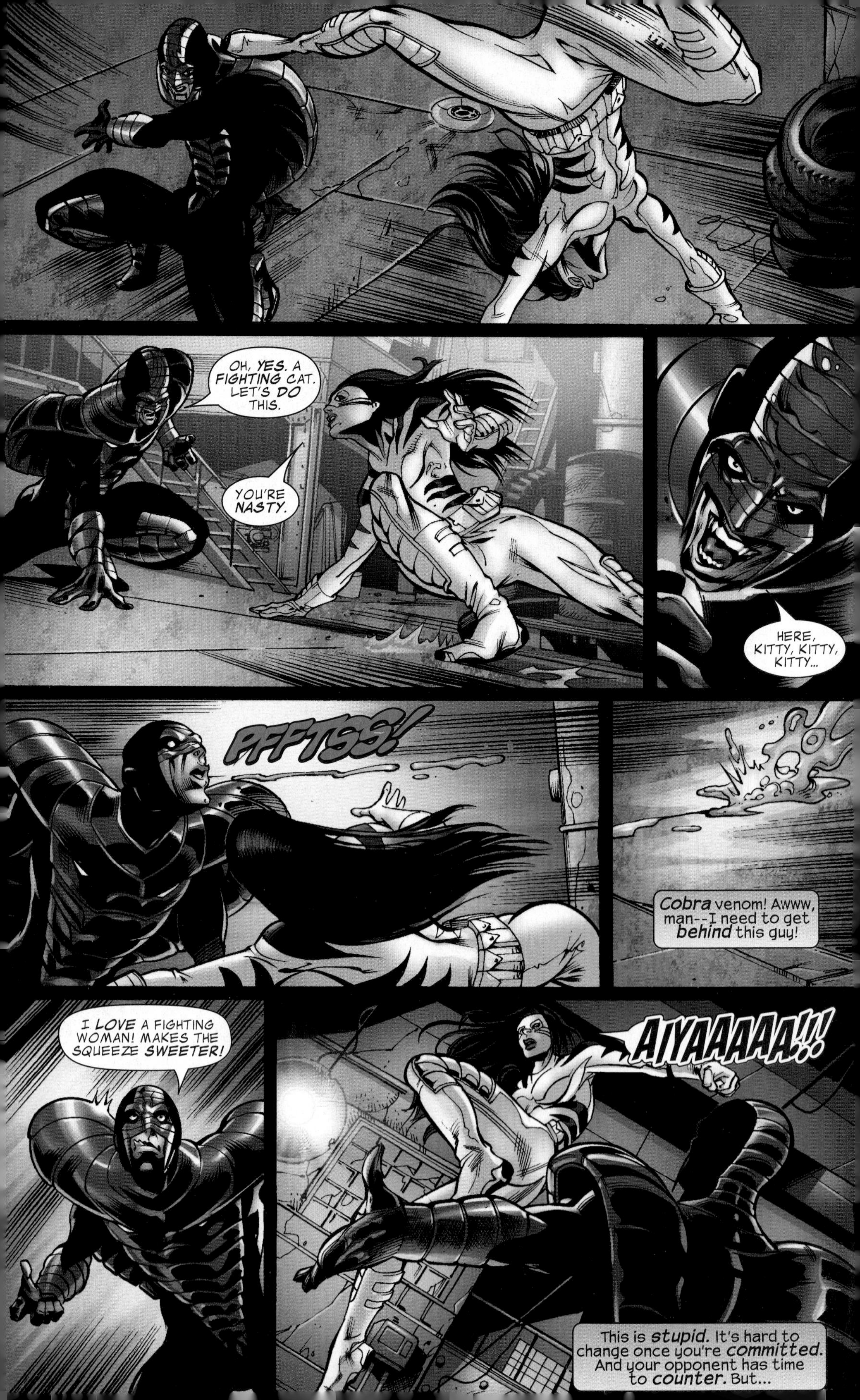
OH, YES. A FIGHTING CAT. LET'S DO THIS.
YOU'RE NASTY.
HERE, KITTY, KITTY, KITTY...
PFFTSS!
Cobra venom! Awww, man--I need to get behind this guy!
I LOVE A FIGHTING WOMAN! MAKES THE SQUEEZE SWEETER!
AIYAAAAA!!!
This is stupid. It's hard to change once you're committed. And your opponent has time to counter. But...

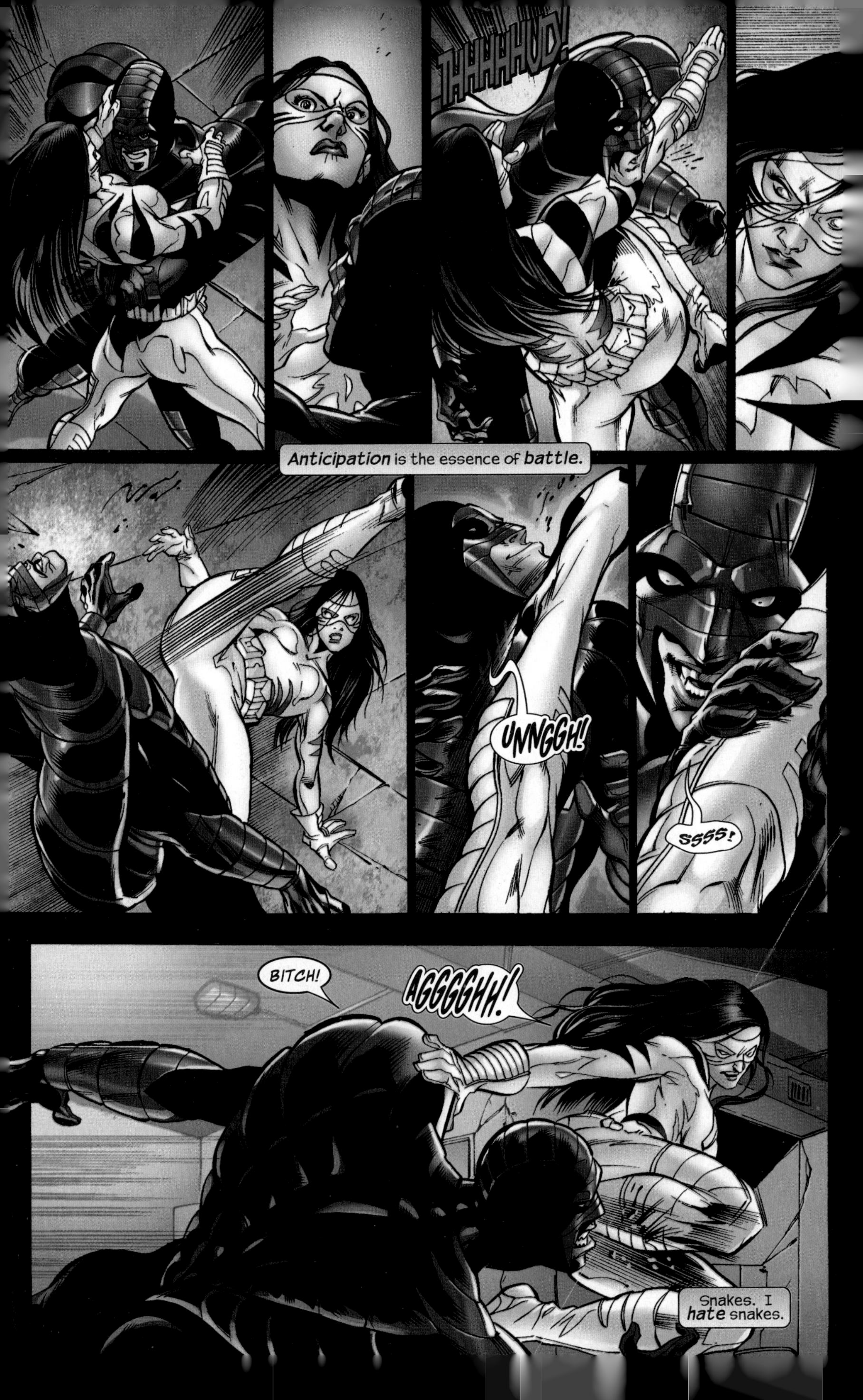
THHHHUD!
Anticipation is the essence of battle.
UNNGGH!
SSSS!
BITCH!
AGGGGHH!
Snakes. I hate snakes.

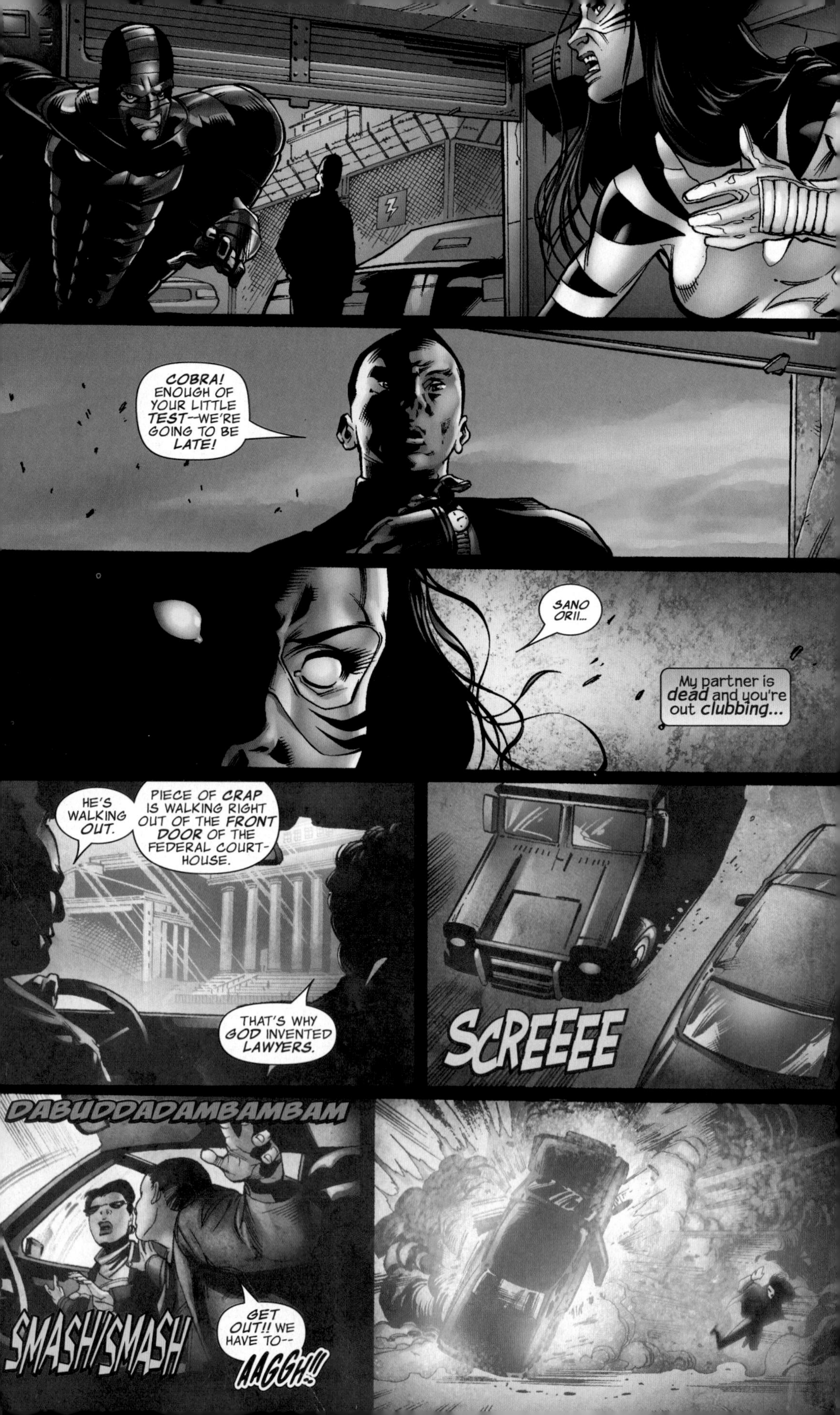
COBRA! ENOUGH OF YOUR LITTLE TEST--WE'RE GOING TO BE LATE!
SANO ORII...
My partner is dead and you're out clubbing...
HE'S WALKING OUT.
PIECE OF CRAP IS WALKING RIGHT OUT OF THE FRONT DOOR OF THE FEDERAL COURT-HOUSE.
THAT'S WHY GOD INVENTED LAWYERS.
SCREEEE
DABUDDADAMBAMBAM
SMASH! SMASH
GET OUT!! WE HAVE TO--
AAGGH!!

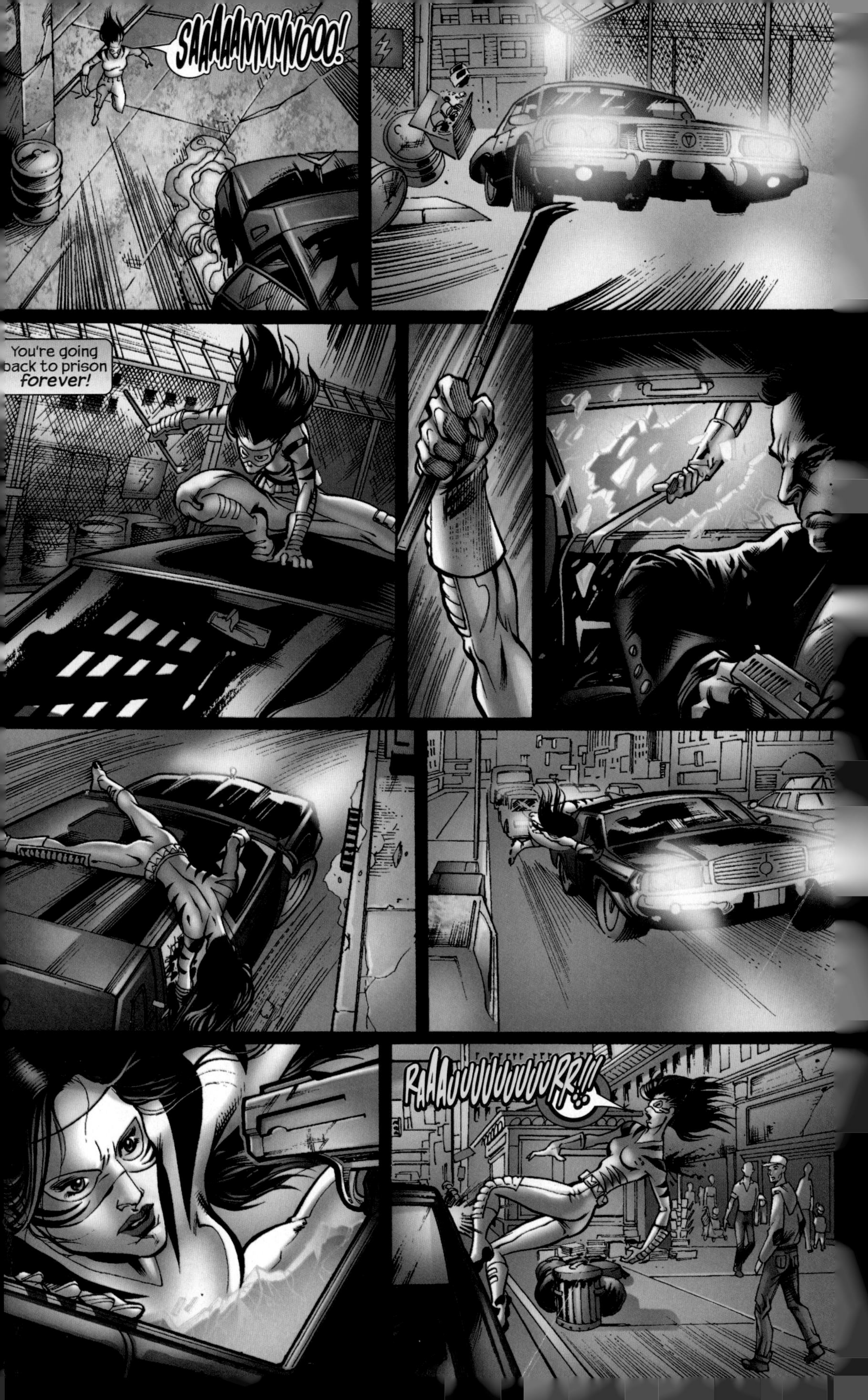
SAAAAANNNNOOO!
You're going back to prison forever!
RAAAUUUUUUUUUURR!!!

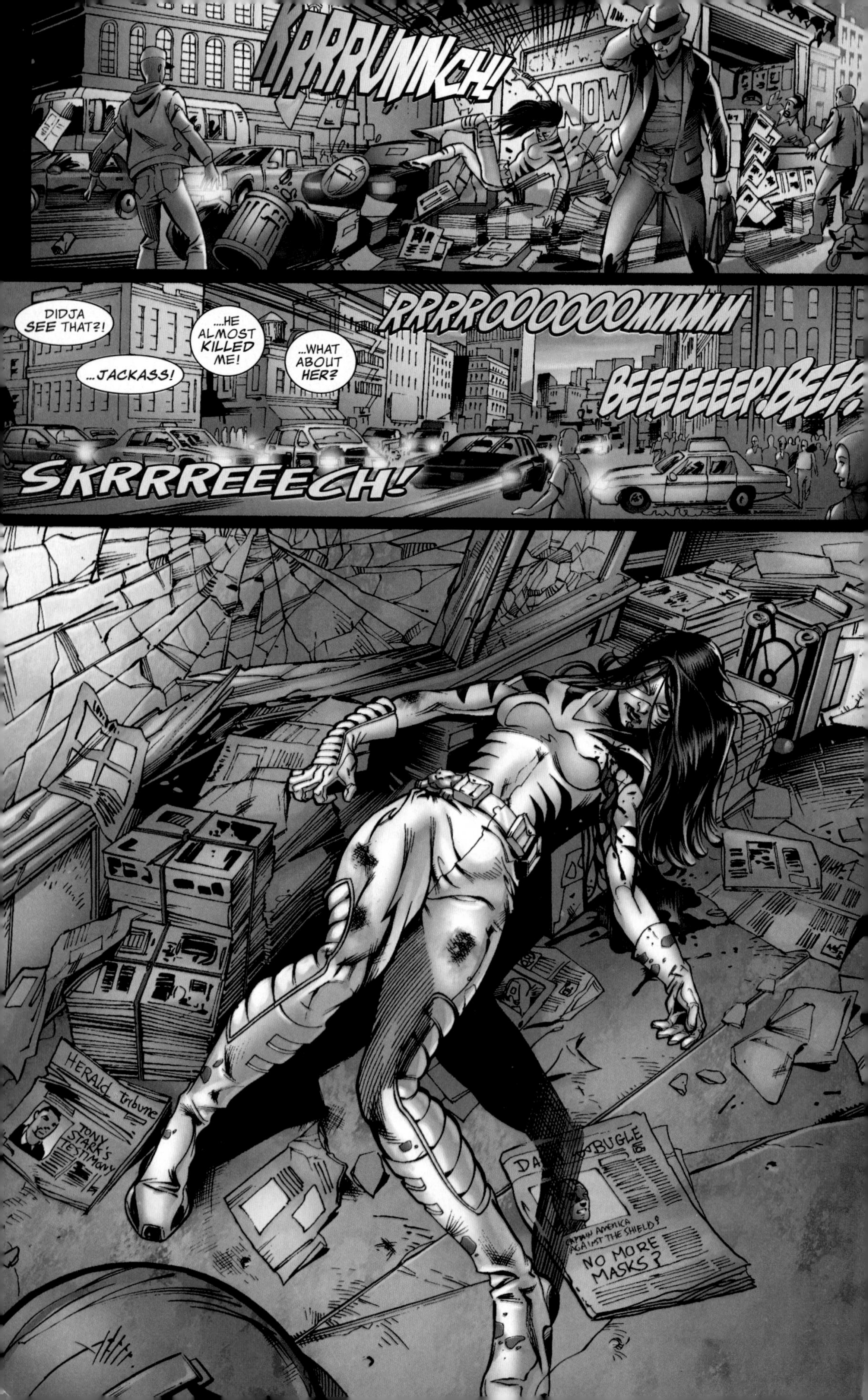
KRRRUNNCH!
NOW
DIDJA SEE THAT?!
...JACKASS!
...HE ALMOST KILLED ME!
...WHAT ABOUT HER?
RRRRROOOOOOOMMMMM
BEEEEEEEP! BEEP!
SKRRRREEEECH!
HERALD Tribune
TONY STARK'S TESTIMONY
BUGLE
CAPTAIN AMERICA AGAINST THE SHIELD?
NO MORE MASKS?

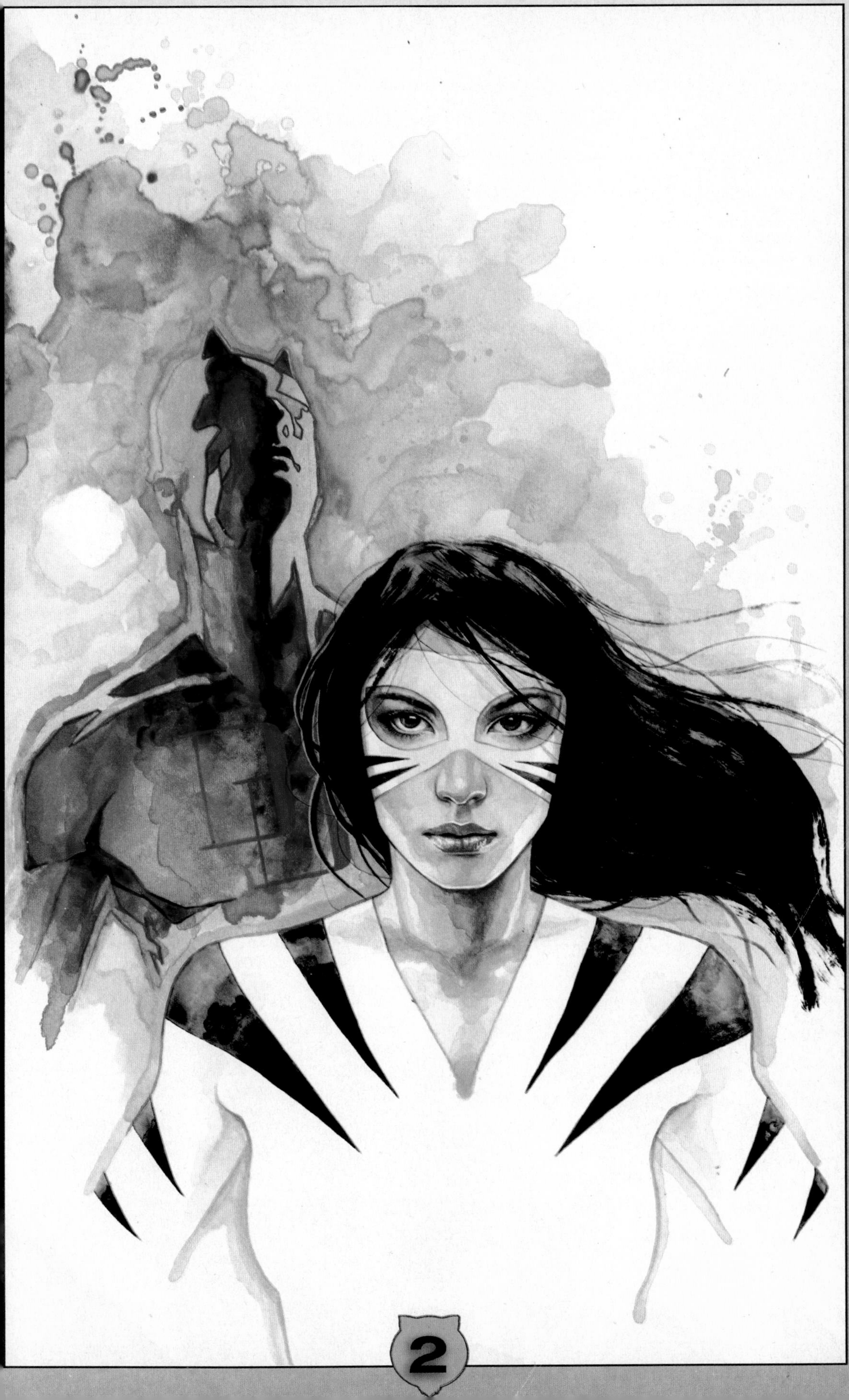
2

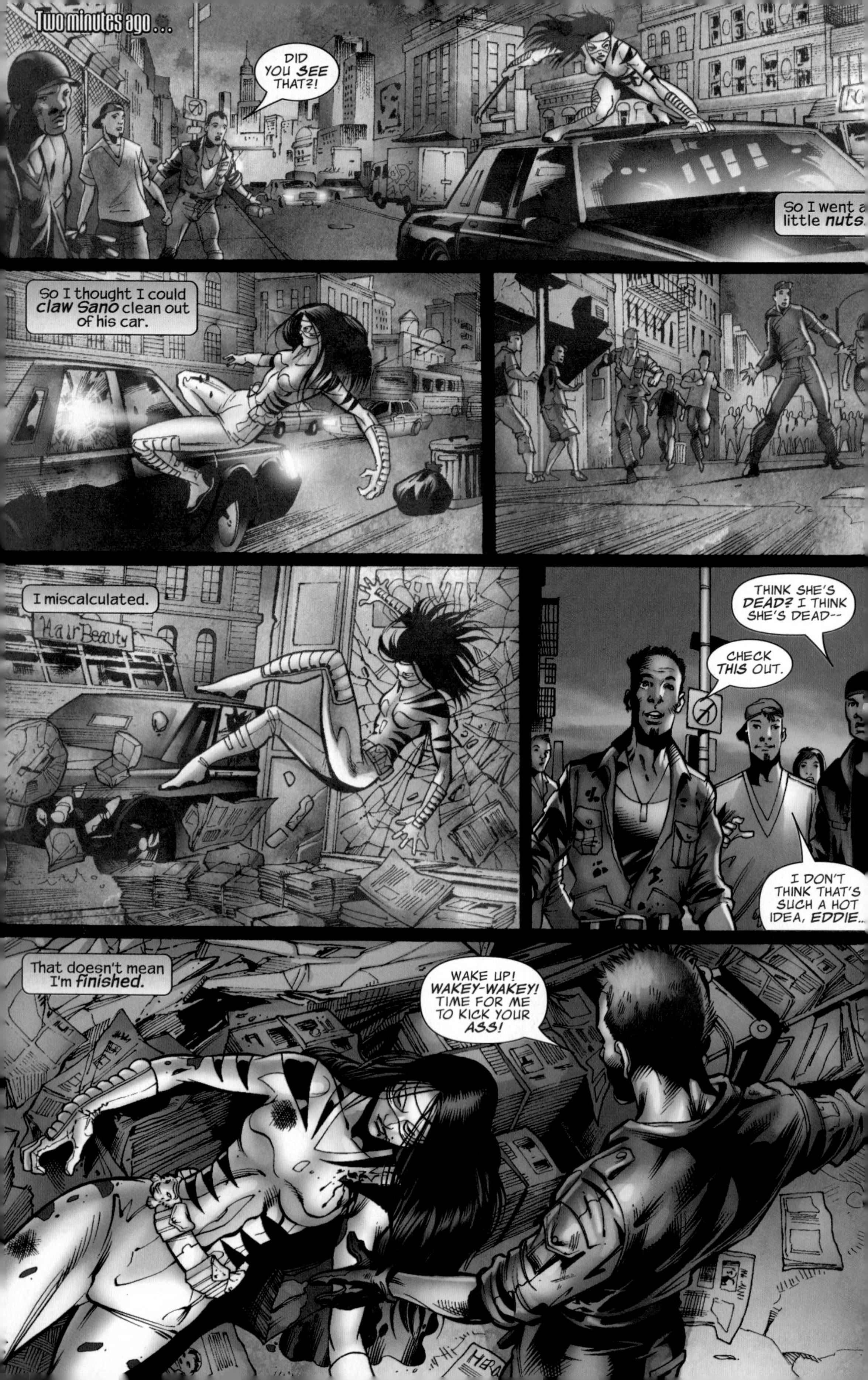
Two minutes ago . . .
DID YOU SEE THAT?!
So I went a little nuts.
So I thought I could claw Sano clean out of his car.
I miscalculated.
Hair Beauty
THINK SHE'S DEAD? I THINK SHE'S DEAD--
CHECK THIS OUT.
I DON'T THINK THAT'S SUCH A HOT IDEA, EDDIE...
That doesn't mean I'm finished.
WAKE UP! WAKEY-WAKEY! TIME FOR ME TO KICK YOUR ASS!

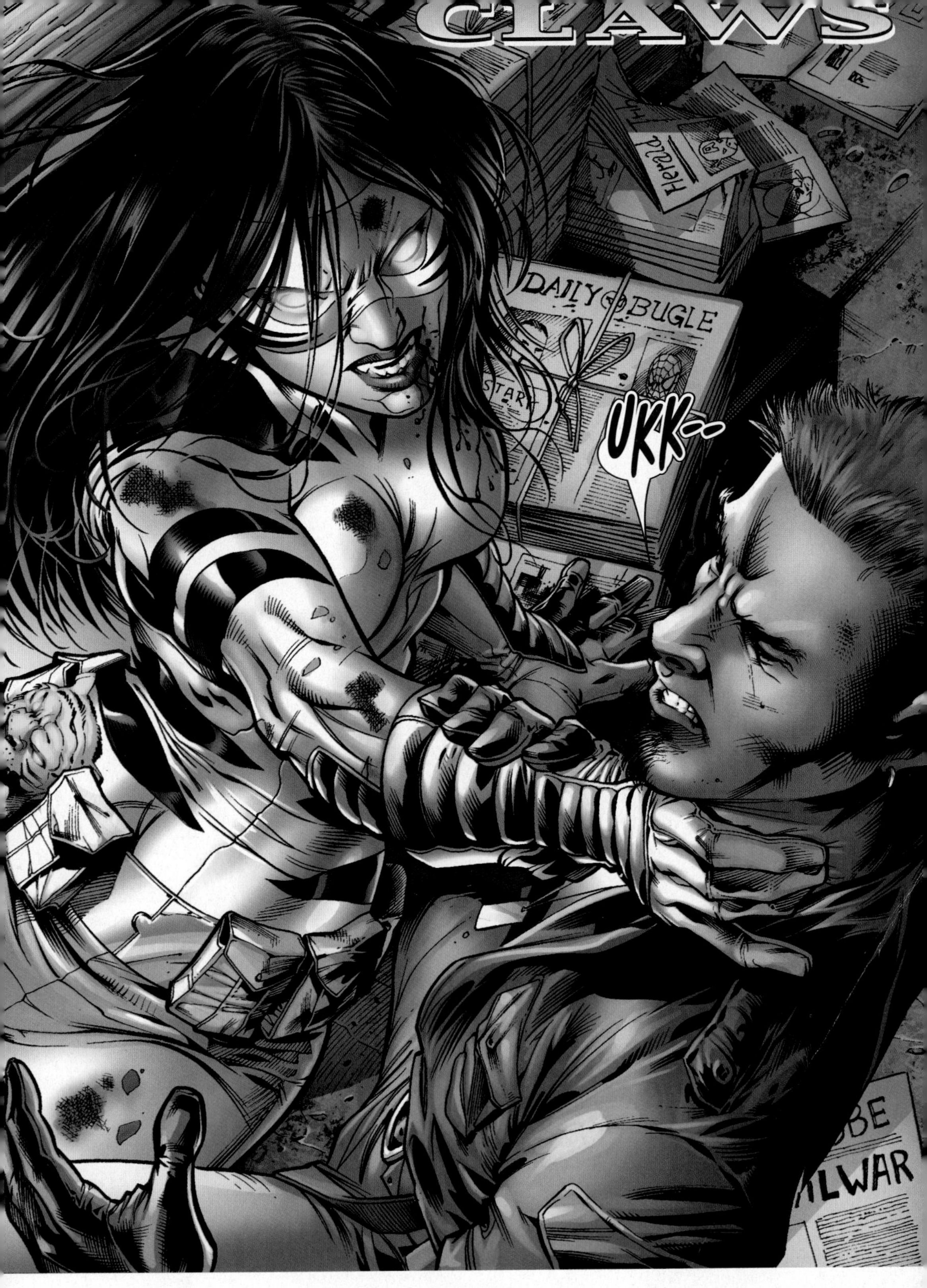
CLAWS
Herald
DAILY BUGLE
UKK--

A HERO'S COMPULSION
PART TWO OF SIX

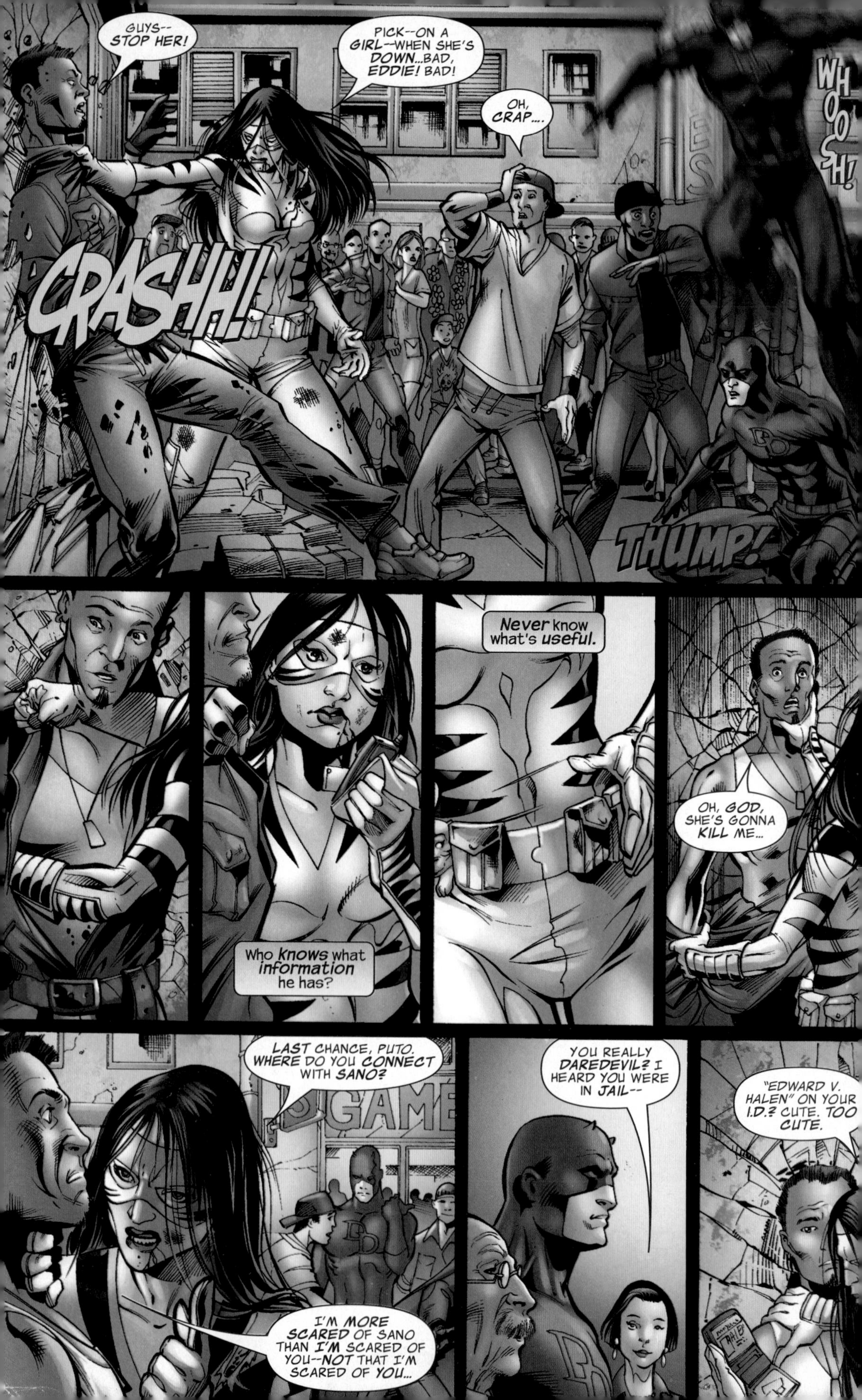

GUYS-- STOP HER!
PICK--ON A GIRL--WHEN SHE'S DOWN...BAD, EDDIE! BAD!
OH, CRAP....
WHOOOSH!
CRASHH!
THUMP!
Never know what's useful.
Who knows what information he has?
OH, GOD, SHE'S GONNA KILL ME...
LAST CHANCE, PUTO. WHERE DO YOU CONNECT WITH SANO?
I'M MORE SCARED OF SANO THAN I'M SCARED OF YOU--NOT THAT I'M SCARED OF YOU...
YOU REALLY DAREDEVIL? I HEARD YOU WERE IN JAIL--
"EDWARD V. HALEN" ON YOUR I.D.? CUTE. TOO CUTE.

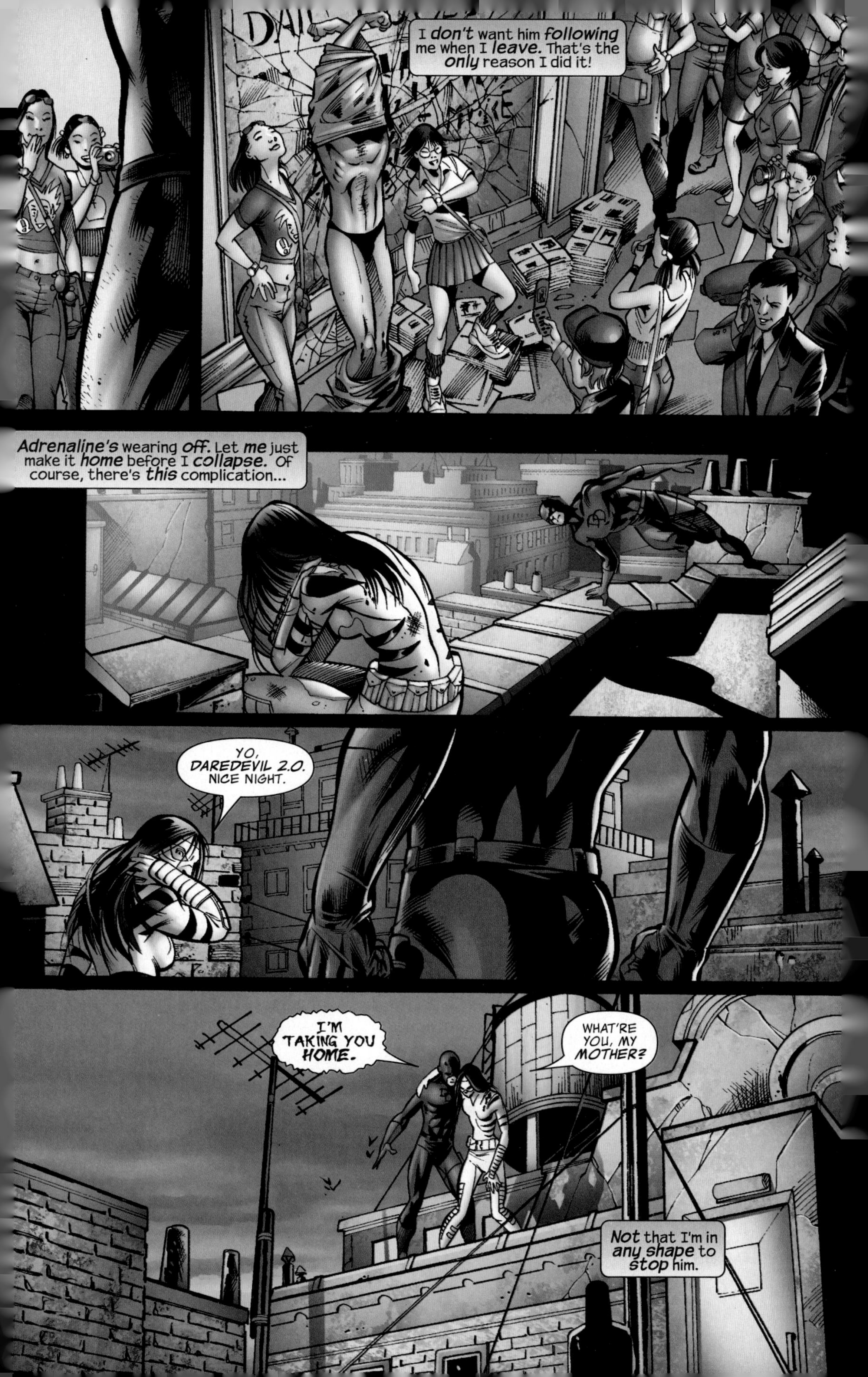
I don't want him following me when I leave. That's the only reason I did it!
Adrenaline's wearing off. Let me just make it home before I collapse. Of course, there's this complication...
YO, DAREDEVIL 2.0. NICE NIGHT.
I'M TAKING YOU HOME.
WHAT'RE YOU, MY MOTHER?
Not that I'm in any shape to stop him.

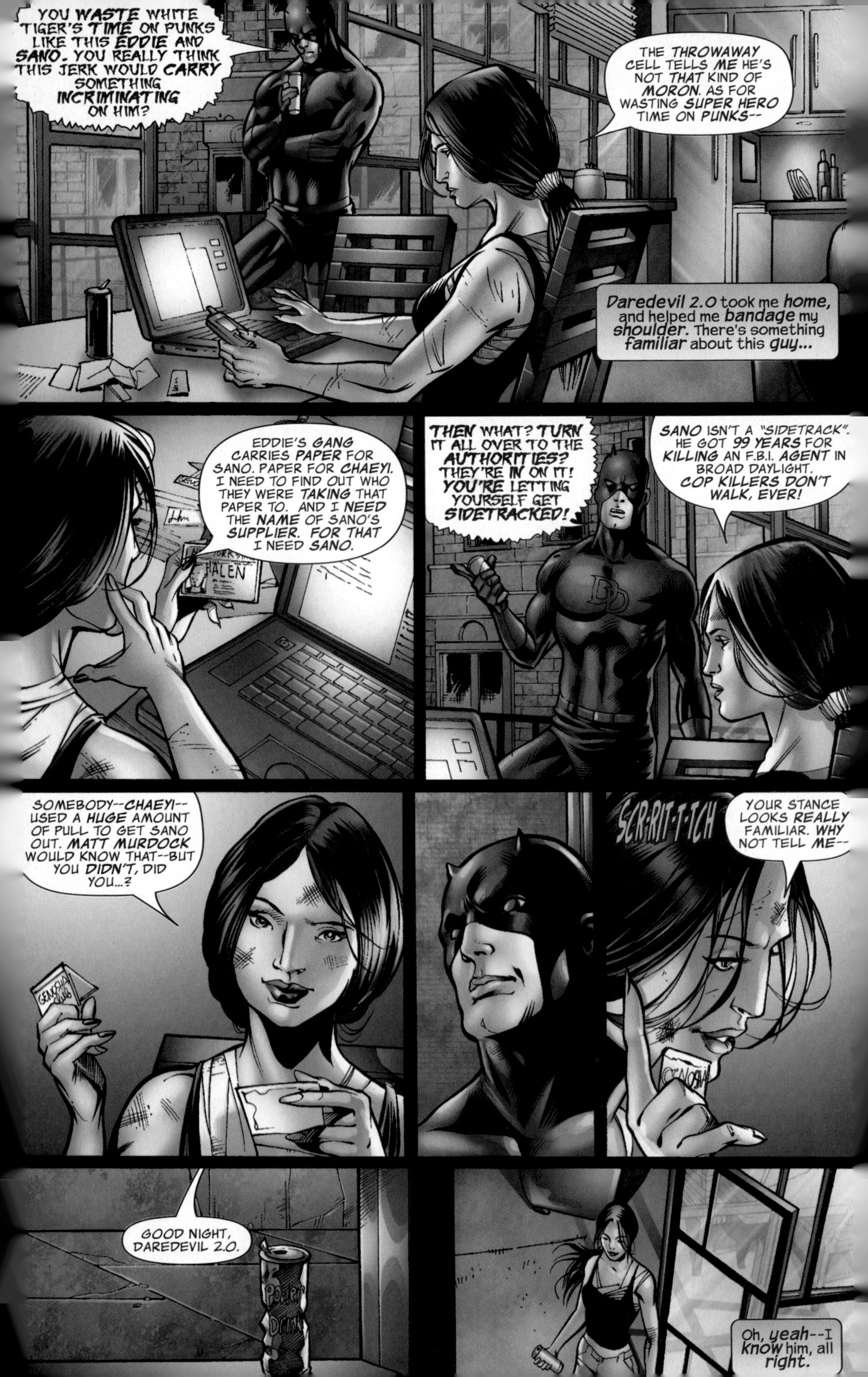
YOU WASTE WHITE TIGER'S TIME ON PUNKS LIKE THIS EDDIE AND SANO. YOU REALLY THINK THIS JERK WOULD CARRY SOMETHING INCRIMINATING ON HIM?
THE THROWAWAY CELL TELLS ME HE'S NOT THAT KIND OF MORON. AS FOR WASTING SUPER HERO TIME ON PUNKS--
Daredevil 2.0 took me home, and helped me bandage my shoulder. There's something familiar about this guy...
EDDIE'S GANG CARRIES PAPER FOR SANO. PAPER FOR CHAEYI. I NEED TO FIND OUT WHO THEY WERE TAKING THAT PAPER TO. AND I NEED THE NAME OF SANO'S SUPPLIER. FOR THAT I NEED SANO.
THEN WHAT? TURN IT ALL OVER TO THE AUTHORITIES? THEY'RE IN ON IT! YOU'RE LETTING YOURSELF GET SIDETRACKED!
SANO ISN'T A "SIDETRACK". HE GOT 99 YEARS FOR KILLING AN F.B.I. AGENT IN BROAD DAYLIGHT. COP KILLERS DON'T WALK, EVER!
SOMEBODY--CHAEYI--USED A HUGE AMOUNT OF PULL TO GET SANO OUT. MATT MURDOCK WOULD KNOW THAT--BUT YOU DIDN'T, DID YOU...?
SCR-RIT-T-TCH
YOUR STANCE LOOKS REALLY FAMILIAR. WHY NOT TELL ME--
GOOD NIGHT, DAREDEVIL 2.0.
Oh, yeah--I know him, all right.

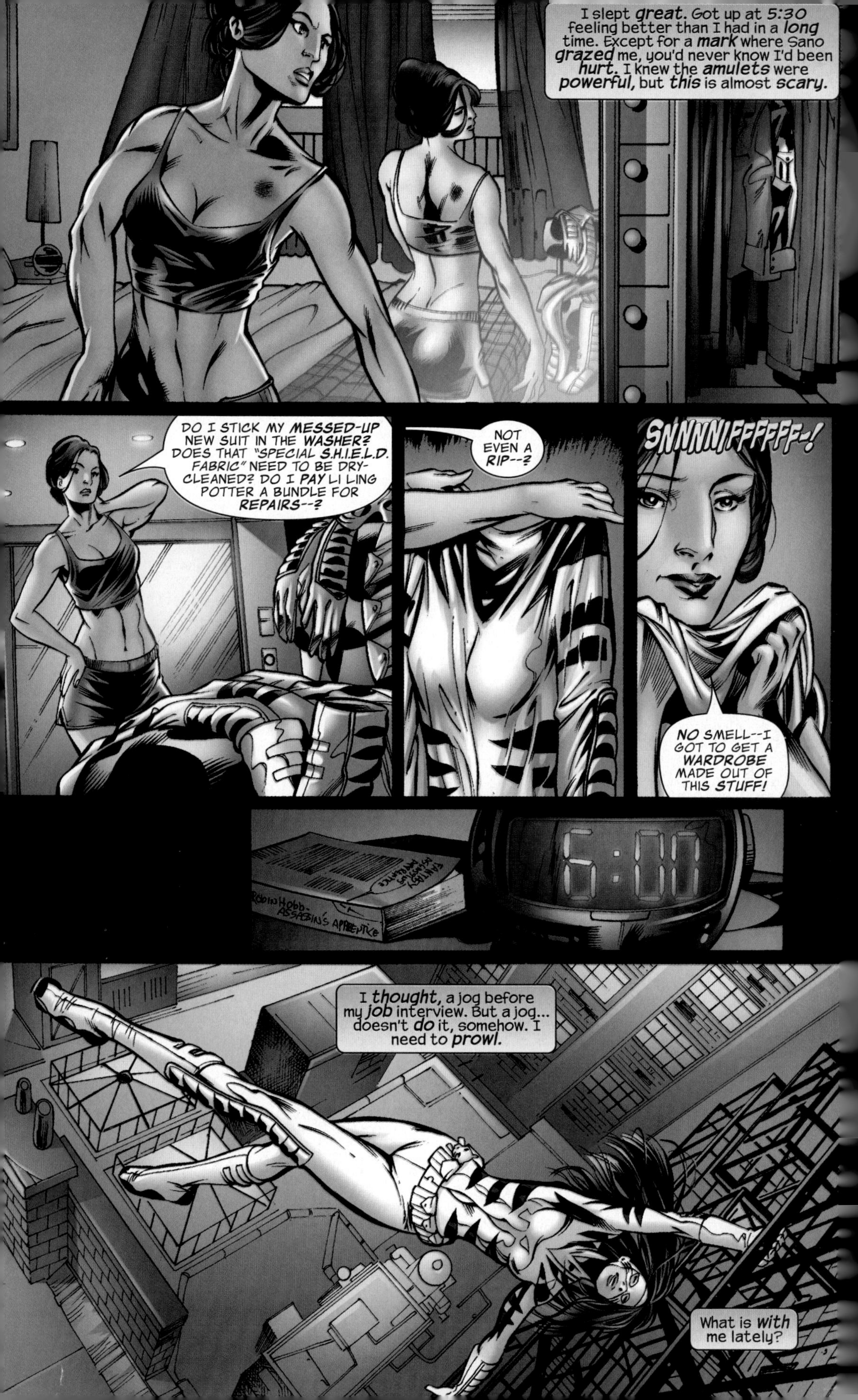

I slept great. Got up at 5:30 feeling better than I had in a long time. Except for a mark where Sano grazed me, you'd never know I'd been hurt. I knew the amulets were powerful, but this is almost scary.
DO I STICK MY MESSED-UP NEW SUIT IN THE WASHER? DOES THAT "SPECIAL S.H.I.E.L.D. FABRIC" NEED TO BE DRY-CLEANED? DO I PAY LI LING POTTER A BUNDLE FOR REPAIRS--?
NOT EVEN A RIP--?
SNNNNIFFFFFF-!
NO SMELL--I GOT TO GET A WARDROBE MADE OUT OF THIS STUFF!
6:00
ROBIN HOBB ASSASSIN'S APPRENTICE
I thought, a jog before my job interview. But a jog... doesn't do it, somehow. I need to prowl.
What is with me lately?

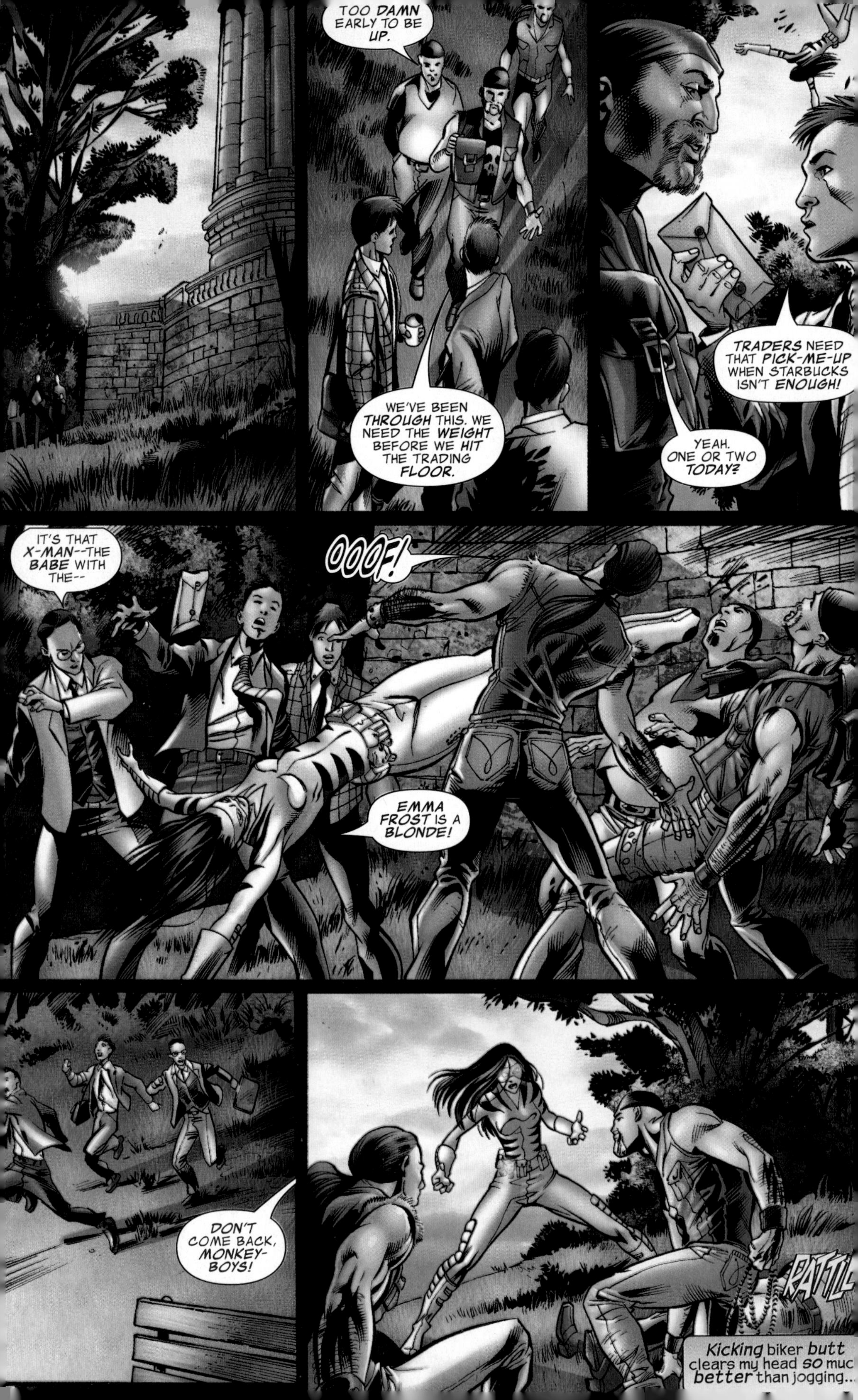

TOO DAMN EARLY TO BE UP.
WE'VE BEEN THROUGH THIS. WE NEED THE WEIGHT BEFORE WE HIT THE TRADING FLOOR.
TRADERS NEED THAT PICK-ME-UP WHEN STARBUCKS ISN'T ENOUGH!
YEAH. ONE OR TWO TODAY?
IT'S THAT X-MAN--THE BABE WITH THE--
OOOF!
EMMA FROST IS A BLONDE!
DON'T COME BACK, MONKEY-BOYS!
RATTL
Kicking biker butt clears my head so muc better than jogging...

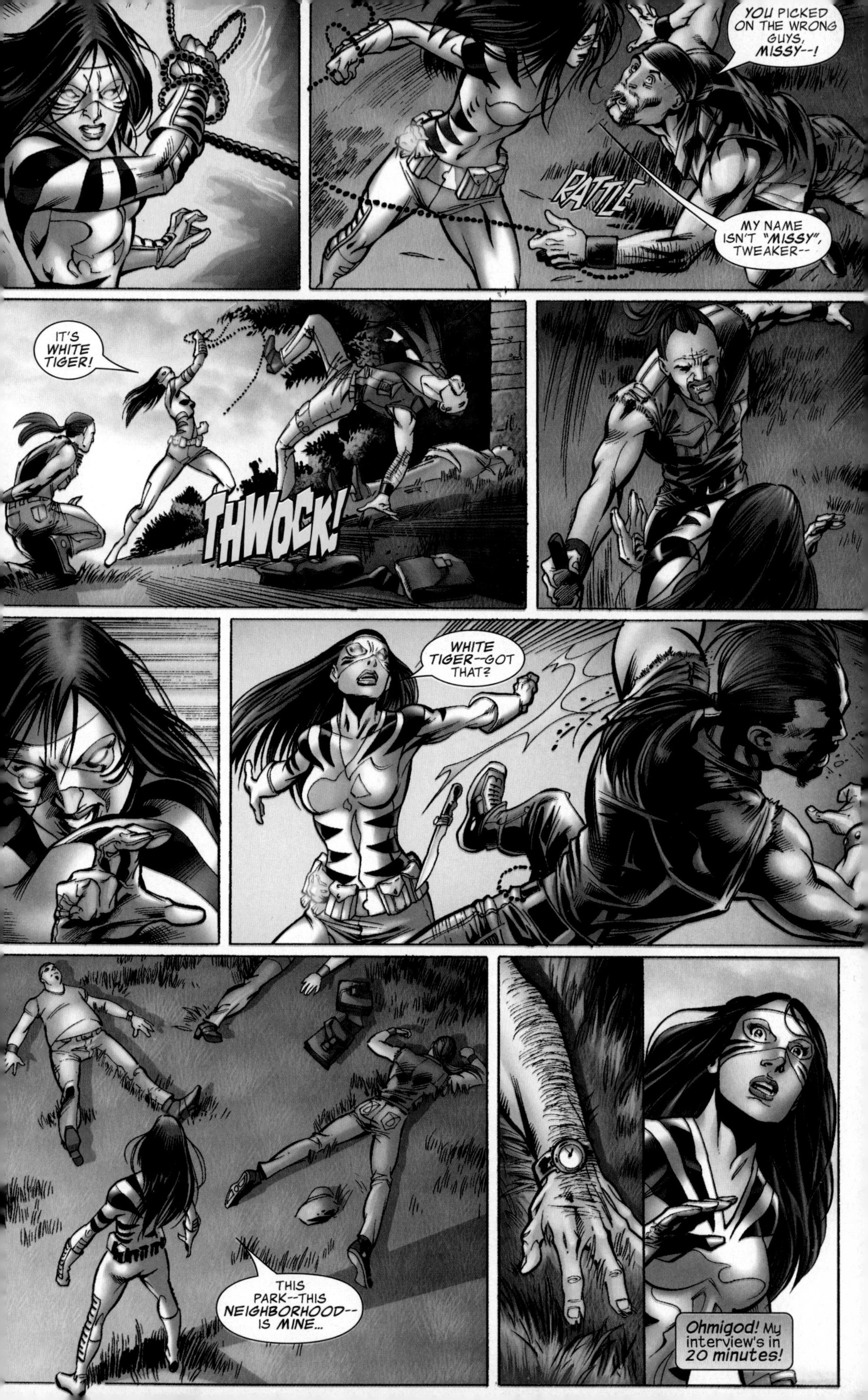
YOU PICKED ON THE WRONG GUYS, MISSY--!
RATTLE
MY NAME ISN'T "MISSY", TWEAKER--
IT'S WHITE TIGER!
THWOCK!
WHITE TIGER--GOT THAT?
THIS PARK--THIS NEIGHBORHOOD--IS MINE...
Ohmigod! My interview's in 20 minutes!

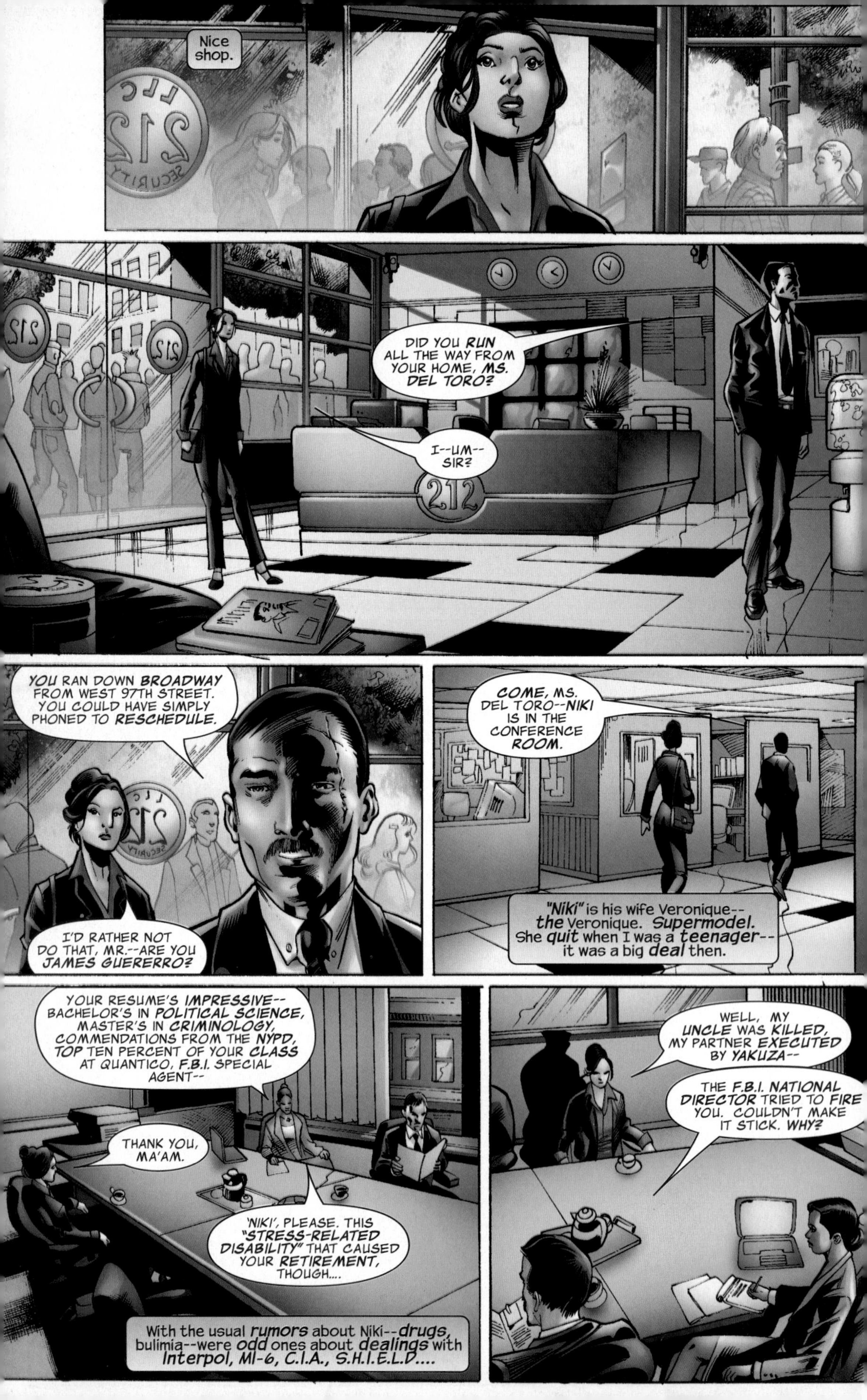
Nice shop.
DID YOU RUN ALL THE WAY FROM YOUR HOME, MS. DEL TORO?
I--UM--SIR?
YOU RAN DOWN BROADWAY FROM WEST 97TH STREET. YOU COULD HAVE SIMPLY PHONED TO RESCHEDULE.
I'D RATHER NOT DO THAT, MR.--ARE YOU JAMES GUERERRO?
COME, MS. DEL TORO--NIKI IS IN THE CONFERENCE ROOM.
"Niki" is his wife Veronique--the Veronique. Supermodel. She quit when I was a teenager--it was a big deal then.
YOUR RESUME'S IMPRESSIVE--BACHELOR'S IN POLITICAL SCIENCE, MASTER'S IN CRIMINOLOGY, COMMENDATIONS FROM THE NYPD, TOP TEN PERCENT OF YOUR CLASS AT QUANTICO, F.B.I. SPECIAL AGENT--
THANK YOU, MA'AM.
'NIKI', PLEASE. THIS "STRESS-RELATED DISABILITY" THAT CAUSED YOUR RETIREMENT, THOUGH....
With the usual rumors about Niki--drugs, bulimia--were odd ones about dealings with Interpol, MI-6, C.I.A., S.H.I.E.L.D....
WELL, MY UNCLE WAS KILLED, MY PARTNER EXECUTED BY YAKUZA--
THE F.B.I. NATIONAL DIRECTOR TRIED TO FIRE YOU. COULDN'T MAKE IT STICK. WHY?

THE DIRECTOR AND I DISAGREED OVER THE HANDLING OF A CASE--

--TASK FORCE MURDOCK. YOU FELT THAT, IN HIS DESIRE TO APPREHEND MATT MURDOCK, THE DIRECTOR HAD CLIMBED INTO BED WITH A KNOWN CRIME BOSS.

I AM NOT AT LIBERTY TO DISCUSS AN INVESTIGATION THAT IS STILL UNDERWAY. SIR.

He's a good guy, or Coville never would have sent me to him.

DO YOU OFTEN ARGUE WITH A SUPERIOR'S HANDLING OF A CASE, MS. DEL TORO?

I AM NOT AT LIBERTY TO DISCUSS AN ONGOING INVESTIGATION.

There went this job. Is Gourmet Garage hiring...?

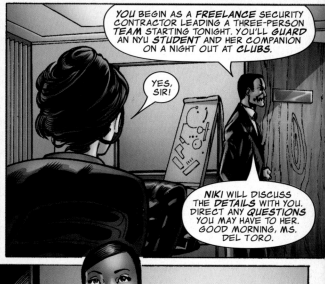

YOU BEGIN AS A FREELANCE SECURITY CONTRACTOR LEADING A THREE-PERSON TEAM STARTING TONIGHT. YOU'LL GUARD AN NYU STUDENT AND HER COMPANION ON A NIGHT OUT AT CLUBS.

YES, SIR!

NIKI WILL DISCUSS THE DETAILS WITH YOU. DIRECT ANY QUESTIONS YOU MAY HAVE TO HER. GOOD MORNING, MS. DEL TORO.

WELCOME ABOARD, LUV! JAMIE'S VERY IMPRESSED-- I KNOW YOU'LL DO WONDERFULLY!

ARE YOU SURE? HE...UH...

NEVER MADE EYE CONTACT? SPOKE SO QUIETLY YOU COULD BARELY HEAR HIM? WAS BRUSQUE TO THE POINT OF RUDENESS?

YEAH, THAT.

DON'T TAKE IT PERSONALLY, LUV! JAMIE'S LIKE THAT WITH EVERYBODY. HE'S SHY, POOR DARLING.

SHY-- RIGHT.

If you consider a waiting panther "shy"...

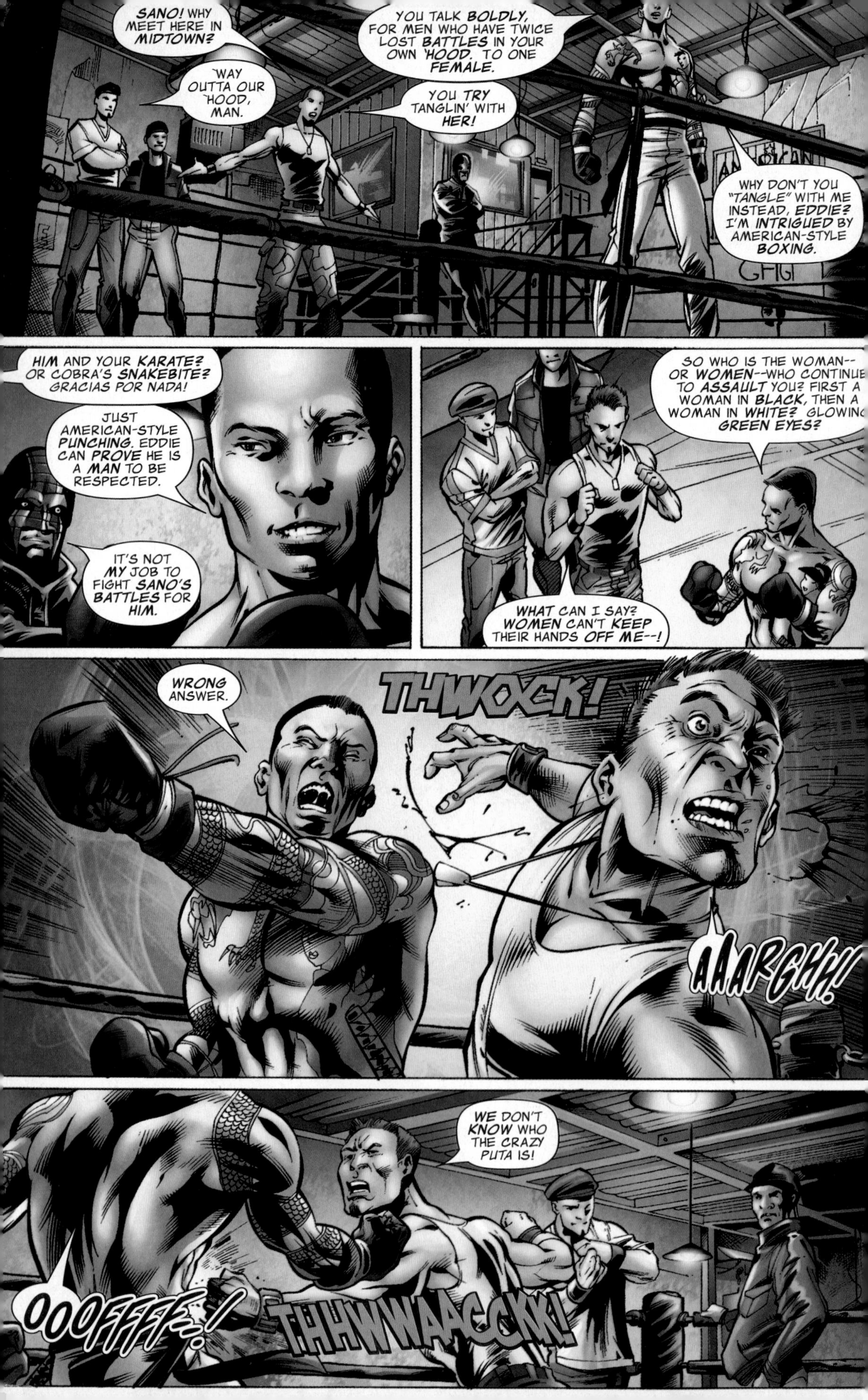
SANO! WHY MEET HERE IN MIDTOWN?
'WAY OUTTA OUR 'HOOD, MAN.
YOU TALK BOLDLY, FOR MEN WHO HAVE TWICE LOST BATTLES IN YOUR OWN 'HOOD. TO ONE FEMALE.
YOU TRY TANGLIN' WITH HER!
WHY DON'T YOU "TANGLE" WITH ME INSTEAD, EDDIE? I'M INTRIGUED BY AMERICAN-STYLE BOXING.
HIM AND YOUR KARATE? OR COBRA'S SNAKEBITE? GRACIAS POR NADA!
JUST AMERICAN-STYLE PUNCHING. EDDIE CAN PROVE HE IS A MAN TO BE RESPECTED.
IT'S NOT MY JOB TO FIGHT SANO'S BATTLES FOR HIM.
SO WHO IS THE WOMAN--OR WOMEN--WHO CONTINUE TO ASSAULT YOU? FIRST A WOMAN IN BLACK, THEN A WOMAN IN WHITE? GLOWING GREEN EYES?
WHAT CAN I SAY? WOMEN CAN'T KEEP THEIR HANDS OFF ME--!
WRONG ANSWER.
THWOCK!
AAARGHH!
WE DON'T KNOW WHO THE CRAZY PUTA IS!
OOOFFFF--!
THHWWAACCKK!

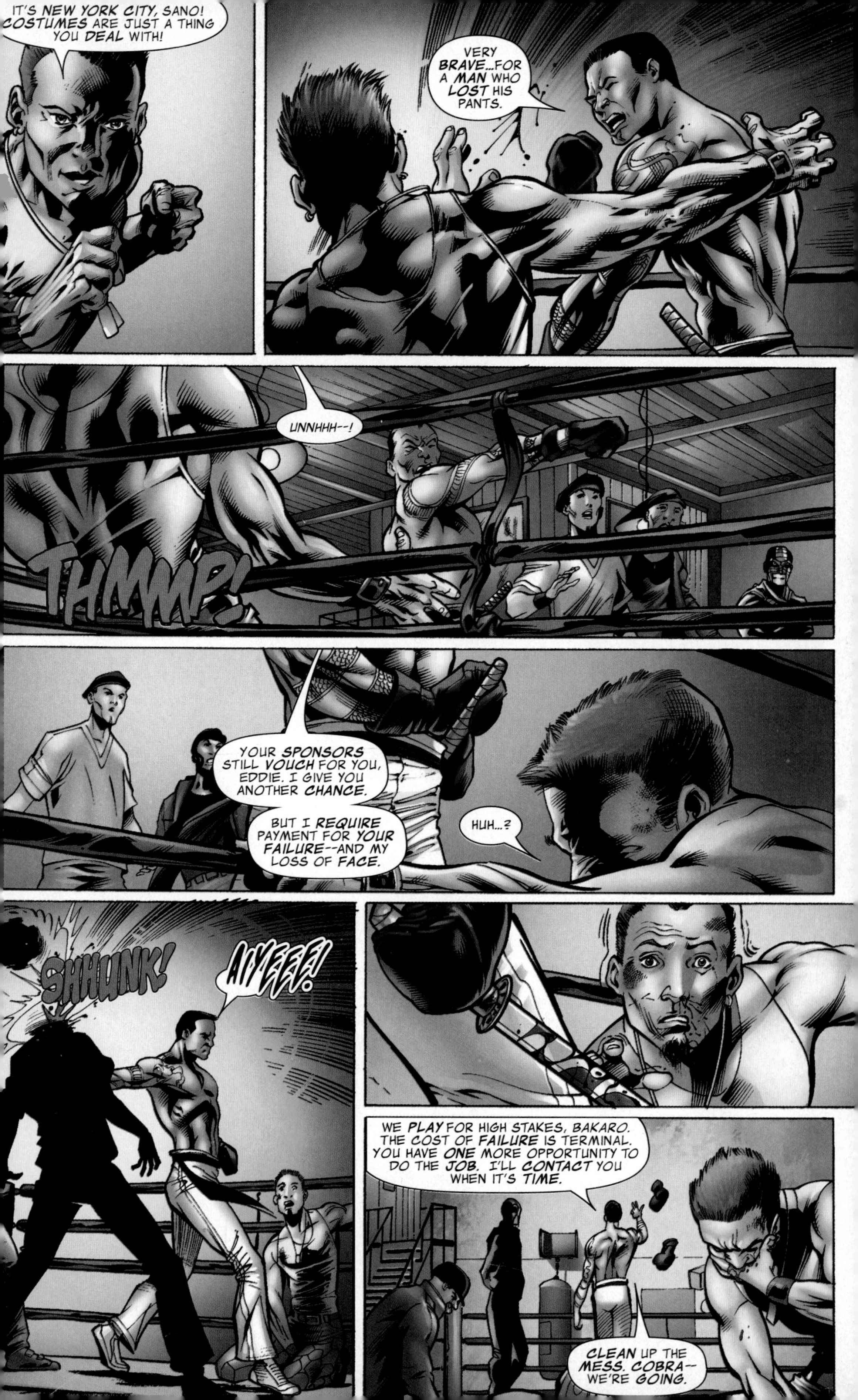
IT'S NEW YORK CITY, SANO! COSTUMES ARE JUST A THING YOU DEAL WITH!
VERY BRAVE...FOR A MAN WHO LOST HIS PANTS.
UNNHHH--!
THMMP!
YOUR SPONSORS STILL VOUCH FOR YOU, EDDIE. I GIVE YOU ANOTHER CHANCE.
BUT I REQUIRE PAYMENT FOR YOUR FAILURE--AND MY LOSS OF FACE.
HUH...?
SHHUNK!
AIYEEE!
WE PLAY FOR HIGH STAKES, BAKARO. THE COST OF FAILURE IS TERMINAL. YOU HAVE ONE MORE OPPORTUNITY TO DO THE JOB. I'LL CONTACT YOU WHEN IT'S TIME.
CLEAN UP THE MESS. COBRA-- WE'RE GOING.

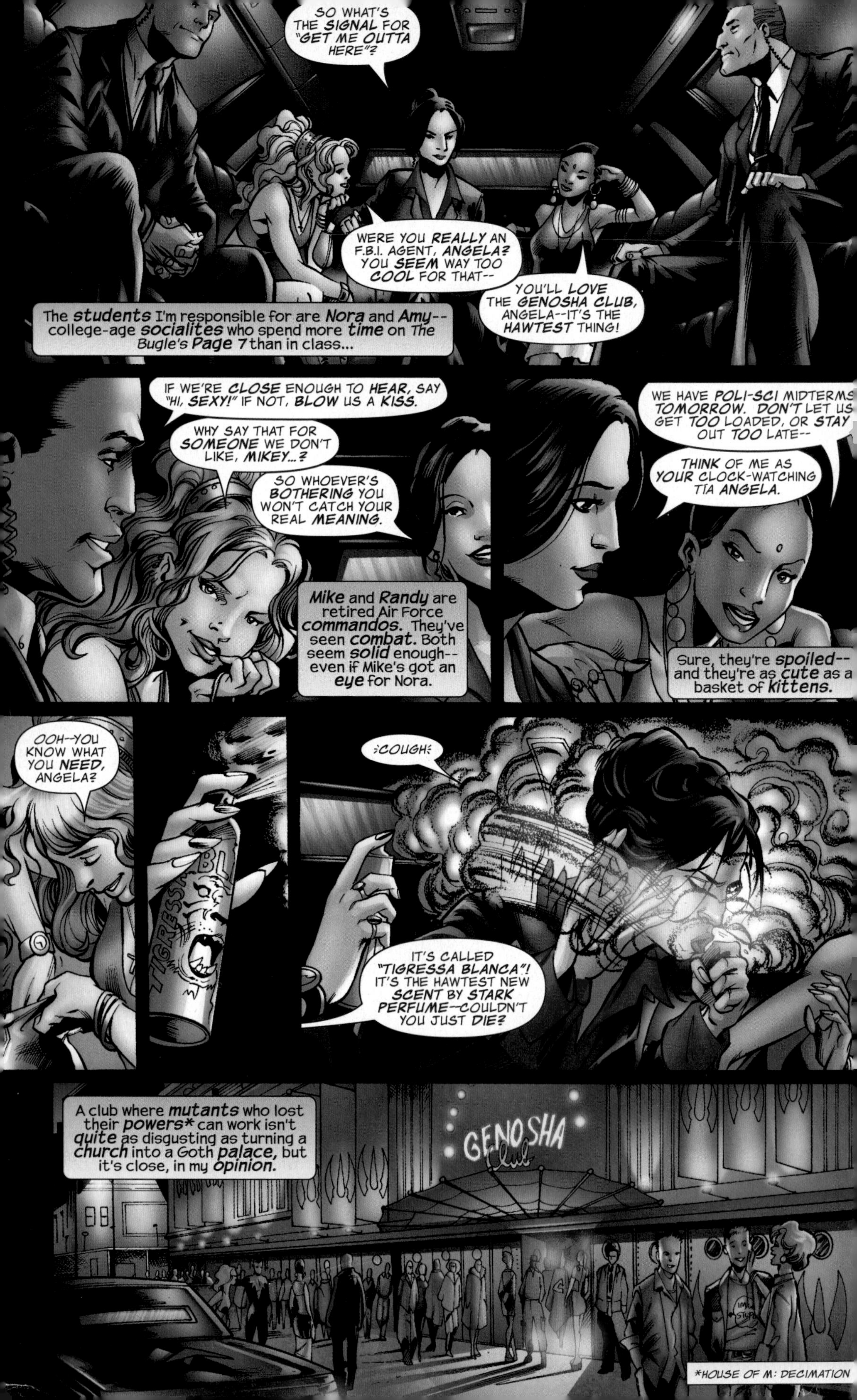

SO WHAT'S THE SIGNAL FOR "GET ME OUTTA HERE"?
WERE YOU REALLY AN F.B.I. AGENT, ANGELA? YOU SEEM WAY TOO COOL FOR THAT--
YOU'LL LOVE THE GENOSHA CLUB, ANGELA--IT'S THE HAWTEST THING!
The students I'm responsible for are Nora and Amy-- college-age socialites who spend more time on The Bugle's Page 7 than in class...
IF WE'RE CLOSE ENOUGH TO HEAR, SAY "HI, SEXY!" IF NOT, BLOW US A KISS.
WHY SAY THAT FOR SOMEONE WE DON'T LIKE, MIKEY...?
SO WHOEVER'S BOTHERING YOU WON'T CATCH YOUR REAL MEANING.
Mike and Randy are retired Air Force commandos. They've seen combat. Both seem solid enough-- even if Mike's got an eye for Nora.
WE HAVE POLI-SCI MIDTERMS TOMORROW. DON'T LET US GET TOO LOADED, OR STAY OUT TOO LATE--
THINK OF ME AS YOUR CLOCK-WATCHING TIA ANGELA.
Sure, they're spoiled-- and they're as cute as a basket of kittens.
OOH--YOU KNOW WHAT YOU NEED, ANGELA?
TIGRESSA BL
:COUGH:
IT'S CALLED "TIGRESSA BLANCA"! IT'S THE HAWTEST NEW SCENT BY STARK PERFUME--COULDN'T YOU JUST DIE?
A club where mutants who lost their powers* can work isn't quite as disgusting as turning a church into a Goth palace, but it's close, in my opinion.
GENOSHA Club
*HOUSE OF M: DECIMATION

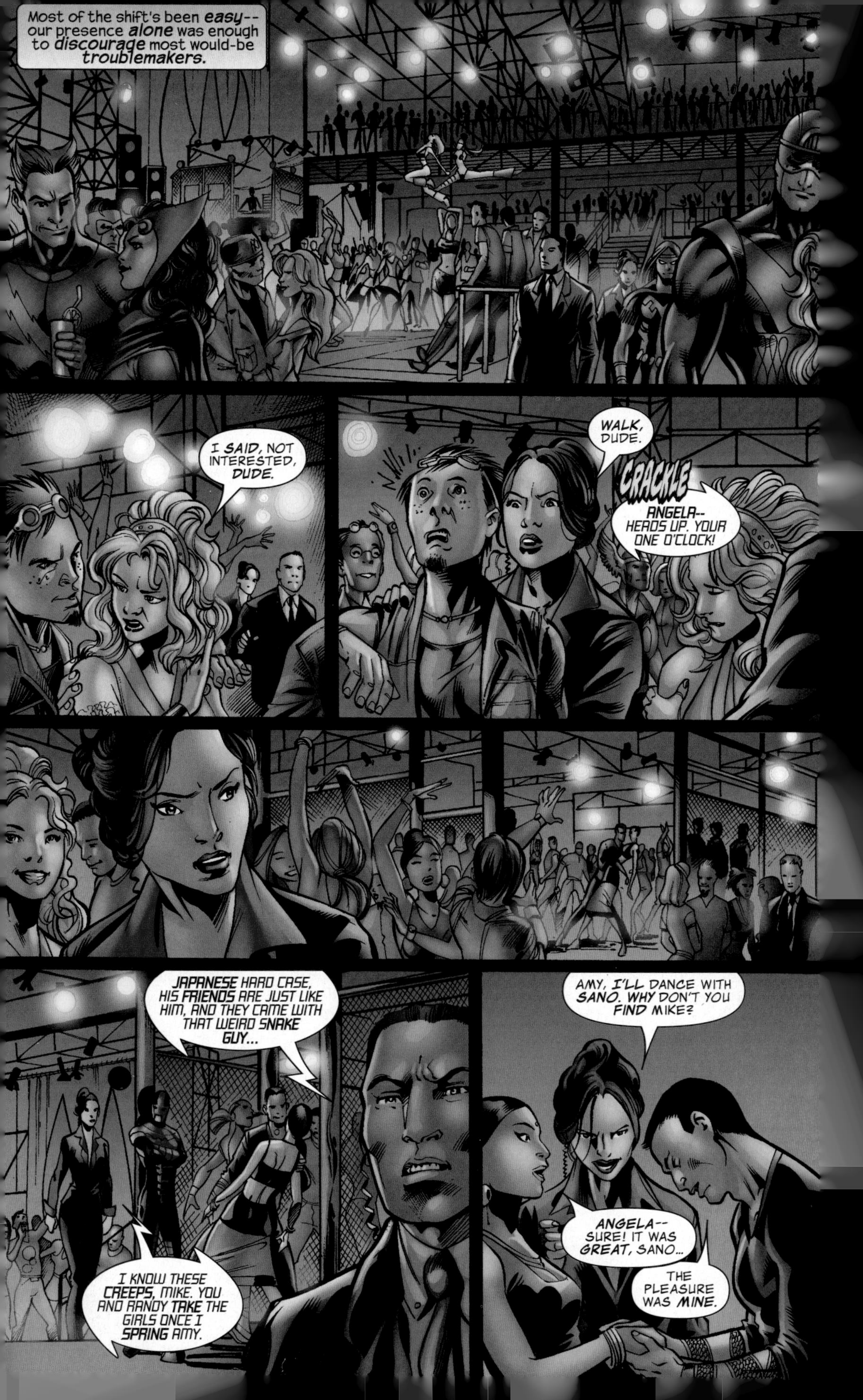
Most of the shift's been easy--our presence alone was enough to discourage most would-be troublemakers.
I SAID, NOT INTERESTED, DUDE.
WALK, DUDE.
CRACKLE
ANGELA--HEADS UP. YOUR ONE O'CLOCK!
JAPANESE HARD CASE, HIS FRIENDS ARE JUST LIKE HIM, AND THEY CAME WITH THAT WEIRD SNAKE GUY...
I KNOW THESE CREEPS, MIKE. YOU AND RANDY TAKE THE GIRLS ONCE I SPRING AMY.
AMY, I'LL DANCE WITH SANO. WHY DON'T YOU FIND MIKE?
ANGELA--SURE! IT WAS GREAT, SANO...
THE PLEASURE WAS MINE.

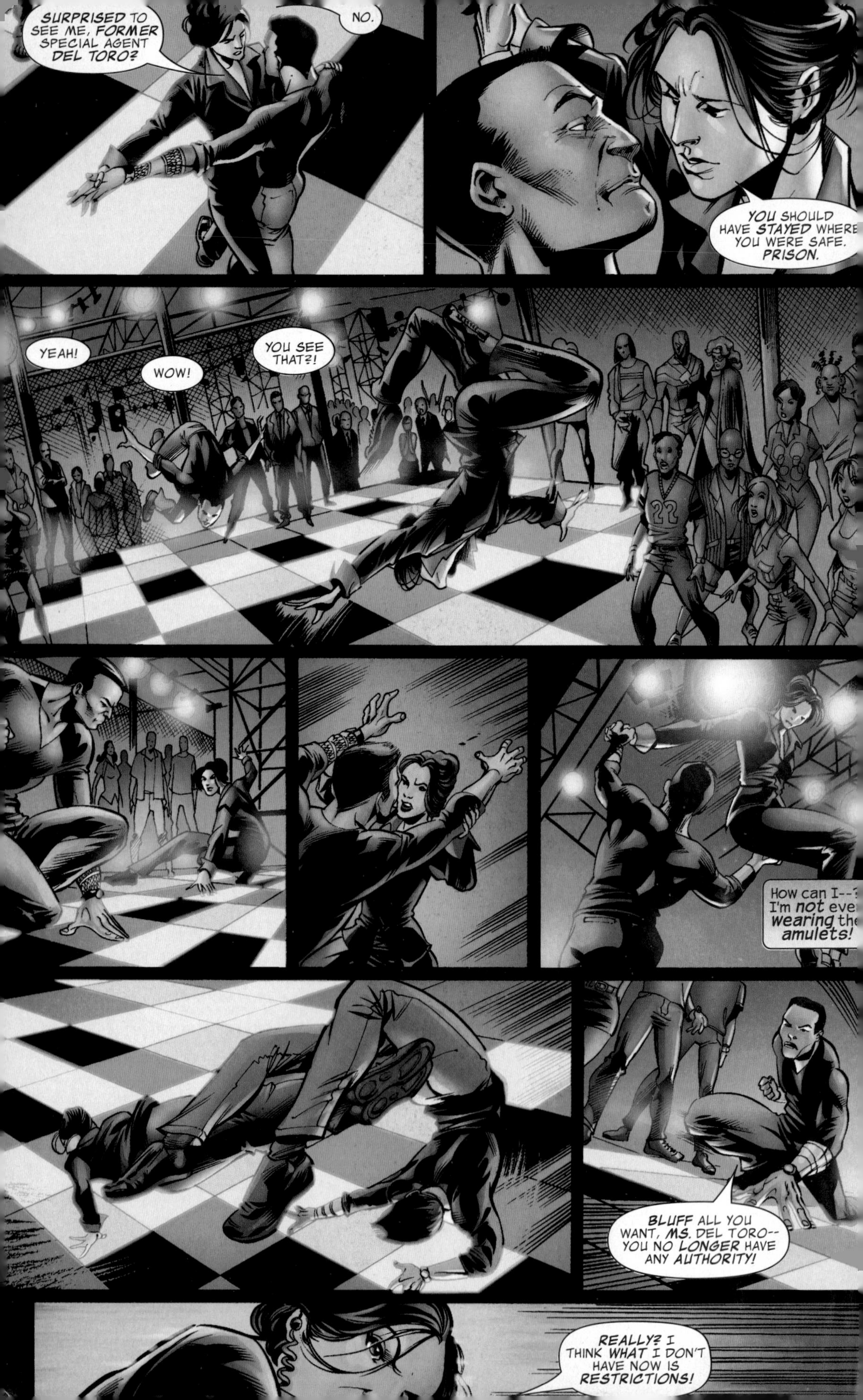
SURPRISED TO SEE ME, FORMER SPECIAL AGENT DEL TORO?
NO.
YOU SHOULD HAVE STAYED WHERE YOU WERE SAFE. PRISON.
YEAH!
WOW!
YOU SEE THAT?!
How can I--? I'm not even wearing the amulets!
BLUFF ALL YOU WANT, MS. DEL TORO-- YOU NO LONGER HAVE ANY AUTHORITY!
REALLY? I THINK WHAT I DON'T HAVE NOW IS RESTRICTIONS!

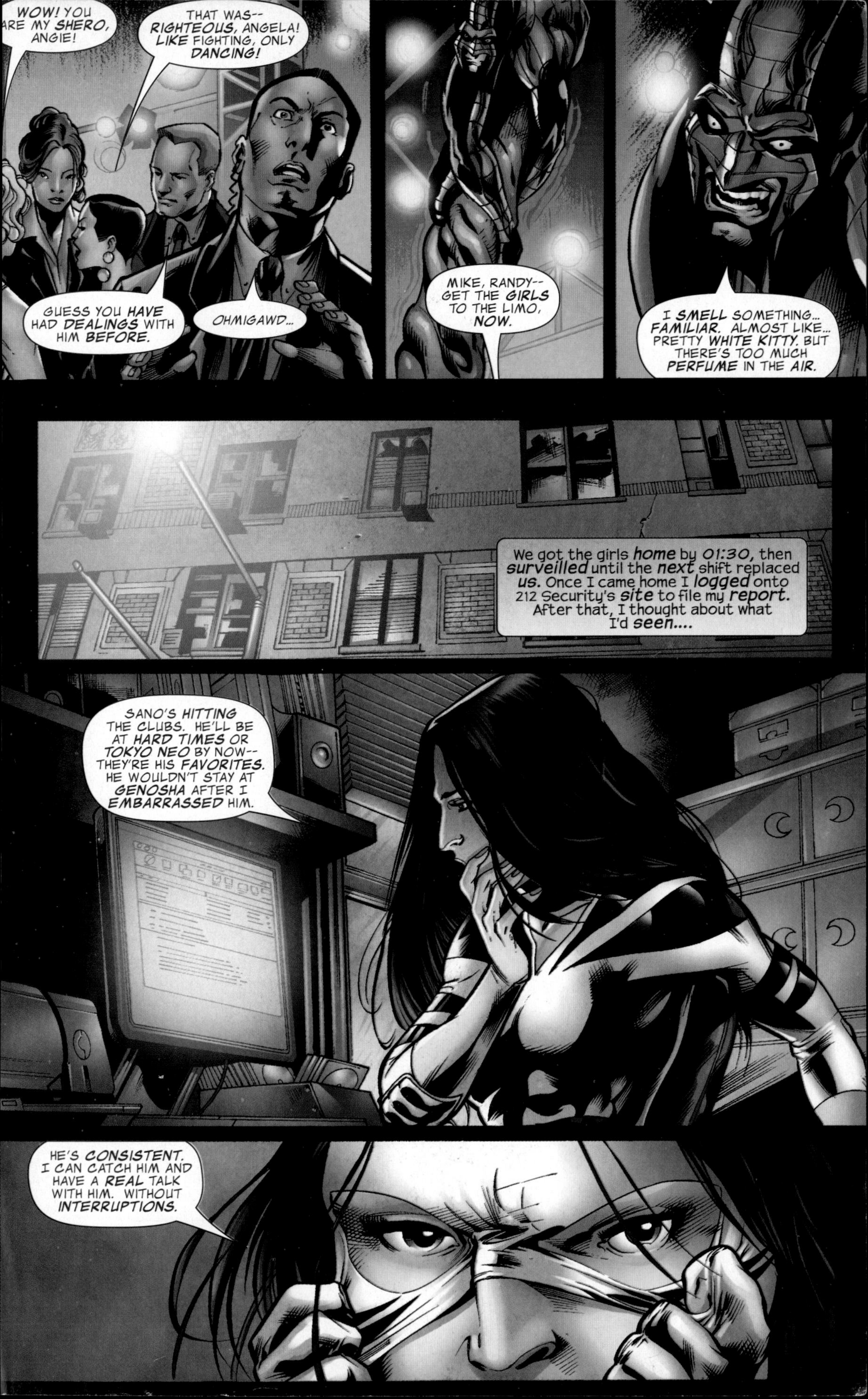
WOW! YOU ARE MY SHERO, ANGIE!
THAT WAS-- RIGHTEOUS, ANGELA! LIKE FIGHTING, ONLY DANCING!
GUESS YOU HAVE HAD DEALINGS WITH HIM BEFORE.
OHMIGAWD...
MIKE, RANDY-- GET THE GIRLS TO THE LIMO, NOW.
I SMELL SOMETHING... FAMILIAR. ALMOST LIKE... PRETTY WHITE KITTY. BUT THERE'S TOO MUCH PERFUME IN THE AIR.
We got the girls home by 01:30, then surveilled until the next shift replaced us. Once I came home I logged onto 212 Security's site to file my report. After that, I thought about what I'd seen....
SANO'S HITTING THE CLUBS. HE'LL BE AT HARD TIMES OR TOKYO NEO BY NOW-- THEY'RE HIS FAVORITES. HE WOULDN'T STAY AT GENOSHA AFTER I EMBARRASSED HIM.
HE'S CONSISTENT. I CAN CATCH HIM AND HAVE A REAL TALK WITH HIM. WITHOUT INTERRUPTIONS.

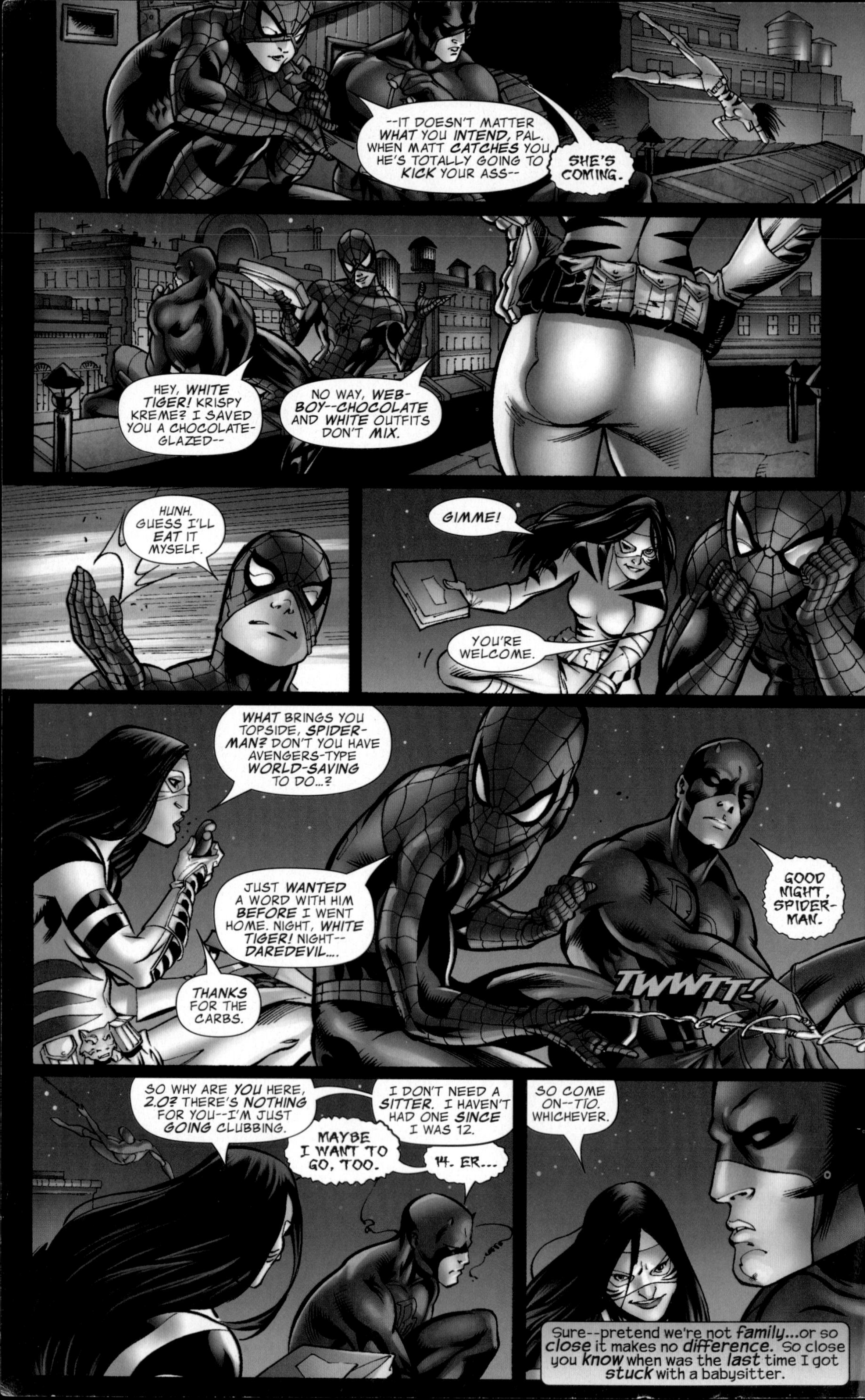

--IT DOESN'T MATTER WHAT YOU INTEND, PAL. WHEN MATT CATCHES YOU HE'S TOTALLY GOING TO KICK YOUR ASS--
SHE'S COMING.
HEY, WHITE TIGER! KRISPY KREME? I SAVED YOU A CHOCOLATE-GLAZED--
NO WAY, WEB-BOY--CHOCOLATE AND WHITE OUTFITS DON'T MIX.
HUNH. GUESS I'LL EAT IT MYSELF.
GIMME!
YOU'RE WELCOME.
WHAT BRINGS YOU TOPSIDE, SPIDER-MAN? DON'T YOU HAVE AVENGERS-TYPE WORLD-SAVING TO DO...?
JUST WANTED A WORD WITH HIM BEFORE I WENT HOME. NIGHT, WHITE TIGER! NIGHT--DAREDEVIL....
THANKS FOR THE CARBS.
GOOD NIGHT, SPIDER-MAN.
TWWTT!
SO WHY ARE YOU HERE, 2.0? THERE'S NOTHING FOR YOU--I'M JUST GOING CLUBBING.
I DON'T NEED A SITTER. I HAVEN'T HAD ONE SINCE I WAS 12.
MAYBE I WANT TO GO, TOO.
14. ER...
SO COME ON--TIO. WHICHEVER.
Sure--pretend we're not family...or so close it makes no difference. So close you know when was the last time I got stuck with a babysitter.

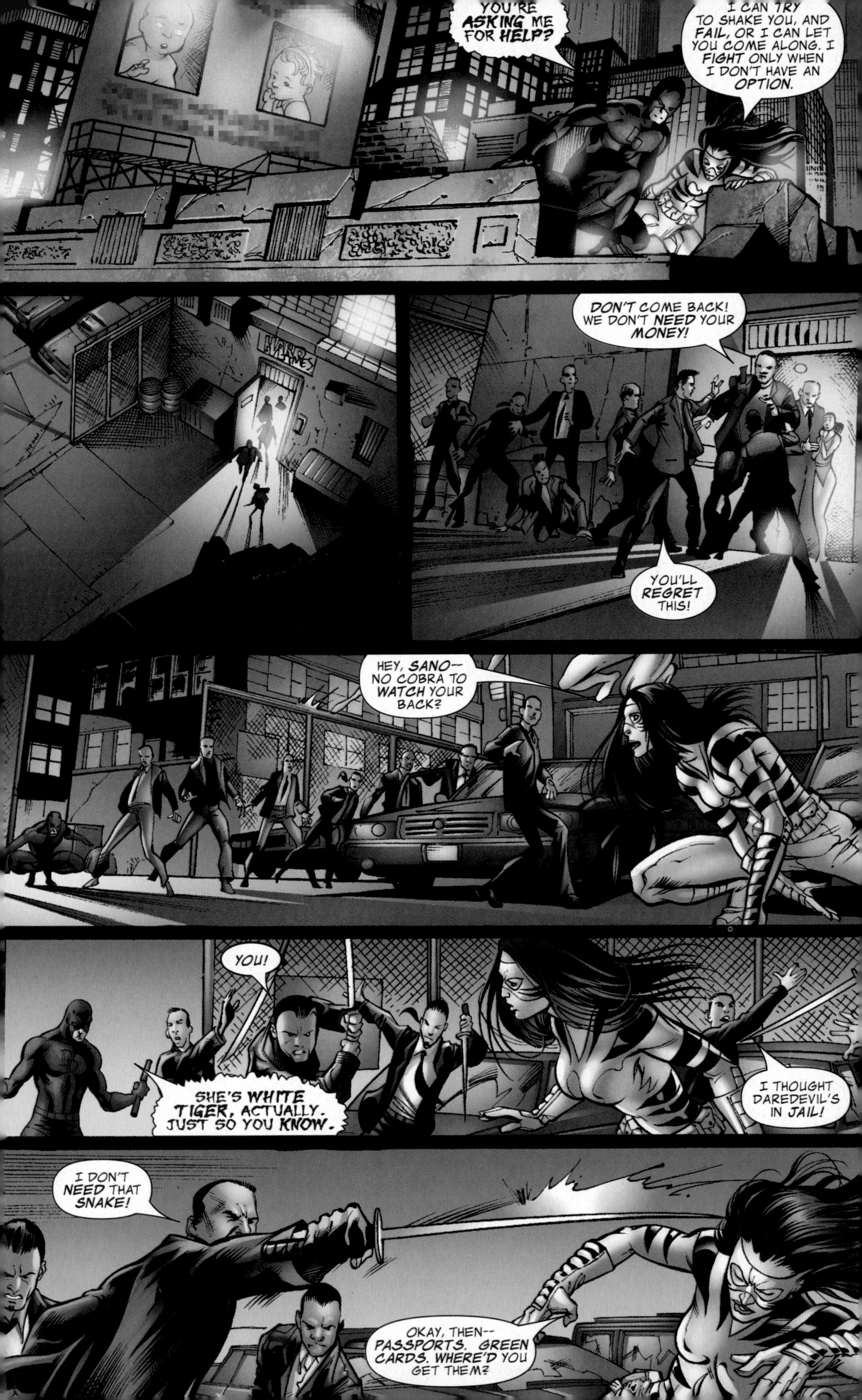

YOU'RE ASKING ME FOR HELP?
I CAN TRY TO SHAKE YOU, AND FAIL, OR I CAN LET YOU COME ALONG. I FIGHT ONLY WHEN I DON'T HAVE AN OPTION.
HARD TIMES
DON'T COME BACK! WE DON'T NEED YOUR MONEY!
YOU'LL REGRET THIS!
HEY, SANO-- NO COBRA TO WATCH YOUR BACK?
YOU!
SHE'S WHITE TIGER, ACTUALLY. JUST SO YOU KNOW.
I THOUGHT DAREDEVIL'S IN JAIL!
I DON'T NEED THAT SNAKE!
OKAY, THEN-- PASSPORTS. GREEN CARDS. WHERE'D YOU GET THEM?

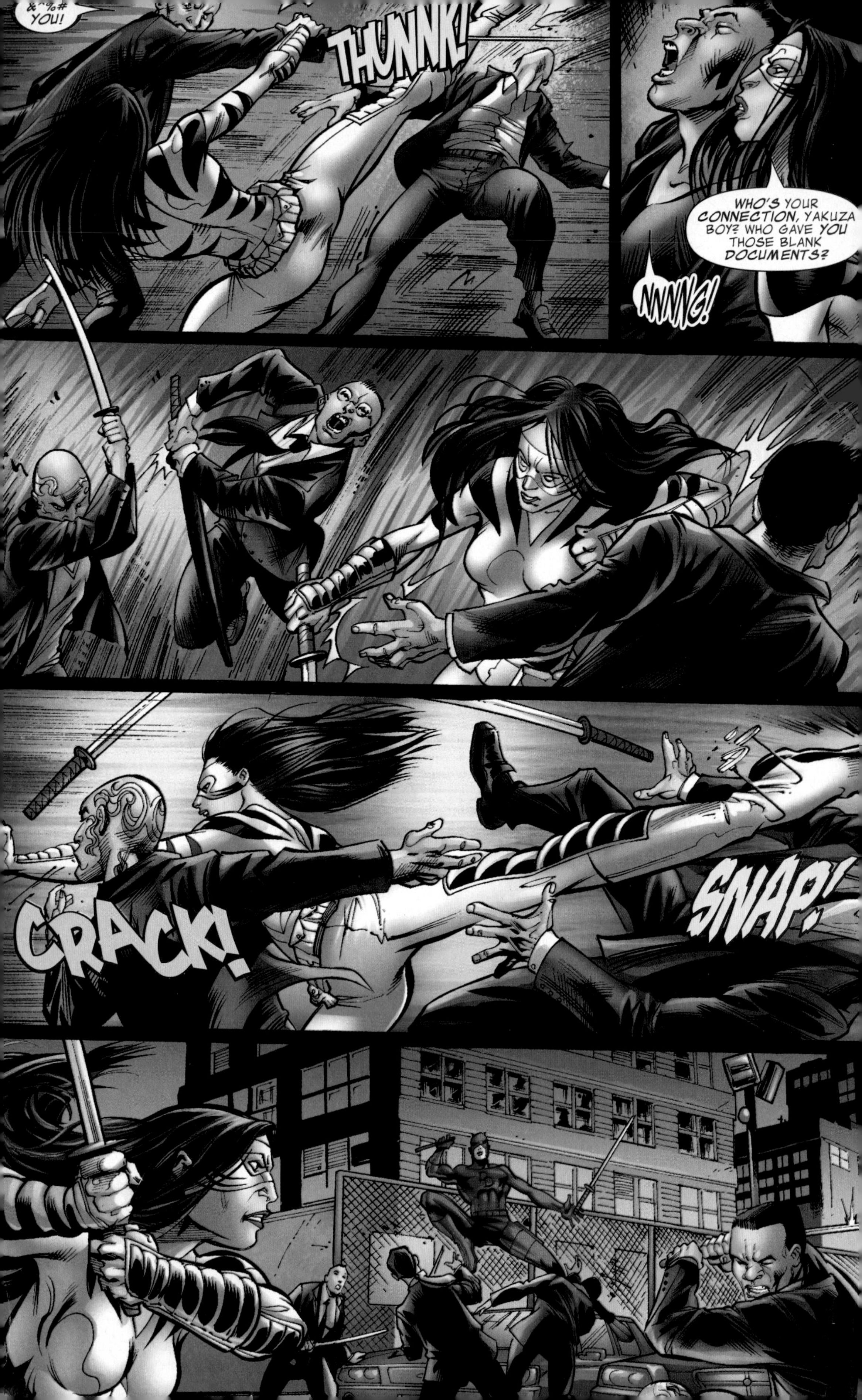
&^%# YOU!
THUNNK!
WHO'S YOUR CONNECTION, YAKUZA BOY? WHO GAVE YOU THOSE BLANK DOCUMENTS?
NNNNG!
CRACK!
SNAP!

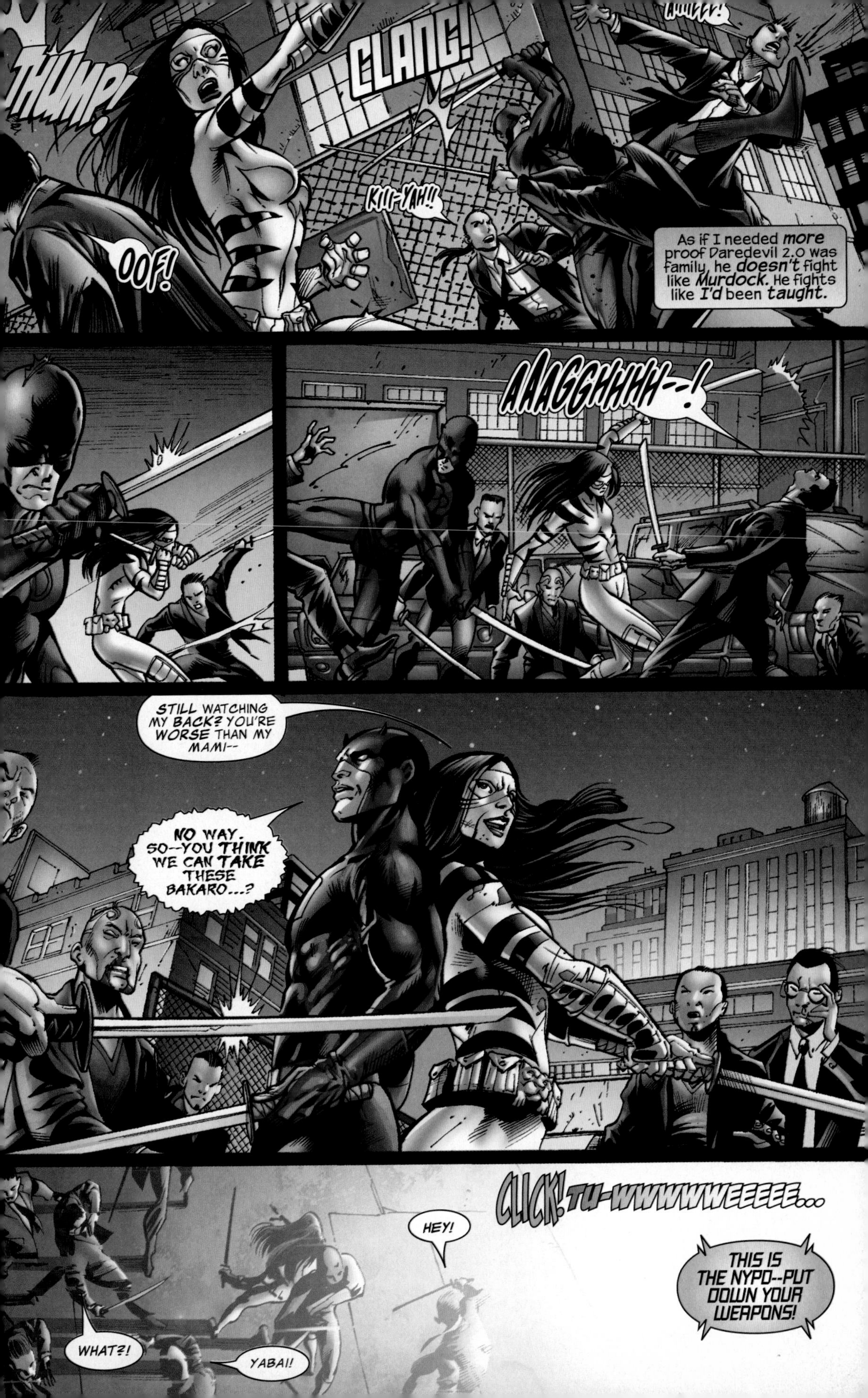
THUMP!
CLANG!
KIII-YAH!!
OOF!
As if I needed more proof Daredevil 2.0 was family, he doesn't fight like Murdock. He fights like I'd been taught.
AAAGGHHHH--!
STILL WATCHING MY BACK? YOU'RE WORSE THAN MY MAMI--
NO WAY. SO--YOU THINK WE CAN TAKE THESE BAKARO...?
CLICK! TU-WWWWWEEEEE...
HEY!
THIS IS THE NYPD--PUT DOWN YOUR WEAPONS!
WHAT?!
YABAI!

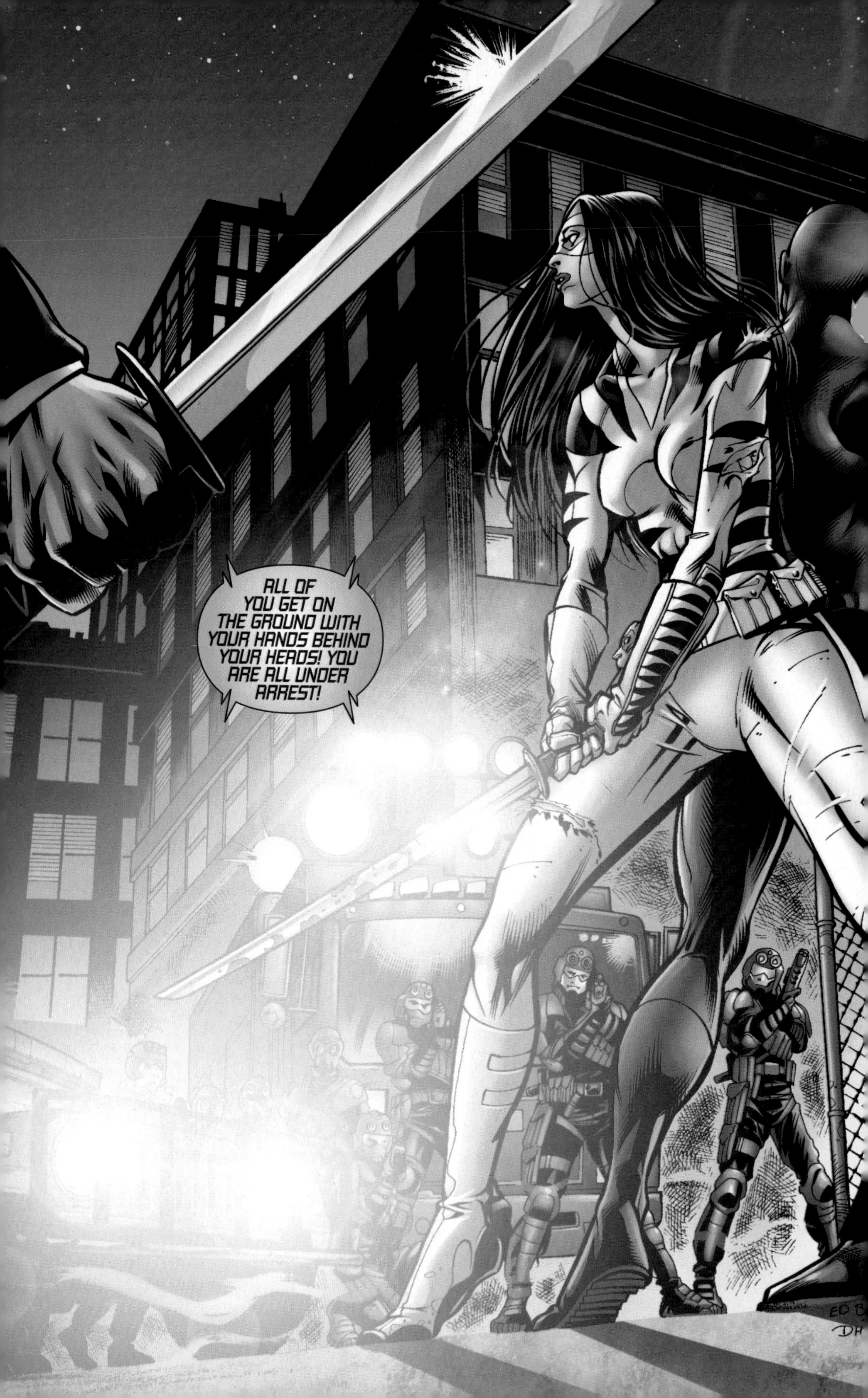
ALL OF YOU GET ON THE GROUND WITH YOUR HANDS BEHIND YOUR HEADS! YOU ARE ALL UNDER ARREST!

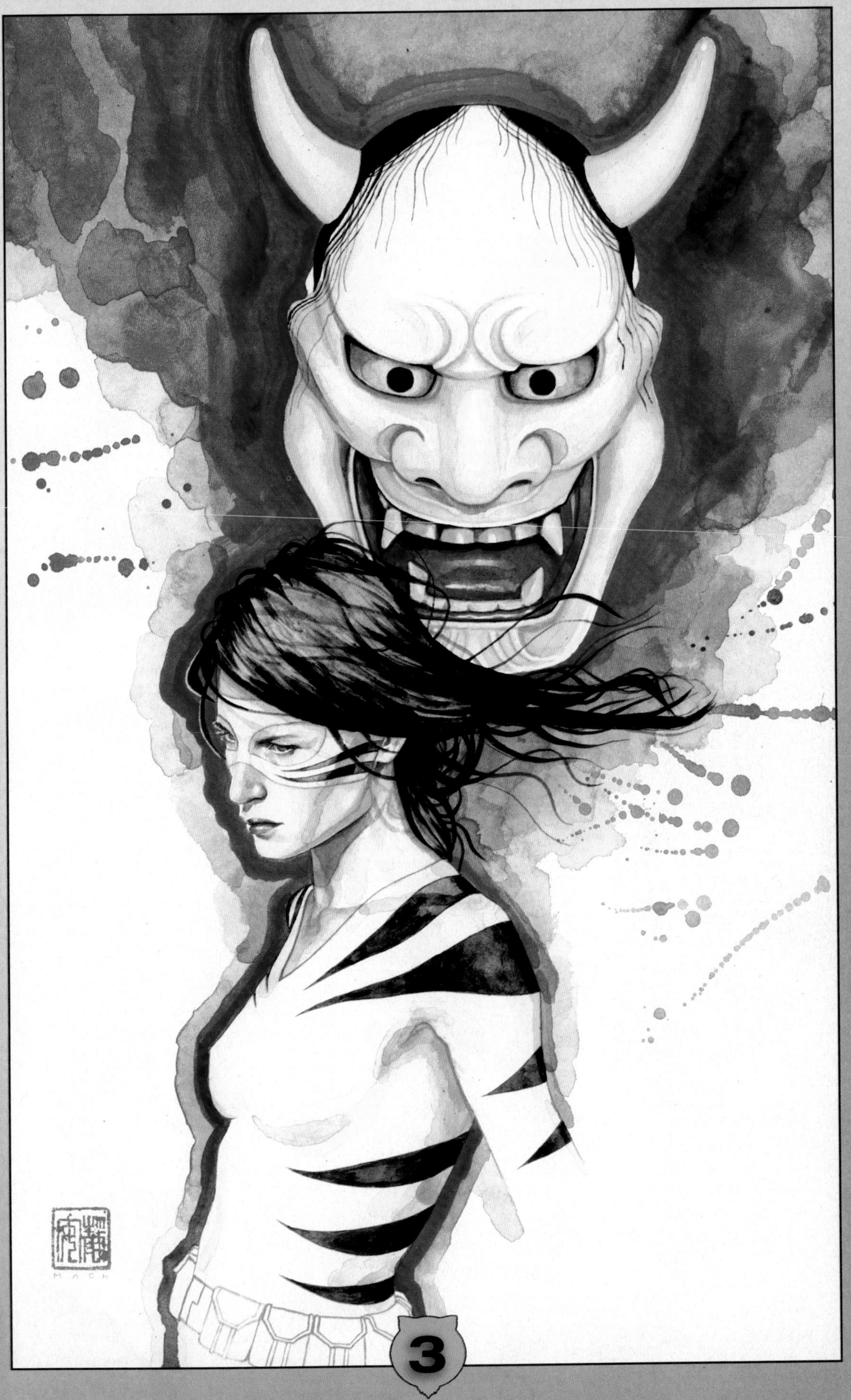
MACH
3

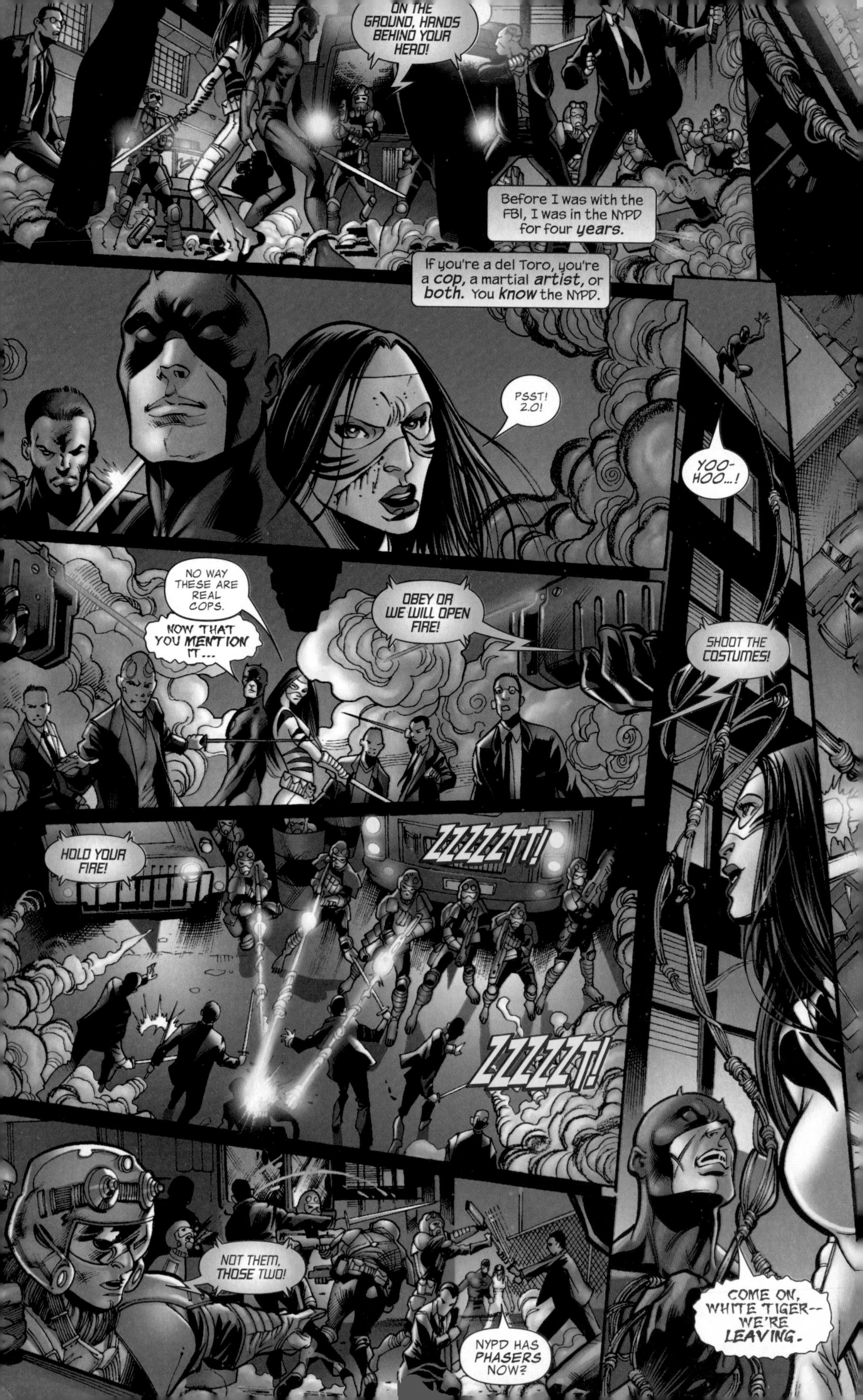
ON THE GROUND, HANDS BEHIND YOUR HEAD!
Before I was with the FBI, I was in the NYPD for four years.
If you're a del Toro, you're a cop, a martial artist, or both. You know the NYPD.
PSST! 2.0!
YOO-HOO...!
NO WAY THESE ARE REAL COPS.
NOW THAT YOU MENTION IT...
OBEY OR WE WILL OPEN FIRE!
SHOOT THE COSTUMES!
HOLD YOUR FIRE!
ZZZZZZTT!
ZZZZZZT!
NOT THEM, THOSE TWO!
NYPD HAS PHASERS NOW?
COME ON, WHITE TIGER-- WE'RE LEAVING.

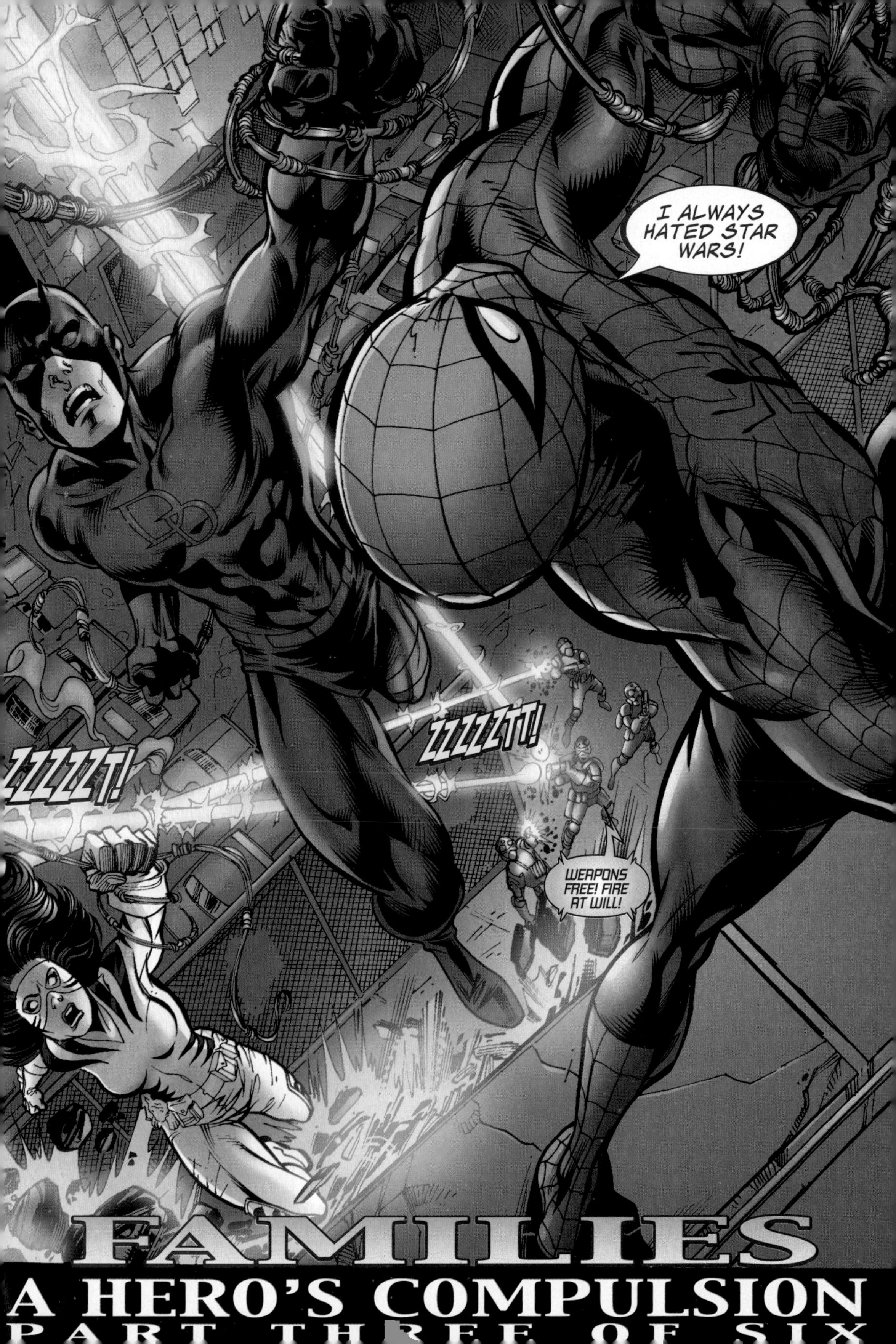
I ALWAYS HATED STAR WARS!
ZZZZZTT!
ZZZZZT!
WEAPONS FREE! FIRE AT WILL!
FAMILIES
A HERO'S COMPULSION
PART THREE OF SIX

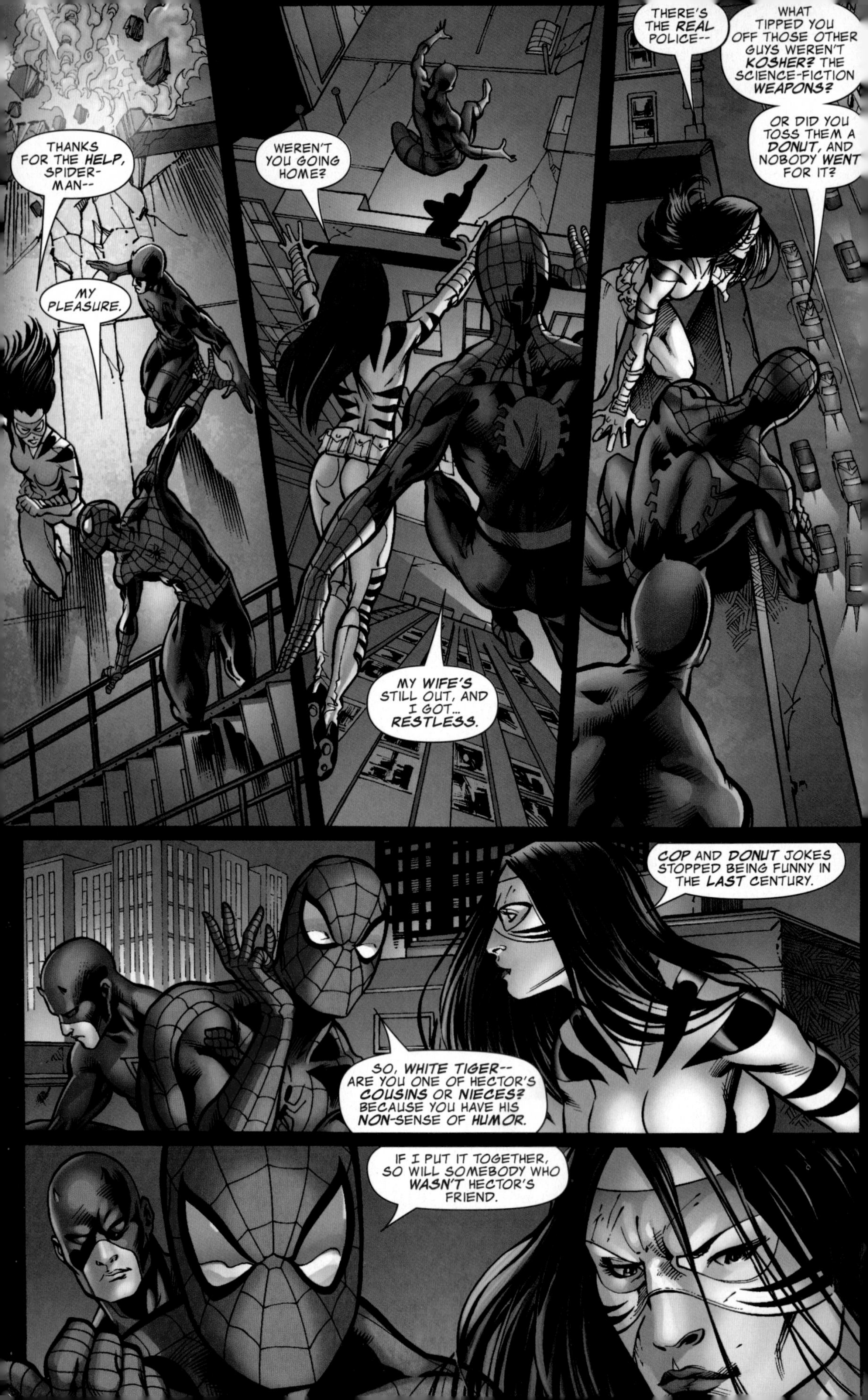
THANKS FOR THE HELP, SPIDER-MAN--
MY PLEASURE.
WEREN'T YOU GOING HOME?
MY WIFE'S STILL OUT, AND I GOT... RESTLESS.
THERE'S THE REAL POLICE--
WHAT TIPPED YOU OFF THOSE OTHER GUYS WEREN'T KOSHER? THE SCIENCE-FICTION WEAPONS?
OR DID YOU TOSS THEM A DONUT, AND NOBODY WENT FOR IT?
COP AND DONUT JOKES STOPPED BEING FUNNY IN THE LAST CENTURY.
SO, WHITE TIGER-- ARE YOU ONE OF HECTOR'S COUSINS OR NIECES? BECAUSE YOU HAVE HIS NON-SENSE OF HUMOR.
IF I PUT IT TOGETHER, SO WILL SOMEBODY WHO WASN'T HECTOR'S FRIEND.

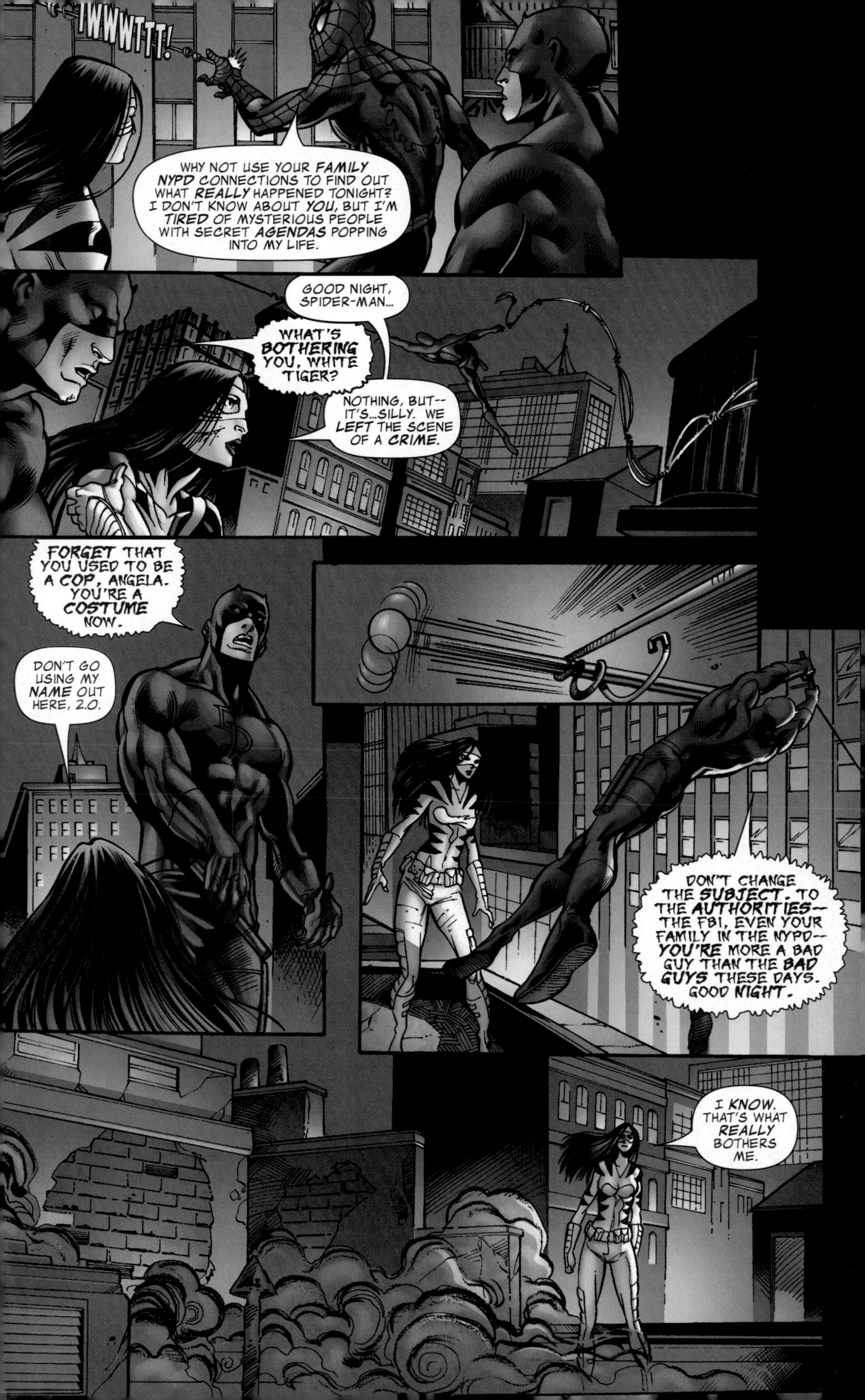
THWWWTTT!
WHY NOT USE YOUR FAMILY NYPD CONNECTIONS TO FIND OUT WHAT REALLY HAPPENED TONIGHT? I DON'T KNOW ABOUT YOU, BUT I'M TIRED OF MYSTERIOUS PEOPLE WITH SECRET AGENDAS POPPING INTO MY LIFE.
GOOD NIGHT, SPIDER-MAN...
WHAT'S BOTHERING YOU, WHITE TIGER?
NOTHING, BUT-- IT'S...SILLY. WE LEFT THE SCENE OF A CRIME.
FORGET THAT YOU USED TO BE A COP, ANGELA. YOU'RE A COSTUME NOW.
DON'T GO USING MY NAME OUT HERE, 2.0.
DON'T CHANGE THE SUBJECT. TO THE AUTHORITIES-- THE FBI, EVEN YOUR FAMILY IN THE NYPD-- YOU'RE MORE A BAD GUY THAN THE BAD GUYS THESE DAYS. GOOD NIGHT.
I KNOW. THAT'S WHAT REALLY BOTHERS ME.

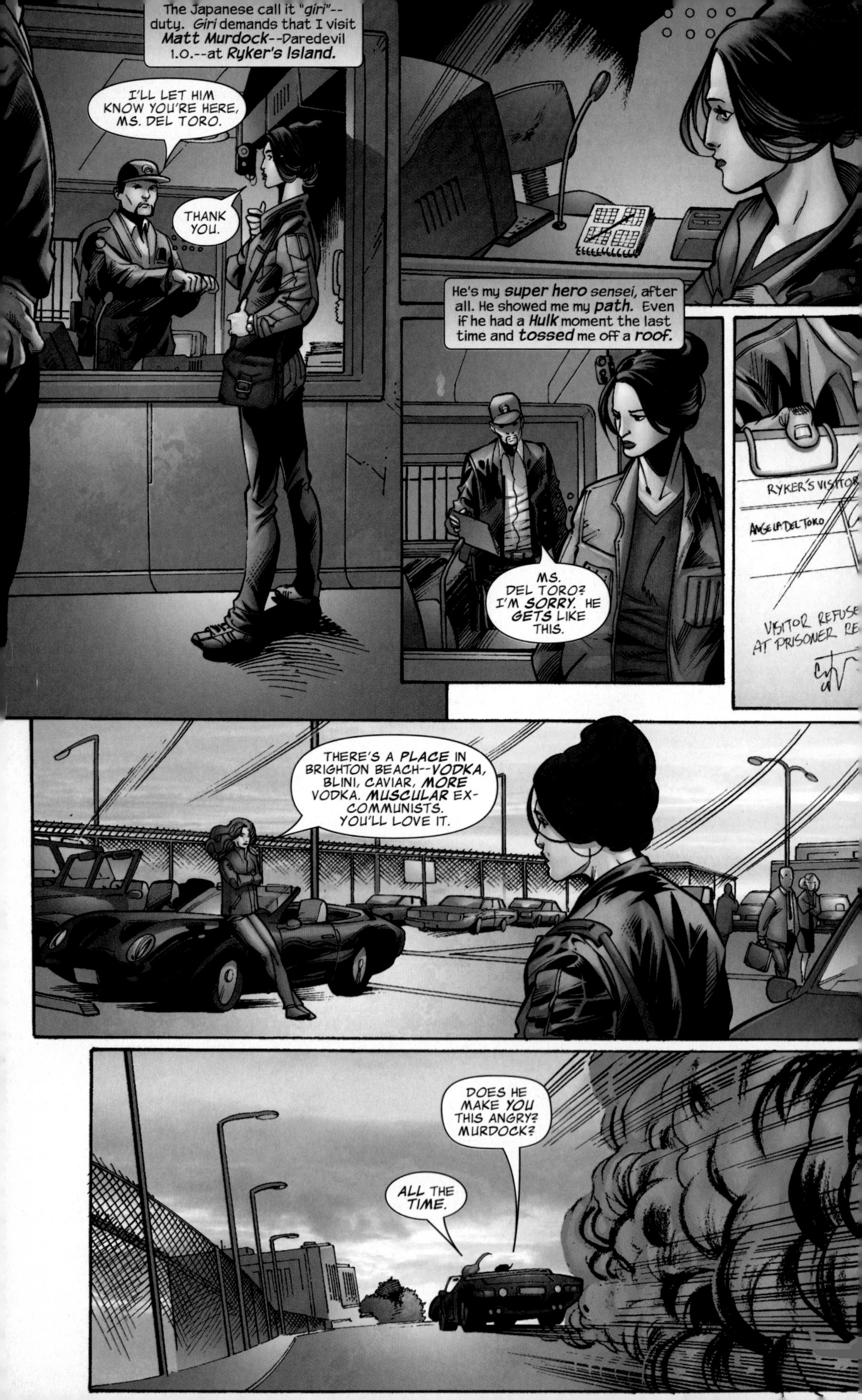

The Japanese call it "giri"--duty. Giri demands that I visit Matt Murdock--Daredevil 1.0.--at Ryker's Island.
I'LL LET HIM KNOW YOU'RE HERE, MS. DEL TORO.
THANK YOU.
He's my super hero sensei, after all. He showed me my path. Even if he had a Hulk moment the last time and tossed me off a roof.
MS. DEL TORO? I'M SORRY. HE GETS LIKE THIS.
RYKER'S VISITOR
ANGELA DEL TORO
VISITOR REFUSE
AT PRISONER RE
THERE'S A PLACE IN BRIGHTON BEACH--VODKA, BLINI, CAVIAR, MORE VODKA. MUSCULAR EX-COMMUNISTS. YOU'LL LOVE IT.
DOES HE MAKE YOU THIS ANGRY? MURDOCK?
ALL THE TIME.

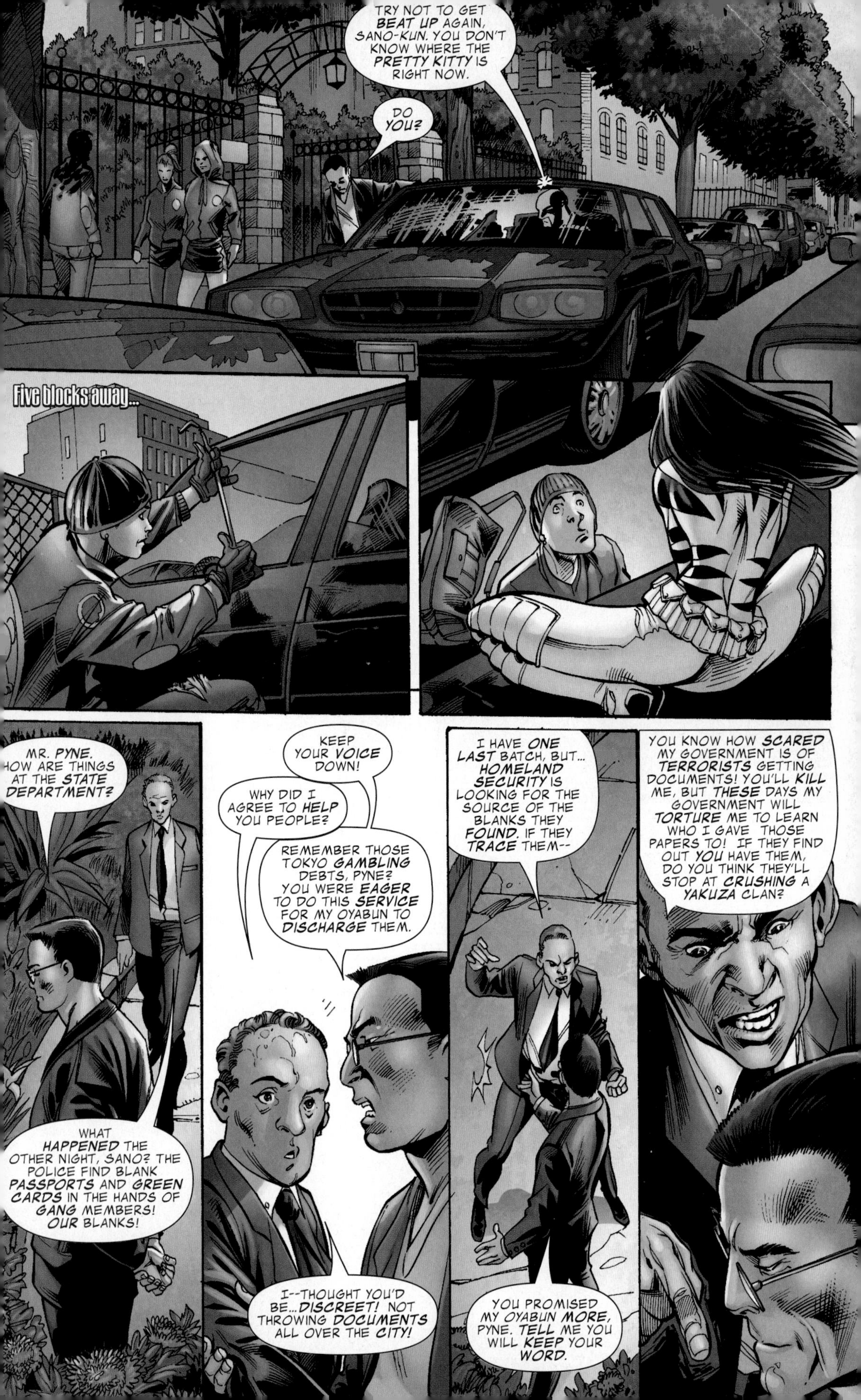
TRY NOT TO GET BEAT UP AGAIN, SANO-KUN. YOU DON'T KNOW WHERE THE PRETTY KITTY IS RIGHT NOW.
DO YOU?
Five blocks away...
MR. PYNE. HOW ARE THINGS AT THE STATE DEPARTMENT?
WHAT HAPPENED THE OTHER NIGHT, SANO? THE POLICE FIND BLANK PASSPORTS AND GREEN CARDS IN THE HANDS OF GANG MEMBERS! OUR BLANKS!
KEEP YOUR VOICE DOWN!
WHY DID I AGREE TO HELP YOU PEOPLE?
REMEMBER THOSE TOKYO GAMBLING DEBTS, PYNE? YOU WERE EAGER TO DO THIS SERVICE FOR MY OYABUN TO DISCHARGE THEM.
I--THOUGHT YOU'D BE...DISCREET! NOT THROWING DOCUMENTS ALL OVER THE CITY!
I HAVE ONE LAST BATCH, BUT... HOMELAND SECURITY IS LOOKING FOR THE SOURCE OF THE BLANKS THEY FOUND. IF THEY TRACE THEM--
YOU PROMISED MY OYABUN MORE, PYNE. TELL ME YOU WILL KEEP YOUR WORD.
YOU KNOW HOW SCARED MY GOVERNMENT IS OF TERRORISTS GETTING DOCUMENTS! YOU'LL KILL ME, BUT THESE DAYS MY GOVERNMENT WILL TORTURE ME TO LEARN WHO I GAVE THOSE PAPERS TO! IF THEY FIND OUT YOU HAVE THEM, DO YOU THINK THEY'LL STOP AT CRUSHING A YAKUZA CLAN?

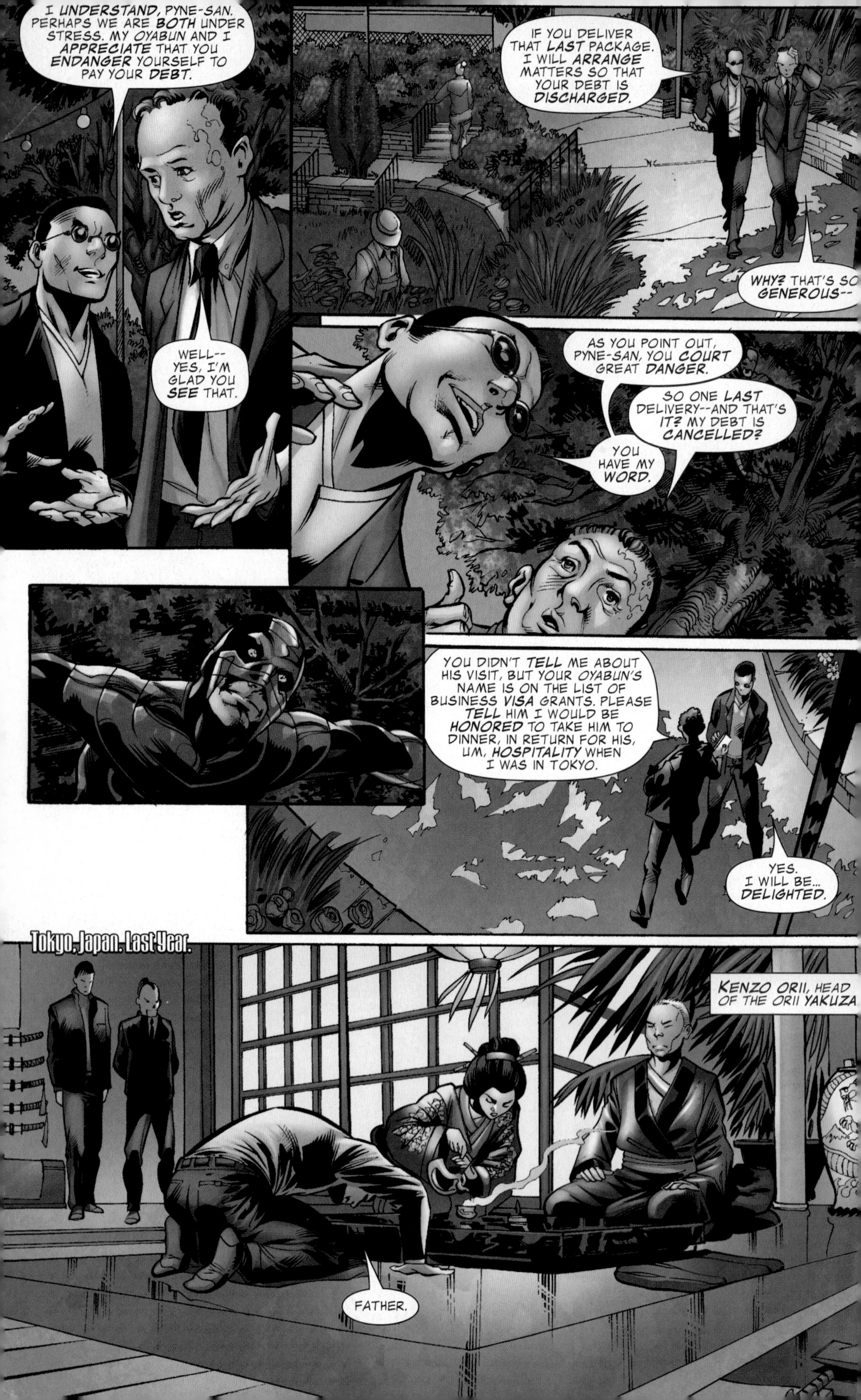
I UNDERSTAND, PYNE-SAN. PERHAPS WE ARE BOTH UNDER STRESS. MY OYABUN AND I APPRECIATE THAT YOU ENDANGER YOURSELF TO PAY YOUR DEBT.
WELL-- YES, I'M GLAD YOU SEE THAT.
IF YOU DELIVER THAT LAST PACKAGE. I WILL ARRANGE MATTERS SO THAT YOUR DEBT IS DISCHARGED.
WHY? THAT'S SO GENEROUS--
AS YOU POINT OUT, PYNE-SAN, YOU COURT GREAT DANGER.
SO ONE LAST DELIVERY--AND THAT'S IT? MY DEBT IS CANCELLED?
YOU HAVE MY WORD.
YOU DIDN'T TELL ME ABOUT HIS VISIT, BUT YOUR OYABUN'S NAME IS ON THE LIST OF BUSINESS VISA GRANTS. PLEASE TELL HIM I WOULD BE HONORED TO TAKE HIM TO DINNER, IN RETURN FOR HIS, UM, HOSPITALITY WHEN I WAS IN TOKYO.
YES. I WILL BE... DELIGHTED.
Tokyo, Japan. Last Year.
KENZO ORII, HEAD OF THE ORII YAKUZA
FATHER.

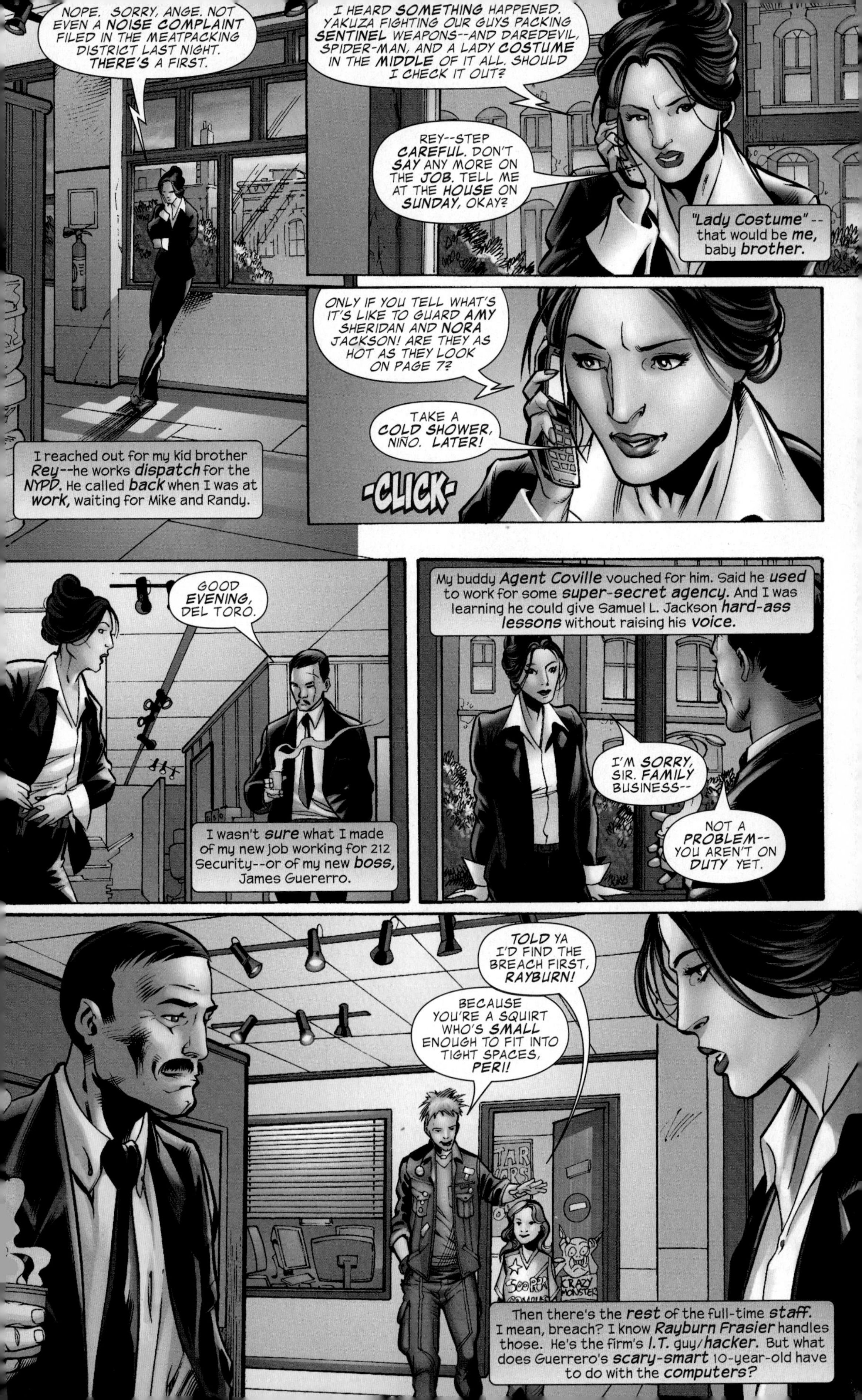
NOPE. SORRY, ANGE. NOT EVEN A NOISE COMPLAINT FILED IN THE MEATPACKING DISTRICT LAST NIGHT. THERE'S A FIRST.
I HEARD SOMETHING HAPPENED. YAKUZA FIGHTING OUR GUYS PACKING SENTINEL WEAPONS--AND DAREDEVIL, SPIDER-MAN, AND A LADY COSTUME IN THE MIDDLE OF IT ALL. SHOULD I CHECK IT OUT?
REY--STEP CAREFUL. DON'T SAY ANY MORE ON THE JOB. TELL ME AT THE HOUSE ON SUNDAY, OKAY?
"Lady Costume"--that would be me, baby brother.
I reached out for my kid brother Rey--he works dispatch for the NYPD. He called back when I was at work, waiting for Mike and Randy.
ONLY IF YOU TELL WHAT'S IT'S LIKE TO GUARD AMY SHERIDAN AND NORA JACKSON! ARE THEY AS HOT AS THEY LOOK ON PAGE 7?
TAKE A COLD SHOWER, NIÑO. LATER!
-CLICK-
GOOD EVENING, DEL TORO.
I wasn't sure what I made of my new job working for 212 Security--or of my new boss, James Guerrero.
My buddy Agent Coville vouched for him. Said he used to work for some super-secret agency. And I was learning he could give Samuel L. Jackson hard-ass lessons without raising his voice.
I'M SORRY, SIR. FAMILY BUSINESS--
NOT A PROBLEM--YOU AREN'T ON DUTY YET.
TOLD YA I'D FIND THE BREACH FIRST, RAYBURN!
BECAUSE YOU'RE A SQUIRT WHO'S SMALL ENOUGH TO FIT INTO TIGHT SPACES, PERI!
Then there's the rest of the full-time staff. I mean, breach? I know Rayburn Frasier handles those. He's the firm's I.T. guy/hacker. But what does Guerrero's scary-smart 10-year-old have to do with the computers?

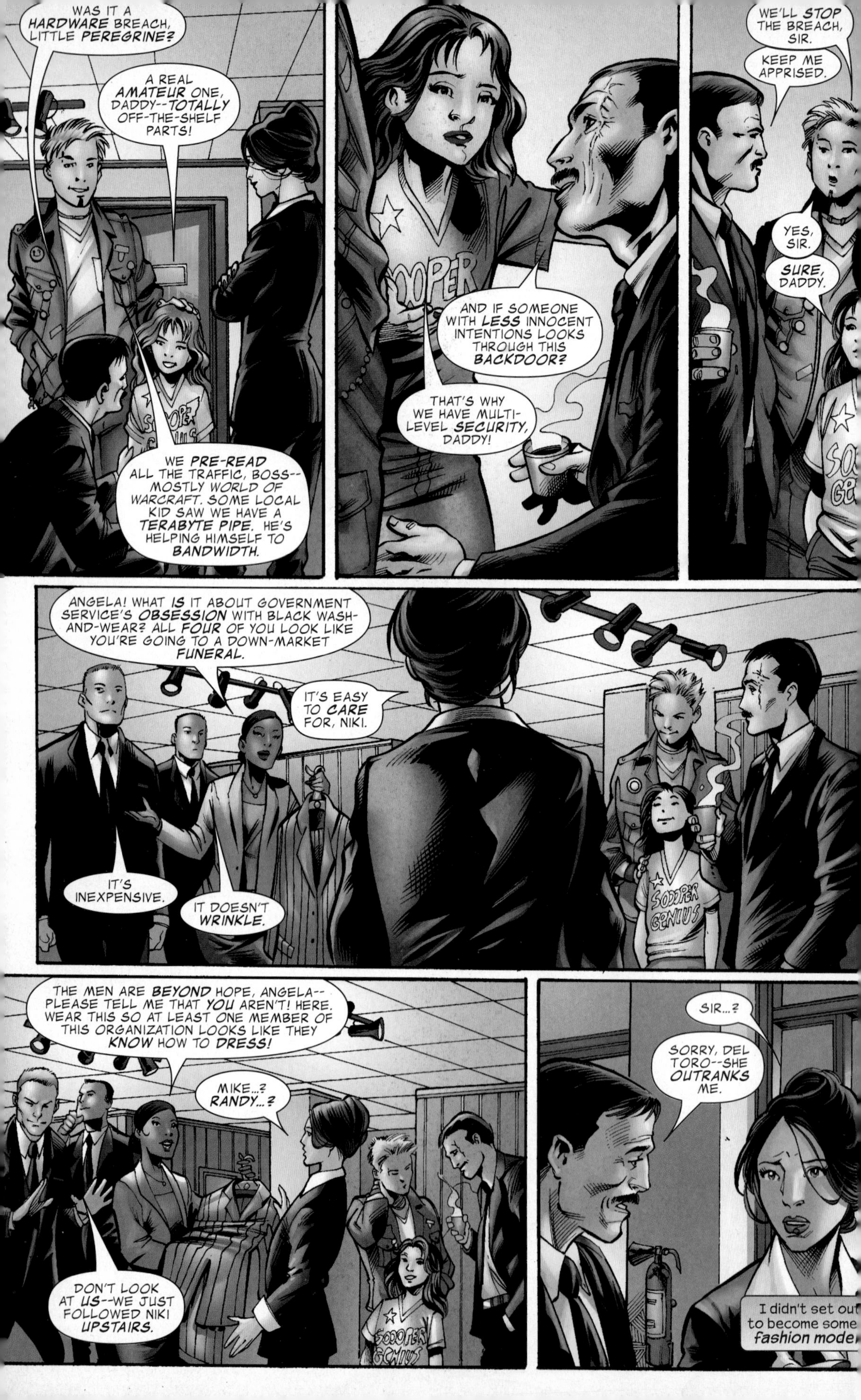
WAS IT A HARDWARE BREACH, LITTLE PEREGRINE?
A REAL AMATEUR ONE, DADDY--TOTALLY OFF-THE-SHELF PARTS!
WE PRE-READ ALL THE TRAFFIC, BOSS--MOSTLY WORLD OF WARCRAFT. SOME LOCAL KID SAW WE HAVE A TERABYTE PIPE. HE'S HELPING HIMSELF TO BANDWIDTH.
AND IF SOMEONE WITH LESS INNOCENT INTENTIONS LOOKS THROUGH THIS BACKDOOR?
THAT'S WHY WE HAVE MULTI-LEVEL SECURITY, DADDY!
WE'LL STOP THE BREACH, SIR.
KEEP ME APPRISED.
YES, SIR.
SURE, DADDY.
ANGELA! WHAT IS IT ABOUT GOVERNMENT SERVICE'S OBSESSION WITH BLACK WASH-AND-WEAR? ALL FOUR OF YOU LOOK LIKE YOU'RE GOING TO A DOWN-MARKET FUNERAL.
IT'S EASY TO CARE FOR, NIKI.
IT'S INEXPENSIVE.
IT DOESN'T WRINKLE.
THE MEN ARE BEYOND HOPE, ANGELA--PLEASE TELL ME THAT YOU AREN'T! HERE. WEAR THIS SO AT LEAST ONE MEMBER OF THIS ORGANIZATION LOOKS LIKE THEY KNOW HOW TO DRESS!
MIKE...? RANDY...?
DON'T LOOK AT US--WE JUST FOLLOWED NIKI UPSTAIRS.
SIR...?
SORRY, DEL TORO--SHE OUTRANKS ME.
I didn't set out to become some fashion mode

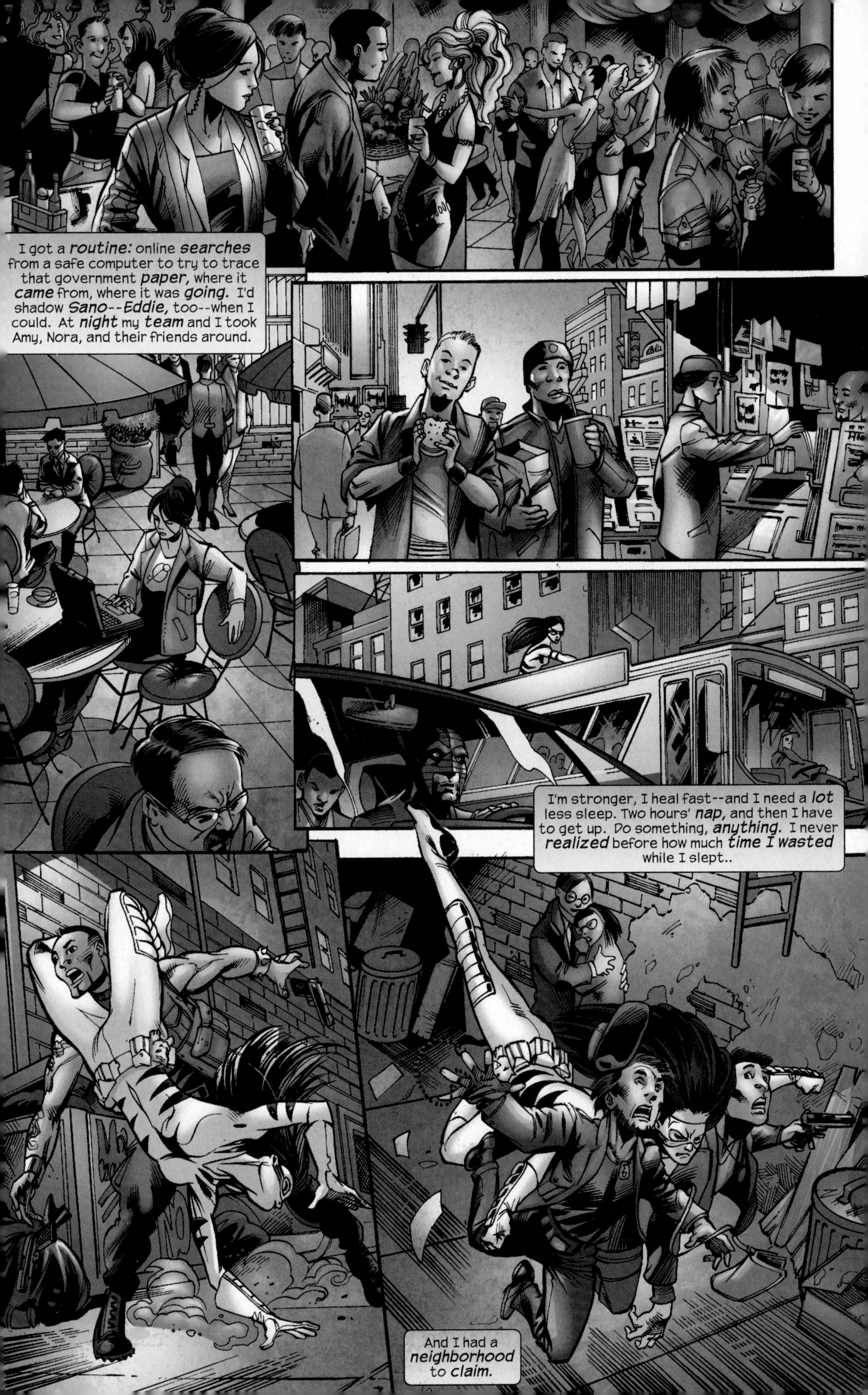
I got a routine: online searches from a safe computer to try to trace that government paper, where it came from, where it was going. I'd shadow Sano--Eddie, too--when I could. At night my team and I took Amy, Nora, and their friends around.
I'm stronger, I heal fast--and I need a lot less sleep. Two hours' nap, and then I have to get up. Do something, anything. I never realized before how much time I wasted while I slept..
And I had a neighborhood to claim.

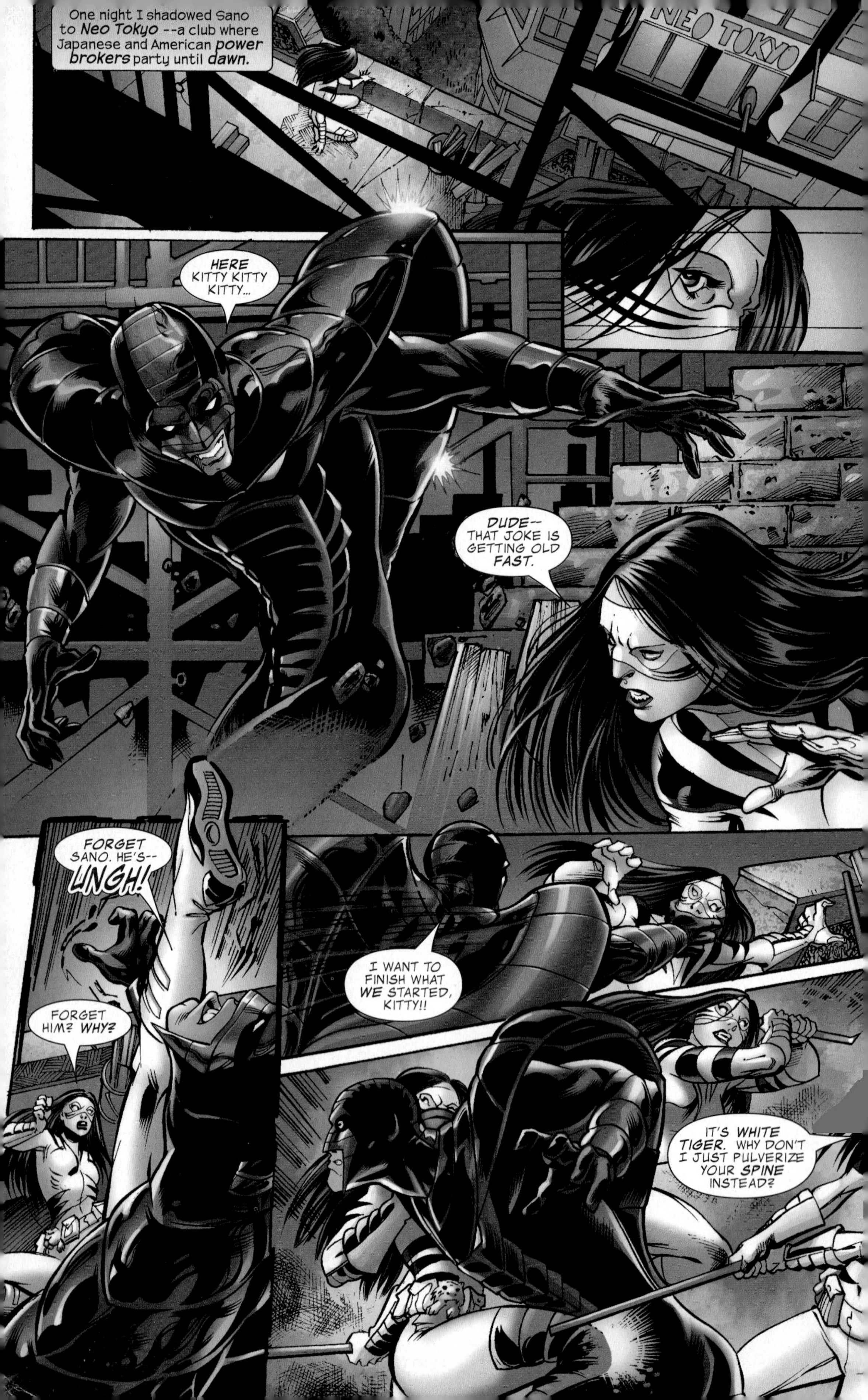

One night I shadowed Sano to Neo Tokyo --a club where Japanese and American power brokers party until dawn.
NEO TOKYO
HERE KITTY KITTY KITTY...
DUDE-- THAT JOKE IS GETTING OLD FAST.
FORGET SANO. HE'S-- UNGH!
I WANT TO FINISH WHAT WE STARTED, KITTY!!
FORGET HIM? WHY?
IT'S WHITE TIGER. WHY DON'T I JUST PULVERIZE YOUR SPINE INSTEAD?

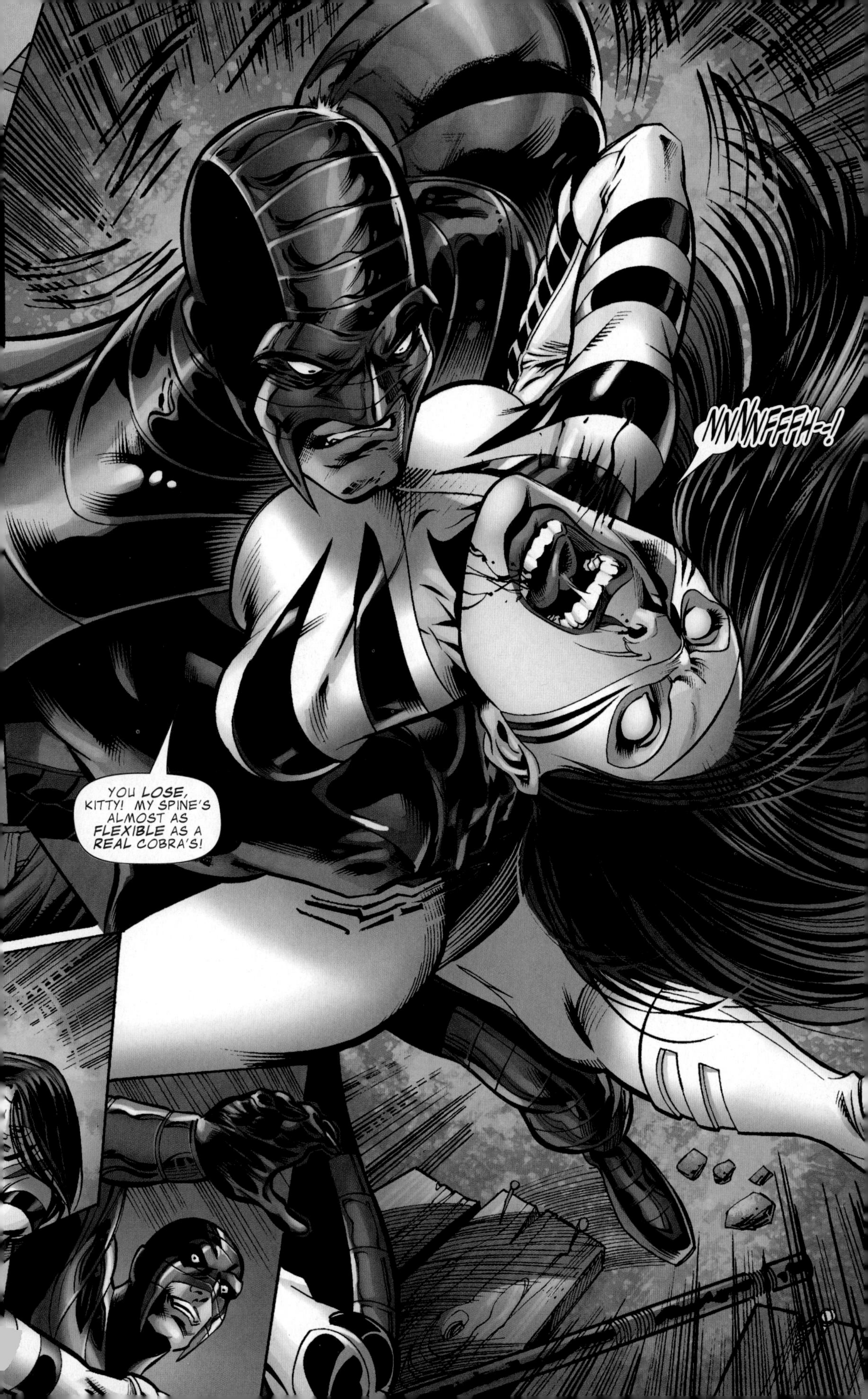
NNNNFFFH--!
YOU LOSE, KITTY! MY SPINE'S ALMOST AS FLEXIBLE AS A REAL COBRA'S!

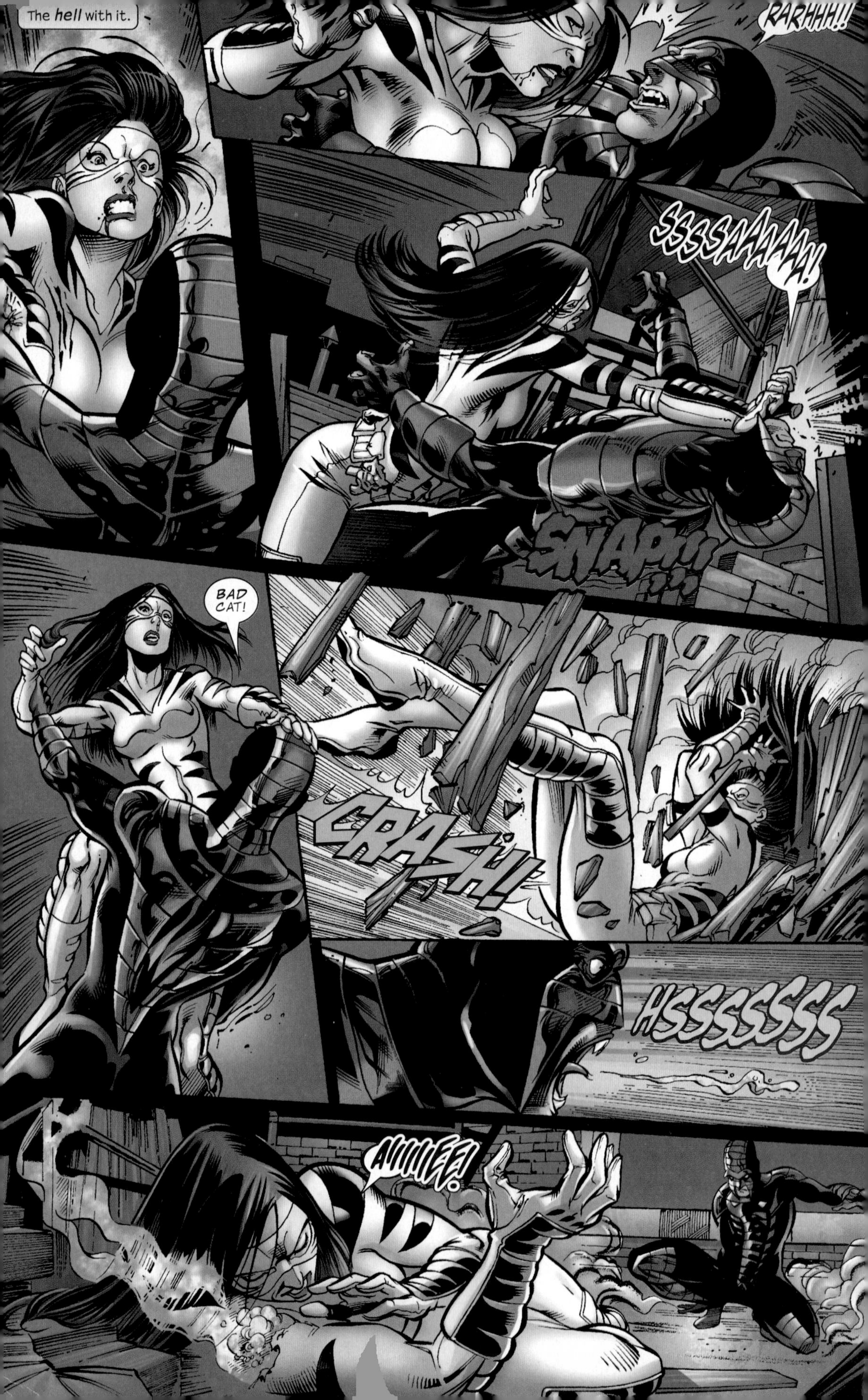
The hell with it.
RARHHH!!
SSSSAAAAAAA!
SNAP!!
BAD CAT!
CRASH!
HSSSSSSS
AIIIIEEE!

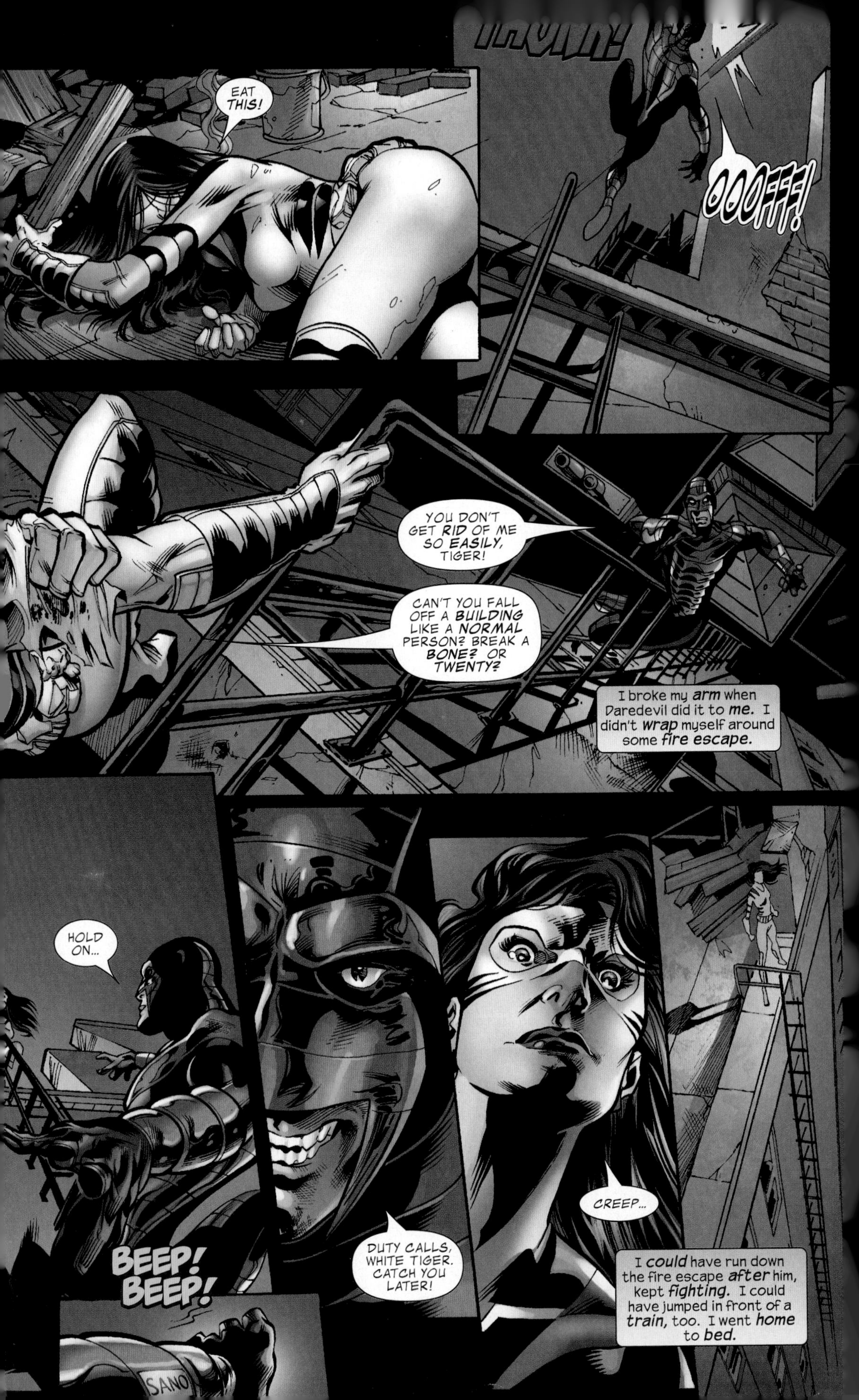
EAT THIS!
OOOFFF!
YOU DON'T GET RID OF ME SO EASILY, TIGER!
CAN'T YOU FALL OFF A BUILDING LIKE A NORMAL PERSON? BREAK A BONE? OR TWENTY?
I broke my arm when Daredevil did it to me. I didn't wrap myself around some fire escape.
HOLD ON...
BEEP! BEEP!
DUTY CALLS, WHITE TIGER. CATCH YOU LATER!
CREEP...
I could have run down the fire escape after him, kept fighting. I could have jumped in front of a train, too. I went home to bed.

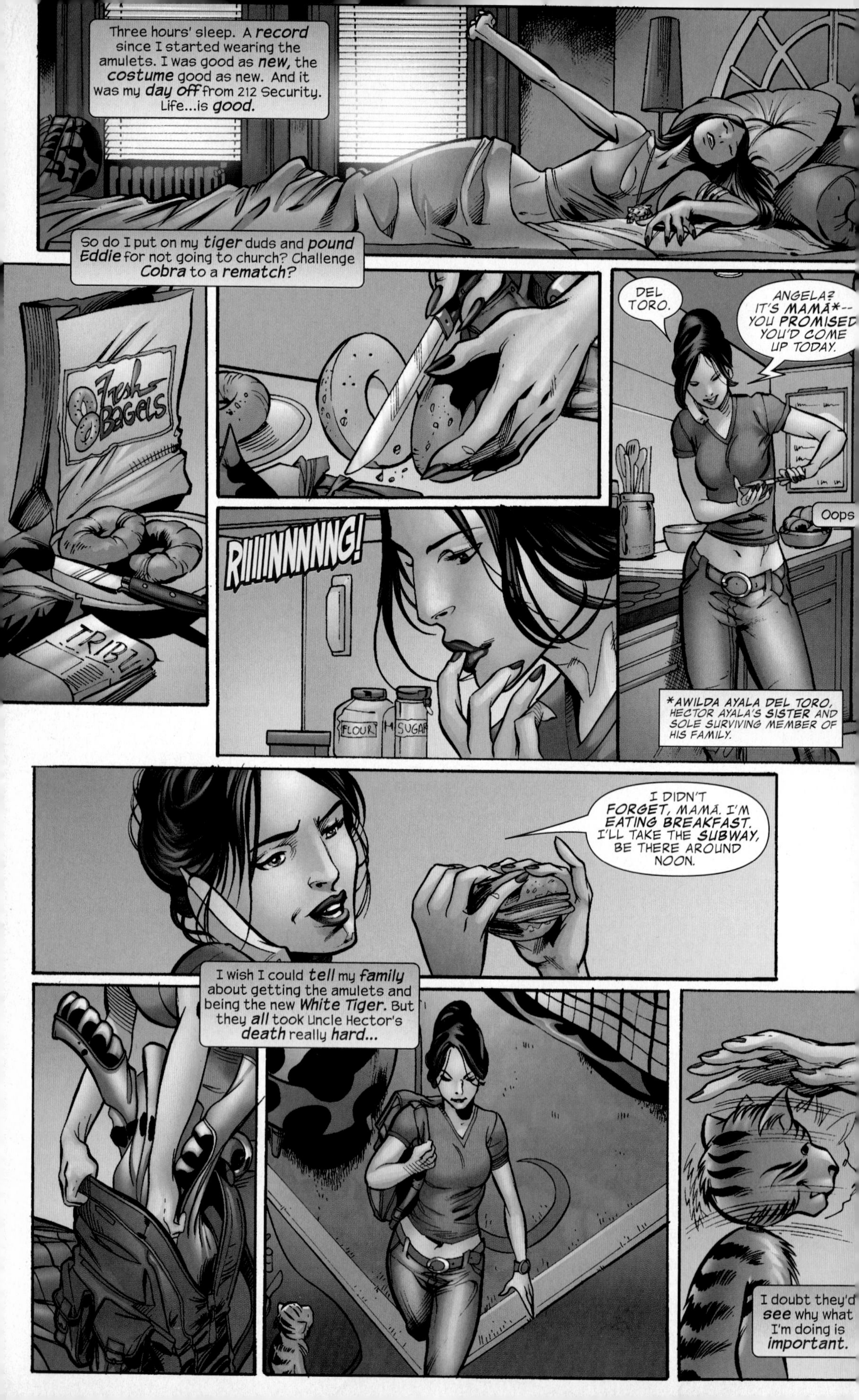
Three hours' sleep. A record since I started wearing the amulets. I was good as new, the costume good as new. And it was my day off from 212 Security. Life...is good.
So do I put on my tiger duds and pound Eddie for not going to church? Challenge Cobra to a rematch?
Fresh Bagels
TRIBU
RIIIINNNNNG!
FLOUR
SUGAR
DEL TORO.
ANGELA? IT'S MAMÁ*-- YOU PROMISED YOU'D COME UP TODAY.
Oops
*AWILDA AYALA DEL TORO, HECTOR AYALA'S SISTER AND SOLE SURVIVING MEMBER OF HIS FAMILY.
I DIDN'T FORGET, MAMÁ. I'M EATING BREAKFAST. I'LL TAKE THE SUBWAY, BE THERE AROUND NOON.
I wish I could tell my family about getting the amulets and being the new White Tiger. But they all took Uncle Hector's death really hard...
I doubt they'd see why what I'm doing is important.

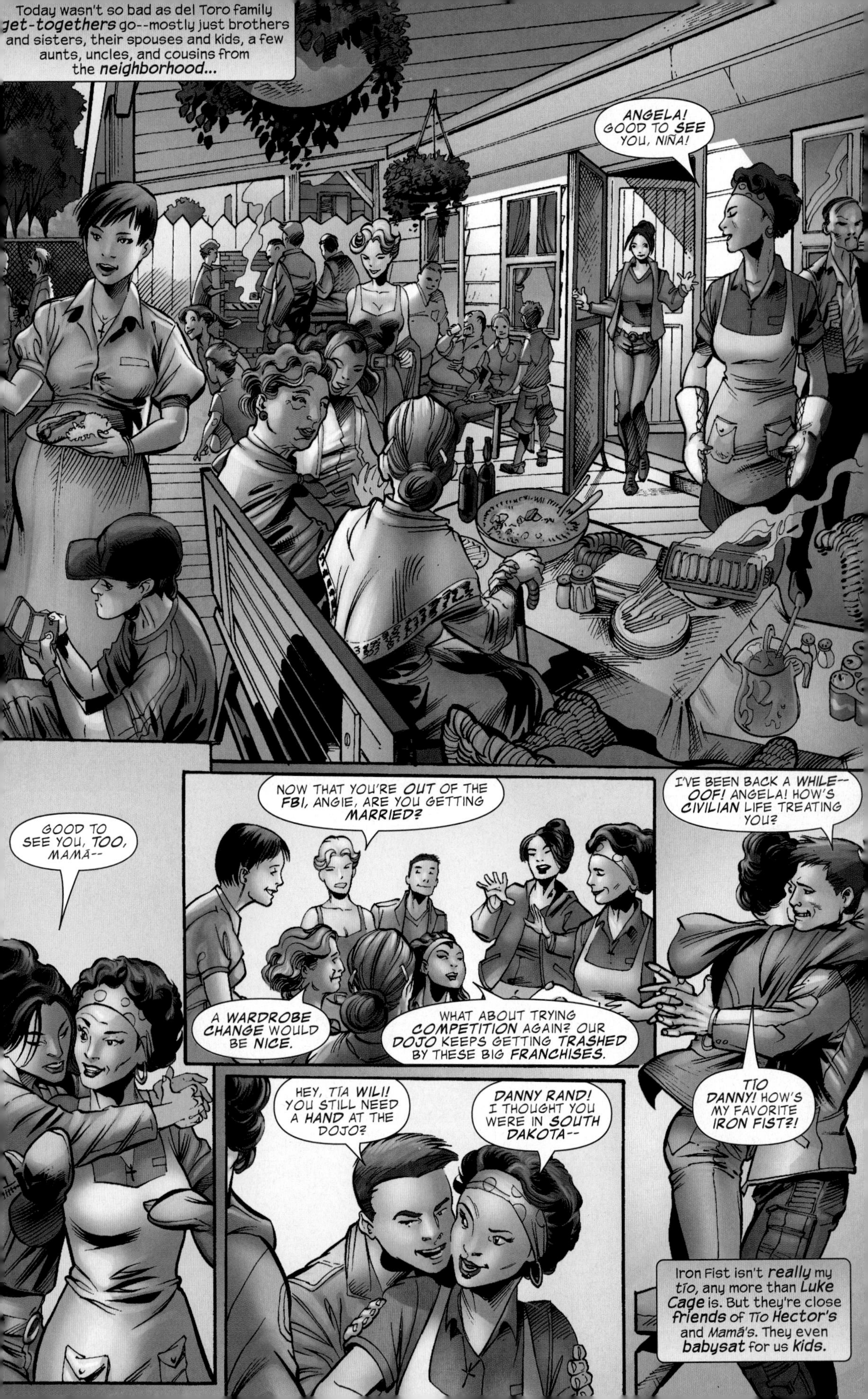
Today wasn't so bad as del Toro family get-togethers go--mostly just brothers and sisters, their spouses and kids, a few aunts, uncles, and cousins from the neighborhood...
ANGELA! GOOD TO SEE YOU, NIÑA!
GOOD TO SEE YOU, TOO, MAMÁ--
NOW THAT YOU'RE OUT OF THE FBI, ANGIE, ARE YOU GETTING MARRIED?
A WARDROBE CHANGE WOULD BE NICE.
WHAT ABOUT TRYING COMPETITION AGAIN? OUR DOJO KEEPS GETTING TRASHED BY THESE BIG FRANCHISES.
I'VE BEEN BACK A WHILE-- OOF! ANGELA! HOW'S CIVILIAN LIFE TREATING YOU?
TÍO DANNY! HOW'S MY FAVORITE IRON FIST?!
HEY, TÍA WILI! YOU STILL NEED A HAND AT THE DOJO?
DANNY RAND! I THOUGHT YOU WERE IN SOUTH DAKOTA--
Iron Fist isn't really my tío, any more than Luke Cage is. But they're close friends of Tío Hector's and Mamá's. They even babysat for us kids.

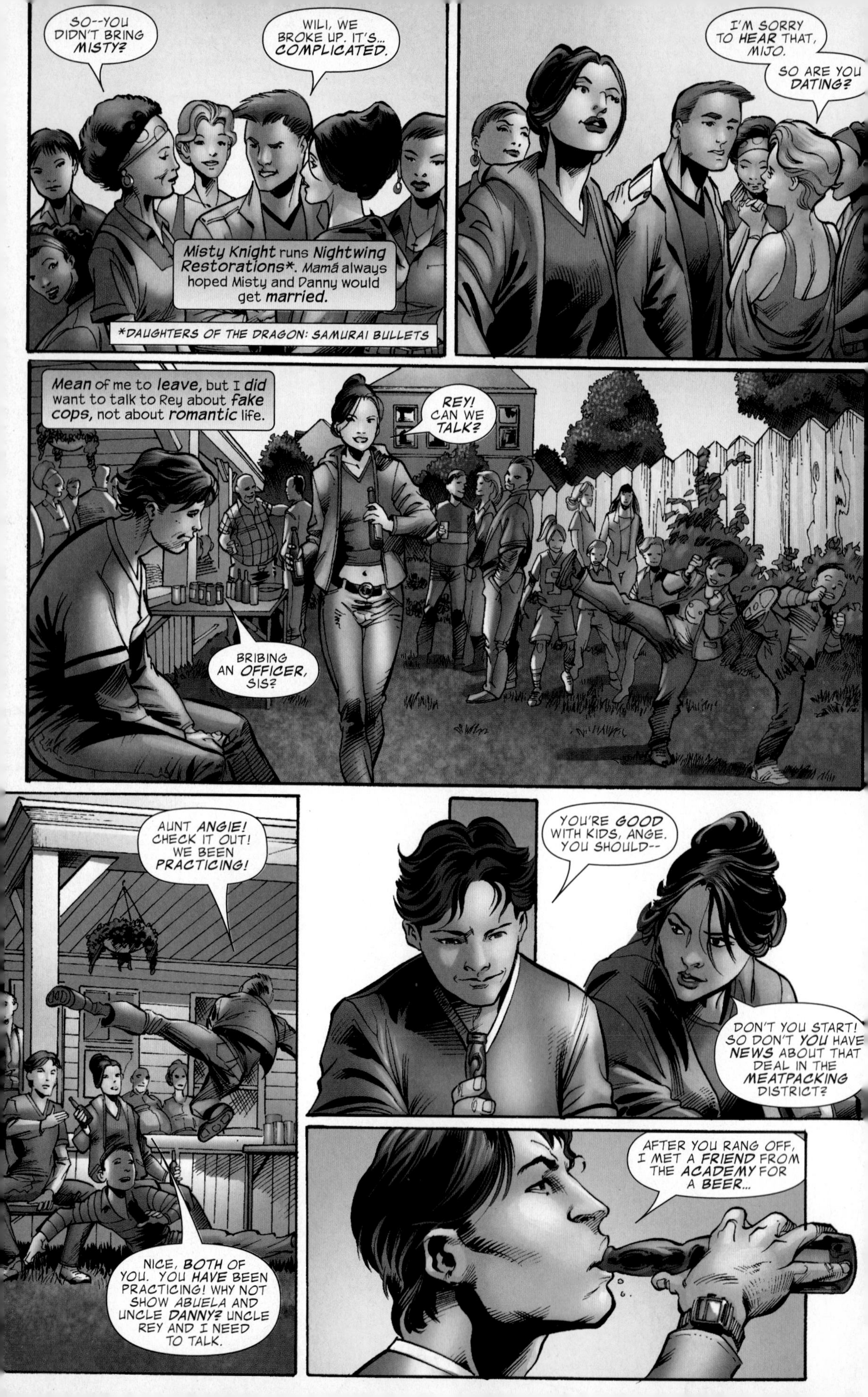
SO--YOU DIDN'T BRING MISTY?
WILI, WE BROKE UP. IT'S... COMPLICATED.
Misty Knight runs Nightwing Restorations*. Mamá always hoped Misty and Danny would get married.
*DAUGHTERS OF THE DRAGON: SAMURAI BULLETS
I'M SORRY TO HEAR THAT, MIJO.
SO ARE YOU DATING?
Mean of me to leave, but I did want to talk to Rey about fake cops, not about romantic life.
REY! CAN WE TALK?
BRIBING AN OFFICER, SIS?
AUNT ANGIE! CHECK IT OUT! WE BEEN PRACTICING!
NICE, BOTH OF YOU. YOU HAVE BEEN PRACTICING! WHY NOT SHOW ABUELA AND UNCLE DANNY? UNCLE REY AND I NEED TO TALK.
YOU'RE GOOD WITH KIDS, ANGE. YOU SHOULD--
DON'T YOU START! SO DON'T YOU HAVE NEWS ABOUT THAT DEAL IN THE MEATPACKING DISTRICT?
AFTER YOU RANG OFF, I MET A FRIEND FROM THE ACADEMY FOR A BEER...

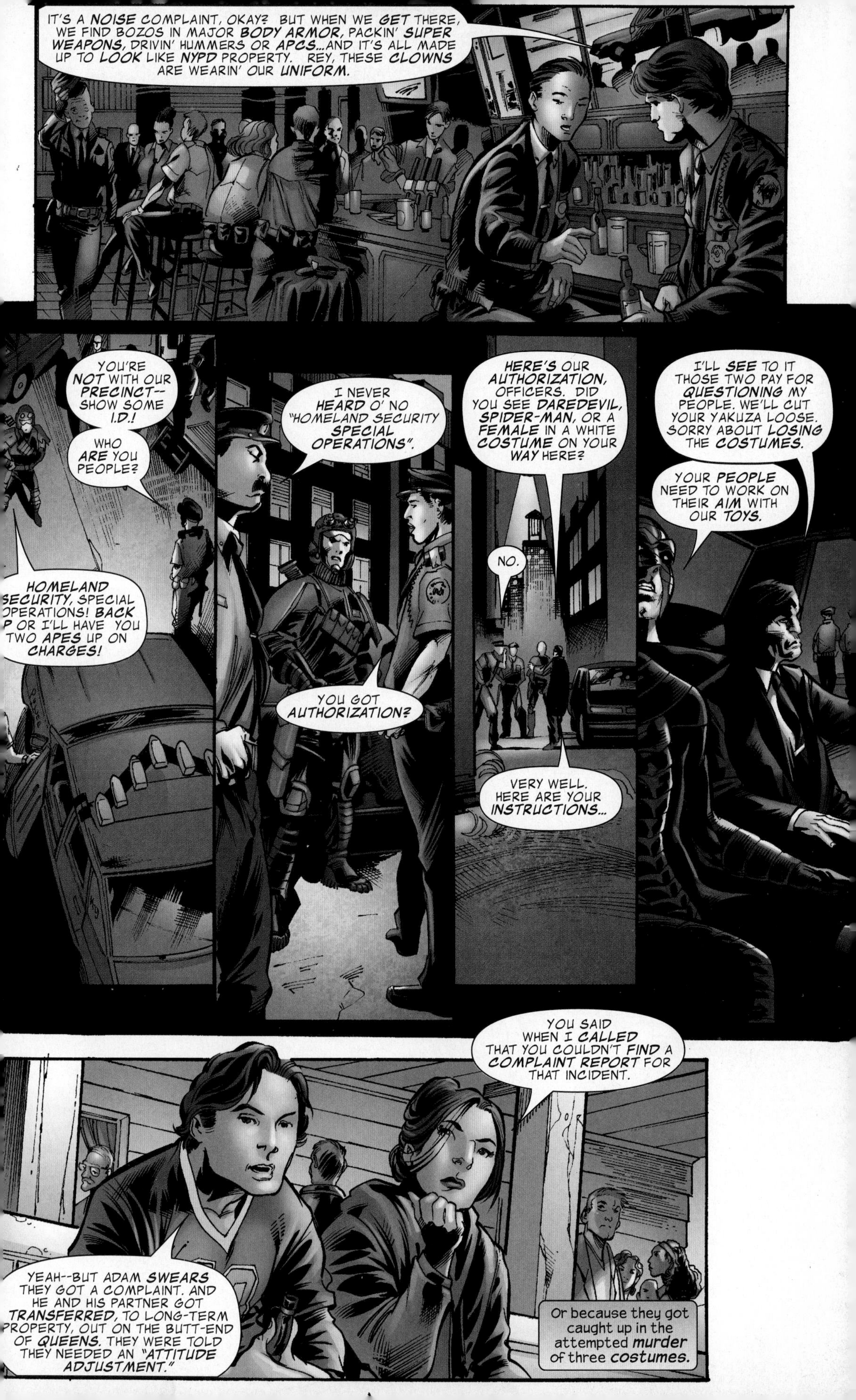
IT'S A NOISE COMPLAINT, OKAY? BUT WHEN WE GET THERE, WE FIND BOZOS IN MAJOR BODY ARMOR, PACKIN' SUPER WEAPONS, DRIVIN' HUMMERS OR APCS...AND IT'S ALL MADE UP TO LOOK LIKE NYPD PROPERTY. REY, THESE CLOWNS ARE WEARIN' OUR UNIFORM.
YOU'RE NOT WITH OUR PRECINCT--SHOW SOME I.D.!
WHO ARE YOU PEOPLE?
HOMELAND SECURITY, SPECIAL OPERATIONS! BACK P OR I'LL HAVE YOU TWO APES UP ON CHARGES!
I NEVER HEARD O' NO "HOMELAND SECURITY SPECIAL OPERATIONS".
YOU GOT AUTHORIZATION?
HERE'S OUR AUTHORIZATION, OFFICERS. DID YOU SEE DAREDEVIL, SPIDER-MAN, OR A FEMALE IN A WHITE COSTUME ON YOUR WAY HERE?
NO.
VERY WELL. HERE ARE YOUR INSTRUCTIONS...
I'LL SEE TO IT THOSE TWO PAY FOR QUESTIONING MY PEOPLE. WE'LL CUT YOUR YAKUZA LOOSE. SORRY ABOUT LOSING THE COSTUMES.
YOUR PEOPLE NEED TO WORK ON THEIR AIM WITH OUR TOYS.
YOU SAID WHEN I CALLED THAT YOU COULDN'T FIND A COMPLAINT REPORT FOR THAT INCIDENT.
YEAH--BUT ADAM SWEARS THEY GOT A COMPLAINT. AND HE AND HIS PARTNER GOT TRANSFERRED, TO LONG-TERM PROPERTY, OUT ON THE BUTT-END OF QUEENS. THEY WERE TOLD THEY NEEDED AN "ATTITUDE ADJUSTMENT."
Or because they got caught up in the attempted murder of three costumes.

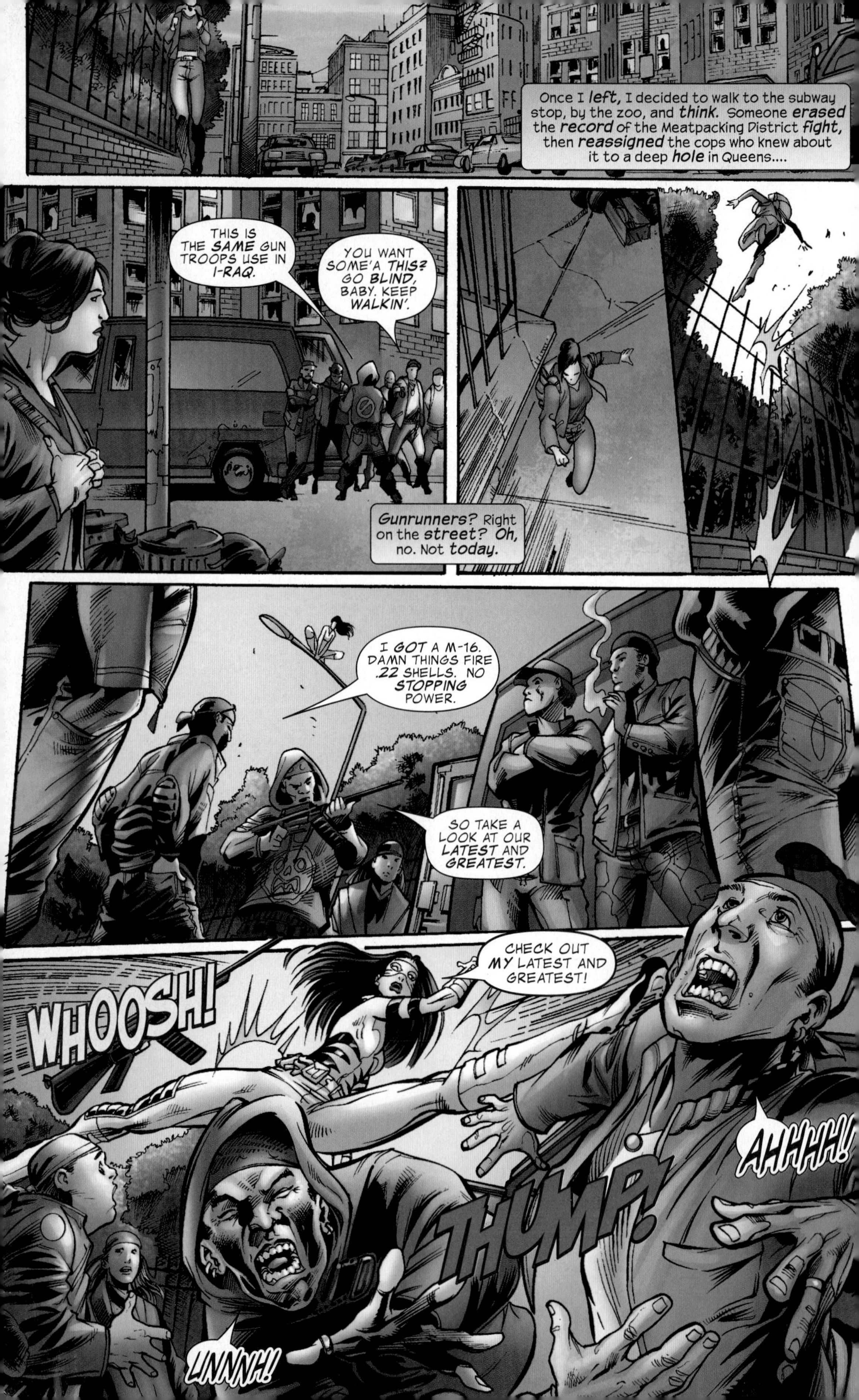
Once I left, I decided to walk to the subway stop, by the zoo, and think. Someone erased the record of the Meatpacking District fight, then reassigned the cops who knew about it to a deep hole in Queens....
THIS IS THE SAME GUN TROOPS USE IN I-RAQ.
YOU WANT SOME'A THIS? GO BLIND, BABY. KEEP WALKIN'.
Gunrunners? Right on the street? Oh, no. Not today.
I GOT A M-16. DAMN THINGS FIRE .22 SHELLS. NO STOPPING POWER.
SO TAKE A LOOK AT OUR LATEST AND GREATEST.
CHECK OUT MY LATEST AND GREATEST!
WHOOSH!
AHHHH!
THUMP!
UNNNH!

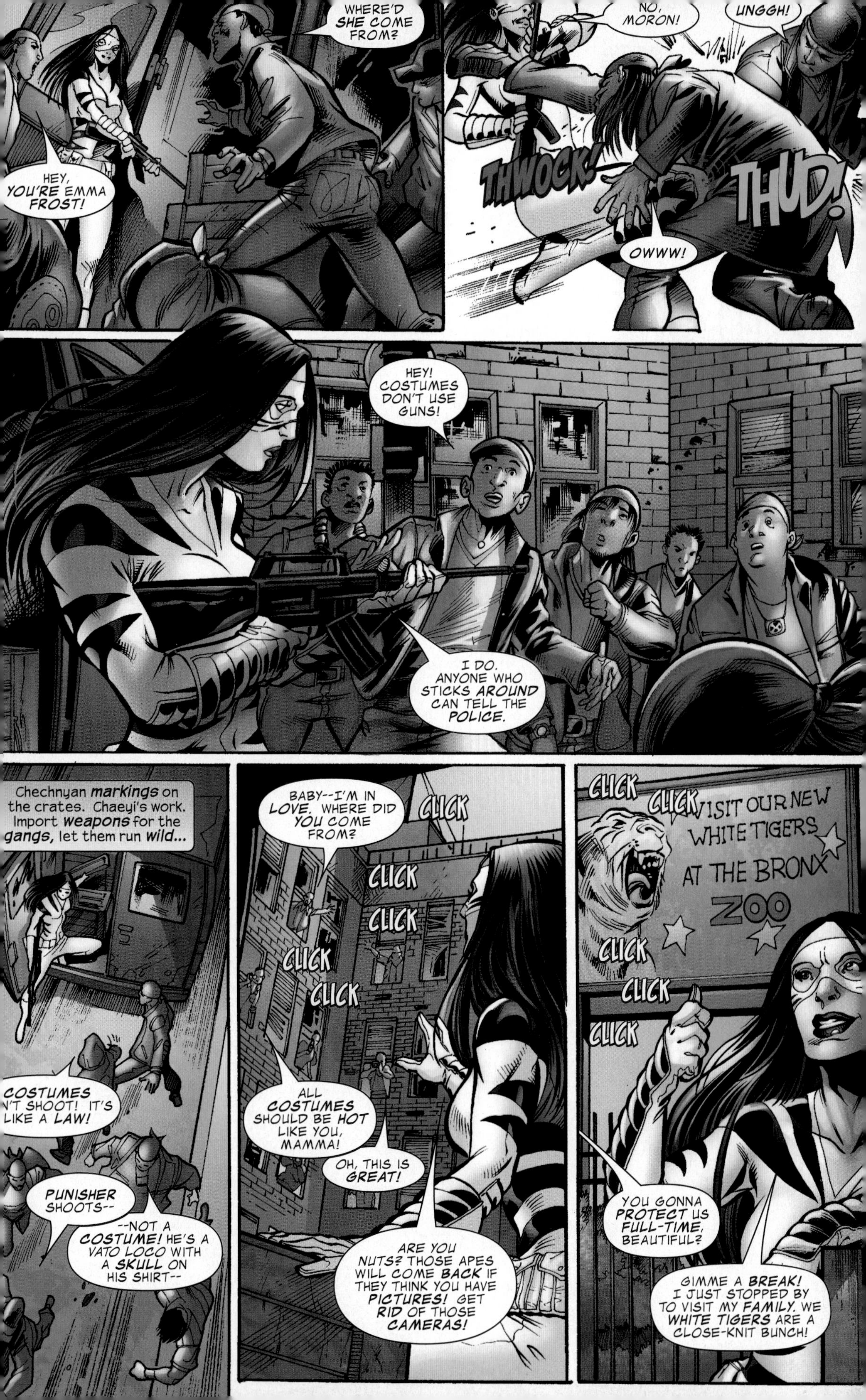
WHERE'D SHE COME FROM?
HEY, YOU'RE EMMA FROST!
NO, MORON!
UNGGH!
THWOCK!
THUD!
OWWW!
HEY! COSTUMES DON'T USE GUNS!
I DO. ANYONE WHO STICKS AROUND CAN TELL THE POLICE.
Chechnyan markings on the crates. Chaeyi's work. Import weapons for the gangs, let them run wild...
COSTUMES N'T SHOOT! IT'S LIKE A LAW!
PUNISHER SHOOTS--
--NOT A COSTUME! HE'S A VATO LOCO WITH A SKULL ON HIS SHIRT--
BABY--I'M IN LOVE. WHERE DID YOU COME FROM?
CLICK
CLICK
CLICK
CLICK
CLICK
ALL COSTUMES SHOULD BE HOT LIKE YOU, MAMMA!
OH, THIS IS GREAT!
ARE YOU NUTS? THOSE APES WILL COME BACK IF THEY THINK YOU HAVE PICTURES! GET RID OF THOSE CAMERAS!
CLICK
CLICK
VISIT OUR NEW WHITE TIGERS AT THE BRONX ZOO
CLICK
CLICK
CLICK
YOU GONNA PROTECT US FULL-TIME, BEAUTIFUL?
GIMME A BREAK! I JUST STOPPED BY TO VISIT MY FAMILY. WE WHITE TIGERS ARE A CLOSE-KNIT BUNCH!

DAILY BUGLE

PAGE 7

Costume Redesign?

by Sean O'Reilly

With reliable sources telling *The BUGLE* that the government is bent on registering all superhumans, we at *PAGE 7* thought we'd suggest some suit redesigns for some of our most secretive costumes:

Daredevil - We all know he's really jailed liberal lawyer Matt Murdock, so why's he still wear that stupid red hood? As a change, we recommend he go totally saturnine - with a pair of Spock ears! Maybe Prince Namor of Atlantis can lend him his...?

Moon Knight - Living proof that masked costumes are secular humanist psychos, this crazy-violent yo-yo is a fan of ancient Egyptian religions. So why not carry the Egypt theme further with a nice Pharoah suit? We bet he'd look just dandy with the fake beard and the funny helmet!

Falcon - Because we're totally equal-opportunity types here at *The BUGLE,* we'd love t see that handsome fac without a distracting mask. S what do you say we replace i with a helpful, and safe, crasl helmet? If he insists on som kind of theme, he can pain wings on it.

Spider-Man - Oh, we reall want to see who's the fac behind this mask! You thinl teaming up with the Avenger will save you, Web-Head Think again! For him, w suggest an orange jumpsuit same as that lawyer Murdock' wearing right now!

Trevor Parsons

Creamy White Goodness!

Normally we at *The BUGLE* don't like Costumes – but in your case, baby, we'll make an exception! This hard-fightin', gun-totin' hot tamale was seen beating the stuffing out of a bunch of gang punks near the Bronx Zoo – when she wasn't blinding them with her white skintight outfit that hugs her curves in all the right places.

PAGE 7
T-SHIRT NOW AVAILABLE ON DAILYBUGLE STORE.COM

FACTORY

GRADE POINT BELOW AVERAGE?

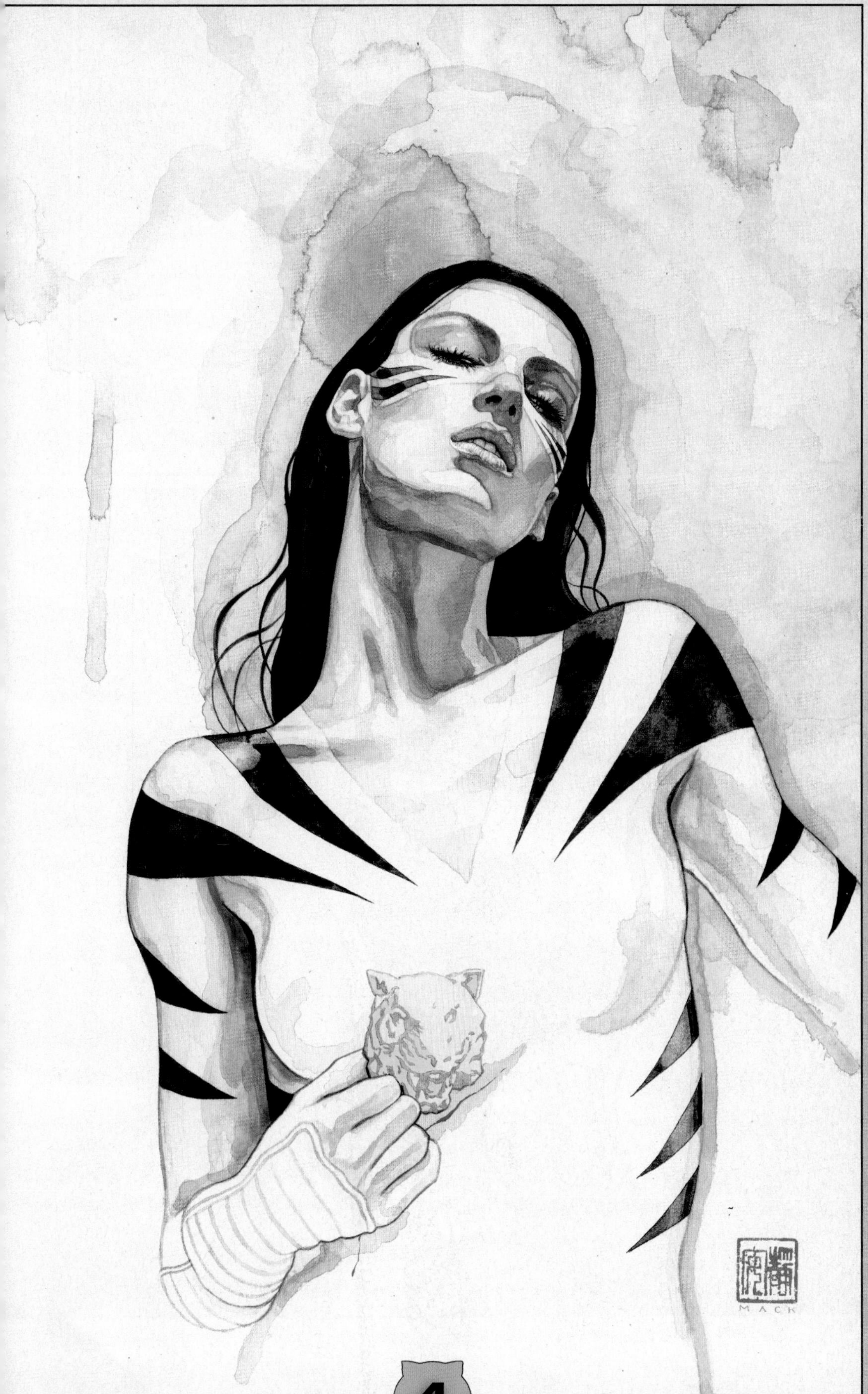
MACK

4

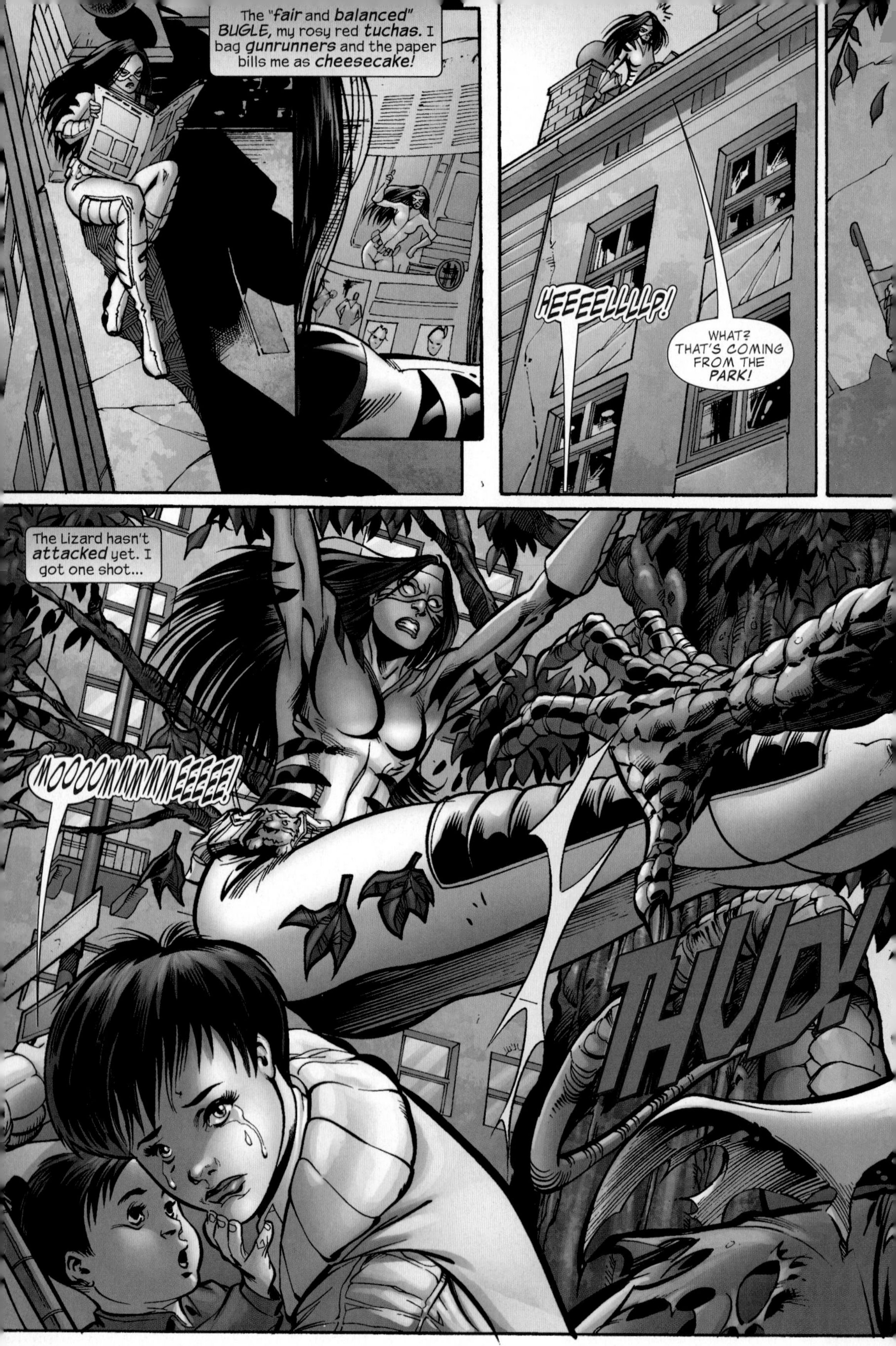

The "fair and balanced" BUGLE, my rosy red tuchas. I bag gunrunners and the paper bills me as cheesecake!
HEEEELLLLP!
WHAT? THAT'S COMING FROM THE PARK!
The Lizard hasn't attacked yet. I got one shot...
MOOOOMMMMMEEEEE!
THUD!

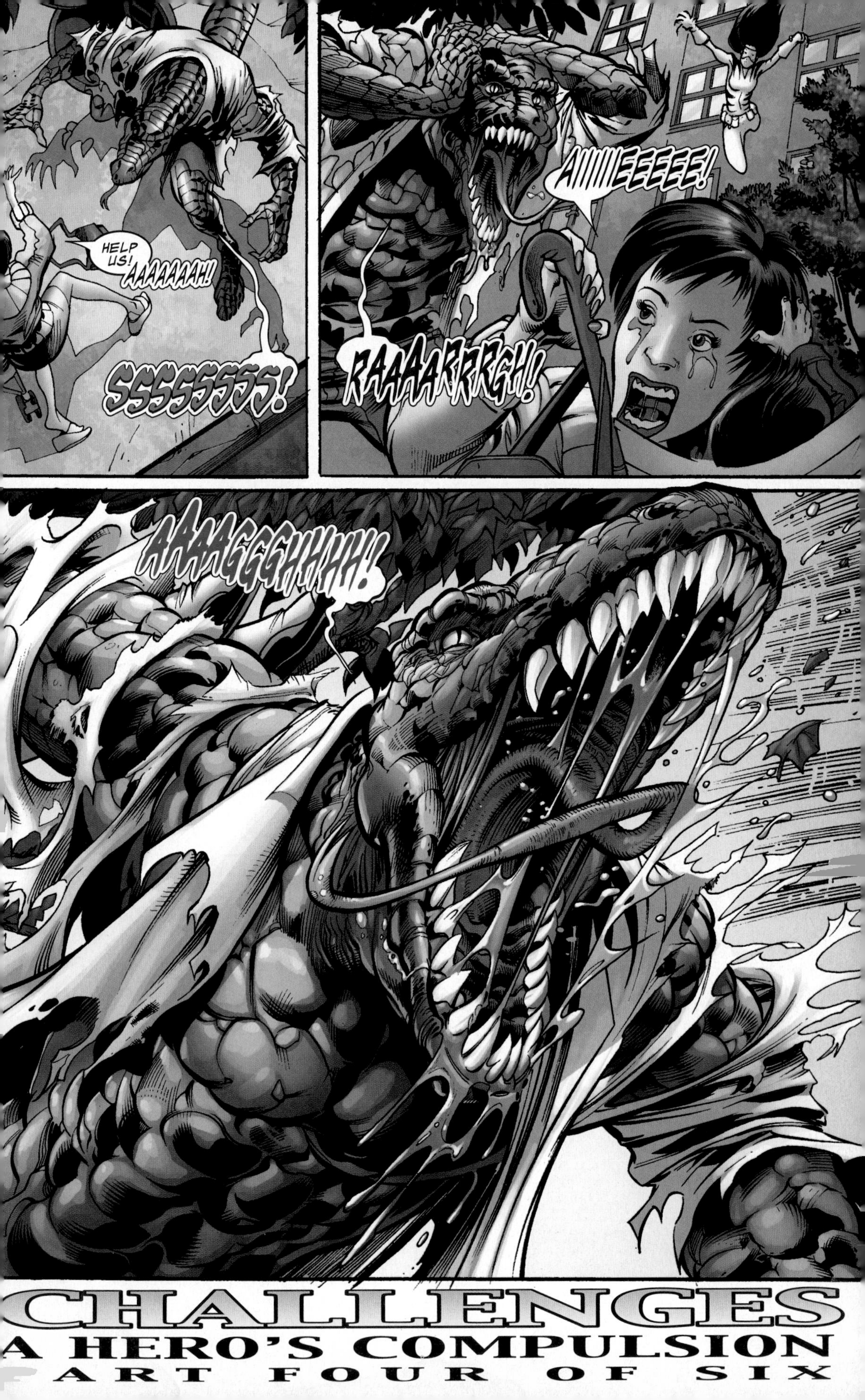
HELP US! AAAAAAH!
SSSSSSSS!
AIIIIEEEEE!
RAAAARRRGH!
AAAAGGGHHHH!
CHALLENGES
A HERO'S COMPULSION
ART FOUR OF SIX

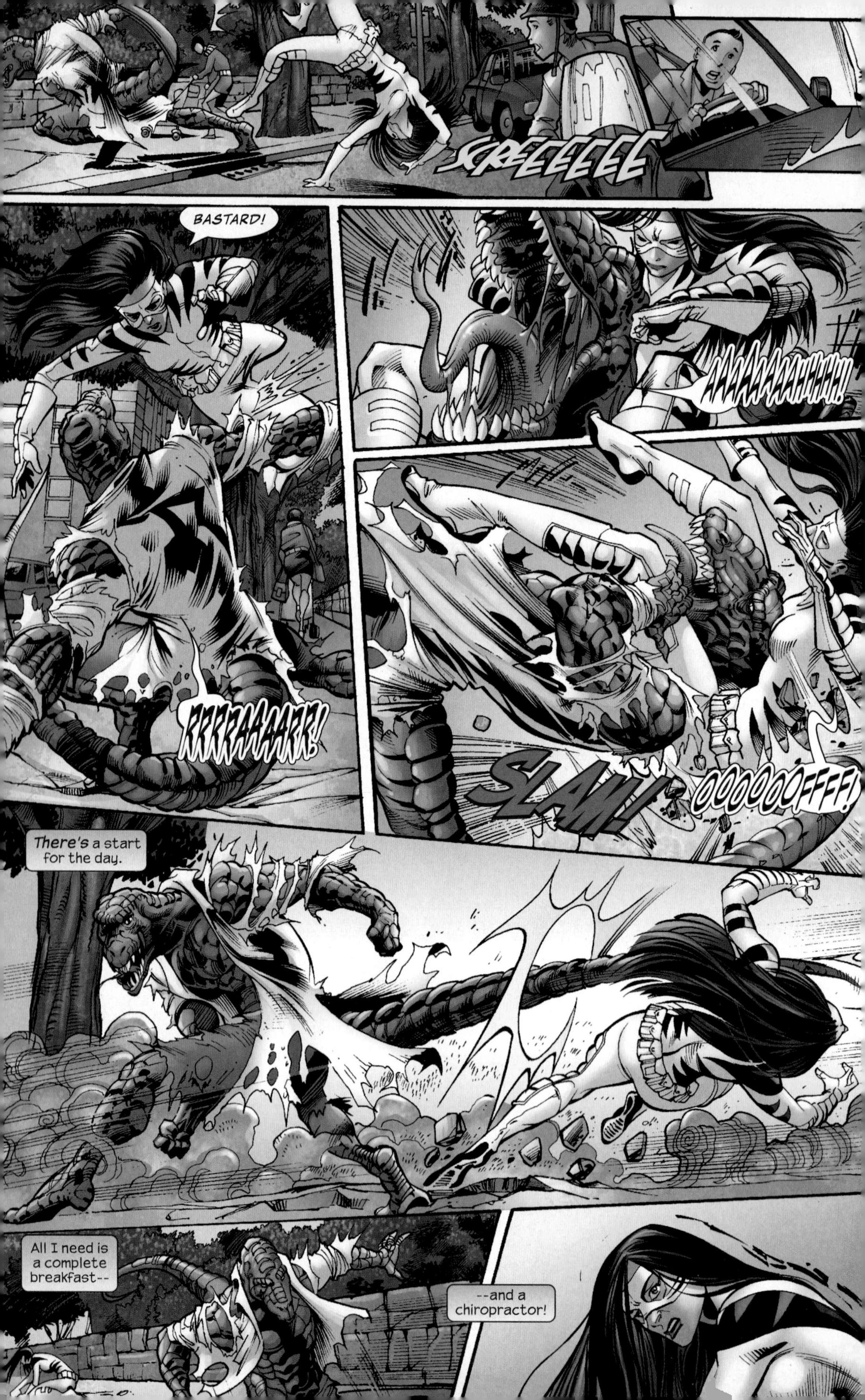

SCREEEEEEE
BASTARD!
RRRRAAAARR!
AAAAAAAAHHHH!
SLAM!
OOOOOOFFFF!
There's a start for the day.
All I need is a complete breakfast--
--and a chiropractor!

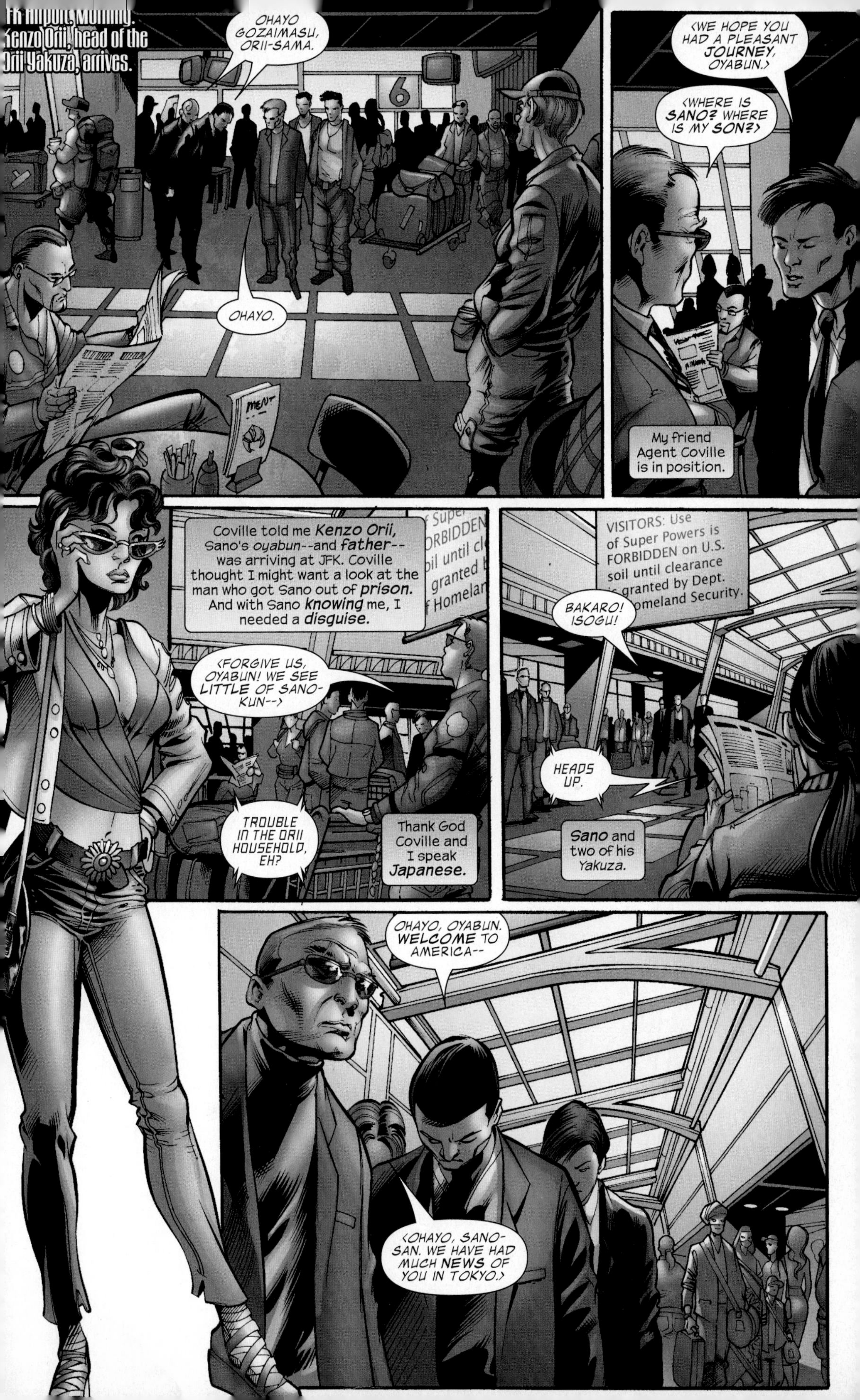

Kenzo Orii, head of the Orii Yakuza, arrives.
OHAYO GOZAIMASU, ORII-SAMA.
OHAYO.
6
MENU
<WE HOPE YOU HAD A PLEASANT JOURNEY, OYABUN.>
<WHERE IS SANO? WHERE IS MY SON?>
My friend Agent Coville is in position.
Coville told me Kenzo Orii, Sano's oyabun--and father--was arriving at JFK. Coville thought I might want a look at the man who got Sano out of prison. And with Sano knowing me, I needed a disguise.
<FORGIVE US, OYABUN! WE SEE LITTLE OF SANO-KUN-->
TROUBLE IN THE ORII HOUSEHOLD, EH?
Thank God Coville and I speak Japanese.
VISITORS: Use of Super Powers is FORBIDDEN on U.S. soil until clearance is granted by Dept. of Homeland Security.
BAKARO! ISOGU!
HEADS UP.
Sano and two of his Yakuza.
OHAYO, OYABUN. WELCOME TO AMERICA--
<OHAYO, SANO-SAN. WE HAVE HAD MUCH NEWS OF YOU IN TOKYO.>

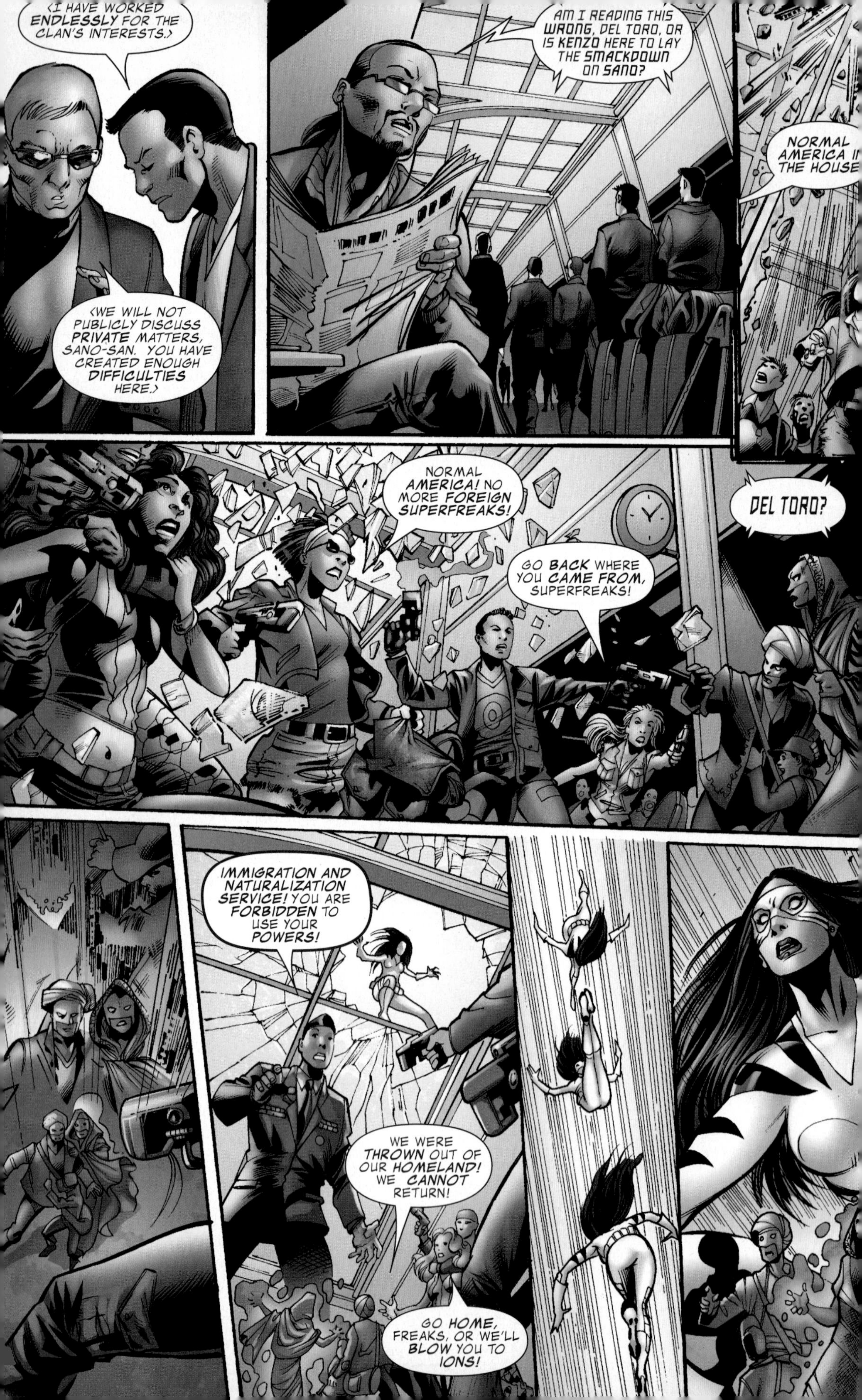

<I HAVE WORKED ENDLESSLY FOR THE CLAN'S INTERESTS.>
<WE WILL NOT PUBLICLY DISCUSS PRIVATE MATTERS, SANO-SAN. YOU HAVE CREATED ENOUGH DIFFICULTIES HERE.>
AM I READING THIS WRONG, DEL TORO, OR IS KENZO HERE TO LAY THE SMACKDOWN ON SANO?
NORMAL AMERICA II THE HOUSE
NORMAL AMERICA! NO MORE FOREIGN SUPERFREAKS!
DEL TORO?
GO BACK WHERE YOU CAME FROM, SUPERFREAKS!
IMMIGRATION AND NATURALIZATION SERVICE! YOU ARE FORBIDDEN TO USE YOUR POWERS!
WE WERE THROWN OUT OF OUR HOMELAND! WE CANNOT RETURN!
GO HOME, FREAKS, OR WE'LL BLOW YOU TO IONS!

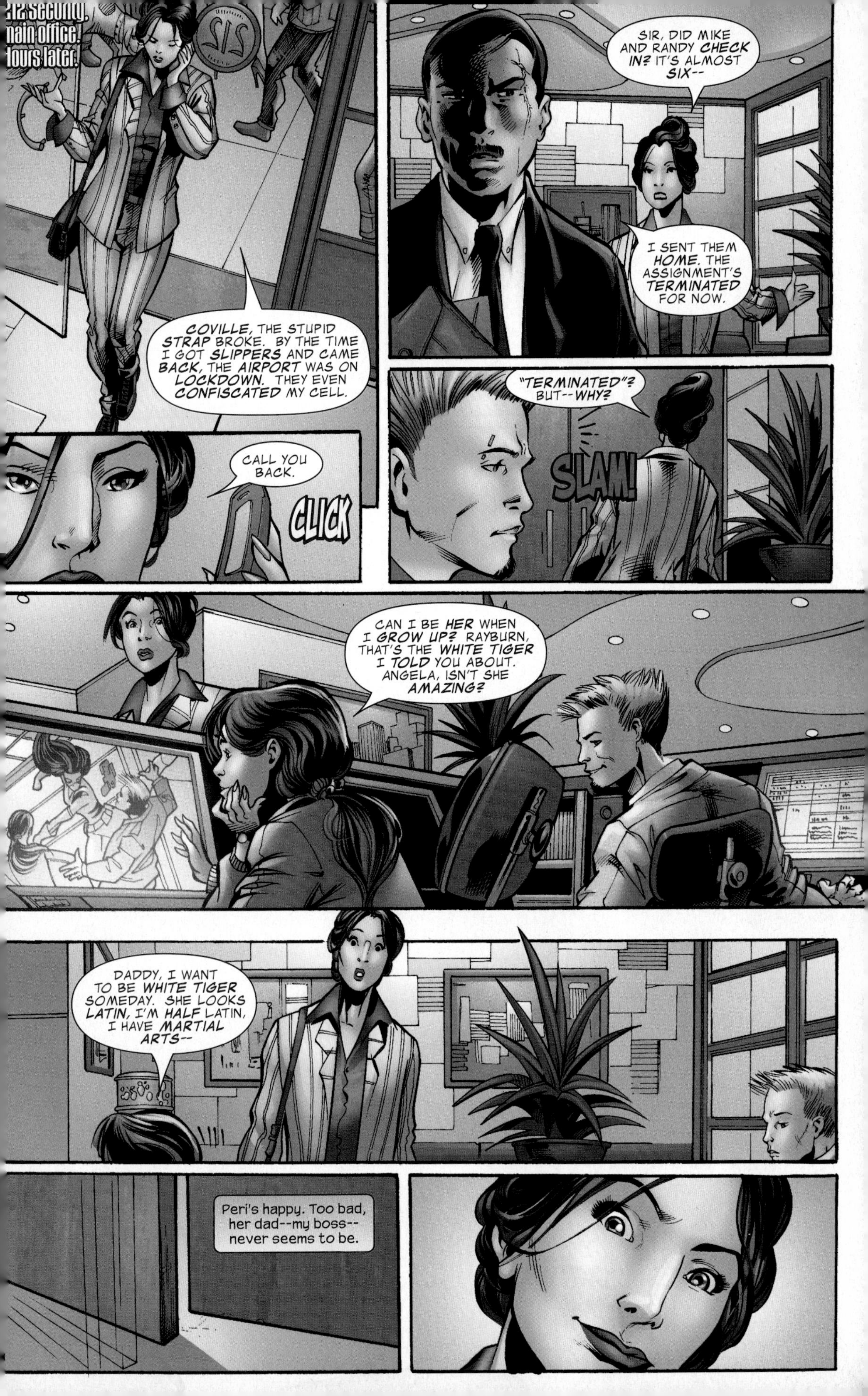

212 Security, nain office. lours later.
COVILLE, THE STUPID STRAP BROKE. BY THE TIME I GOT SLIPPERS AND CAME BACK, THE AIRPORT WAS ON LOCKDOWN. THEY EVEN CONFISCATED MY CELL.
SIR, DID MIKE AND RANDY CHECK IN? IT'S ALMOST SIX--
I SENT THEM HOME. THE ASSIGNMENT'S TERMINATED FOR NOW.
CALL YOU BACK.
CLICK
"TERMINATED"? BUT--WHY?
SLAM!
CAN I BE HER WHEN I GROW UP? RAYBURN, THAT'S THE WHITE TIGER I TOLD YOU ABOUT. ANGELA, ISN'T SHE AMAZING?
DADDY, I WANT TO BE WHITE TIGER SOMEDAY. SHE LOOKS LATIN, I'M HALF LATIN, I HAVE MARTIAL ARTS--
Peri's happy. Too bad, her dad--my boss--never seems to be.

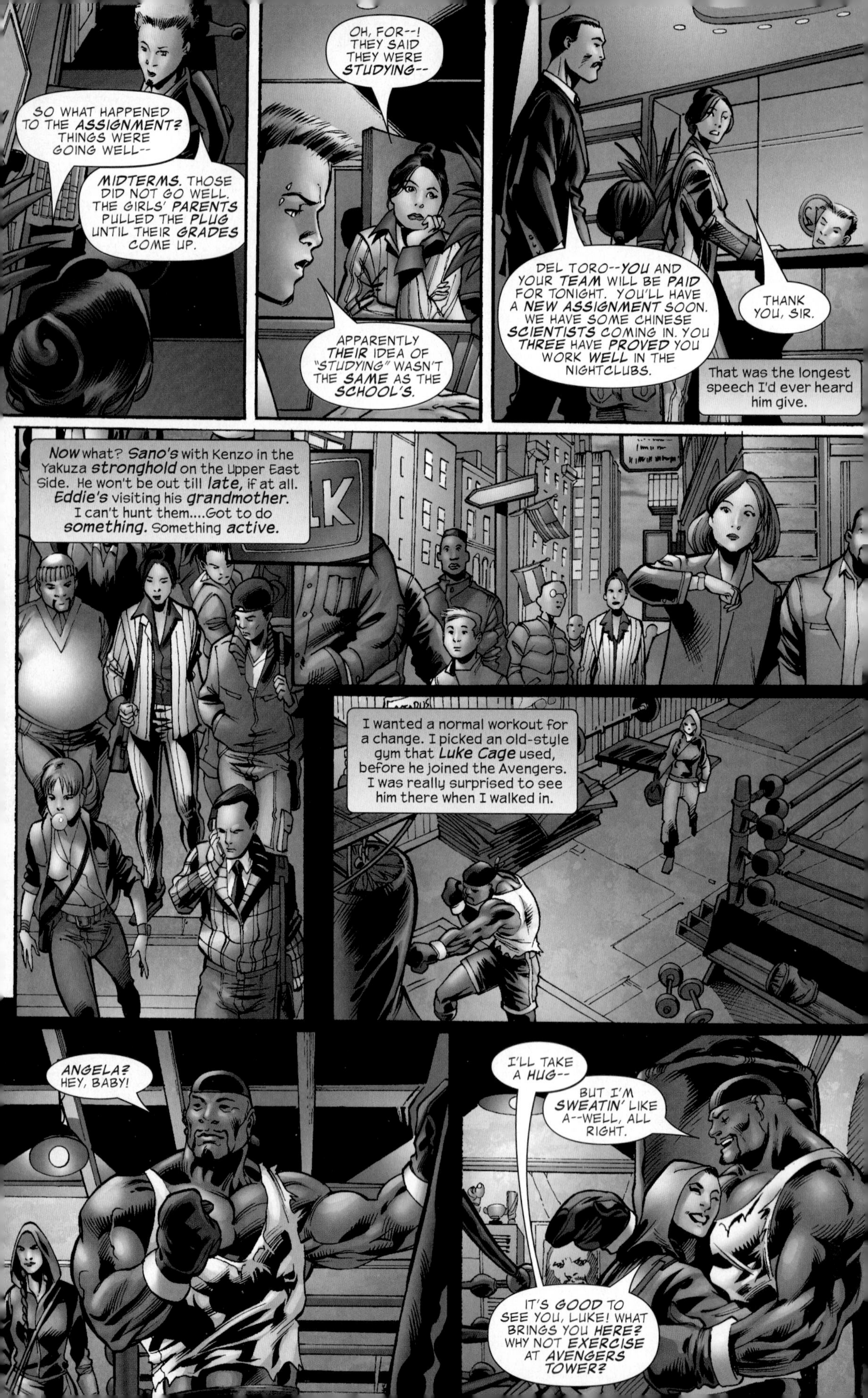
SO WHAT HAPPENED TO THE ASSIGNMENT? THINGS WERE GOING WELL--
MIDTERMS. THOSE DID NOT GO WELL. THE GIRLS' PARENTS PULLED THE PLUG UNTIL THEIR GRADES COME UP.
OH, FOR--! THEY SAID THEY WERE STUDYING--
APPARENTLY THEIR IDEA OF "STUDYING" WASN'T THE SAME AS THE SCHOOL'S.
DEL TORO--YOU AND YOUR TEAM WILL BE PAID FOR TONIGHT. YOU'LL HAVE A NEW ASSIGNMENT SOON. WE HAVE SOME CHINESE SCIENTISTS COMING IN. YOU THREE HAVE PROVED YOU WORK WELL IN THE NIGHTCLUBS.
THANK YOU, SIR.
That was the longest speech I'd ever heard him give.
Now what? Sano's with Kenzo in the Yakuza stronghold on the Upper East Side. He won't be out till late, if at all. Eddie's visiting his grandmother. I can't hunt them....Got to do something. Something active.
I wanted a normal workout for a change. I picked an old-style gym that Luke Cage used, before he joined the Avengers. I was really surprised to see him there when I walked in.
ANGELA? HEY, BABY!
I'LL TAKE A HUG--
BUT I'M SWEATIN' LIKE A--WELL, ALL RIGHT.
IT'S GOOD TO SEE YOU, LUKE! WHAT BRINGS YOU HERE? WHY NOT EXERCISE AT AVENGERS TOWER?

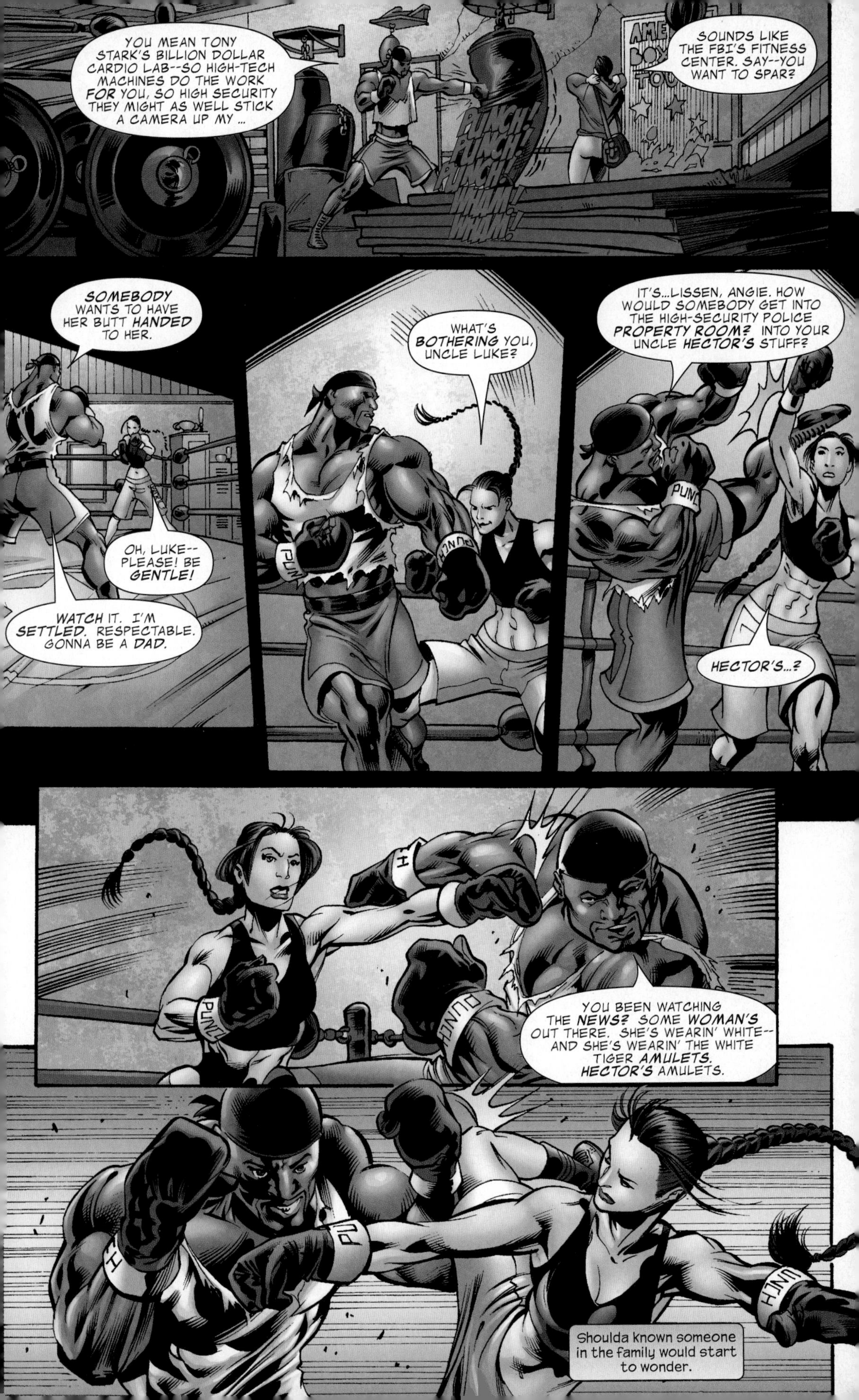
YOU MEAN TONY STARK'S BILLION DOLLAR CARDIO LAB--SO HIGH-TECH MACHINES DO THE WORK FOR YOU, SO HIGH SECURITY THEY MIGHT AS WELL STICK A CAMERA UP MY ...
SOUNDS LIKE THE FBI'S FITNESS CENTER. SAY--YOU WANT TO SPAR?
PUNCH! PUNCH! PUNCH! WHAM! WHAM!
SOMEBODY WANTS TO HAVE HER BUTT HANDED TO HER.
OH, LUKE-- PLEASE! BE GENTLE!
WATCH IT. I'M SETTLED. RESPECTABLE. GONNA BE A DAD.
WHAT'S BOTHERING YOU, UNCLE LUKE?
IT'S...LISSEN, ANGIE. HOW WOULD SOMEBODY GET INTO THE HIGH-SECURITY POLICE PROPERTY ROOM? INTO YOUR UNCLE HECTOR'S STUFF?
HECTOR'S...?
YOU BEEN WATCHING THE NEWS? SOME WOMAN'S OUT THERE. SHE'S WEARIN' WHITE-- AND SHE'S WEARIN' THE WHITE TIGER AMULETS. HECTOR'S AMULETS.
Shoulda known someone in the family would start to wonder.

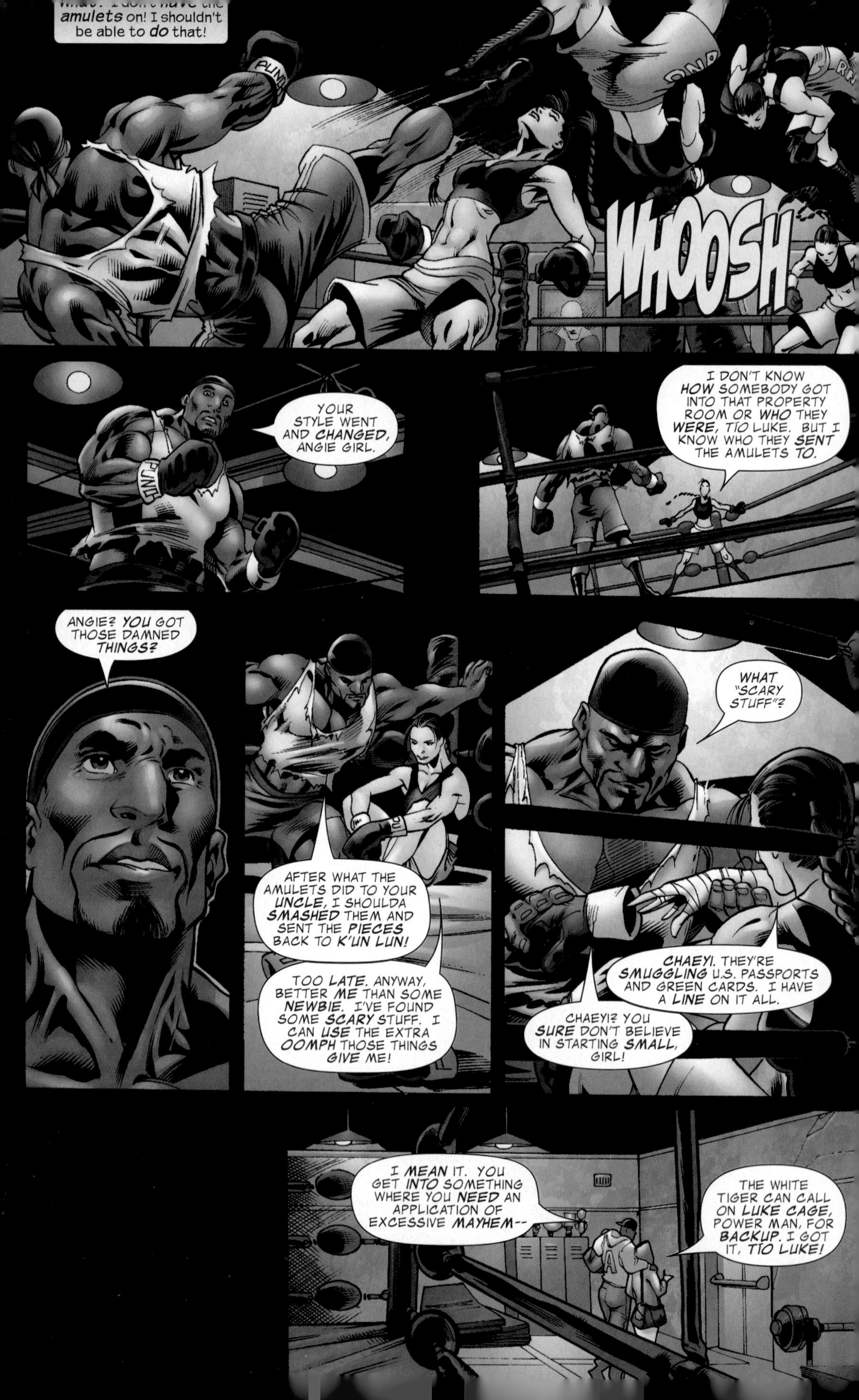
amulets on! I shouldn't be able to do that!
WHOOSH
YOUR STYLE WENT AND CHANGED, ANGIE GIRL.
I DON'T KNOW HOW SOMEBODY GOT INTO THAT PROPERTY ROOM OR WHO THEY WERE, TÍO LUKE. BUT I KNOW WHO THEY SENT THE AMULETS TO.
ANGIE? YOU GOT THOSE DAMNED THINGS?
AFTER WHAT THE AMULETS DID TO YOUR UNCLE, I SHOULDA SMASHED THEM AND SENT THE PIECES BACK TO K'UN LUN!
TOO LATE. ANYWAY, BETTER ME THAN SOME NEWBIE. I'VE FOUND SOME SCARY STUFF. I CAN USE THE EXTRA OOMPH THOSE THINGS GIVE ME!
WHAT "SCARY STUFF"?
CHAEYI. THEY'RE SMUGGLING U.S. PASSPORTS AND GREEN CARDS. I HAVE A LINE ON IT ALL.
CHAEYI? YOU SURE DON'T BELIEVE IN STARTING SMALL, GIRL!
I MEAN IT. YOU GET INTO SOMETHING WHERE YOU NEED AN APPLICATION OF EXCESSIVE MAYHEM--
THE WHITE TIGER CAN CALL ON LUKE CAGE, POWER MAN, FOR BACKUP. I GOT IT, TÍO LUKE!

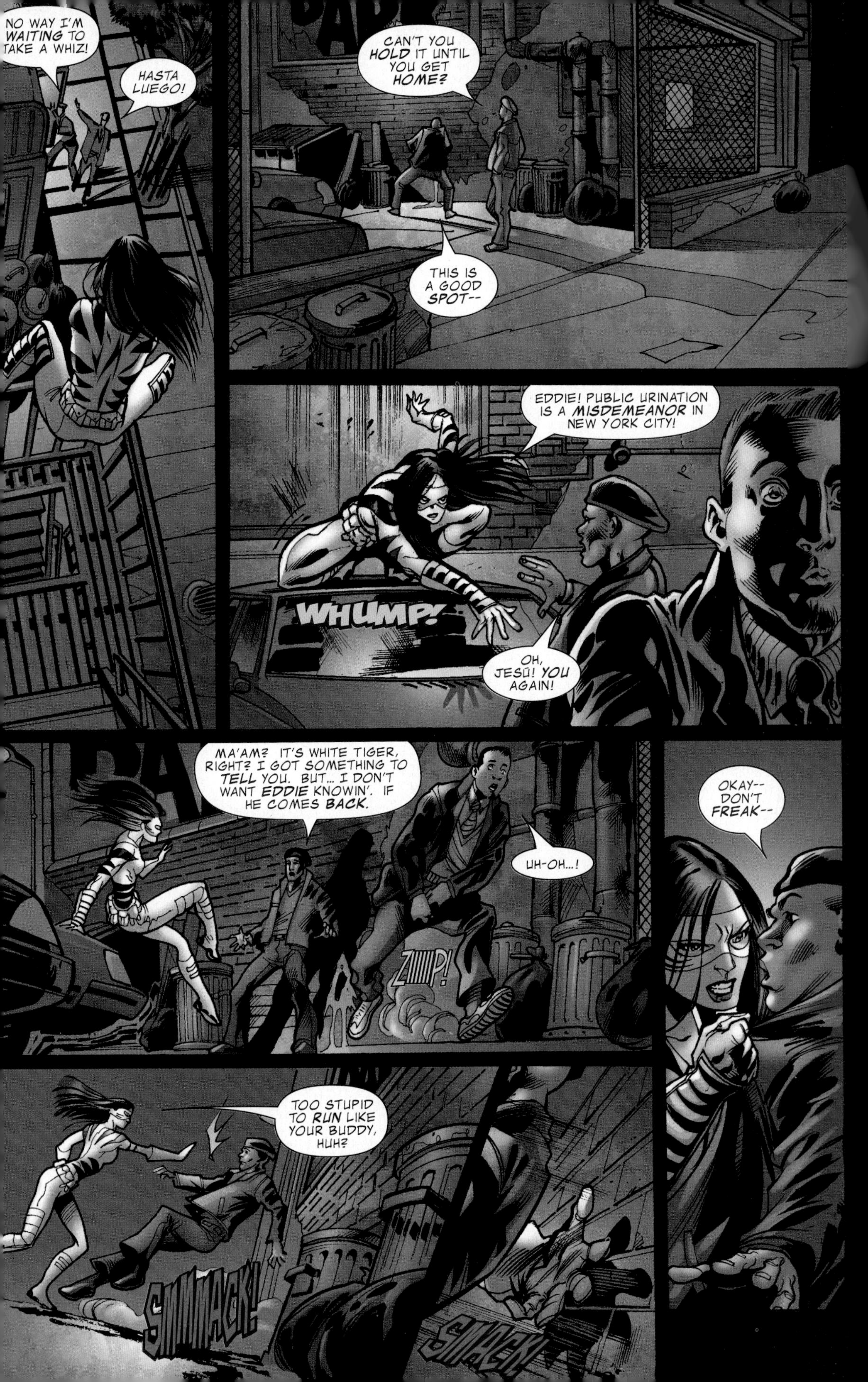
NO WAY I'M WAITING TO TAKE A WHIZ!
HASTA LUEGO!
CAN'T YOU HOLD IT UNTIL YOU GET HOME?
THIS IS A GOOD SPOT--
EDDIE! PUBLIC URINATION IS A MISDEMEANOR IN NEW YORK CITY!
WHUMP!
OH, JESÚ! YOU AGAIN!
MA'AM? IT'S WHITE TIGER, RIGHT? I GOT SOMETHING TO TELL YOU. BUT... I DON'T WANT EDDIE KNOWIN'. IF HE COMES BACK.
UH-OH...!
ZIIIP!
OKAY-- DON'T FREAK--
TOO STUPID TO RUN LIKE YOUR BUDDY, HUH?
SMMMACK!
SHACK!

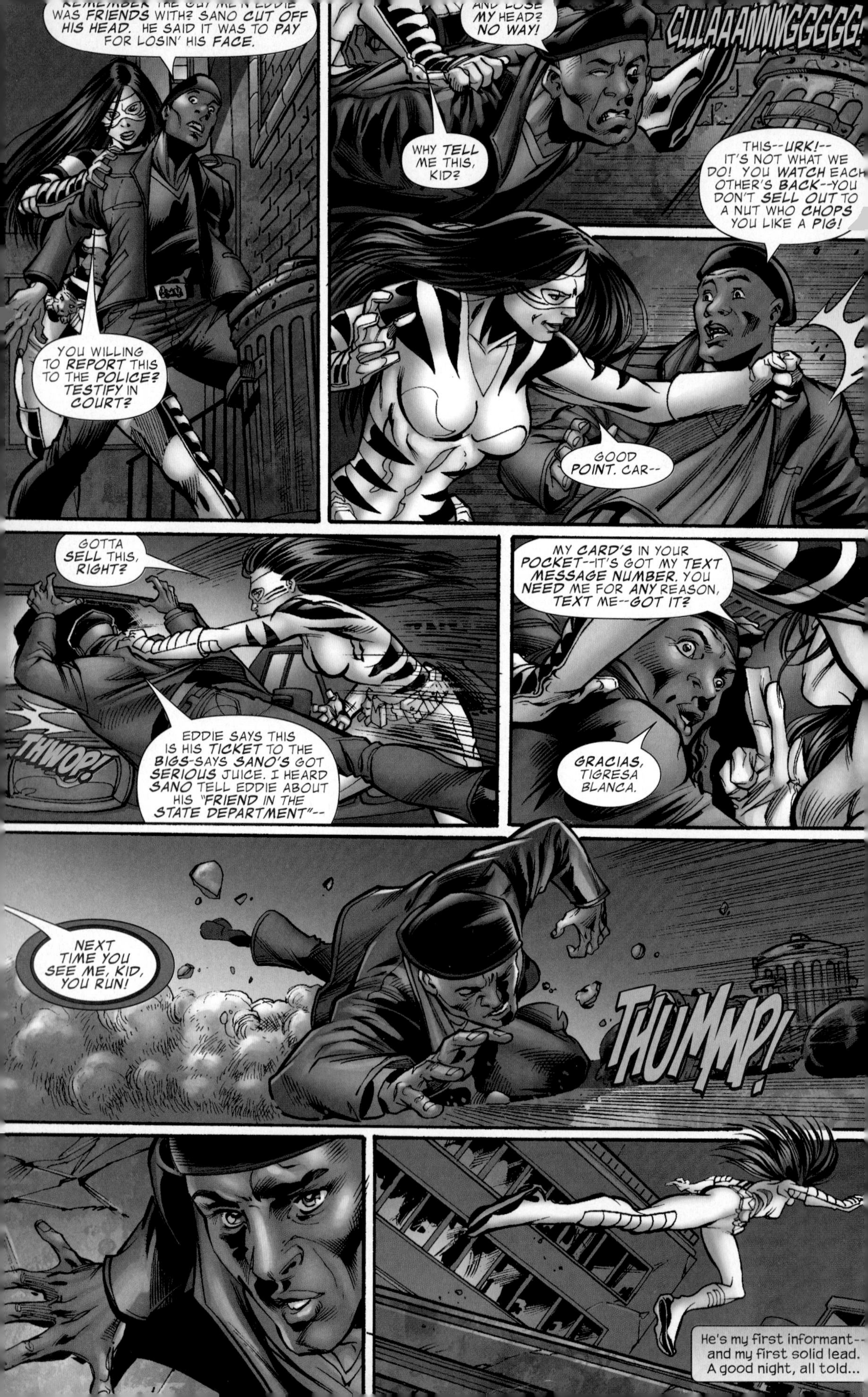

WAS FRIENDS WITH? SANO CUT OFF HIS HEAD. HE SAID IT WAS TO PAY FOR LOSIN' HIS FACE.
YOU WILLING TO REPORT THIS TO THE POLICE? TESTIFY IN COURT?
AND LOSE MY HEAD? NO WAY!
WHY TELL ME THIS, KID?
CLLLAAANNNGGGGG!
THIS--URK!--IT'S NOT WHAT WE DO! YOU WATCH EACH OTHER'S BACK--YOU DON'T SELL OUT TO A NUT WHO CHOPS YOU LIKE A PIG!
GOOD POINT. CAR--
GOTTA SELL THIS, RIGHT?
EDDIE SAYS THIS IS HIS TICKET TO THE BIGS-SAYS SANO'S GOT SERIOUS JUICE. I HEARD SANO TELL EDDIE ABOUT HIS "FRIEND IN THE STATE DEPARTMENT"--
THWOP!
MY CARD'S IN YOUR POCKET--IT'S GOT MY TEXT MESSAGE NUMBER. YOU NEED ME FOR ANY REASON, TEXT ME--GOT IT?
GRACIAS, TIGRESA BLANCA.
NEXT TIME YOU SEE ME, KID, YOU RUN!
THUMMP!
He's my first informant--and my first solid lead. A good night, all told...

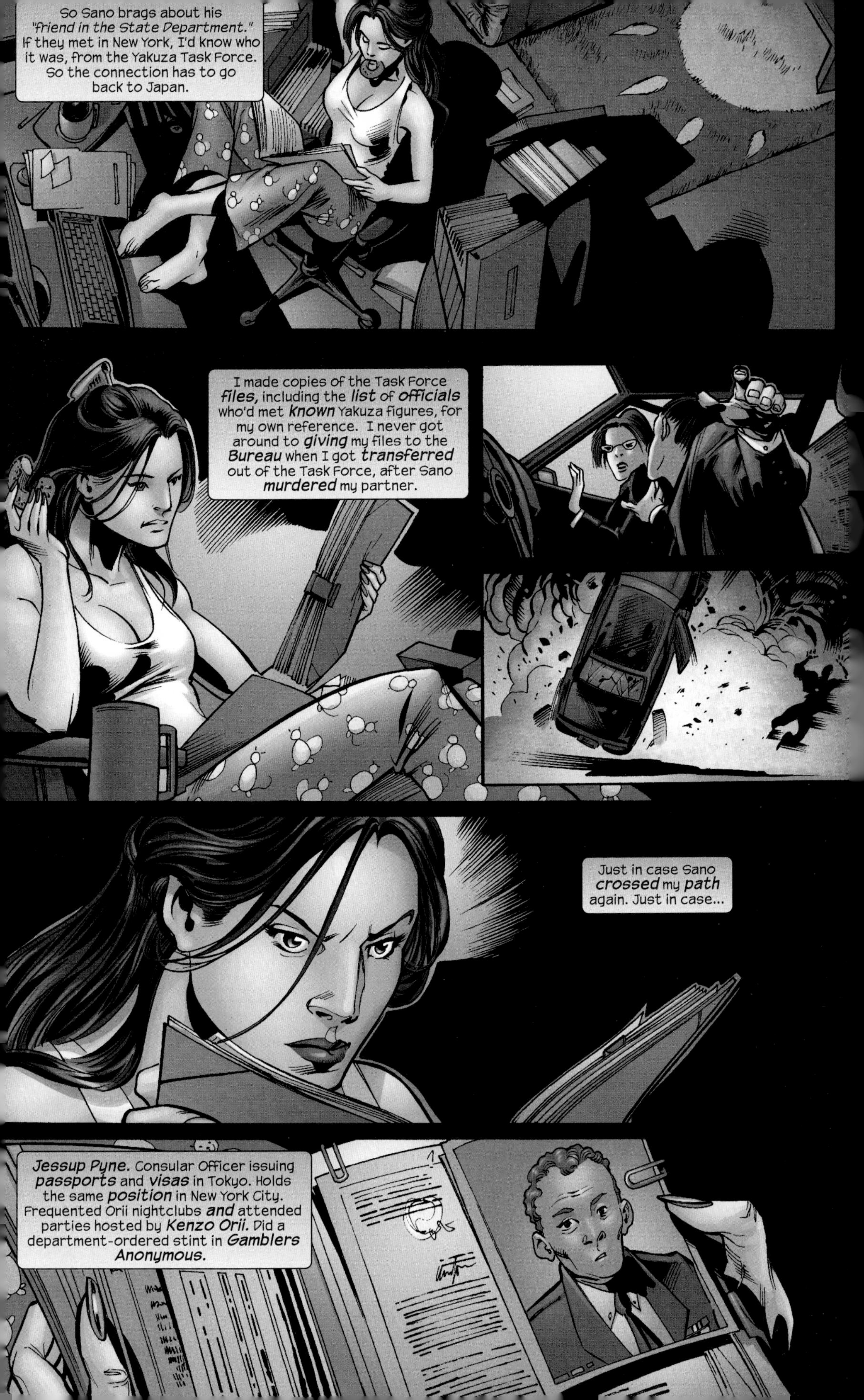
So Sano brags about his "friend in the State Department." If they met in New York, I'd know who it was, from the Yakuza Task Force. So the connection has to go back to Japan.
I made copies of the Task Force files, including the list of officials who'd met known Yakuza figures, for my own reference. I never got around to giving my files to the Bureau when I got transferred out of the Task Force, after Sano murdered my partner.
Just in case Sano crossed my path again. Just in case...
Jessup Pyne. Consular Officer issuing passports and visas in Tokyo. Holds the same position in New York City. Frequented Orii nightclubs and attended parties hosted by Kenzo Orii. Did a department-ordered stint in Gamblers Anonymous.

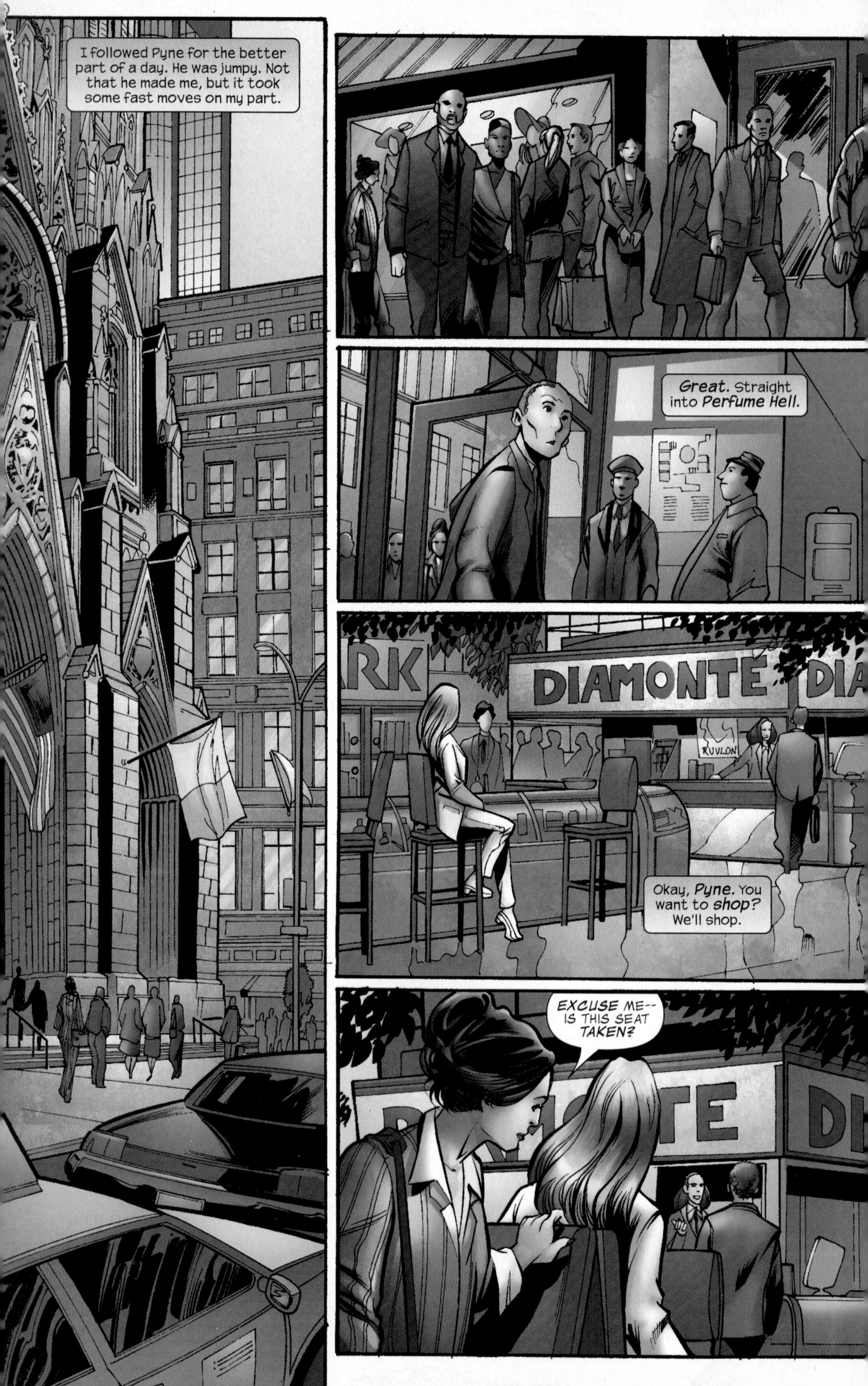

I followed Pyne for the better part of a day. He was jumpy. Not that he made me, but it took some fast moves on my part.
Great. Straight into Perfume Hell.
ARK
DIAMONTE
DIA
RUVLON
Okay, Pyne. You want to shop? We'll shop.
EXCUSE ME-- IS THIS SEAT TAKEN?

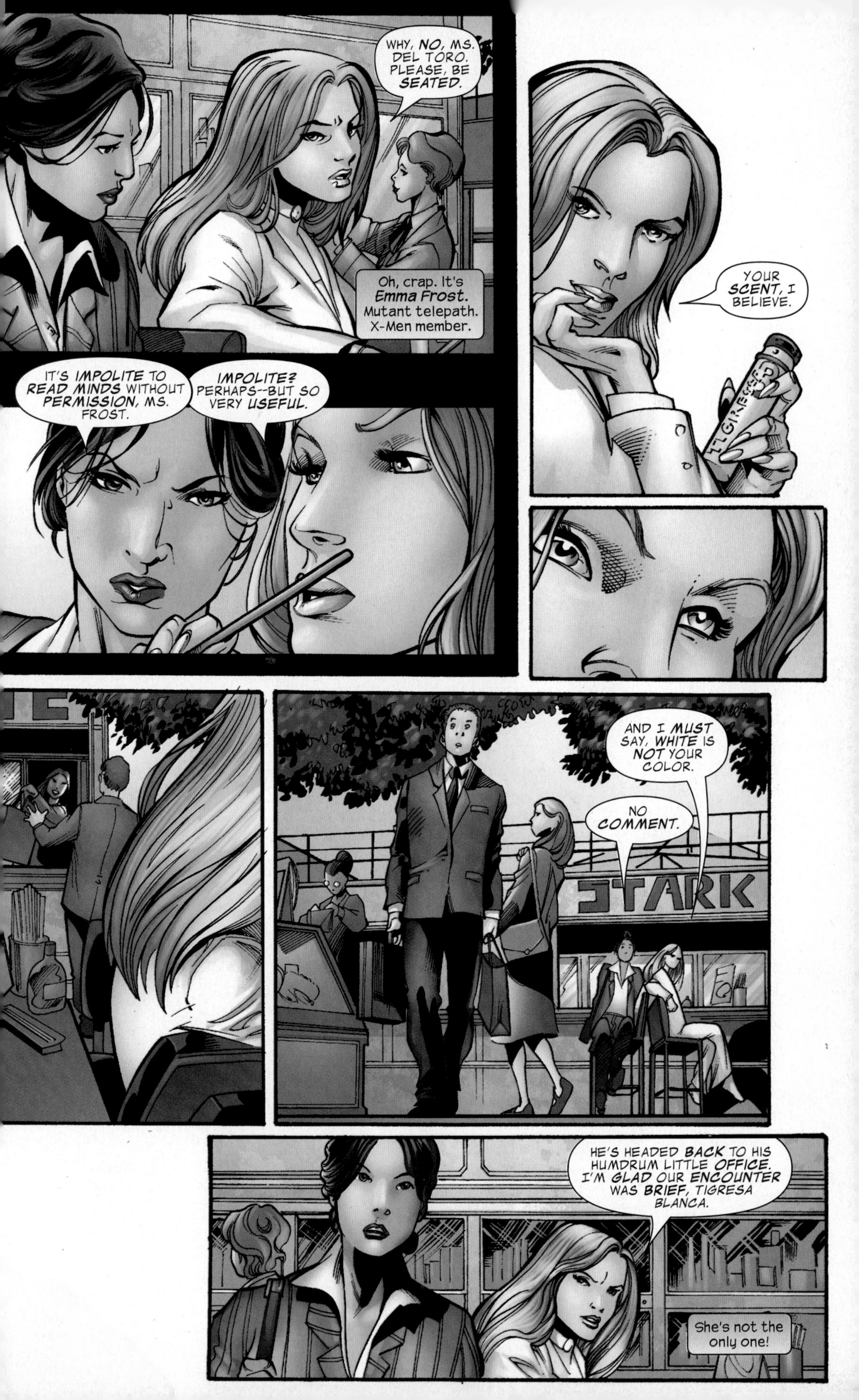
WHY, NO, MS. DEL TORO. PLEASE, BE SEATED.
Oh, crap. It's Emma Frost. Mutant telepath. X-Men member.
YOUR SCENT, I BELIEVE.
TIGRESA
IT'S IMPOLITE TO READ MINDS WITHOUT PERMISSION, MS. FROST.
IMPOLITE? PERHAPS--BUT SO VERY USEFUL.
AND I MUST SAY, WHITE IS NOT YOUR COLOR.
NO COMMENT.
STARK
HE'S HEADED BACK TO HIS HUMDRUM LITTLE OFFICE. I'M GLAD OUR ENCOUNTER WAS BRIEF, TIGRESA BLANCA.
She's not the only one!

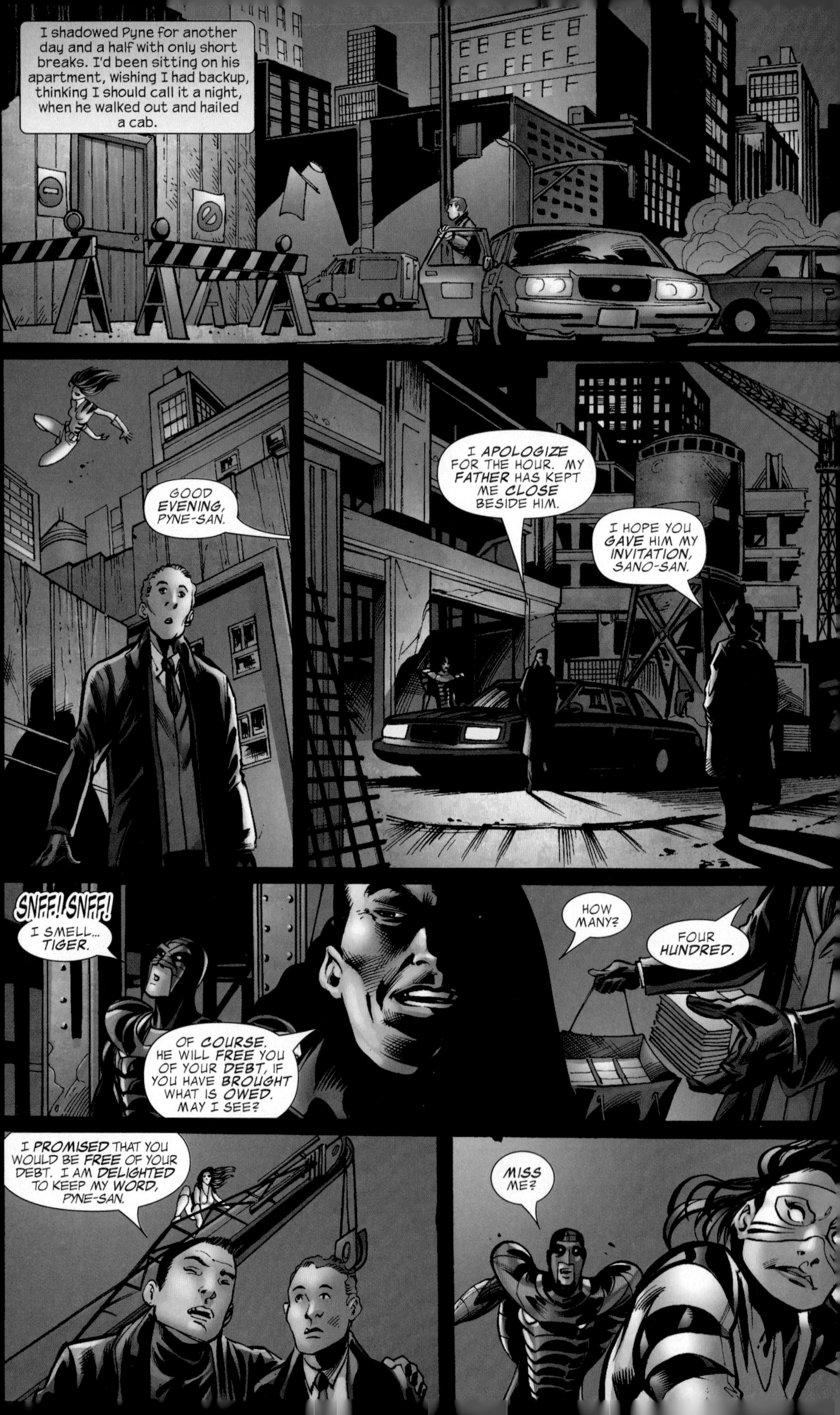
I shadowed Pyne for another day and a half with only short breaks. I'd been sitting on his apartment, wishing I had backup, thinking I should call it a night, when he walked out and hailed a cab.
GOOD EVENING, PYNE-SAN.
I APOLOGIZE FOR THE HOUR. MY FATHER HAS KEPT ME CLOSE BESIDE HIM.
I HOPE YOU GAVE HIM MY INVITATION, SANO-SAN.
SNFF! SNFF!
I SMELL... TIGER.
OF COURSE. HE WILL FREE YOU OF YOUR DEBT, IF YOU HAVE BROUGHT WHAT IS OWED. MAY I SEE?
HOW MANY?
FOUR HUNDRED.
I PROMISED THAT YOU WOULD BE FREE OF YOUR DEBT. I AM DELIGHTED TO KEEP MY WORD, PYNE-SAN.
MISS ME?

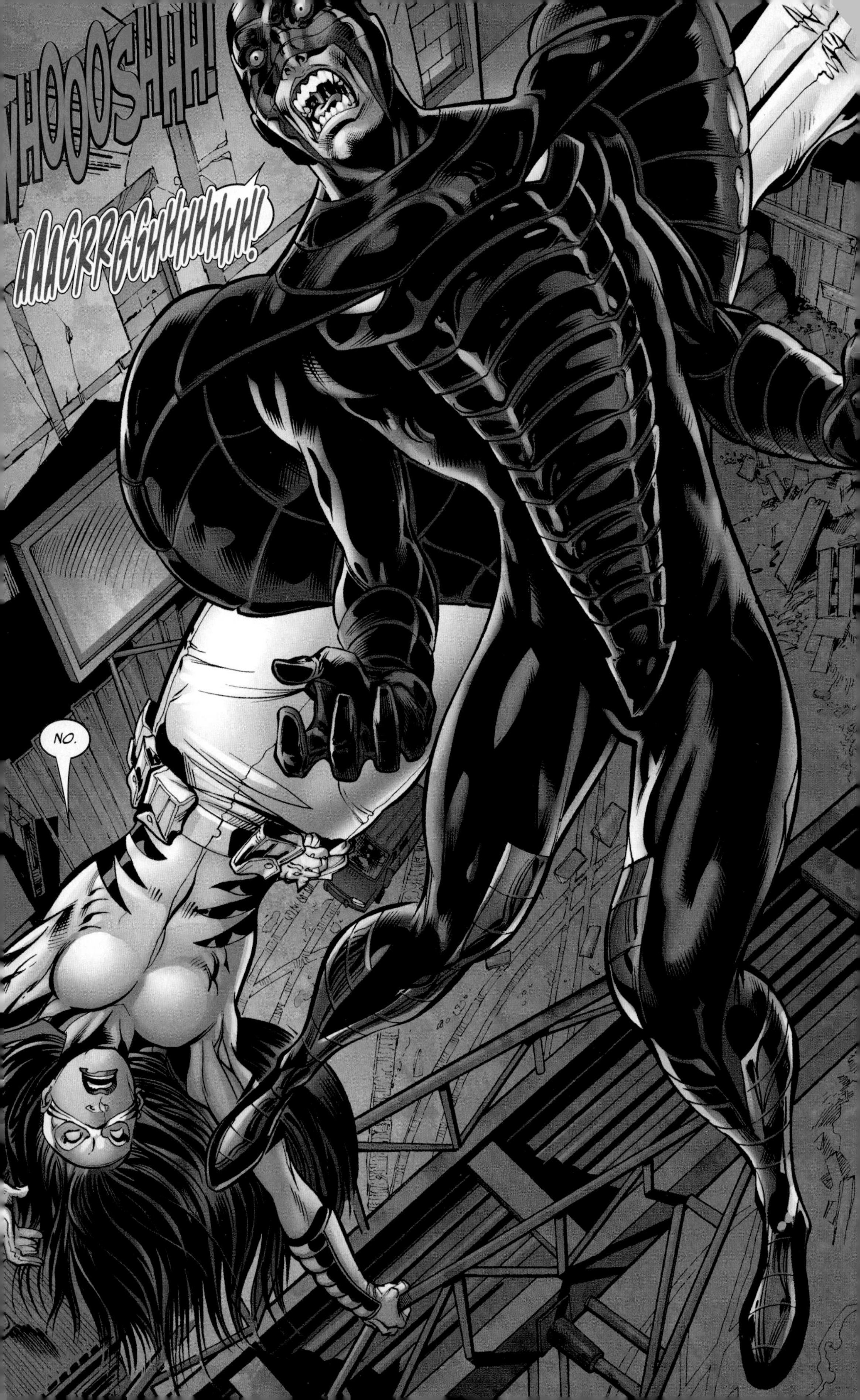
WHOOOSHH!
AAAGRRGGHHHHHHH!
NO.

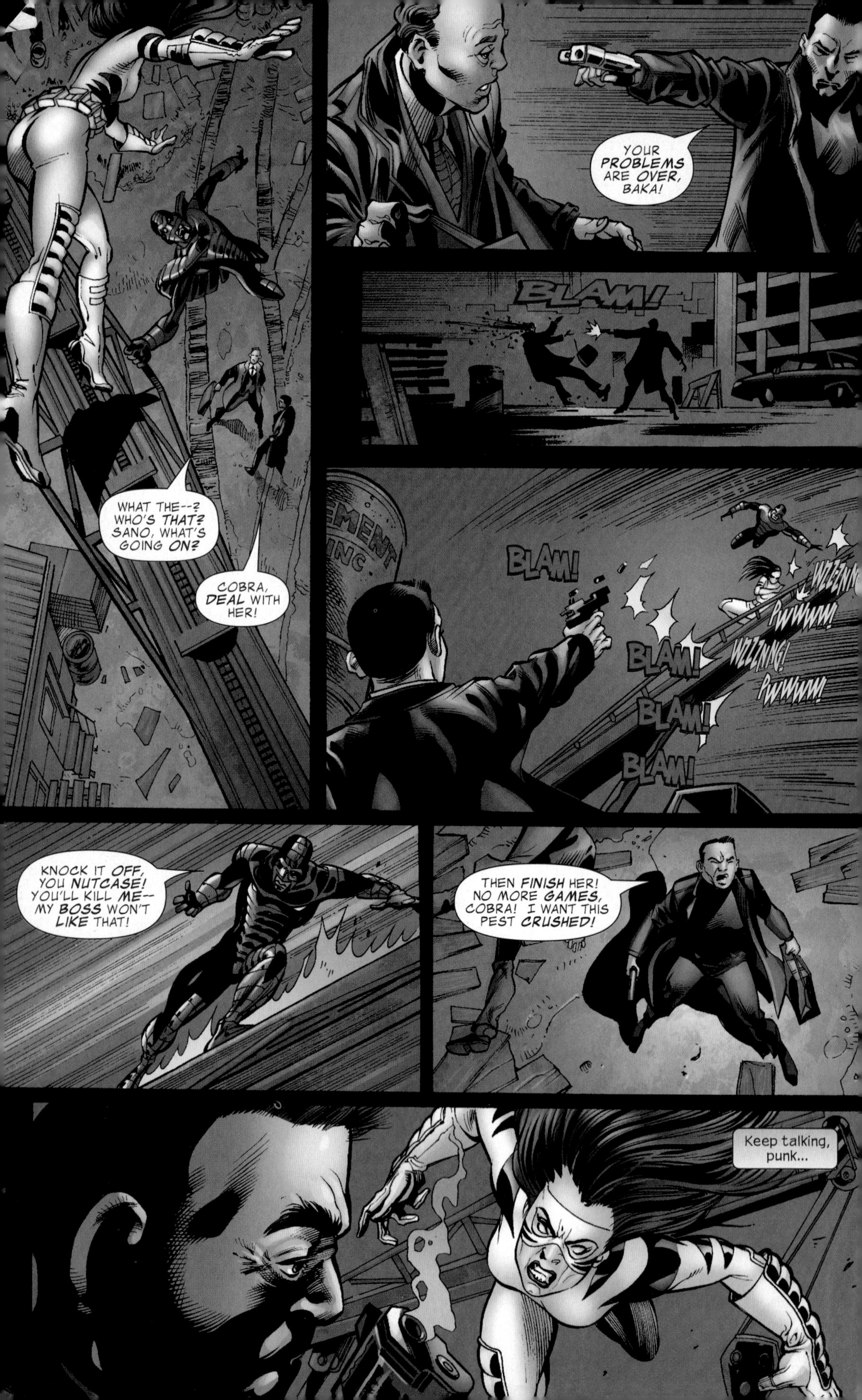
WHAT THE--? WHO'S THAT? SANO, WHAT'S GOING ON?
COBRA, DEAL WITH HER!
YOUR PROBLEMS ARE OVER, BAKA!
BLAM!
BLAM!
WIZZNNG!
PWWWM!
BLAM!
WIZZNNG!
PWWWM!
BLAM!
BLAM!
KNOCK IT OFF, YOU NUTCASE! YOU'LL KILL ME-- MY BOSS WON'T LIKE THAT!
THEN FINISH HER! NO MORE GAMES, COBRA! I WANT THIS PEST CRUSHED!
Keep talking, punk...

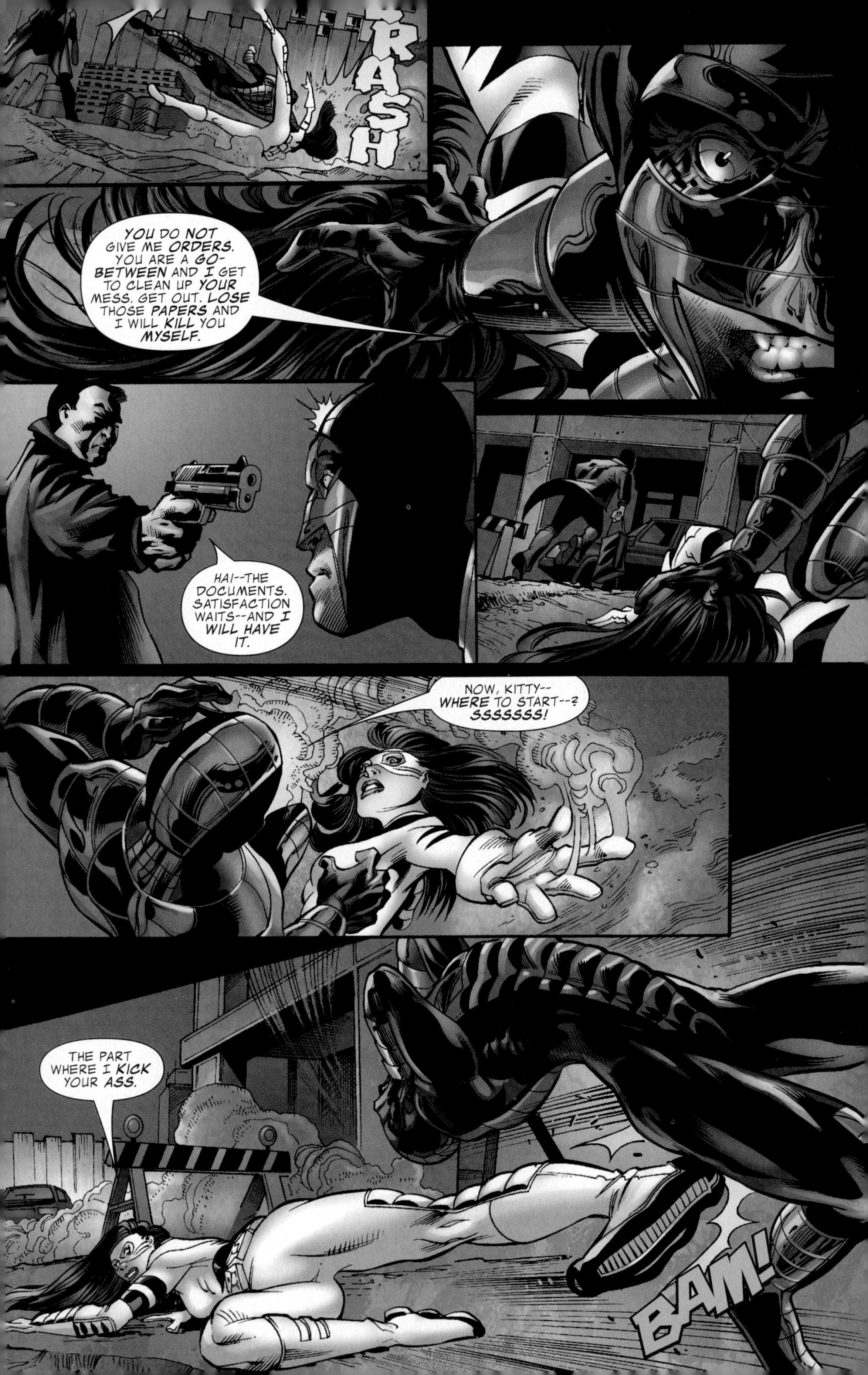
RASH
YOU DO NOT GIVE ME ORDERS. YOU ARE A GO-BETWEEN AND I GET TO CLEAN UP YOUR MESS. GET OUT. LOSE THOSE PAPERS AND I WILL KILL YOU MYSELF.
HAI--THE DOCUMENTS. SATISFACTION WAITS--AND I WILL HAVE IT.
NOW, KITTY-- WHERE TO START--? SSSSSSS!
THE PART WHERE I KICK YOUR ASS.
BAM!

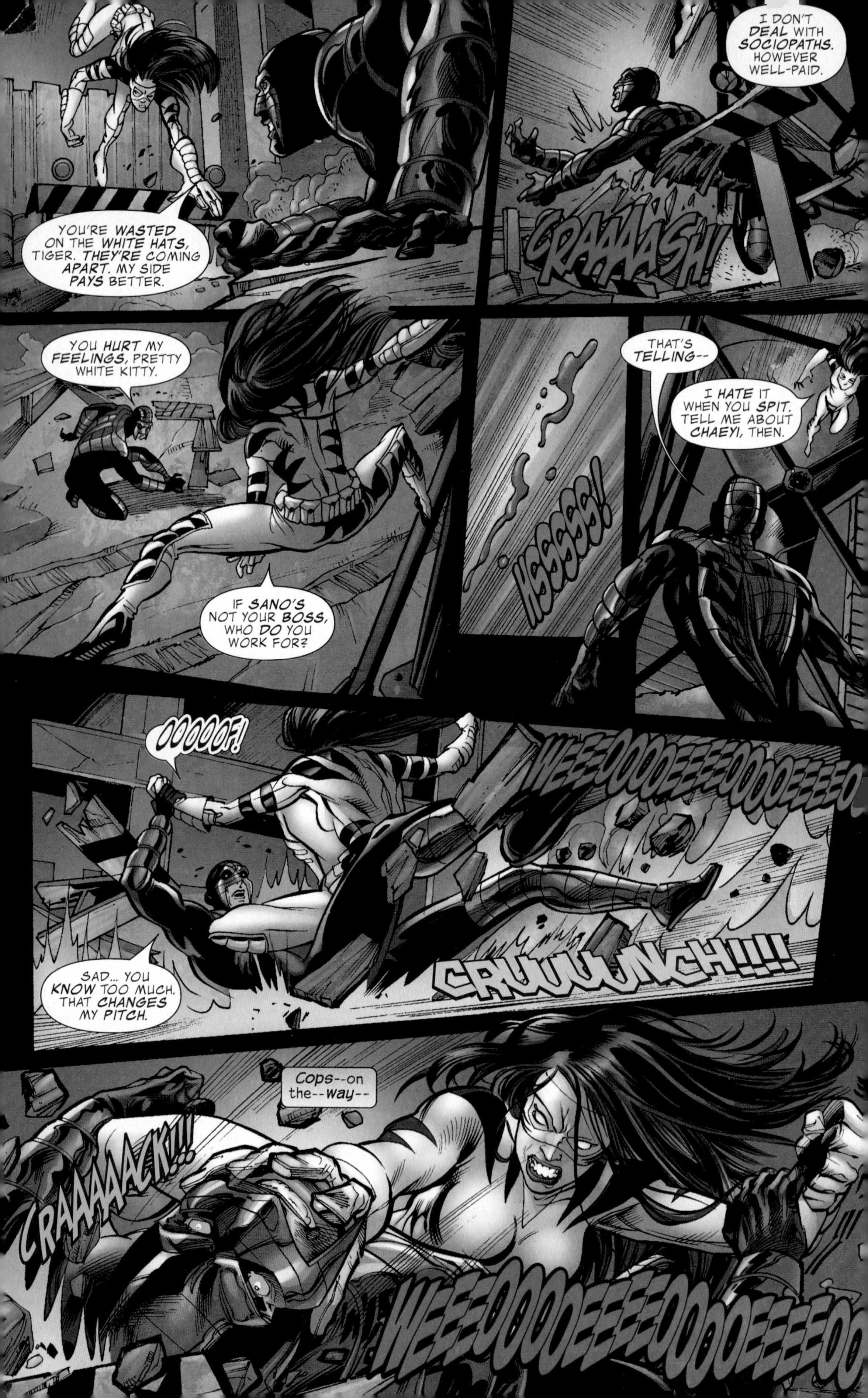
YOU'RE WASTED ON THE WHITE HATS, TIGER. THEY'RE COMING APART. MY SIDE PAYS BETTER.
I DON'T DEAL WITH SOCIOPATHS. HOWEVER WELL-PAID.
CRAAAASH!
YOU HURT MY FEELINGS, PRETTY WHITE KITTY.
IF SANO'S NOT YOUR BOSS, WHO DO YOU WORK FOR?
HSSSSS!
THAT'S TELLING--
I HATE IT WHEN YOU SPIT. TELL ME ABOUT CHAEYI, THEN.
OOOOOF!
WEEEOOOOEEEEOOOOEEEEO
CRUUUUNCH!!!!
SAD... YOU KNOW TOO MUCH. THAT CHANGES MY PITCH.
Cops--on the--way--
CRAAAAACK!!!
WEEEOOOOEEEEOOOOEEEEOO

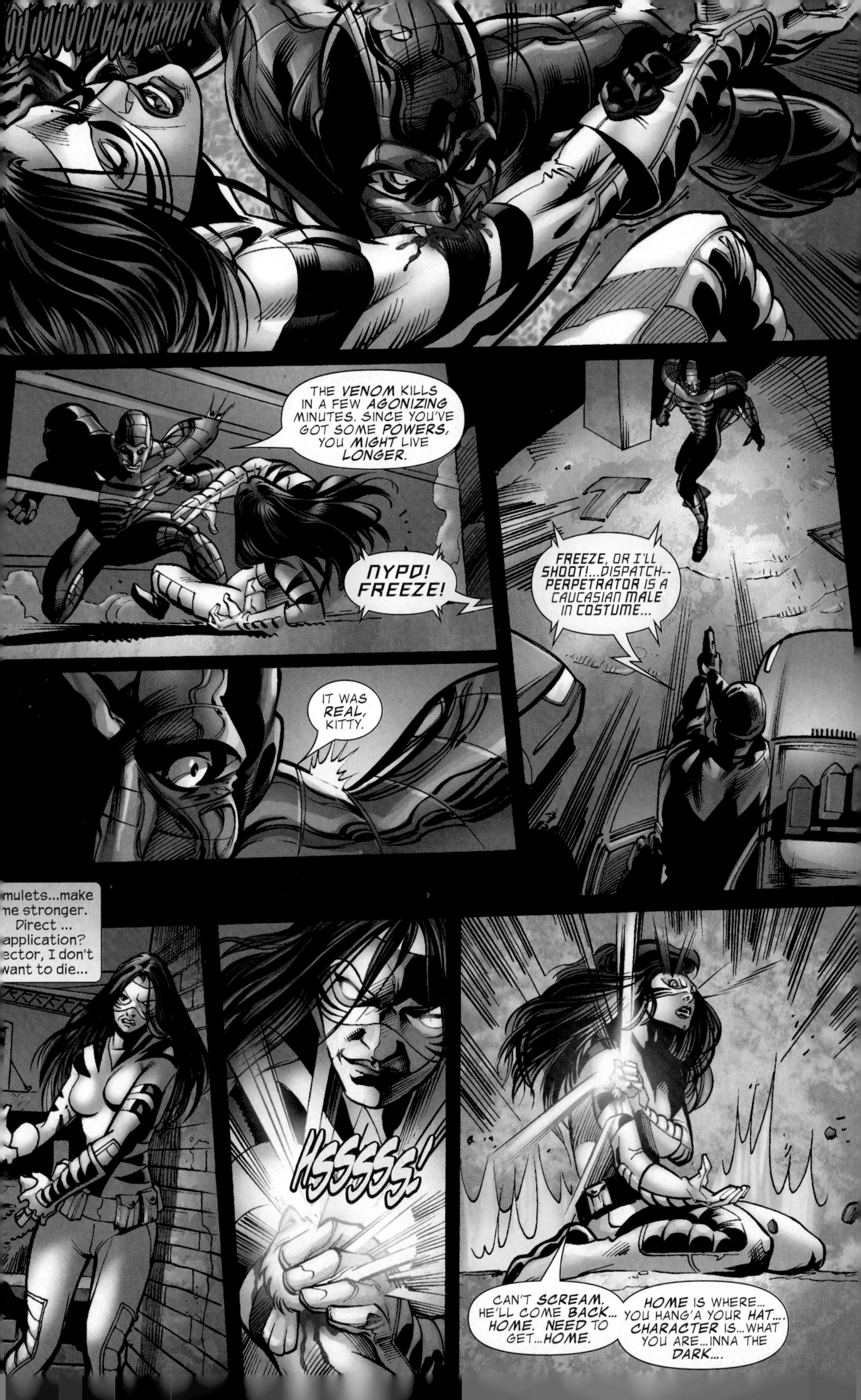
OOOOOOOUGGGAAHH!
THE VENOM KILLS IN A FEW AGONIZING MINUTES. SINCE YOU'VE GOT SOME POWERS, YOU MIGHT LIVE LONGER.
NYPD! FREEZE!
FREEZE, OR I'LL SHOOT!...DISPATCH--PERPETRATOR IS A CAUCASIAN MALE IN COSTUME...
IT WAS REAL, KITTY.
mulets...make me stronger. Direct ... application? ector, I don't want to die...
HSSSSS!
CAN'T SCREAM. HE'LL COME BACK... HOME. NEED TO GET...HOME.
HOME IS WHERE... YOU HANG'A YOUR HAT.... CHARACTER IS...WHAT YOU ARE...INNA THE DARK....

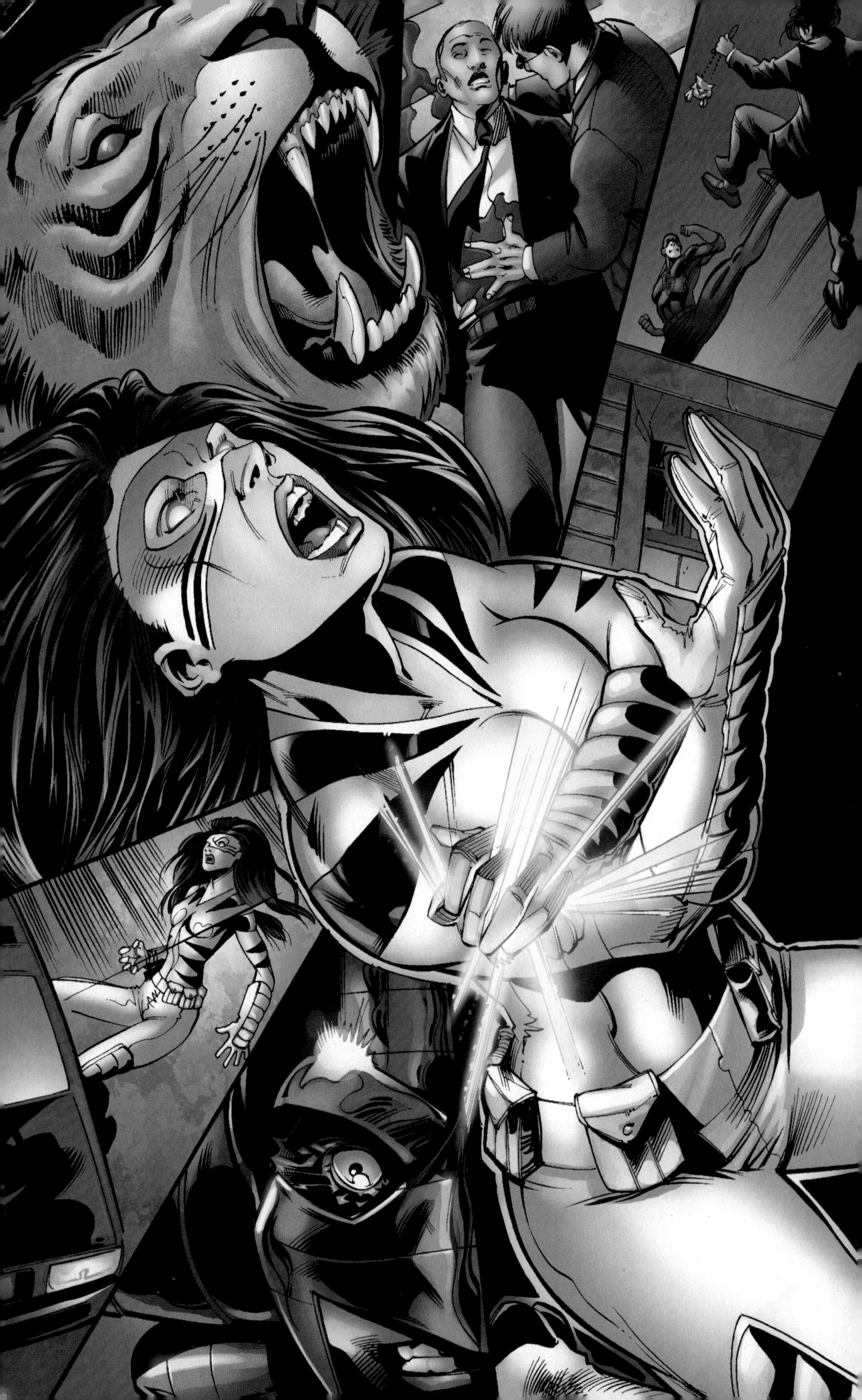

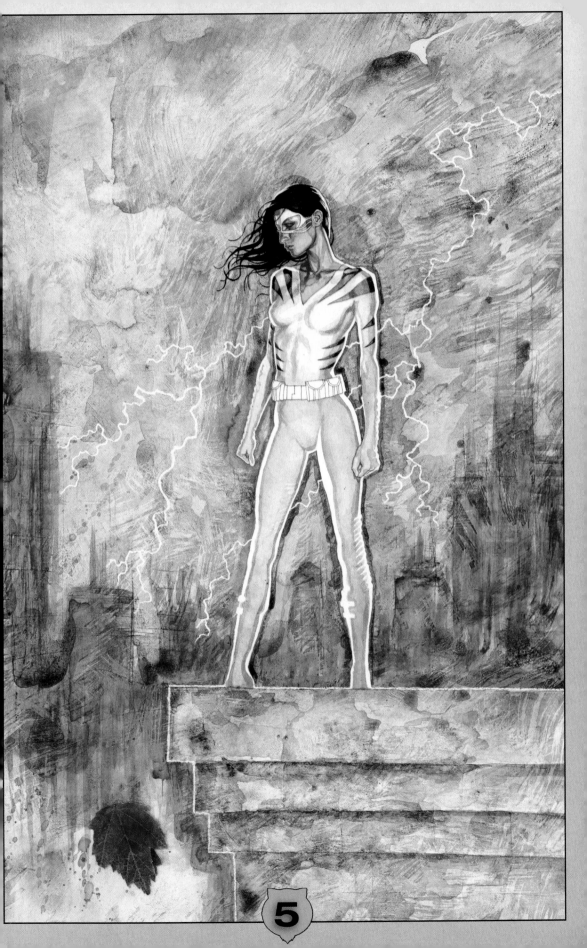

5

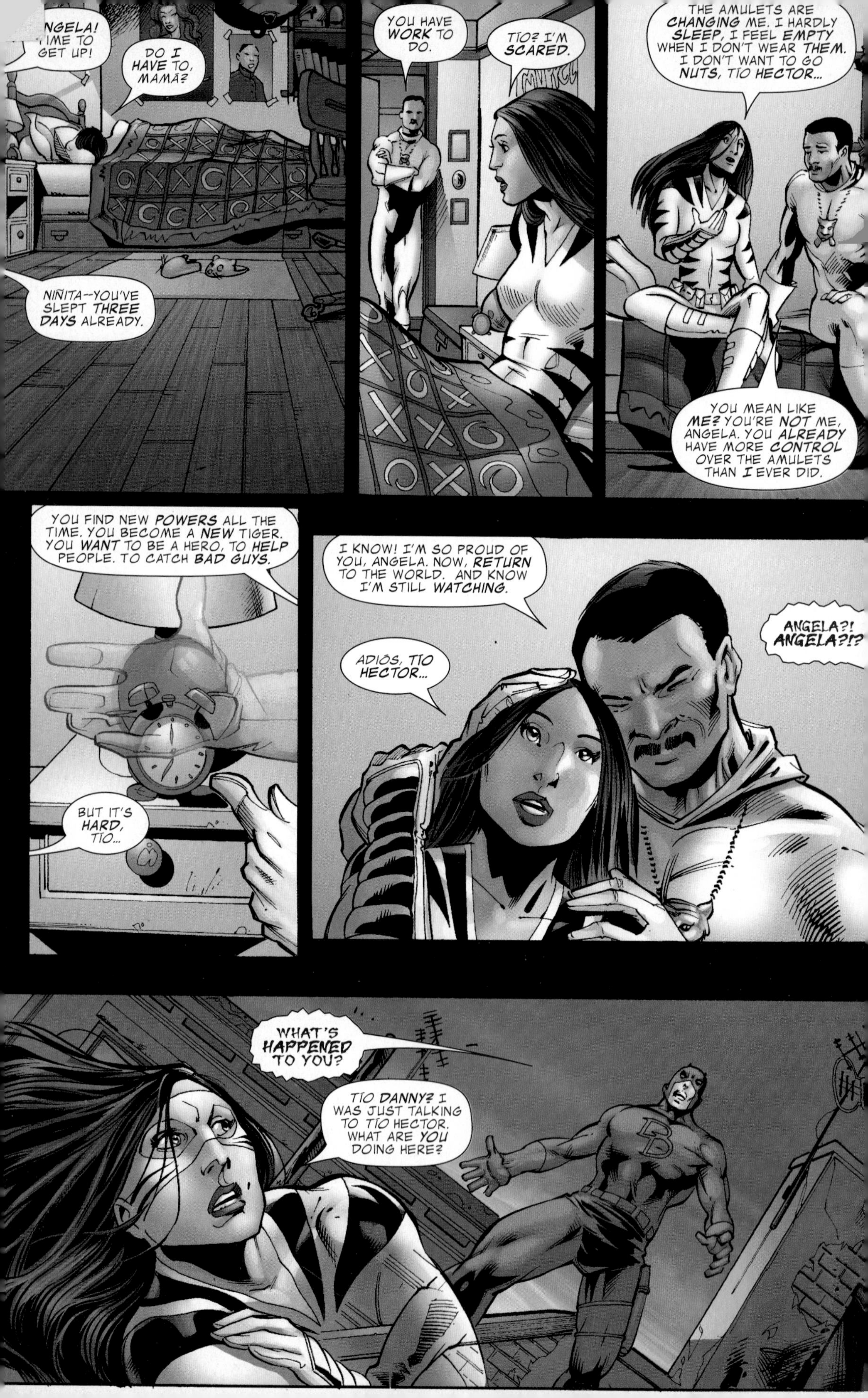
ANGELA! TIME TO GET UP!
DO I HAVE TO, MAMÁ?
NIÑITA--YOU'VE SLEPT THREE DAYS ALREADY.
YOU HAVE WORK TO DO.
TÍO? I'M SCARED.
THE AMULETS ARE CHANGING ME. I HARDLY SLEEP, I FEEL EMPTY WHEN I DON'T WEAR THEM. I DON'T WANT TO GO NUTS, TÍO HECTOR...
YOU MEAN LIKE ME? YOU'RE NOT ME, ANGELA. YOU ALREADY HAVE MORE CONTROL OVER THE AMULETS THAN I EVER DID.
YOU FIND NEW POWERS ALL THE TIME. YOU BECOME A NEW TIGER. YOU WANT TO BE A HERO, TO HELP PEOPLE. TO CATCH BAD GUYS.
BUT IT'S HARD, TÍO...
I KNOW! I'M SO PROUD OF YOU, ANGELA. NOW, RETURN TO THE WORLD. AND KNOW I'M STILL WATCHING.
ADIÓS, TÍO HECTOR...
ANGELA?! ANGELA?!?
WHAT'S HAPPENED TO YOU?
TÍO DANNY? I WAS JUST TALKING TO TÍO HECTOR. WHAT ARE YOU DOING HERE?

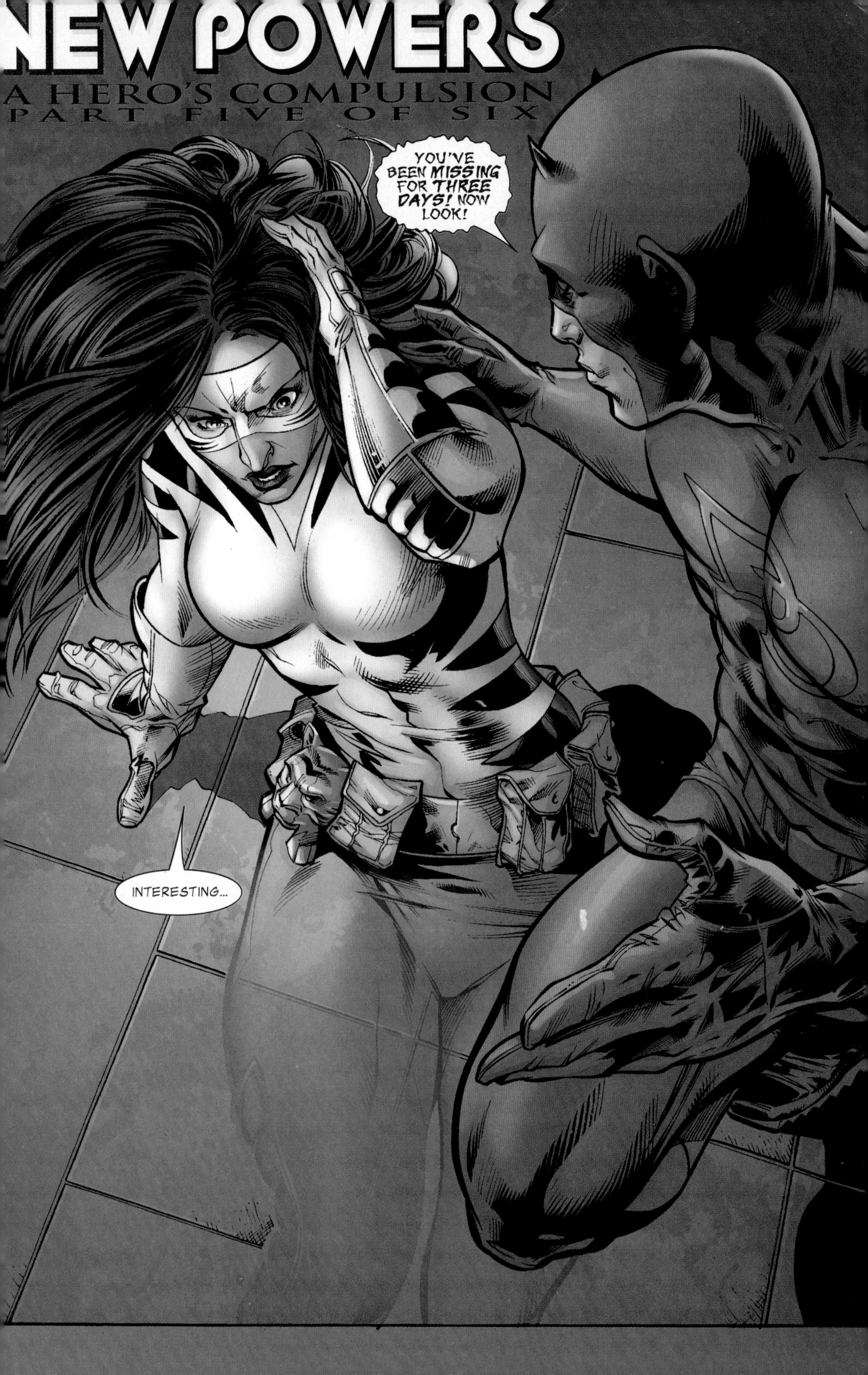
NEW POWERS
A HERO'S COMPULSION
PART FIVE OF SIX
YOU'VE BEEN MISSING FOR THREE DAYS! NOW LOOK!
INTERESTING...

DANNY RAND, PLAYING DAREDEVIL.

I DON'T KNOW WHAT YOU *MEAN*, WHITE TIGER--

SHUT UP. I'M MAD IT TOOK ME *THIS* LONG TO WORK IT OUT.

WHY ARE YOU *DOING* THIS, TIO DANNY? IT DOESN'T *HELP* MURDOCK.

=SIGH= ALL RIGHT--YOU *GOT* ME, ANGELA...

CLICK

THERE--THE *VOICE CHIP'S* OFF, OKAY? THOUGH *HOW* YOU FIGURED IT OUT IS *BEYOND* ME.

STANCE, PUNCHES, KICKS--I ALWAYS *KNEW* YOU WERE *FAMILY*. IT JUST TOOK ME UNTIL *NOW* TO *CONNECT* IT ALL.

I'VE BEEN *OUT* FOR THREE *DAYS*?

YES. THERE WAS A REPORT OF A DEAD *STATE DEPARTMENT* OFFICIAL NEAR HERE LATE *SUNDAY*. THEY TRIED TO *ARREST* A GUY IN A *WEIRD* RED COSTUME WHO *FLED* THE SCENE. SOMEBODY IN *WHITE* WAS SUPPOSEDLY *FIGHTING* WITH THE *SNAKE GUY*.

I FIGURED IT WAS *YOU*. THEN YOU DIDN'T COME *HOME* SUNDAY. I'VE BEEN *LOOKING* FOR YOU EVER SINCE.

DIDN'T YOU *SEE* ME *LYING* UP HERE, DANNY?

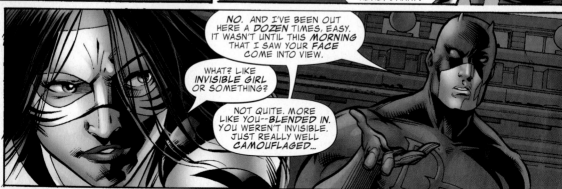

NO. AND I'VE BEEN OUT HERE A *DOZEN* TIMES, EASY. IT WASN'T UNTIL THIS *MORNING* THAT I SAW YOUR *FACE* COME INTO VIEW.

WHAT? LIKE *INVISIBLE GIRL* OR SOMETHING?

NOT QUITE. MORE LIKE YOU--*BLENDED* IN. YOU WEREN'T *INVISIBLE*. JUST REALLY WELL *CAMOUFLAGED*...

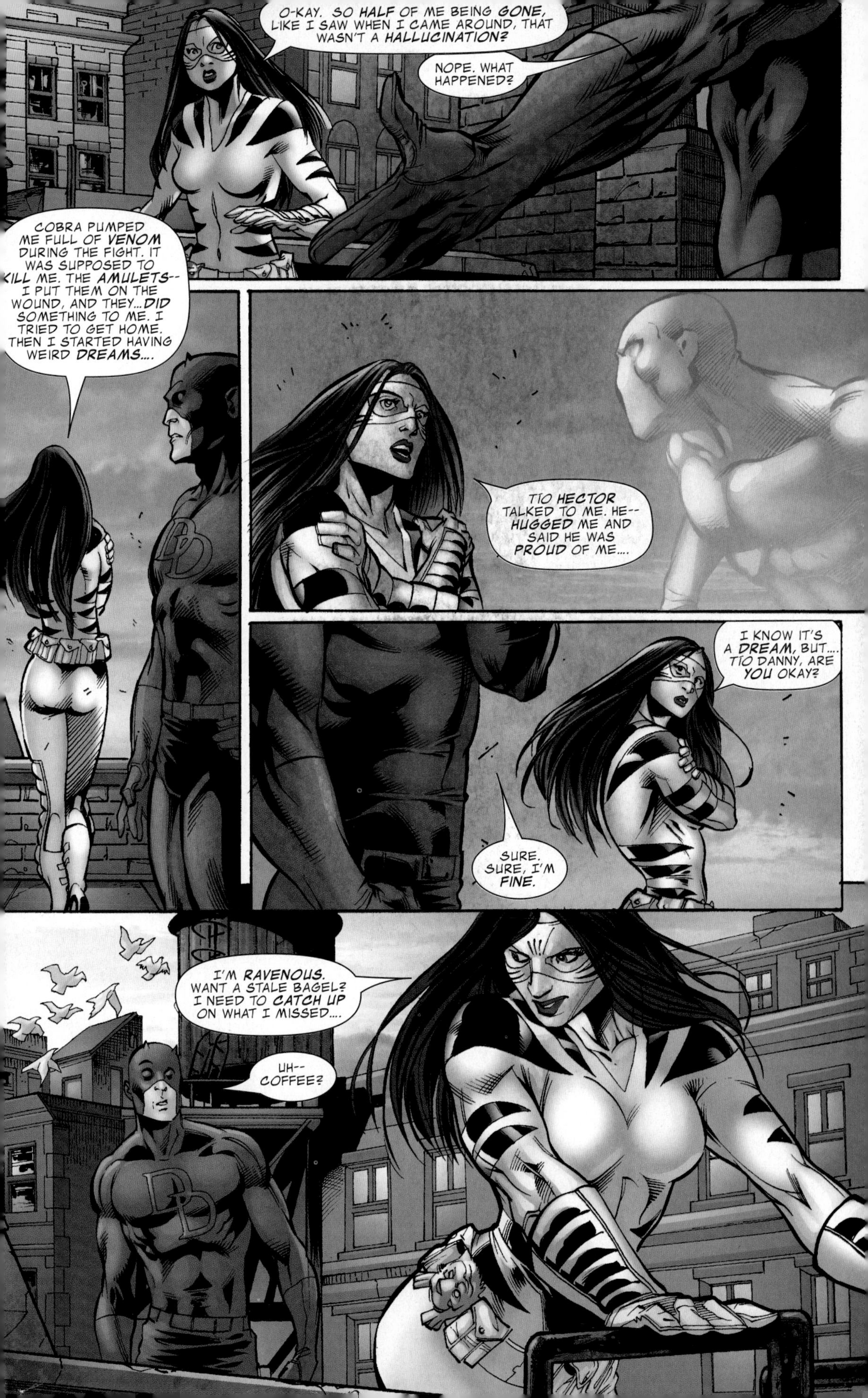

O-KAY. SO HALF OF ME BEING GONE, LIKE I SAW WHEN I CAME AROUND, THAT WASN'T A HALLUCINATION?
NOPE. WHAT HAPPENED?
COBRA PUMPED ME FULL OF VENOM DURING THE FIGHT. IT WAS SUPPOSED TO KILL ME. THE AMULETS-- I PUT THEM ON THE WOUND, AND THEY...DID SOMETHING TO ME. I TRIED TO GET HOME. THEN I STARTED HAVING WEIRD DREAMS....
TÍO HECTOR TALKED TO ME. HE-- HUGGED ME AND SAID HE WAS PROUD OF ME....
I KNOW IT'S A DREAM, BUT.... TÍO DANNY, ARE YOU OKAY?
SURE. SURE, I'M FINE.
I'M RAVENOUS. WANT A STALE BAGEL? I NEED TO CATCH UP ON WHAT I MISSED....
UH-- COFFEE?

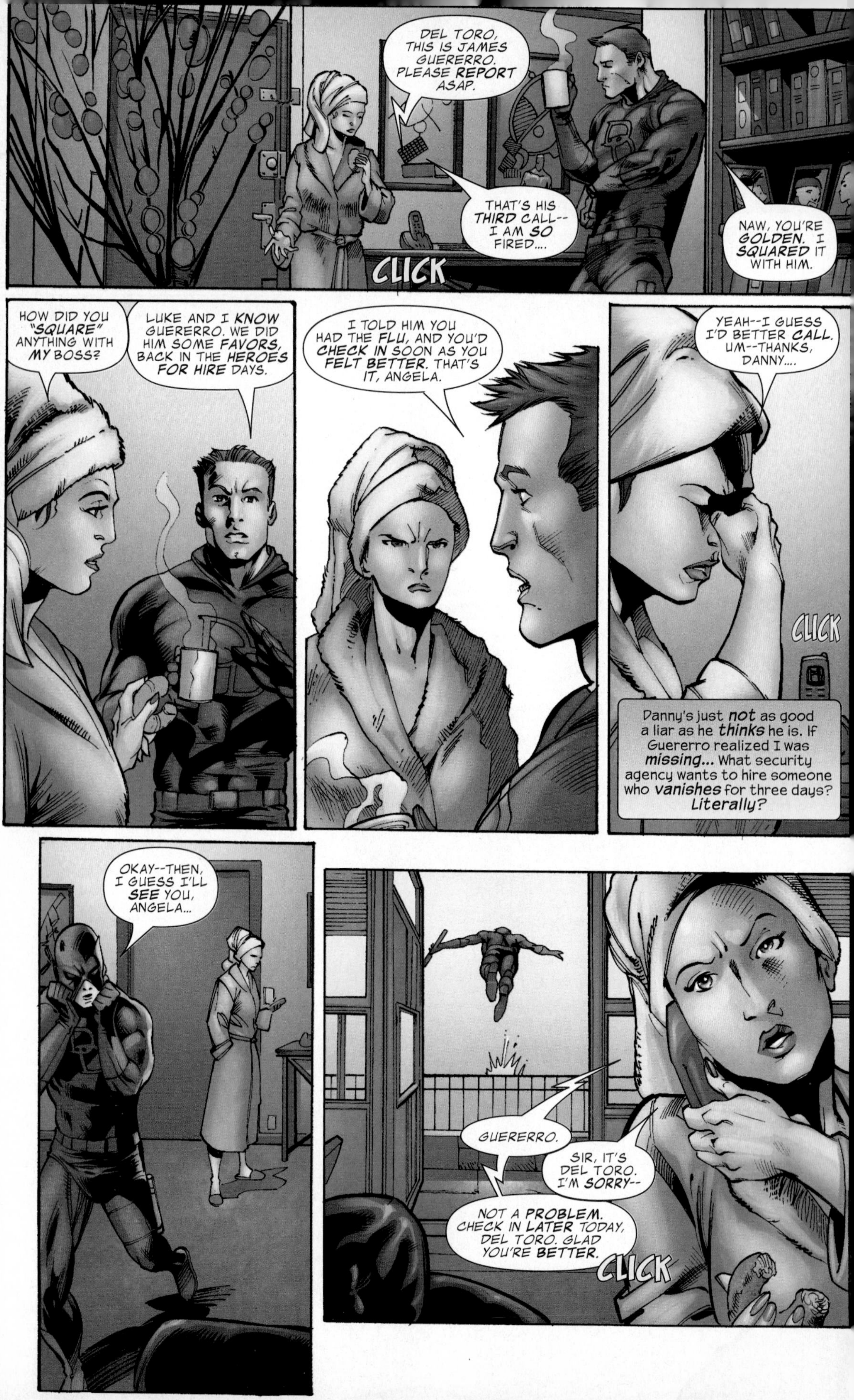
DEL TORO, THIS IS JAMES GUERERRO. PLEASE REPORT ASAP.
CLICK
THAT'S HIS THIRD CALL-- I AM SO FIRED....
NAW, YOU'RE GOLDEN. I SQUARED IT WITH HIM.
HOW DID YOU "SQUARE" ANYTHING WITH MY BOSS?
LUKE AND I KNOW GUERERRO. WE DID HIM SOME FAVORS, BACK IN THE HEROES FOR HIRE DAYS.
I TOLD HIM YOU HAD THE FLU, AND YOU'D CHECK IN SOON AS YOU FELT BETTER. THAT'S IT, ANGELA.
YEAH--I GUESS I'D BETTER CALL. UM--THANKS, DANNY....
CLICK
Danny's just not as good a liar as he thinks he is. If Guererro realized I was missing... What security agency wants to hire someone who vanishes for three days? Literally?
OKAY--THEN, I GUESS I'LL SEE YOU, ANGELA...
GUERERRO.
SIR, IT'S DEL TORO. I'M SORRY--
NOT A PROBLEM. CHECK IN LATER TODAY, DEL TORO. GLAD YOU'RE BETTER.
CLICK

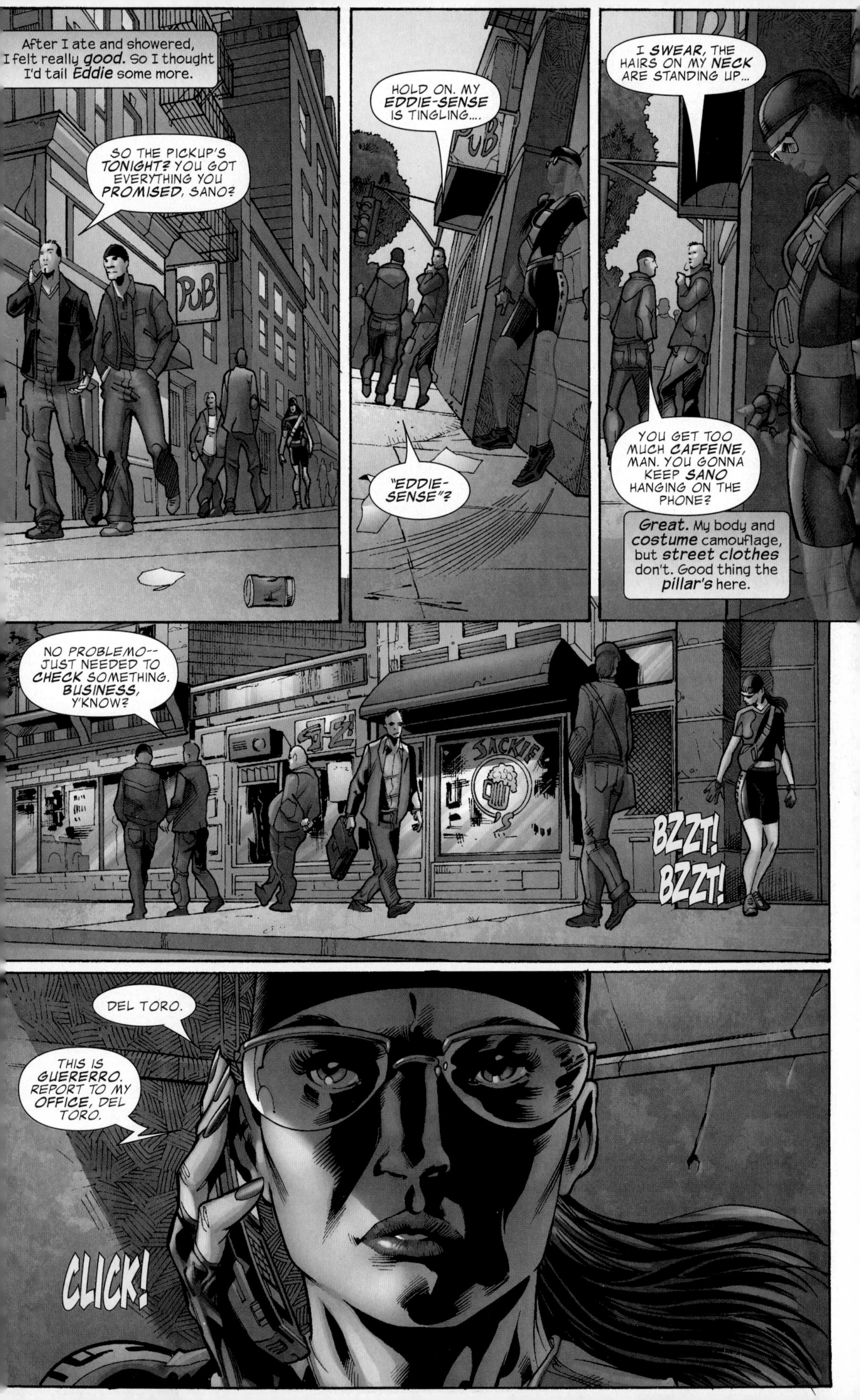
After I ate and showered, I felt really good. So I thought I'd tail Eddie some more.
SO THE PICKUP'S TONIGHT? YOU GOT EVERYTHING YOU PROMISED, SANO?
PUB
HOLD ON. MY EDDIE-SENSE IS TINGLING....
"EDDIE-SENSE"?
I SWEAR, THE HAIRS ON MY NECK ARE STANDING UP...
YOU GET TOO MUCH CAFFEINE, MAN. YOU GONNA KEEP SANO HANGING ON THE PHONE?
Great. My body and costume camouflage, but street clothes don't. Good thing the pillar's here.
NO PROBLEMO-- JUST NEEDED TO CHECK SOMETHING. BUSINESS, Y'KNOW?
JACKIE
BZZT! BZZT!
DEL TORO.
THIS IS GUERERRO. REPORT TO MY OFFICE, DEL TORO.
CLICK!

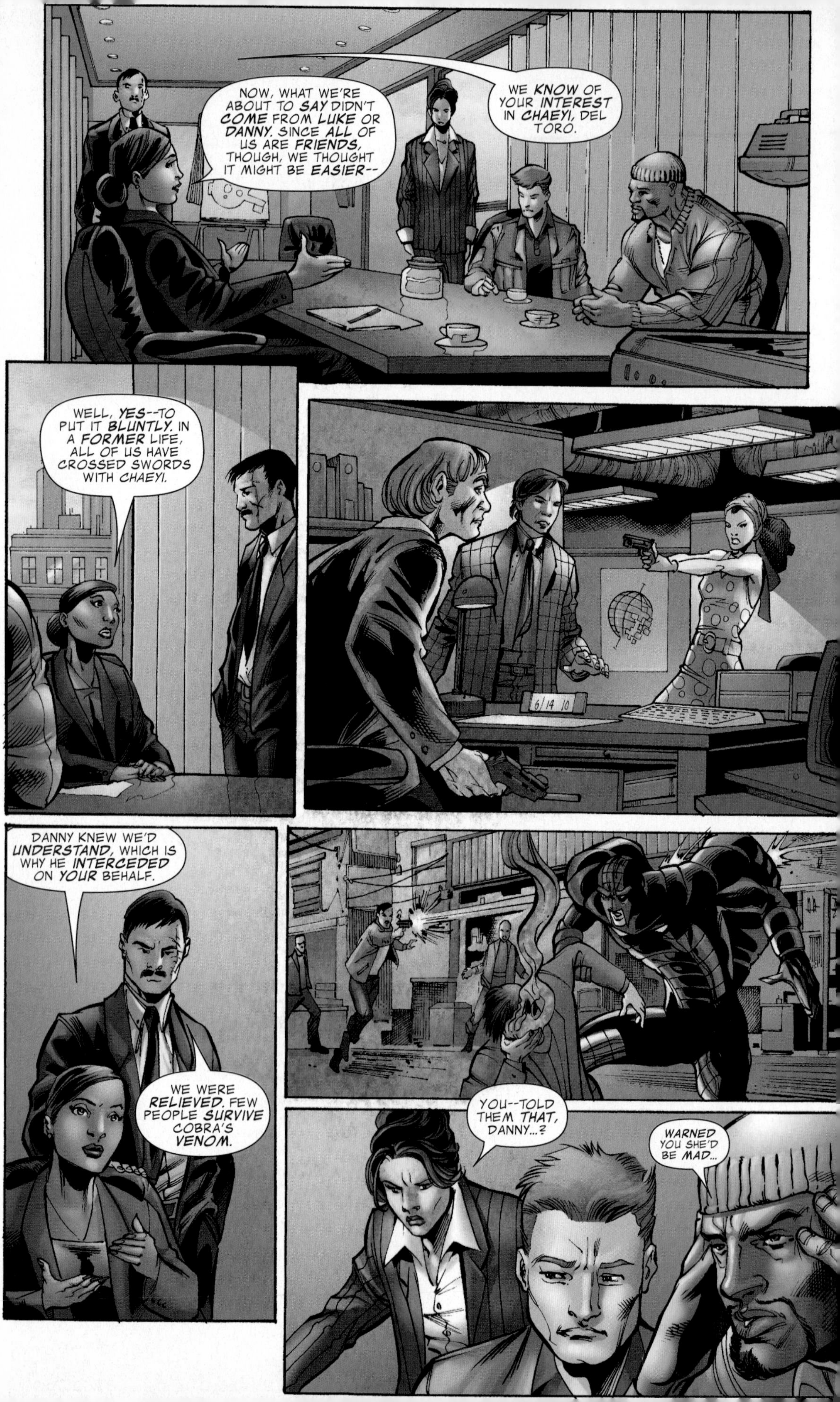
NOW, WHAT WE'RE ABOUT TO SAY DIDN'T COME FROM LUKE OR DANNY. SINCE ALL OF US ARE FRIENDS, THOUGH, WE THOUGHT IT MIGHT BE EASIER--
WE KNOW OF YOUR INTEREST IN CHAEYI, DEL TORO.
WELL, YES--TO PUT IT BLUNTLY. IN A FORMER LIFE, ALL OF US HAVE CROSSED SWORDS WITH CHAEYI.
6/14/10
DANNY KNEW WE'D UNDERSTAND, WHICH IS WHY HE INTERCEDED ON YOUR BEHALF.
WE WERE RELIEVED. FEW PEOPLE SURVIVE COBRA'S VENOM.
YOU--TOLD THEM THAT, DANNY...?
WARNED YOU SHE'D BE MAD...

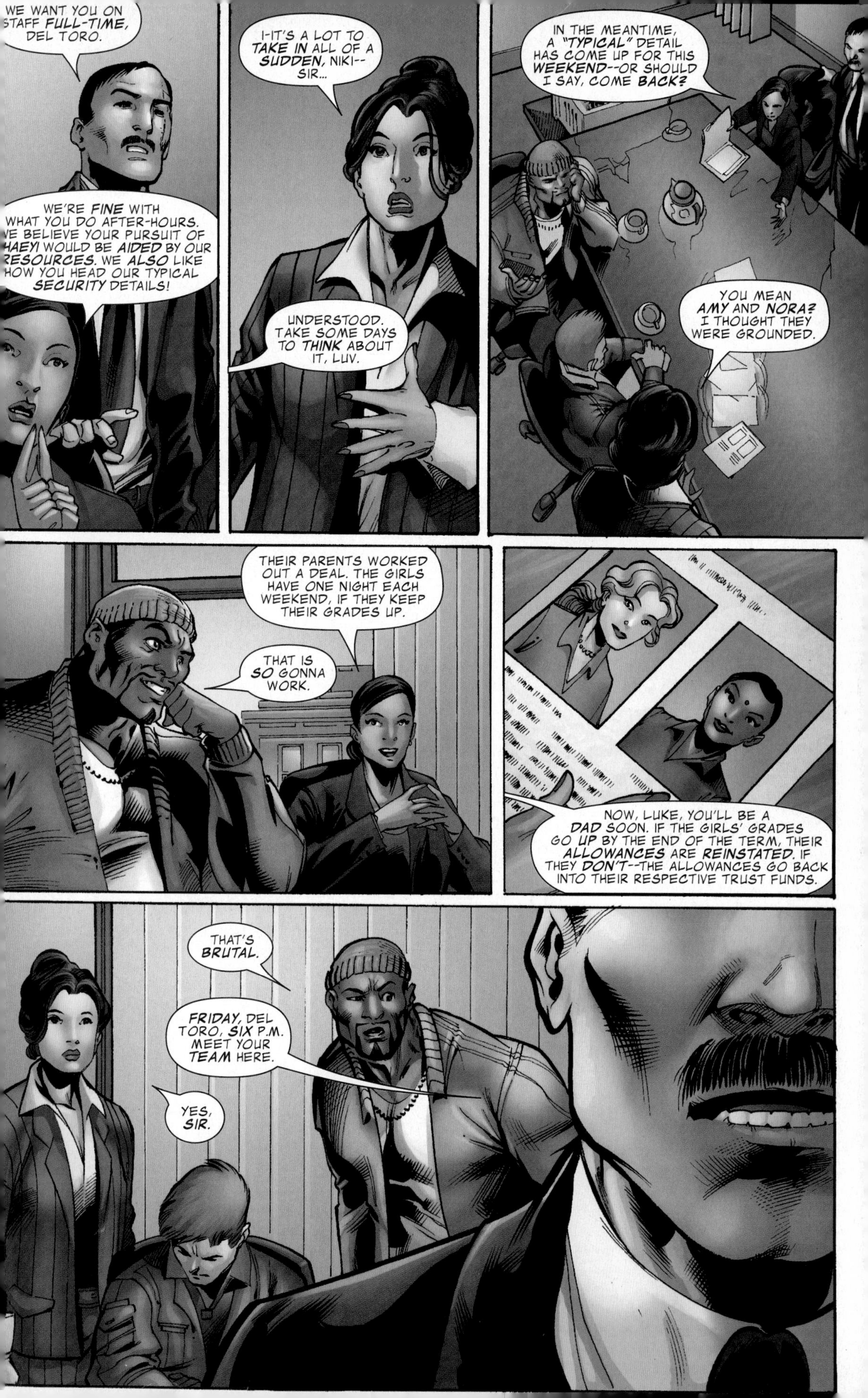
WE WANT YOU ON STAFF FULL-TIME, DEL TORO.
WE'RE FINE WITH WHAT YOU DO AFTER-HOURS. WE BELIEVE YOUR PURSUIT OF HAEYI WOULD BE AIDED BY OUR RESOURCES. WE ALSO LIKE HOW YOU HEAD OUR TYPICAL SECURITY DETAILS!
I-IT'S A LOT TO TAKE IN ALL OF A SUDDEN, NIKI-- SIR...
UNDERSTOOD. TAKE SOME DAYS TO THINK ABOUT IT, LUV.
IN THE MEANTIME, A "TYPICAL" DETAIL HAS COME UP FOR THIS WEEKEND--OR SHOULD I SAY, COME BACK?
YOU MEAN AMY AND NORA? I THOUGHT THEY WERE GROUNDED.
THEIR PARENTS WORKED OUT A DEAL. THE GIRLS HAVE ONE NIGHT EACH WEEKEND, IF THEY KEEP THEIR GRADES UP.
THAT IS SO GONNA WORK.
NOW, LUKE, YOU'LL BE A DAD SOON. IF THE GIRLS' GRADES GO UP BY THE END OF THE TERM, THEIR ALLOWANCES ARE REINSTATED. IF THEY DON'T--THE ALLOWANCES GO BACK INTO THEIR RESPECTIVE TRUST FUNDS.
THAT'S BRUTAL.
FRIDAY, DEL TORO, SIX P.M. MEET YOUR TEAM HERE.
YES, SIR.

ANGELA, LOOK--I--

DON'T SAY IT, DANNY. JUST--DON'T.

LET'S TAKE THIS SOMEPLACE PRIVATE.

212

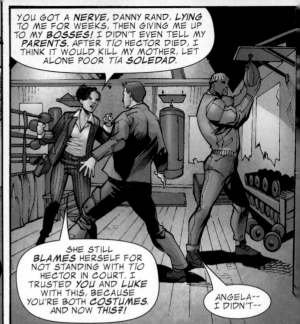

YOU GOT A *NERVE*, DANNY RAND, *LYING* TO ME FOR WEEKS, THEN GIVING ME UP TO MY *BOSSES!* I DIDN'T EVEN TELL MY *PARENTS.* AFTER *TÍO* HECTOR DIED, I THINK IT WOULD KILL MY MOTHER, LET ALONE POOR *TÍA SOLEDAD.*

SHE STILL *BLAMES* HERSELF FOR NOT STANDING WITH *TÍO* HECTOR IN COURT. I TRUSTED *YOU* AND *LUKE* WITH THIS, BECAUSE YOU'RE BOTH *COSTUMES.* AND NOW *THIS?!*

ANGELA-- I DIDN'T--

THANKS. THANKS A LOT!

I TOLD YOU, *WIDOW* TOLD YOU, EVEN THE *AMAZIN' SPIDER-MAN* TOLD YOU. *LEVEL* WITH HER.

RRRRRIIIIINGGG!

BUT YOU HAD TO *LIE* ABOUT YOUR *IDENTITY* AND GIVE *HERS* AWAY. YOU THINK SHE'LL LISTEN TO YOU NOW?

I JUST THOUGHT, LONG AS I WAS WEARING THE *OUTFIT,* I COULD CARRY ON MATT'S MENTORING--

MISTY'S *RIGHT,* YOU REALLY *ARE* CLUELESS.

RRRRRIIIIINGGG!

AVENGER ASSEMBLE.

I'M GONN[A] GET TO HAT[E] THAT....DANN[Y] LATER.

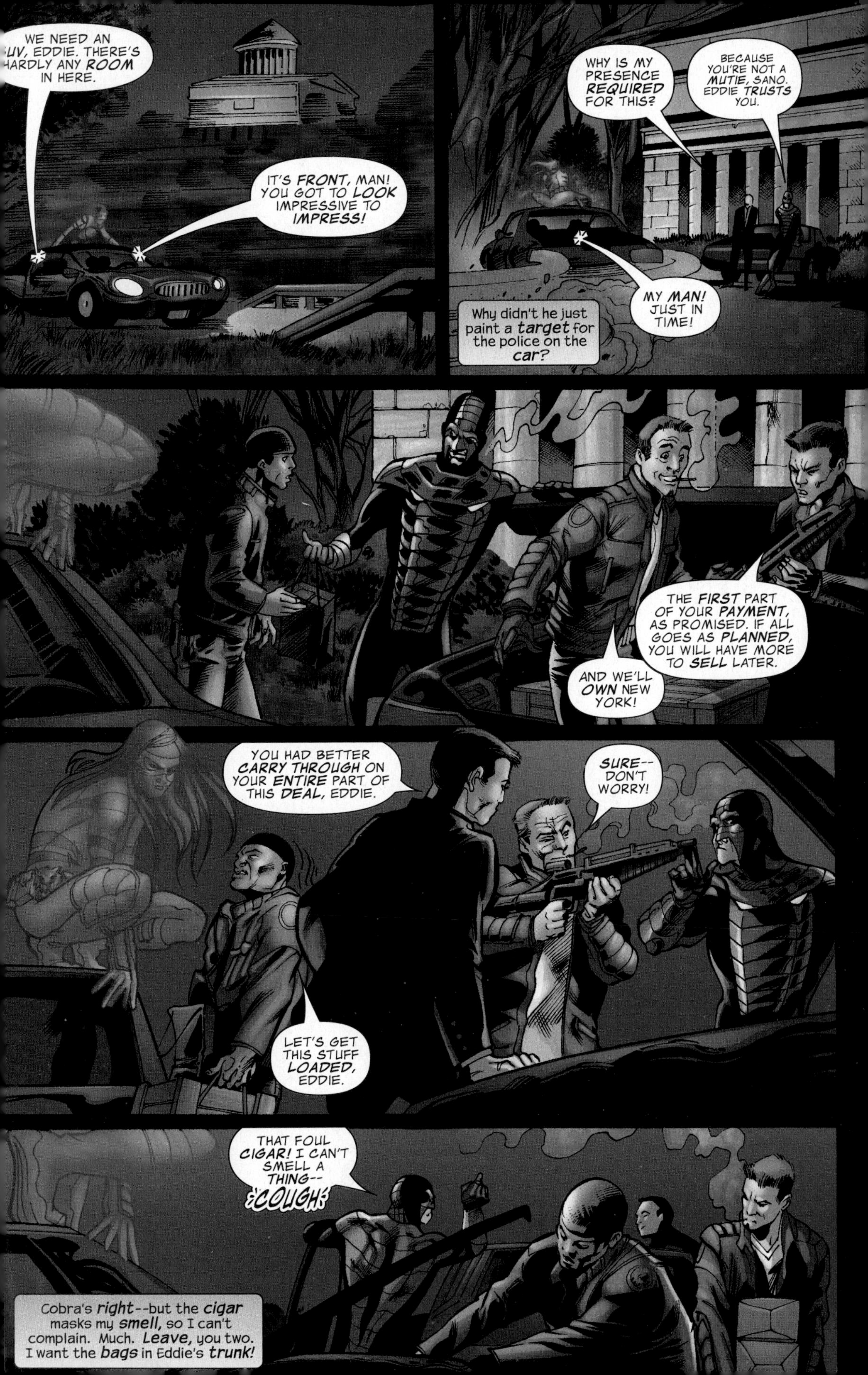
WE NEED AN SUV, EDDIE. THERE'S HARDLY ANY ROOM IN HERE.
IT'S FRONT, MAN! YOU GOT TO LOOK IMPRESSIVE TO IMPRESS!
WHY IS MY PRESENCE REQUIRED FOR THIS?
BECAUSE YOU'RE NOT A MUTIE, SANO. EDDIE TRUSTS YOU.
Why didn't he just paint a target for the police on the car?
MY MAN! JUST IN TIME!
THE FIRST PART OF YOUR PAYMENT, AS PROMISED. IF ALL GOES AS PLANNED, YOU WILL HAVE MORE TO SELL LATER.
AND WE'LL OWN NEW YORK!
YOU HAD BETTER CARRY THROUGH ON YOUR ENTIRE PART OF THIS DEAL, EDDIE.
SURE-- DON'T WORRY!
LET'S GET THIS STUFF LOADED, EDDIE.
THAT FOUL CIGAR! I CAN'T SMELL A THING-- COUGH
Cobra's right--but the cigar masks my smell, so I can't complain. Much. Leave, you two. I want the bags in Eddie's trunk!

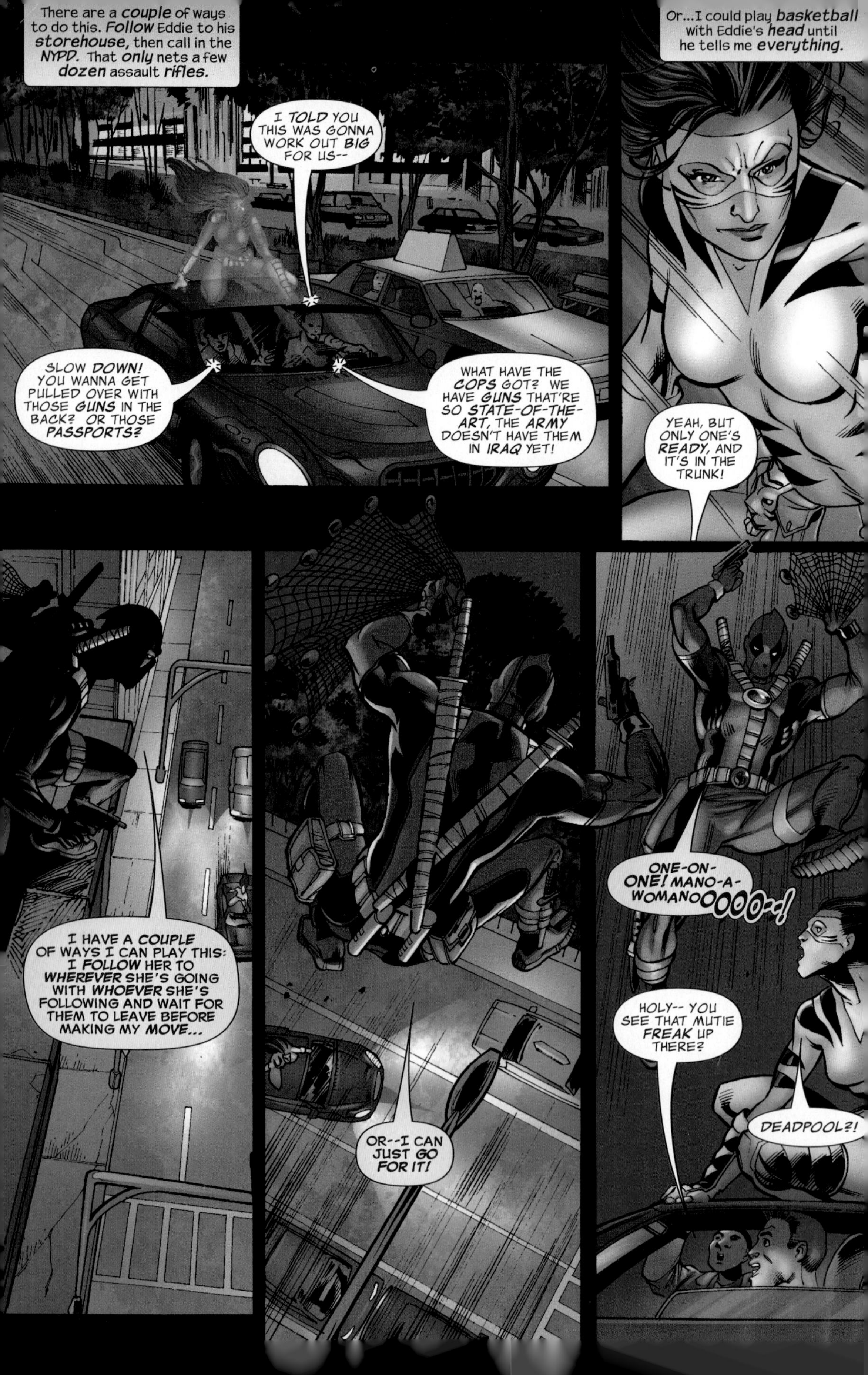
There are a couple of ways to do this. Follow Eddie to his storehouse, then call in the NYPD. That only nets a few dozen assault rifles.
I TOLD YOU THIS WAS GONNA WORK OUT BIG FOR US--
SLOW DOWN! YOU WANNA GET PULLED OVER WITH THOSE GUNS IN THE BACK? OR THOSE PASSPORTS?
WHAT HAVE THE COPS GOT? WE HAVE GUNS THAT'RE SO STATE-OF-THE-ART, THE ARMY DOESN'T HAVE THEM IN IRAQ YET!
Or...I could play basketball with Eddie's head until he tells me everything.
YEAH, BUT ONLY ONE'S READY, AND IT'S IN THE TRUNK!
I HAVE A COUPLE OF WAYS I CAN PLAY THIS: I FOLLOW HER TO WHEREVER SHE'S GOING WITH WHOEVER SHE'S FOLLOWING AND WAIT FOR THEM TO LEAVE BEFORE MAKING MY MOVE...
OR--I CAN JUST GO FOR IT!
ONE-ON-ONE! MANO-A-WOMANOOOOO-o!
HOLY-- YOU SEE THAT MUTIE FREAK UP THERE?
DEADPOOL?!

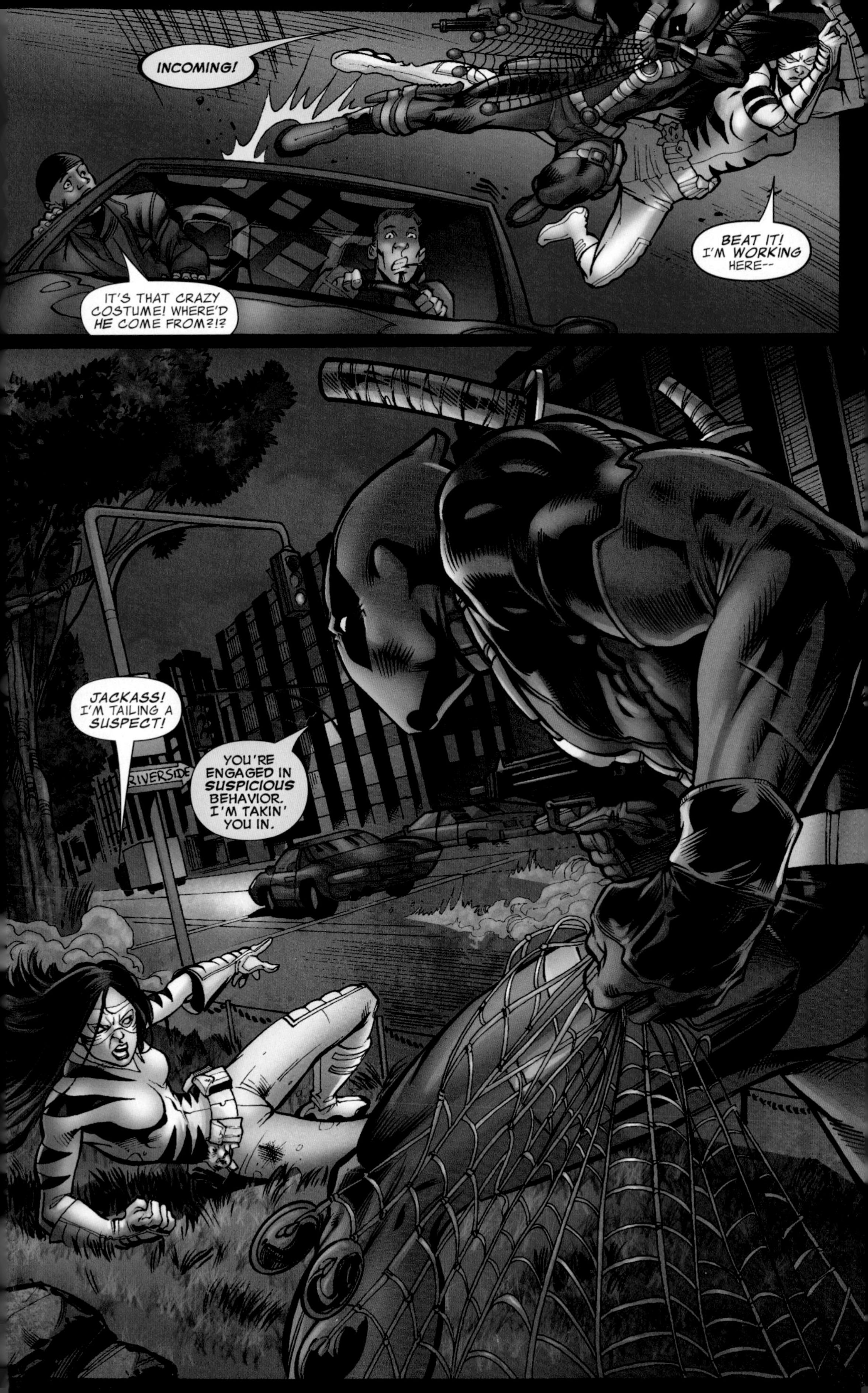
INCOMING!
IT'S THAT CRAZY COSTUME! WHERE'D HE COME FROM?!?
BEAT IT! I'M WORKING HERE--
JACKASS! I'M TAILING A SUSPECT!
RIVERSIDE
YOU'RE ENGAGED IN SUSPICIOUS BEHAVIOR. I'M TAKIN' YOU IN.

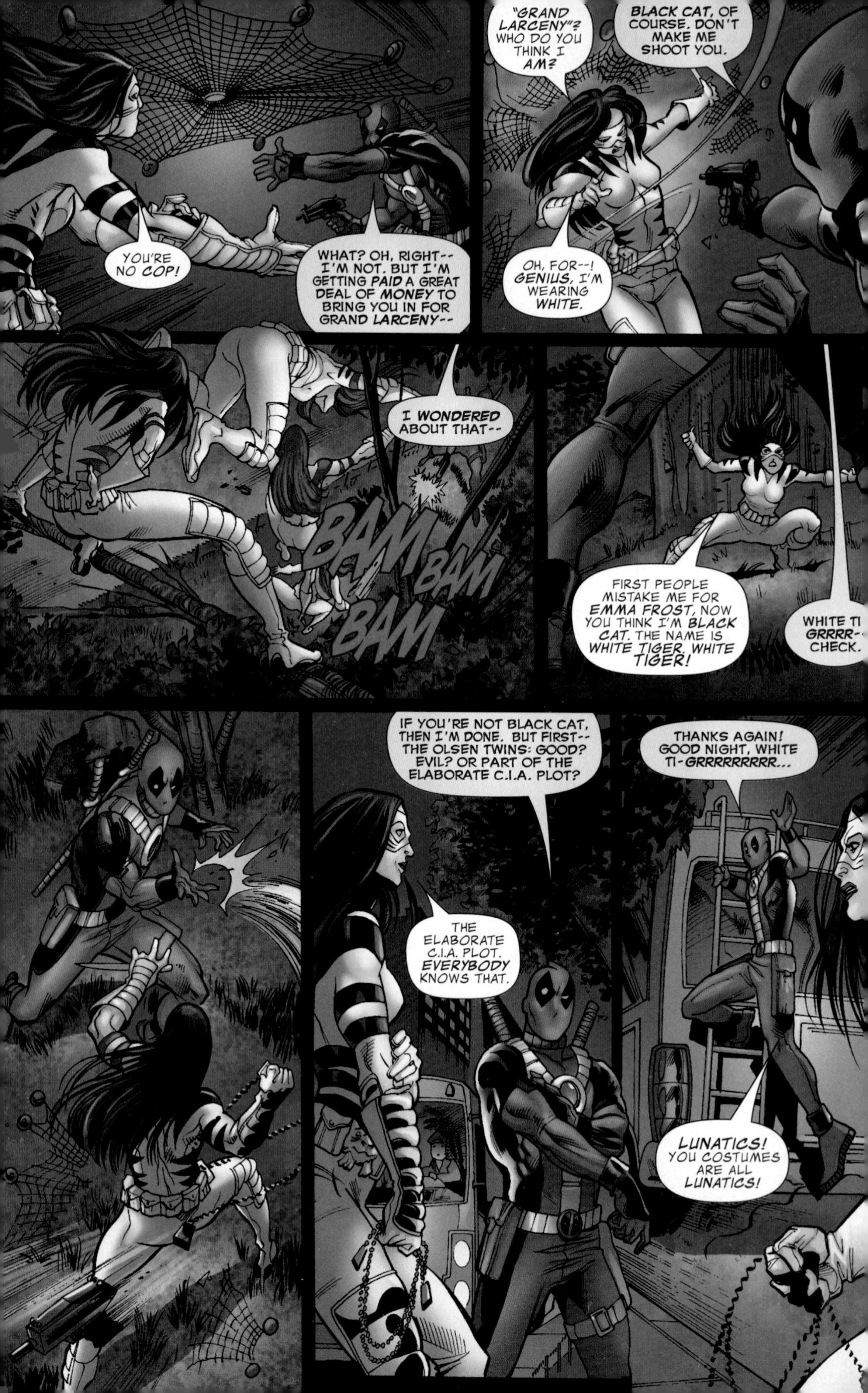
YOU'RE NO COP!
WHAT? OH, RIGHT-- I'M NOT. BUT I'M GETTING PAID A GREAT DEAL OF MONEY TO BRING YOU IN FOR GRAND LARCENY--
"GRAND LARCENY"? WHO DO YOU THINK I AM?
BLACK CAT, OF COURSE. DON'T MAKE ME SHOOT YOU.
OH, FOR--! GENIUS, I'M WEARING WHITE.
I WONDERED ABOUT THAT--
BAM BAM BAM
FIRST PEOPLE MISTAKE ME FOR EMMA FROST, NOW YOU THINK I'M BLACK CAT. THE NAME IS WHITE TIGER. WHITE TIGER!
WHITE TI GRRRR-CHECK.
IF YOU'RE NOT BLACK CAT, THEN I'M DONE. BUT FIRST-- THE OLSEN TWINS: GOOD? EVIL? OR PART OF THE ELABORATE C.I.A. PLOT?
THE ELABORATE C.I.A. PLOT. EVERYBODY KNOWS THAT.
THANKS AGAIN! GOOD NIGHT, WHITE TI-GRRRRRRRR...
LUNATICS! YOU COSTUMES ARE ALL LUNATICS!

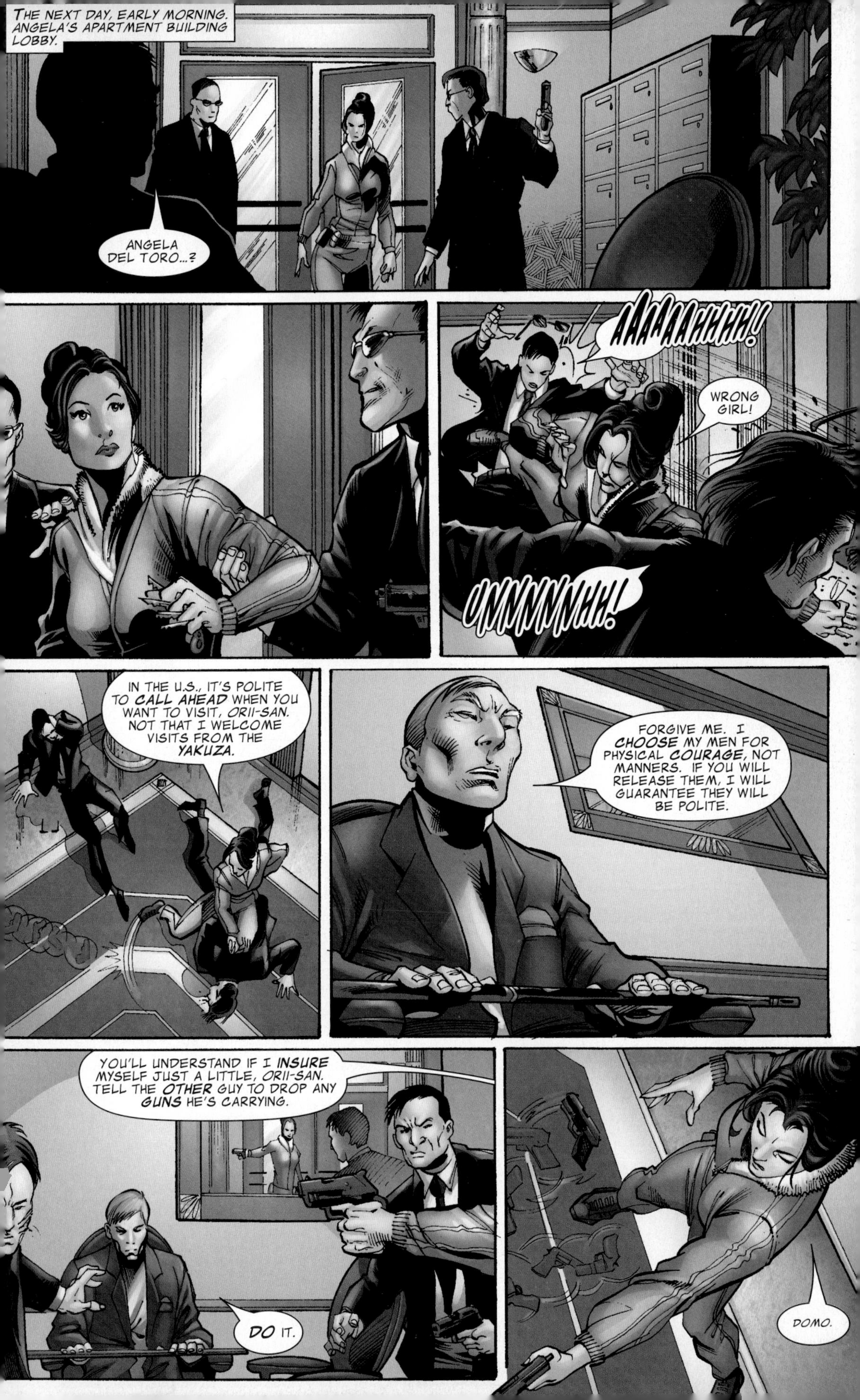
THE NEXT DAY, EARLY MORNING. ANGELA'S APARTMENT BUILDING LOBBY.
ANGELA DEL TORO...?
AAAAAAAHHHH!
WRONG GIRL!
UNNNNNHH!
IN THE U.S., IT'S POLITE TO CALL AHEAD WHEN YOU WANT TO VISIT, ORII-SAN. NOT THAT I WELCOME VISITS FROM THE YAKUZA.
FORGIVE ME. I CHOOSE MY MEN FOR PHYSICAL COURAGE, NOT MANNERS. IF YOU WILL RELEASE THEM, I WILL GUARANTEE THEY WILL BE POLITE.
YOU'LL UNDERSTAND IF I INSURE MYSELF JUST A LITTLE, ORII-SAN. TELL THE OTHER GUY TO DROP ANY GUNS HE'S CARRYING.
DO IT.
DOMO.

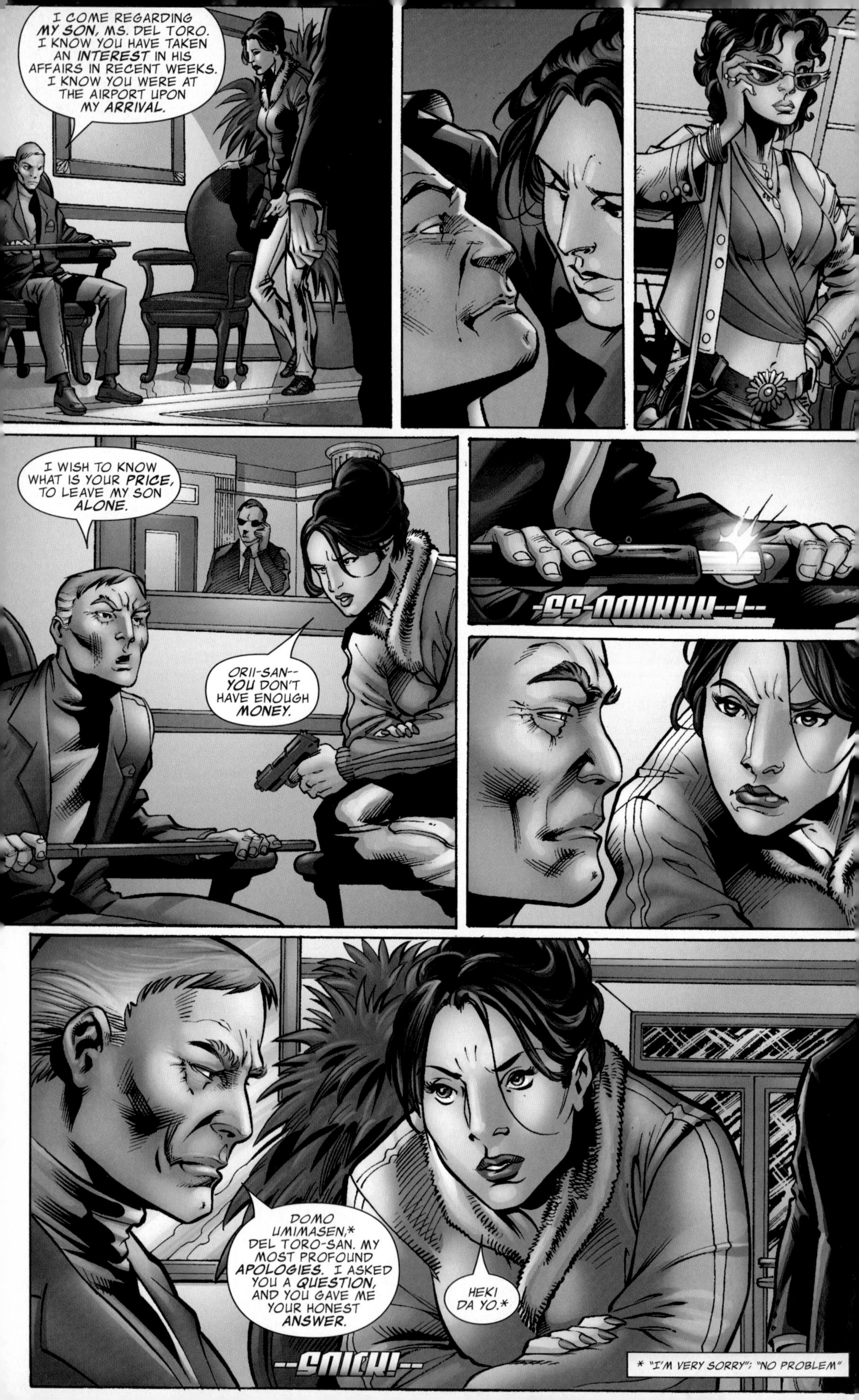
I COME REGARDING MY SON, MS. DEL TORO. I KNOW YOU HAVE TAKEN AN INTEREST IN HIS AFFAIRS IN RECENT WEEKS. I KNOW YOU WERE AT THE AIRPORT UPON MY ARRIVAL.
I WISH TO KNOW WHAT IS YOUR PRICE, TO LEAVE MY SON ALONE.
ORII-SAN-- YOU DON'T HAVE ENOUGH MONEY.
-SS-NNIKKK--!--
DOMO UMIMASEN,* DEL TORO-SAN. MY MOST PROFOUND APOLOGIES. I ASKED YOU A QUESTION, AND YOU GAVE ME YOUR HONEST ANSWER.
HEKI DA YO.*
--SNICK!--
* "I'M VERY SORRY"; "NO PROBLEM"

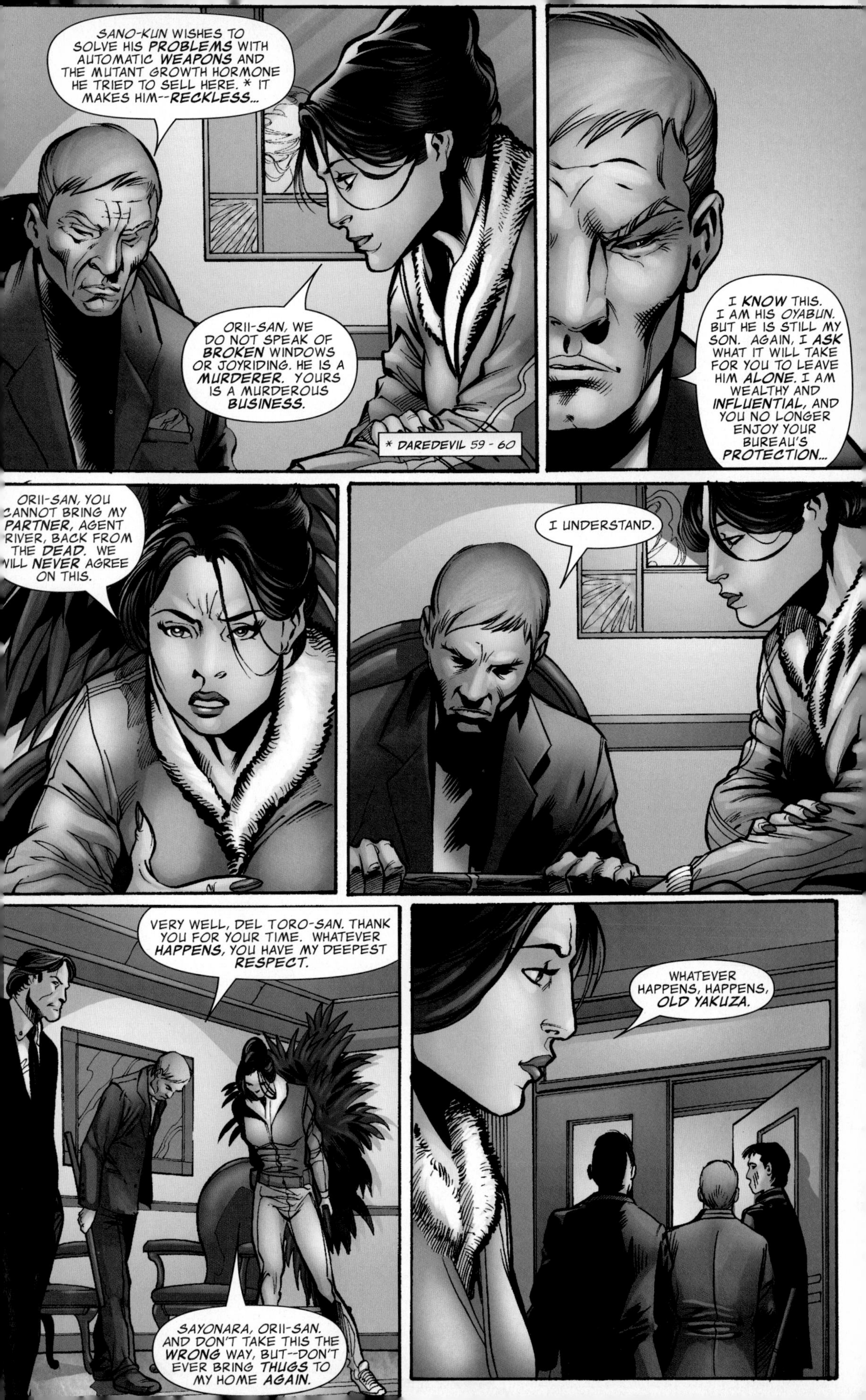
SANO-KUN WISHES TO SOLVE HIS PROBLEMS WITH AUTOMATIC WEAPONS AND THE MUTANT GROWTH HORMONE HE TRIED TO SELL HERE. * IT MAKES HIM--RECKLESS...
ORII-SAN, WE DO NOT SPEAK OF BROKEN WINDOWS OR JOYRIDING. HE IS A MURDERER. YOURS IS A MURDEROUS BUSINESS.
* DAREDEVIL 59 - 60
I KNOW THIS. I AM HIS OYABUN. BUT HE IS STILL MY SON. AGAIN, I ASK WHAT IT WILL TAKE FOR YOU TO LEAVE HIM ALONE. I AM WEALTHY AND INFLUENTIAL, AND YOU NO LONGER ENJOY YOUR BUREAU'S PROTECTION...
ORII-SAN, YOU CANNOT BRING MY PARTNER, AGENT RIVER, BACK FROM THE DEAD. WE WILL NEVER AGREE ON THIS.
I UNDERSTAND.
VERY WELL, DEL TORO-SAN. THANK YOU FOR YOUR TIME. WHATEVER HAPPENS, YOU HAVE MY DEEPEST RESPECT.
SAYONARA, ORII-SAN. AND DON'T TAKE THIS THE WRONG WAY, BUT--DON'T EVER BRING THUGS TO MY HOME AGAIN.
WHATEVER HAPPENS, HAPPENS, OLD YAKUZA.

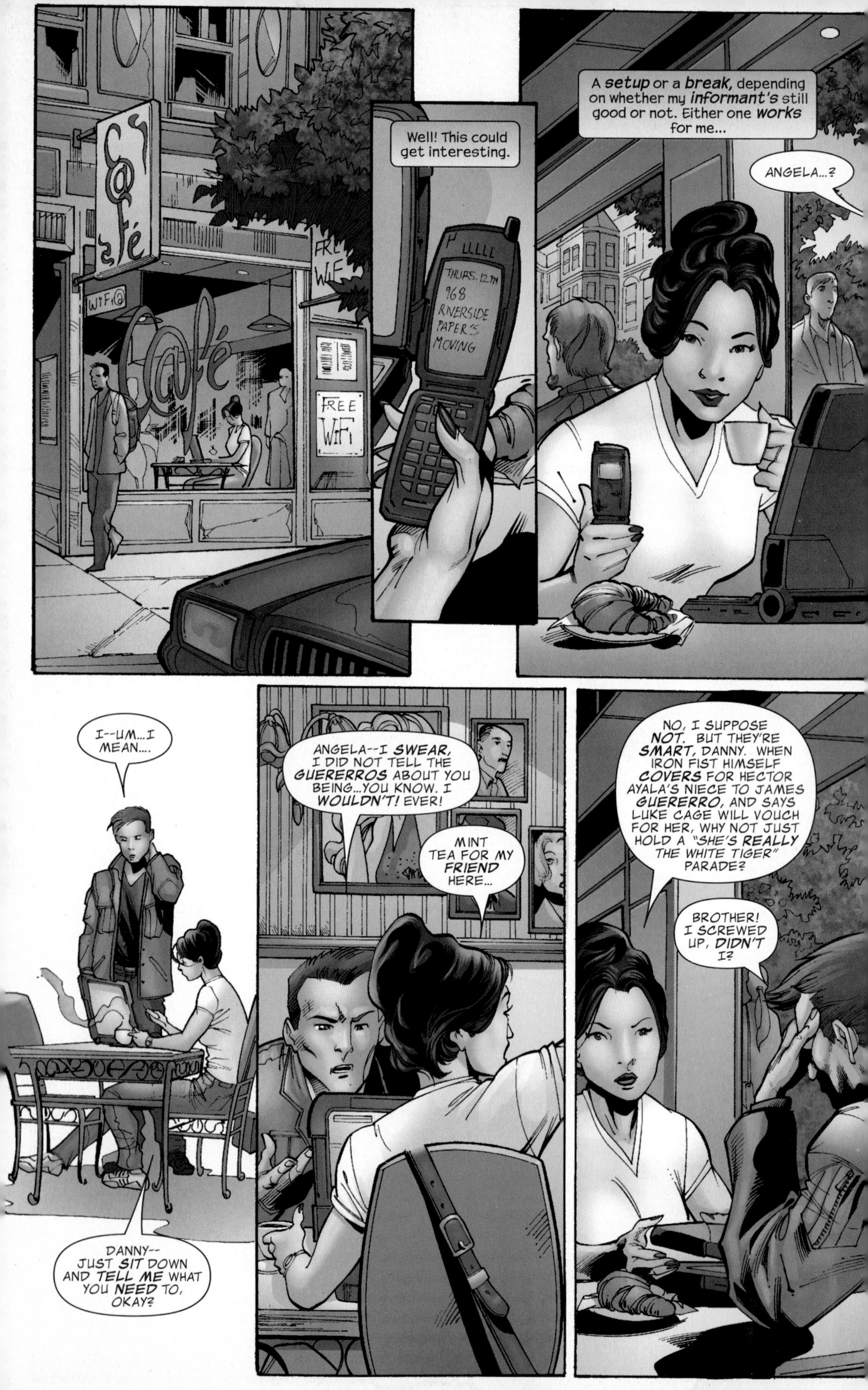
Well! This could get interesting.
THURS. 12 PM
968 RIVERSIDE
PAPER'S MOVING
A setup or a break, depending on whether my informant's still good or not. Either one works for me...
ANGELA...?
I--UM...I MEAN....
DANNY-- JUST SIT DOWN AND TELL ME WHAT YOU NEED TO, OKAY?
ANGELA--I SWEAR, I DID NOT TELL THE GUERERROS ABOUT YOU BEING...YOU KNOW. I WOULDN'T! EVER!
MINT TEA FOR MY FRIEND HERE...
NO, I SUPPOSE NOT. BUT THEY'RE SMART, DANNY. WHEN IRON FIST HIMSELF COVERS FOR HECTOR AYALA'S NIECE TO JAMES GUERERRO, AND SAYS LUKE CAGE WILL VOUCH FOR HER, WHY NOT JUST HOLD A "SHE'S REALLY THE WHITE TIGER" PARADE?
BROTHER! I SCREWED UP, DIDN'T I?

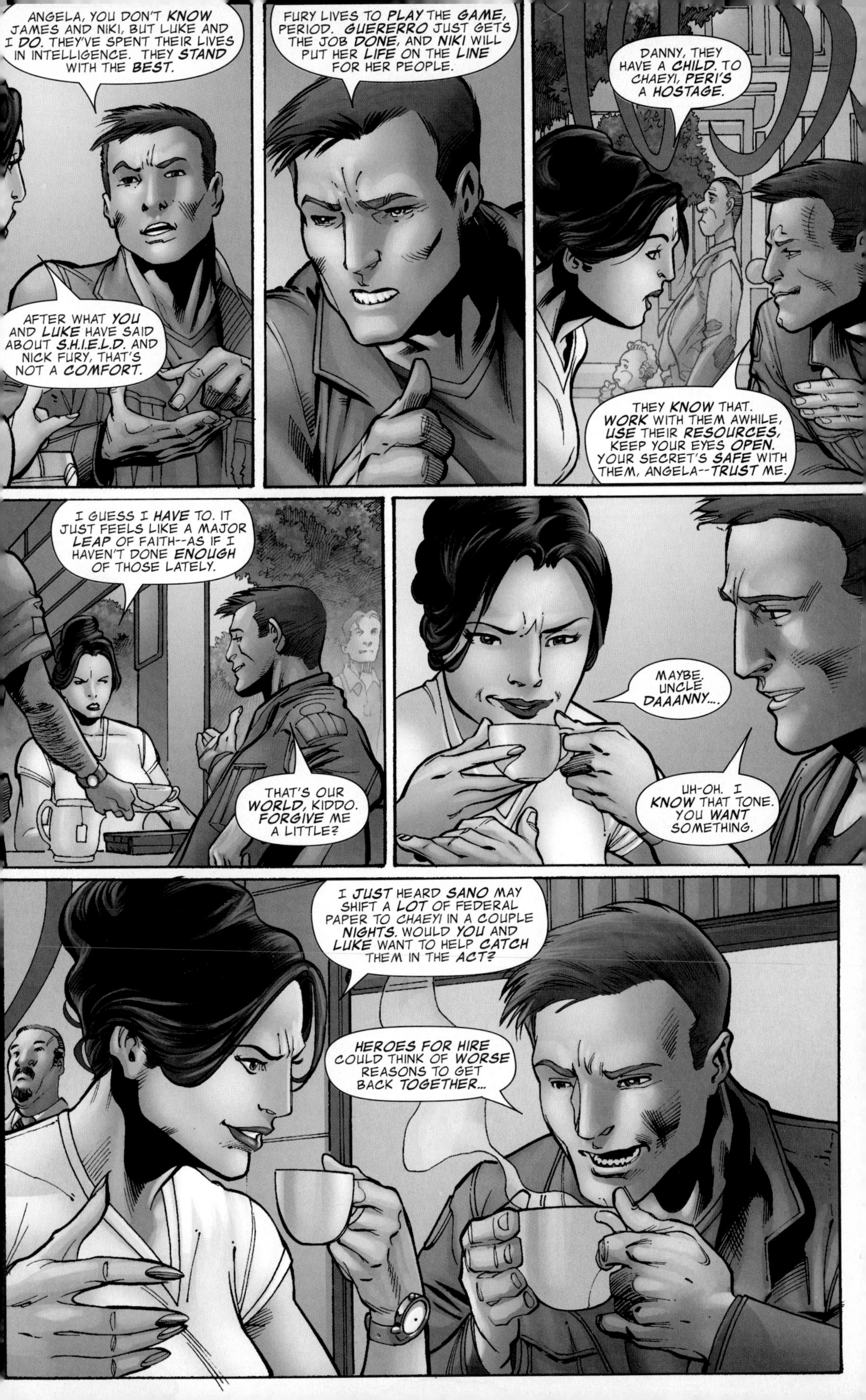
ANGELA, YOU DON'T KNOW JAMES AND NIKI, BUT LUKE AND I DO. THEY'VE SPENT THEIR LIVES IN INTELLIGENCE. THEY STAND WITH THE BEST.
AFTER WHAT YOU AND LUKE HAVE SAID ABOUT S.H.I.E.L.D. AND NICK FURY, THAT'S NOT A COMFORT.
FURY LIVES TO PLAY THE GAME, PERIOD. GUERERRO JUST GETS THE JOB DONE, AND NIKI WILL PUT HER LIFE ON THE LINE FOR HER PEOPLE.
DANNY, THEY HAVE A CHILD. TO CHAEYI, PERI'S A HOSTAGE.
THEY KNOW THAT. WORK WITH THEM AWHILE, USE THEIR RESOURCES, KEEP YOUR EYES OPEN. YOUR SECRET'S SAFE WITH THEM, ANGELA--TRUST ME.
I GUESS I HAVE TO. IT JUST FEELS LIKE A MAJOR LEAP OF FAITH--AS IF I HAVEN'T DONE ENOUGH OF THOSE LATELY.
THAT'S OUR WORLD, KIDDO. FORGIVE ME A LITTLE?
MAYBE. UNCLE DAAANNY....
UH-OH. I KNOW THAT TONE. YOU WANT SOMETHING.
I JUST HEARD SANO MAY SHIFT A LOT OF FEDERAL PAPER TO CHAEYI IN A COUPLE NIGHTS. WOULD YOU AND LUKE WANT TO HELP CATCH THEM IN THE ACT?
HEROES FOR HIRE COULD THINK OF WORSE REASONS TO GET BACK TOGETHER...

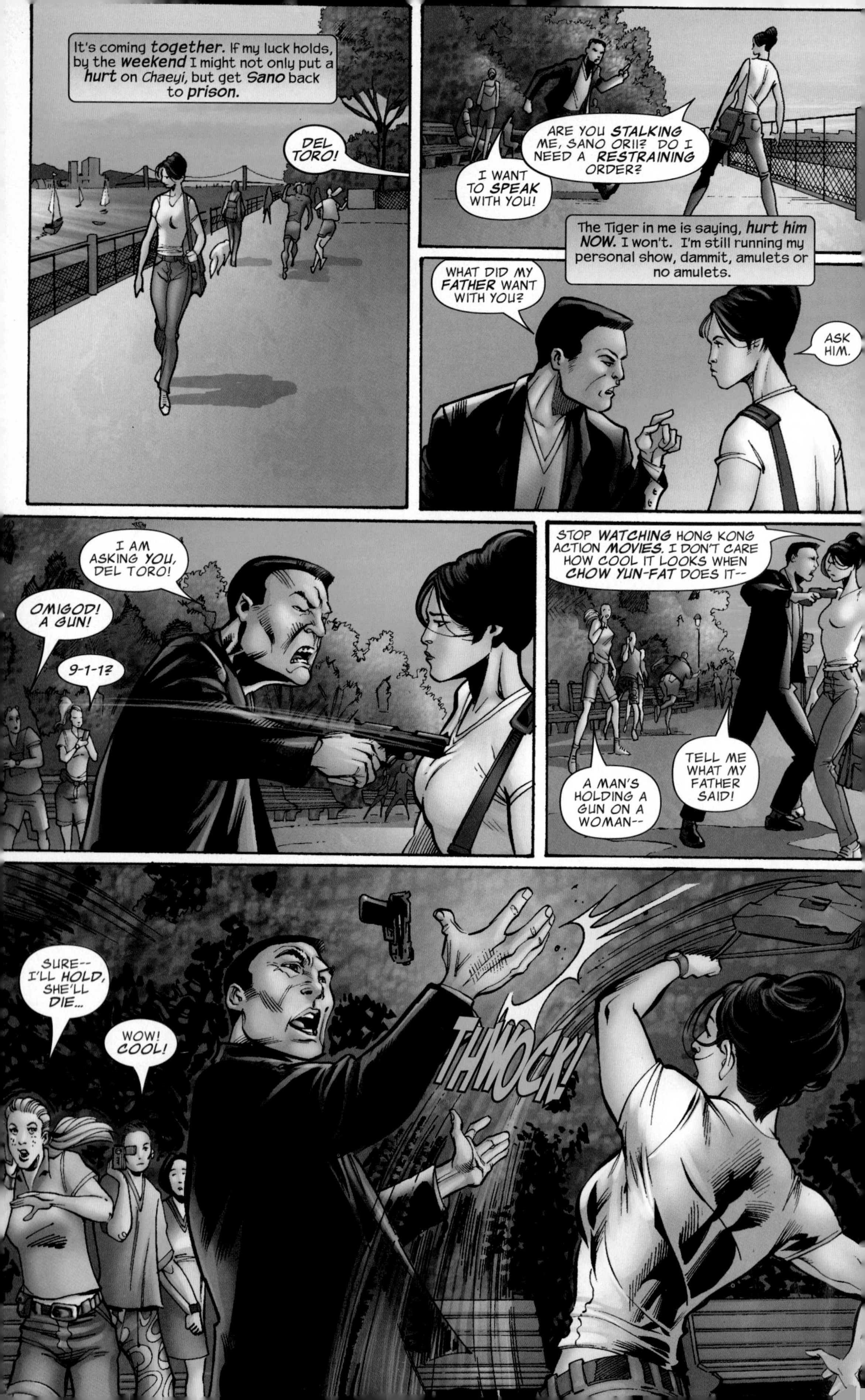
It's coming together. If my luck holds, by the weekend I might not only put a hurt on Chaeyi, but get Sano back to prison.
DEL TORO!
ARE YOU STALKING ME, SANO ORII? DO I NEED A RESTRAINING ORDER?
I WANT TO SPEAK WITH YOU!
The Tiger in me is saying, hurt him NOW. I won't. I'm still running my personal show, dammit, amulets or no amulets.
WHAT DID MY FATHER WANT WITH YOU?
ASK HIM.
I AM ASKING YOU, DEL TORO!
OMIGOD! A GUN!
9-1-1?
STOP WATCHING HONG KONG ACTION MOVIES. I DON'T CARE HOW COOL IT LOOKS WHEN CHOW YUN-FAT DOES IT--
A MAN'S HOLDING A GUN ON A WOMAN--
TELL ME WHAT MY FATHER SAID!
SURE-- I'LL HOLD, SHE'LL DIE...
WOW! COOL!
THWOCK!

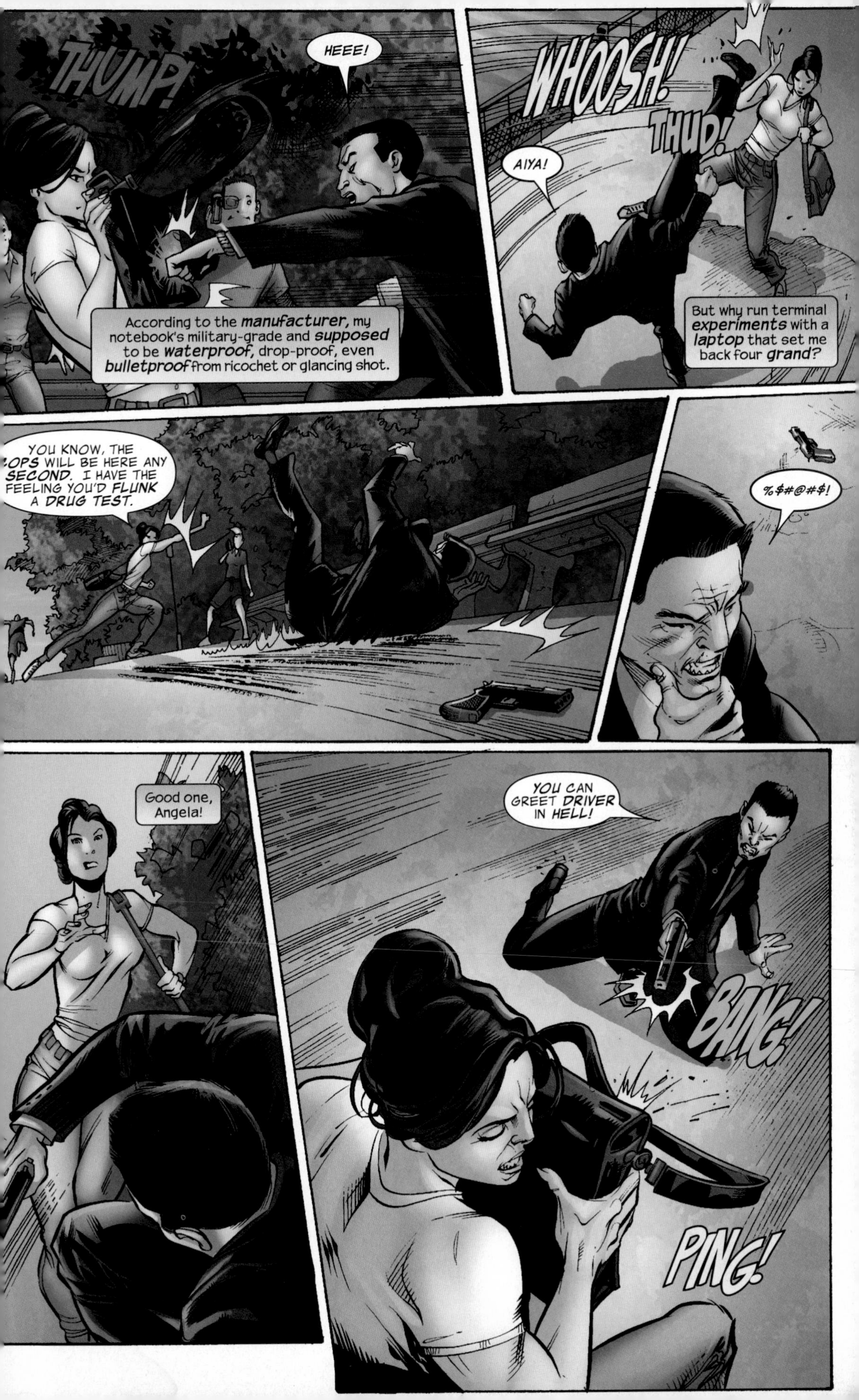
THUMP!
HEEE!
According to the manufacturer, my notebook's military-grade and supposed to be waterproof, drop-proof, even bulletproof from ricochet or glancing shot.
WHOOSH!
THUD!
AIYA!
But why run terminal experiments with a laptop that set me back four grand?
YOU KNOW, THE COPS WILL BE HERE ANY SECOND. I HAVE THE FEELING YOU'D FLUNK A DRUG TEST.
%$#@#$!
Good one, Angela!
YOU CAN GREET DRIVER IN HELL!
BANG!
PING!

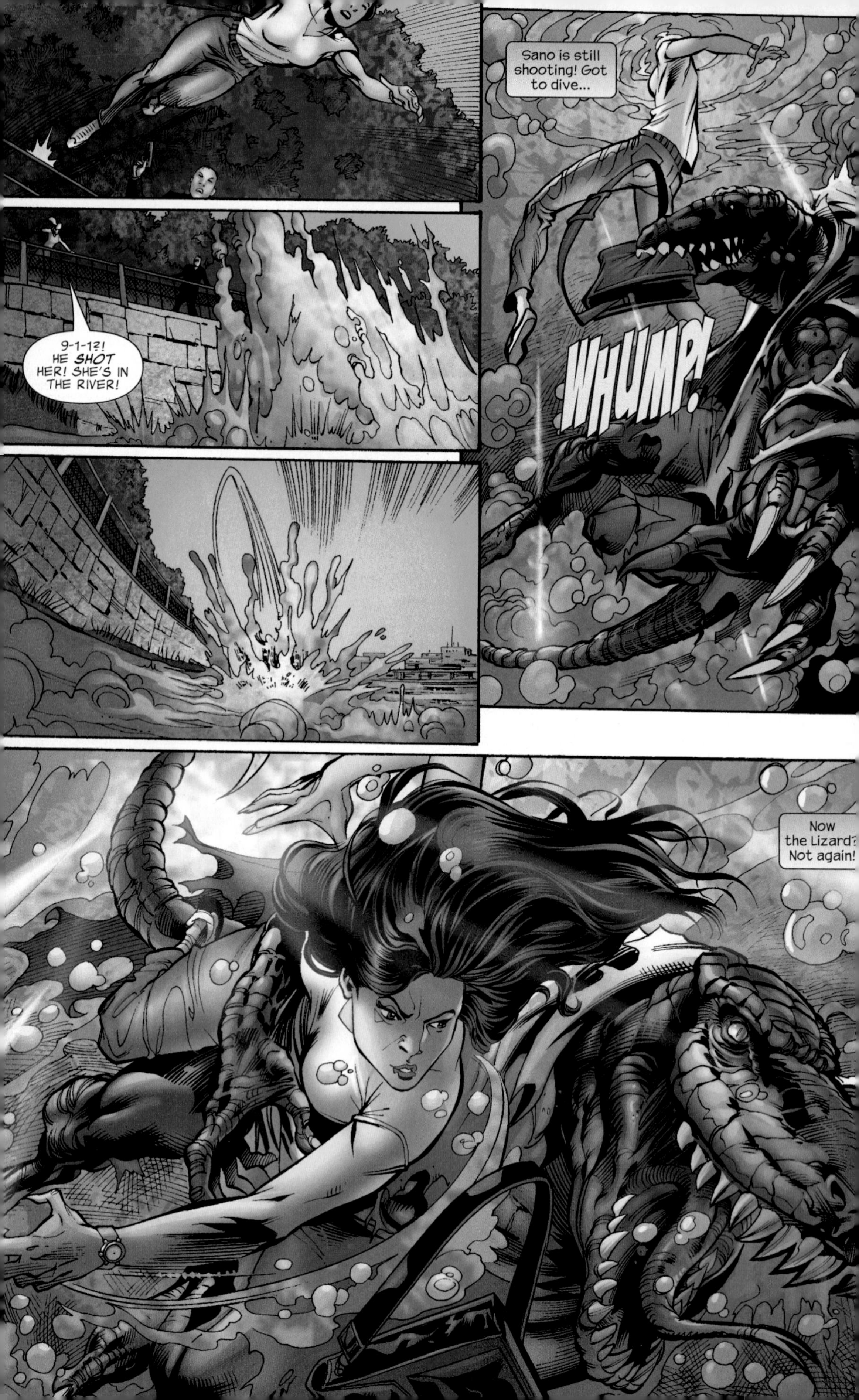
9-1-1?! HE SHOT HER! SHE'S IN THE RIVER!
Sano is still shooting! Got to dive...
WHUMP!
Now the Lizard? Not again!

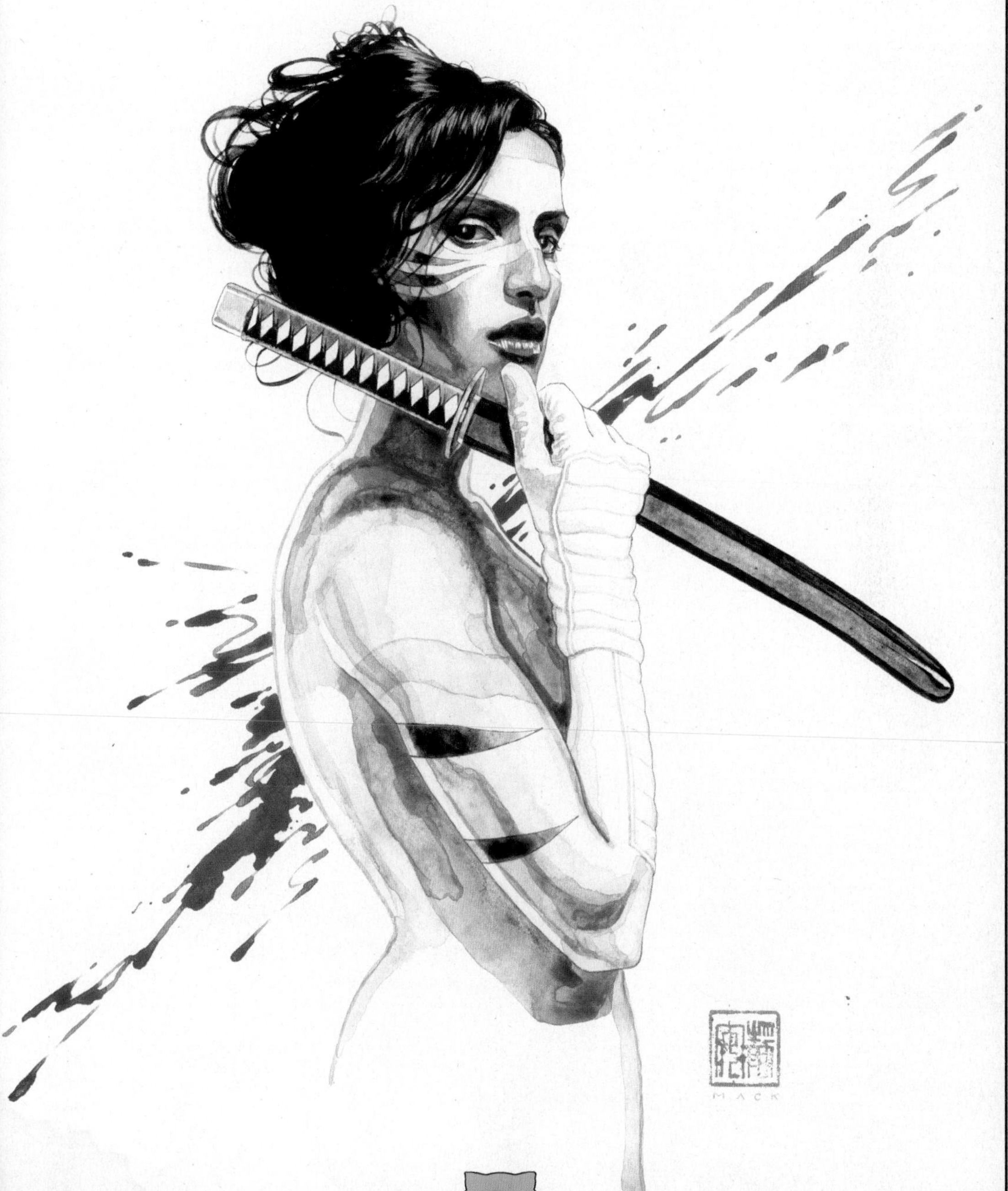
MACK

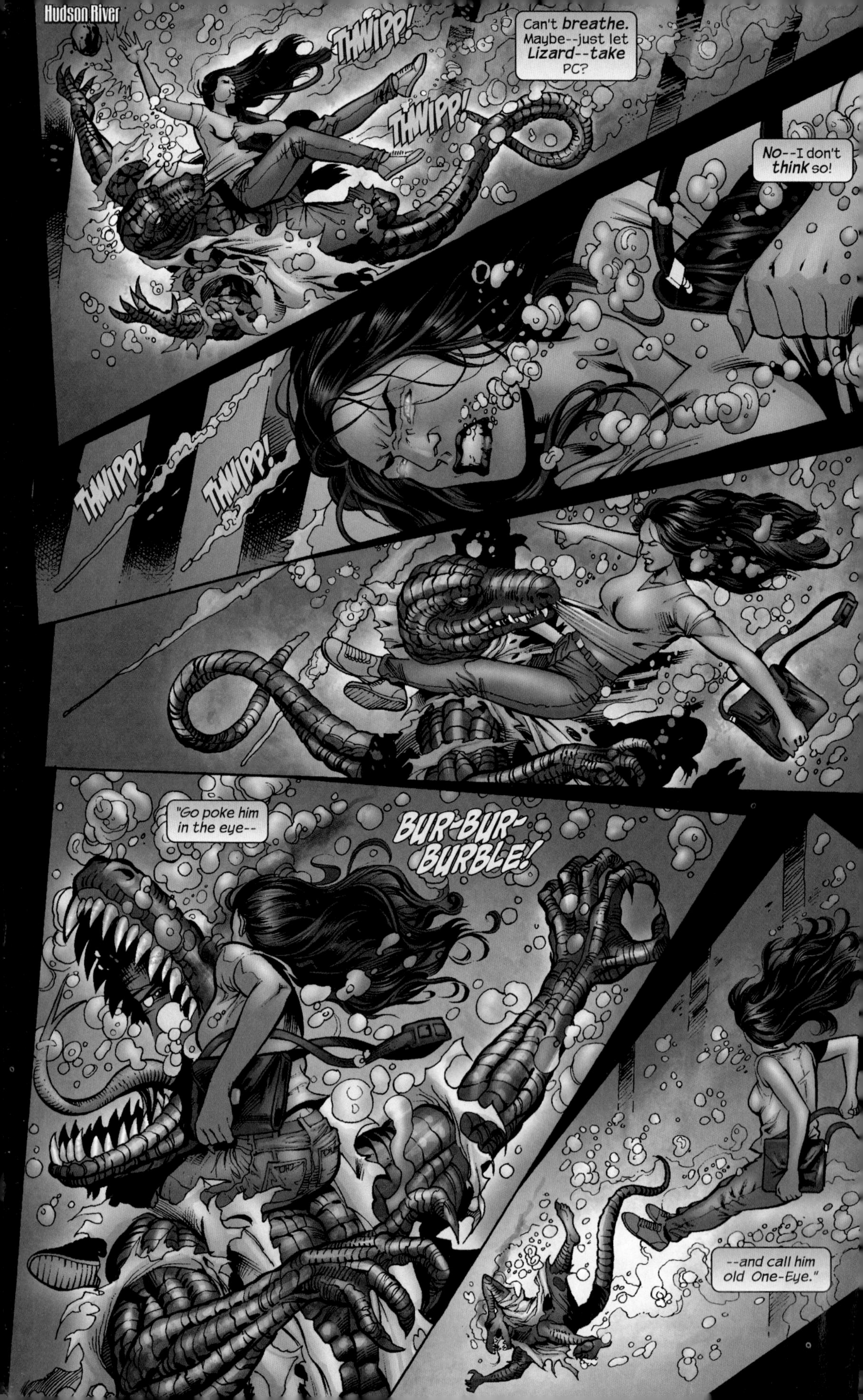
Hudson River
THWIPP!
Can't breathe. Maybe--just let Lizard--take PC?
THWIPP!
No--I don't think so!
THWIPP!
THWIPP!
"Go poke him in the eye--
BUR-BUR-BURBLE!
--and call him old One-Eye."

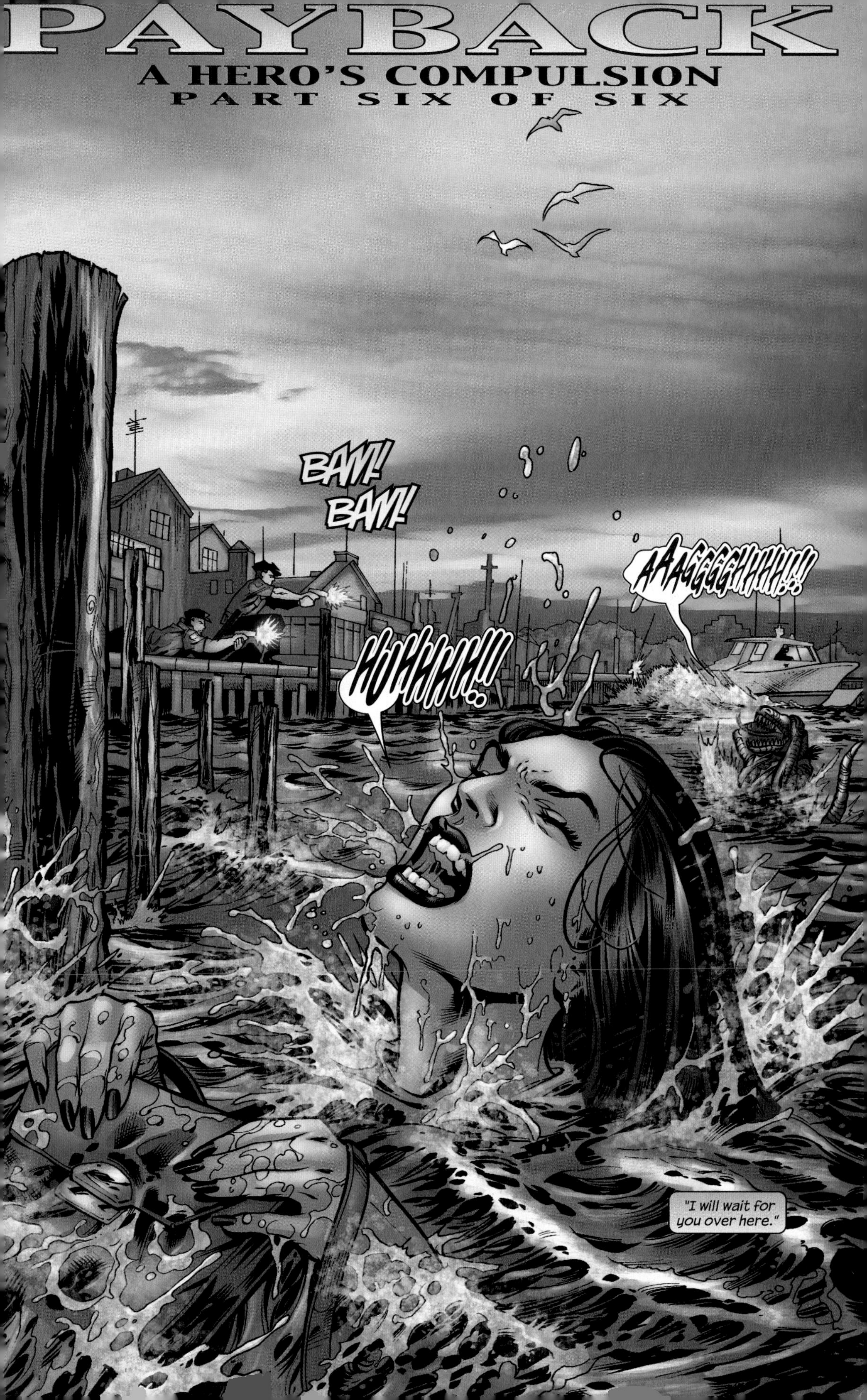
PAYBACK
A HERO'S COMPULSION
PART SIX OF SIX
BAM!
BAM!
HUHHHHH!!..
AAAGGGGHHHHH!!..
"I will wait for you over here."

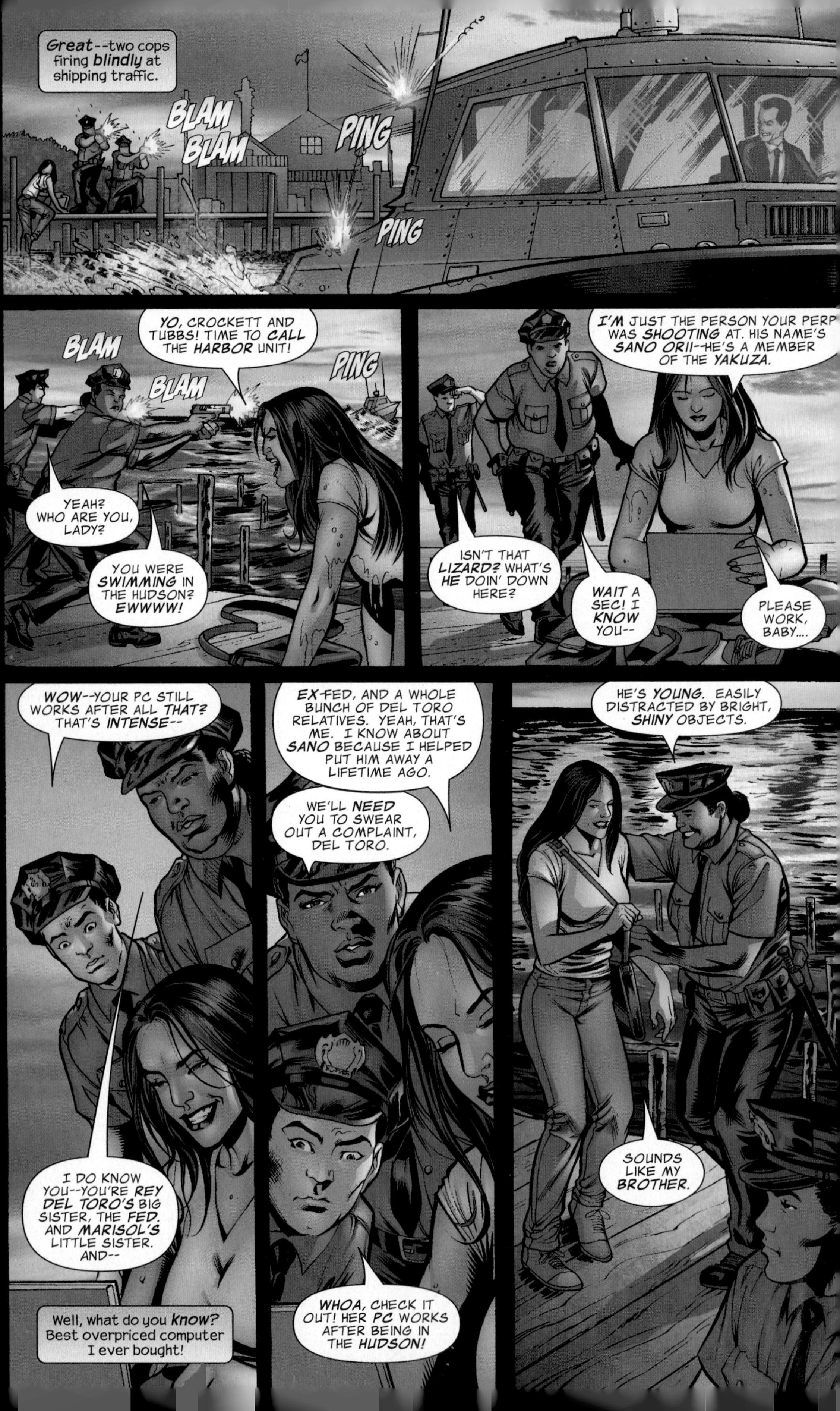

Great--two cops firing blindly at shipping traffic.
BLAM BLAM
PING
PING
BLAM
YO, CROCKETT AND TUBBS! TIME TO CALL THE HARBOR UNIT!
BLAM
PING
YEAH? WHO ARE YOU, LADY?
YOU WERE SWIMMING IN THE HUDSON? EWWWW!
I'M JUST THE PERSON YOUR PERP WAS SHOOTING AT. HIS NAME'S SANO ORII--HE'S A MEMBER OF THE YAKUZA.
ISN'T THAT LIZARD? WHAT'S HE DOIN' DOWN HERE?
WAIT A SEC! I KNOW YOU--
PLEASE WORK, BABY....
WOW--YOUR PC STILL WORKS AFTER ALL THAT? THAT'S INTENSE--
I DO KNOW YOU--YOU'RE REY DEL TORO'S BIG SISTER, THE FED. AND MARISOL'S LITTLE SISTER. AND--
Well, what do you know? Best overpriced computer I ever bought!
EX-FED, AND A WHOLE BUNCH OF DEL TORO RELATIVES. YEAH, THAT'S ME. I KNOW ABOUT SANO BECAUSE I HELPED PUT HIM AWAY A LIFETIME AGO.
WE'LL NEED YOU TO SWEAR OUT A COMPLAINT, DEL TORO.
WHOA, CHECK IT OUT! HER PC WORKS AFTER BEING IN THE HUDSON!
HE'S YOUNG. EASILY DISTRACTED BY BRIGHT, SHINY OBJECTS.
SOUNDS LIKE MY BROTHER.

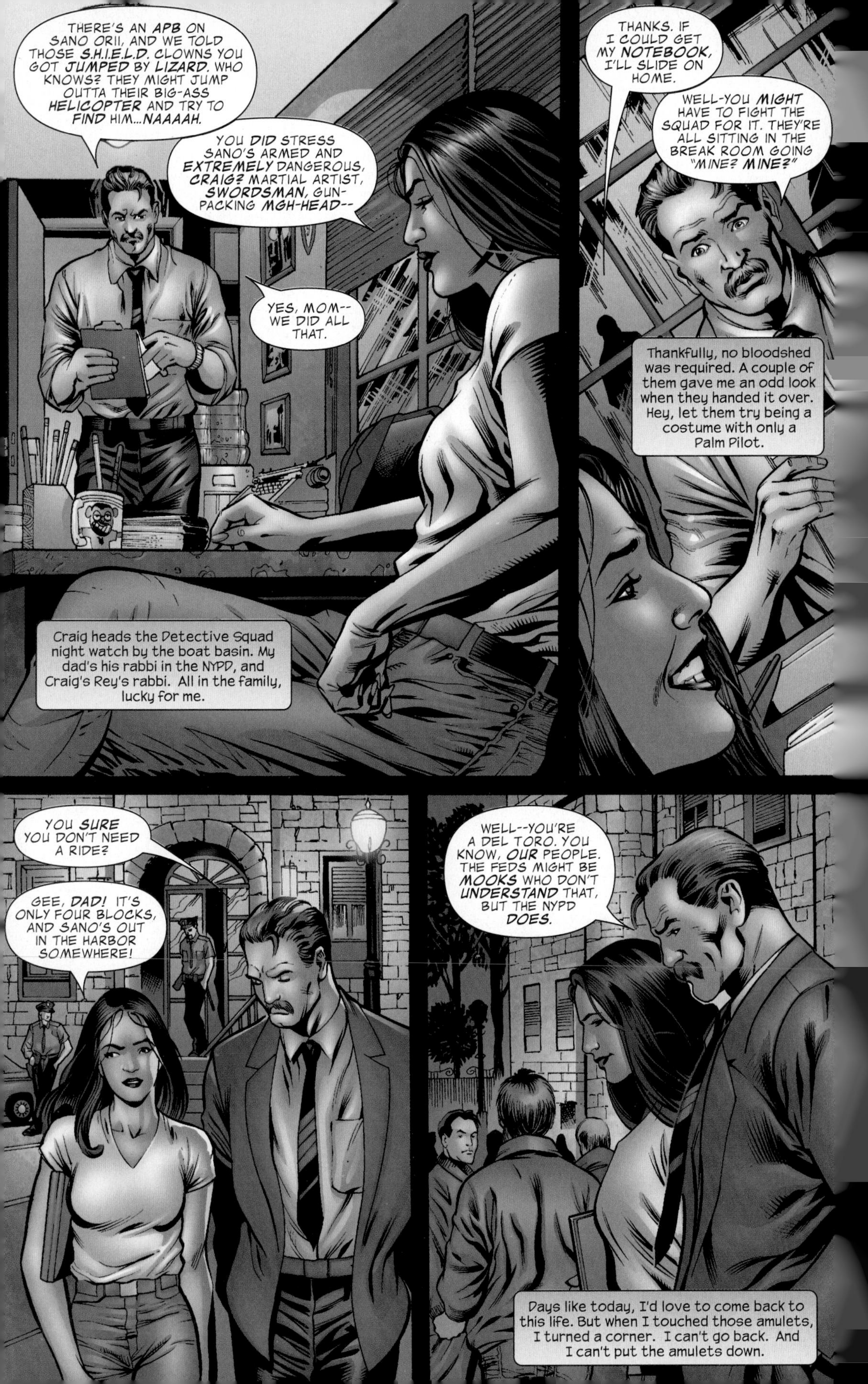
THERE'S AN APB ON SANO ORII, AND WE TOLD THOSE S.H.I.E.L.D. CLOWNS YOU GOT JUMPED BY LIZARD. WHO KNOWS? THEY MIGHT JUMP OUTTA THEIR BIG-ASS HELICOPTER AND TRY TO FIND HIM...NAAAAH.
YOU DID STRESS SANO'S ARMED AND EXTREMELY DANGEROUS, CRAIG? MARTIAL ARTIST, SWORDSMAN, GUN-PACKING MGH-HEAD--
YES, MOM-- WE DID ALL THAT.
Craig heads the Detective Squad night watch by the boat basin. My dad's his rabbi in the NYPD, and Craig's Rey's rabbi. All in the family, lucky for me.
THANKS. IF I COULD GET MY NOTEBOOK, I'LL SLIDE ON HOME.
WELL-YOU MIGHT HAVE TO FIGHT THE SQUAD FOR IT. THEY'RE ALL SITTING IN THE BREAK ROOM GOING "MINE? MINE?"
Thankfully, no bloodshed was required. A couple of them gave me an odd look when they handed it over. Hey, let them try being a costume with only a Palm Pilot.
YOU SURE YOU DON'T NEED A RIDE?
GEE, DAD! IT'S ONLY FOUR BLOCKS, AND SANO'S OUT IN THE HARBOR SOMEWHERE!
WELL--YOU'RE A DEL TORO. YOU KNOW, OUR PEOPLE. THE FEDS MIGHT BE MOOKS WHO DON'T UNDERSTAND THAT, BUT THE NYPD DOES.
Days like today, I'd love to come back to this life. But when I touched those amulets, I turned a corner. I can't go back. And I can't put the amulets down.

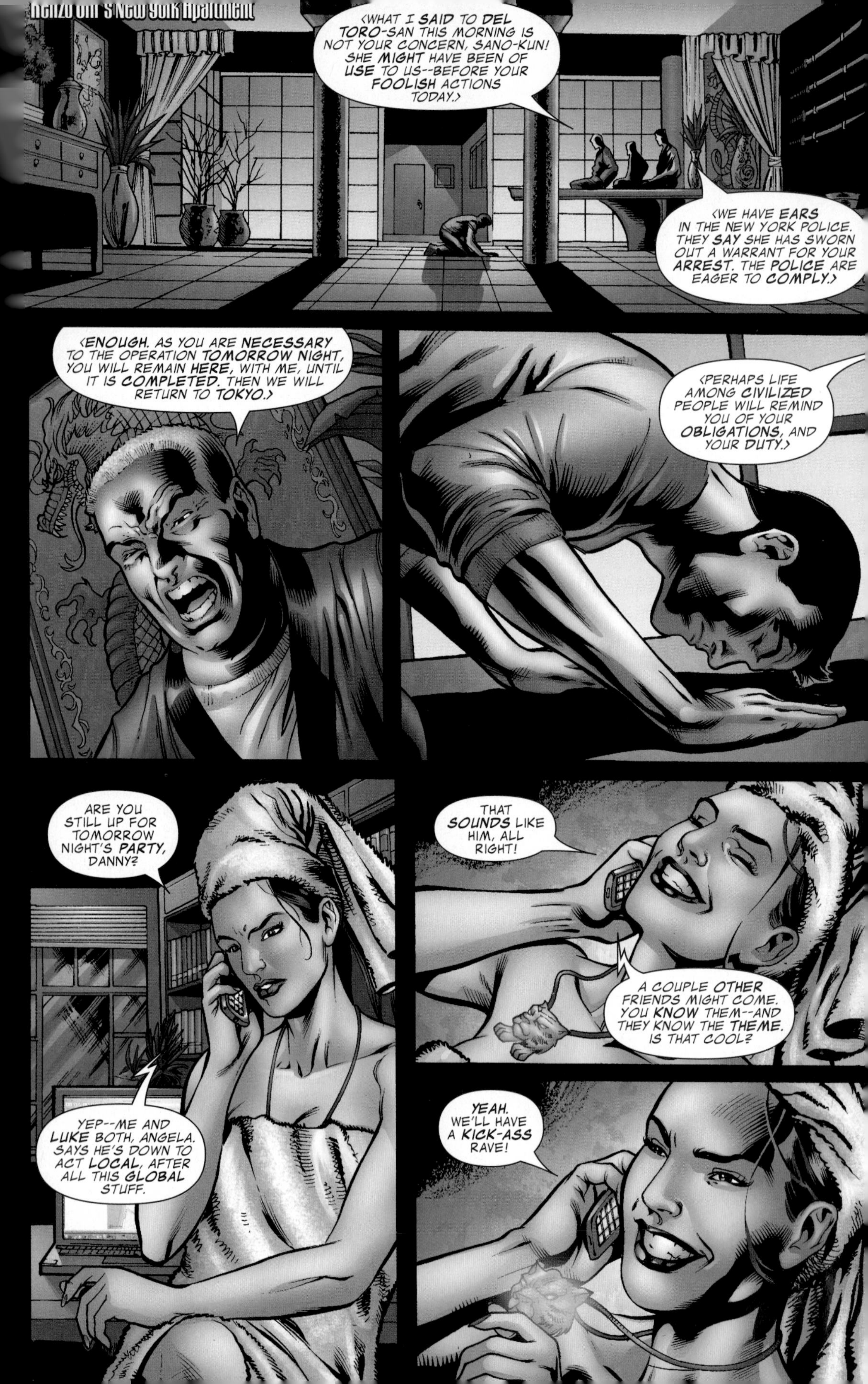
Kenzo Ohr's New York Apartment
<WHAT I SAID TO DEL TORO-SAN THIS MORNING IS NOT YOUR CONCERN, SANO-KUN! SHE MIGHT HAVE BEEN OF USE TO US--BEFORE YOUR FOOLISH ACTIONS TODAY.>
<WE HAVE EARS IN THE NEW YORK POLICE. THEY SAY SHE HAS SWORN OUT A WARRANT FOR YOUR ARREST. THE POLICE ARE EAGER TO COMPLY.>
<ENOUGH. AS YOU ARE NECESSARY TO THE OPERATION TOMORROW NIGHT, YOU WILL REMAIN HERE, WITH ME, UNTIL IT IS COMPLETED. THEN WE WILL RETURN TO TOKYO.>
<PERHAPS LIFE AMONG CIVILIZED PEOPLE WILL REMIND YOU OF YOUR OBLIGATIONS, AND YOUR DUTY.>
ARE YOU STILL UP FOR TOMORROW NIGHT'S PARTY, DANNY?
YEP--ME AND LUKE BOTH, ANGELA. SAYS HE'S DOWN TO ACT LOCAL, AFTER ALL THIS GLOBAL STUFF.
THAT SOUNDS LIKE HIM, ALL RIGHT!
A COUPLE OTHER FRIENDS MIGHT COME. YOU KNOW THEM--AND THEY KNOW THE THEME. IS THAT COOL?
YEAH. WE'LL HAVE A KICK-ASS RAVE!

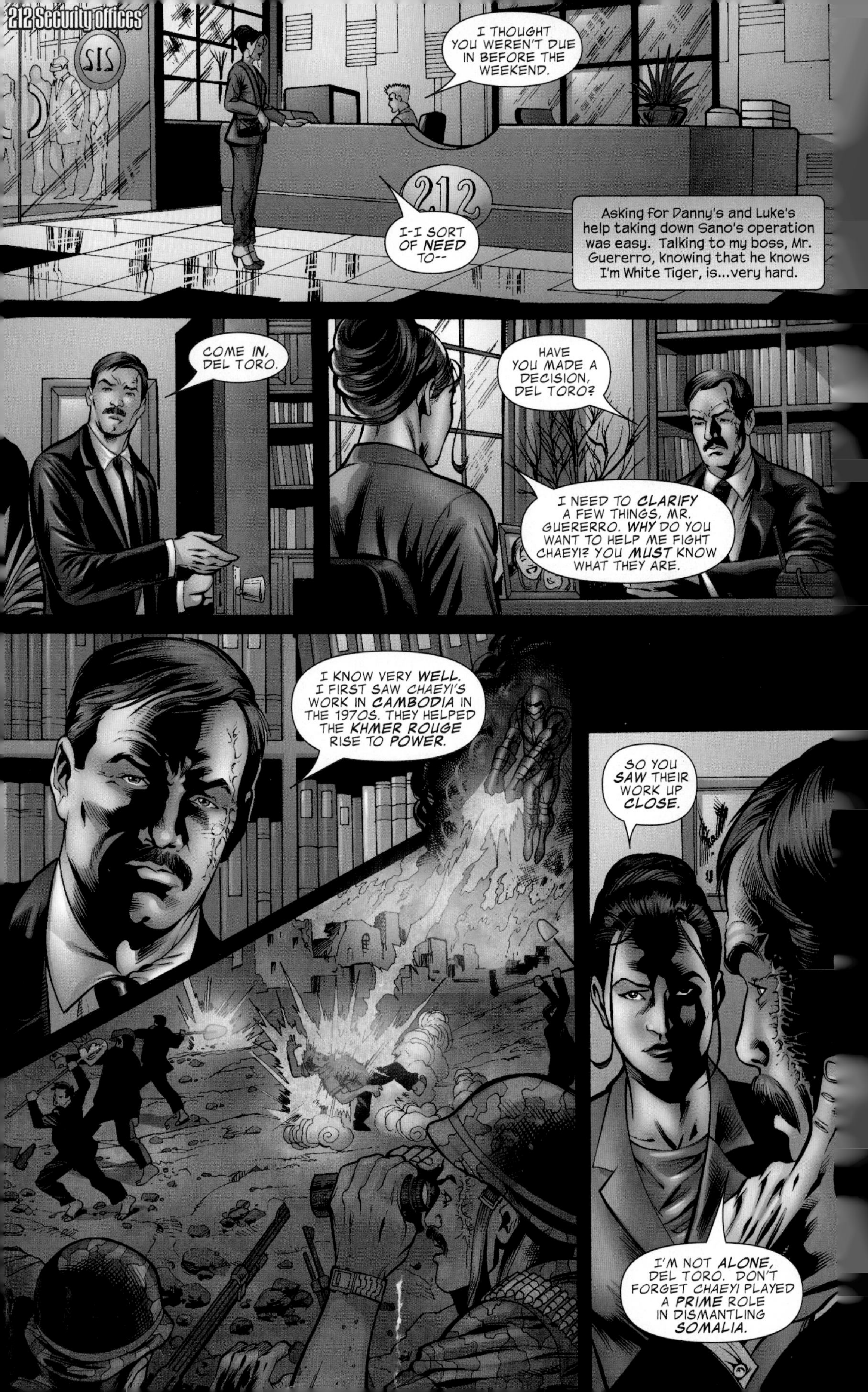
212 Security offices
I THOUGHT YOU WEREN'T DUE IN BEFORE THE WEEKEND.
I-I SORT OF NEED TO--
Asking for Danny's and Luke's help taking down Sano's operation was easy. Talking to my boss, Mr. Guererro, knowing that he knows I'm White Tiger, is...very hard.
COME IN, DEL TORO.
HAVE YOU MADE A DECISION, DEL TORO?
I NEED TO CLARIFY A FEW THINGS, MR. GUERERRO. WHY DO YOU WANT TO HELP ME FIGHT CHAEYI? YOU MUST KNOW WHAT THEY ARE.
I KNOW VERY WELL. I FIRST SAW CHAEYI'S WORK IN CAMBODIA IN THE 1970S. THEY HELPED THE KHMER ROUGE RISE TO POWER.
SO YOU SAW THEIR WORK UP CLOSE.
I'M NOT ALONE, DEL TORO. DON'T FORGET CHAEYI PLAYED A PRIME ROLE IN DISMANTLING SOMALIA.

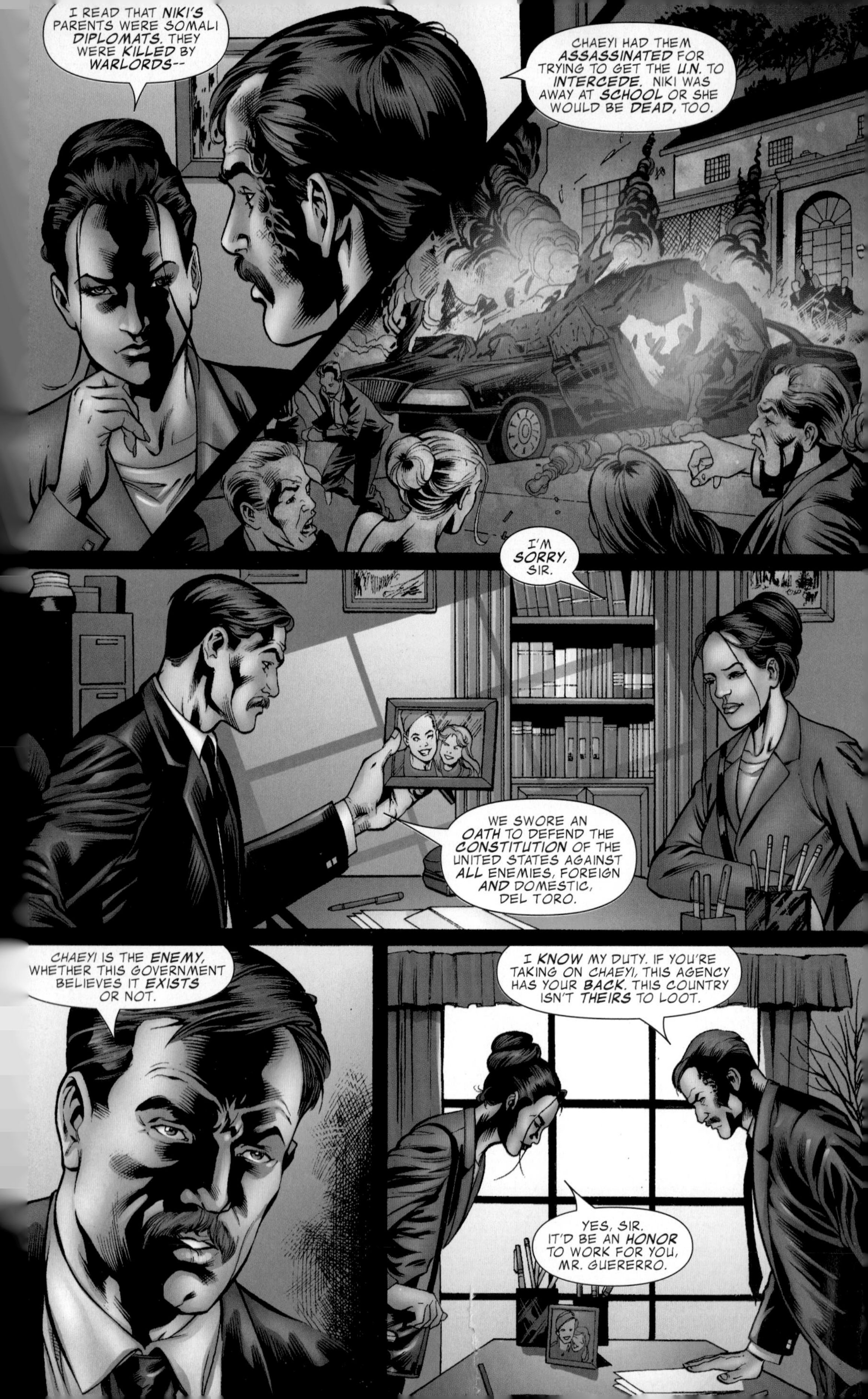
I READ THAT NIKI'S PARENTS WERE SOMALI DIPLOMATS. THEY WERE KILLED BY WARLORDS--
CHAEYI HAD THEM ASSASSINATED FOR TRYING TO GET THE U.N. TO INTERCEDE. NIKI WAS AWAY AT SCHOOL OR SHE WOULD BE DEAD, TOO.
I'M SORRY, SIR.
WE SWORE AN OATH TO DEFEND THE CONSTITUTION OF THE UNITED STATES AGAINST ALL ENEMIES, FOREIGN AND DOMESTIC, DEL TORO.
CHAEYI IS THE ENEMY, WHETHER THIS GOVERNMENT BELIEVES IT EXISTS OR NOT.
I KNOW MY DUTY. IF YOU'RE TAKING ON CHAEYI, THIS AGENCY HAS YOUR BACK. THIS COUNTRY ISN'T THEIRS TO LOOT.
YES, SIR. IT'D BE AN HONOR TO WORK FOR YOU, MR. GUERERRO.

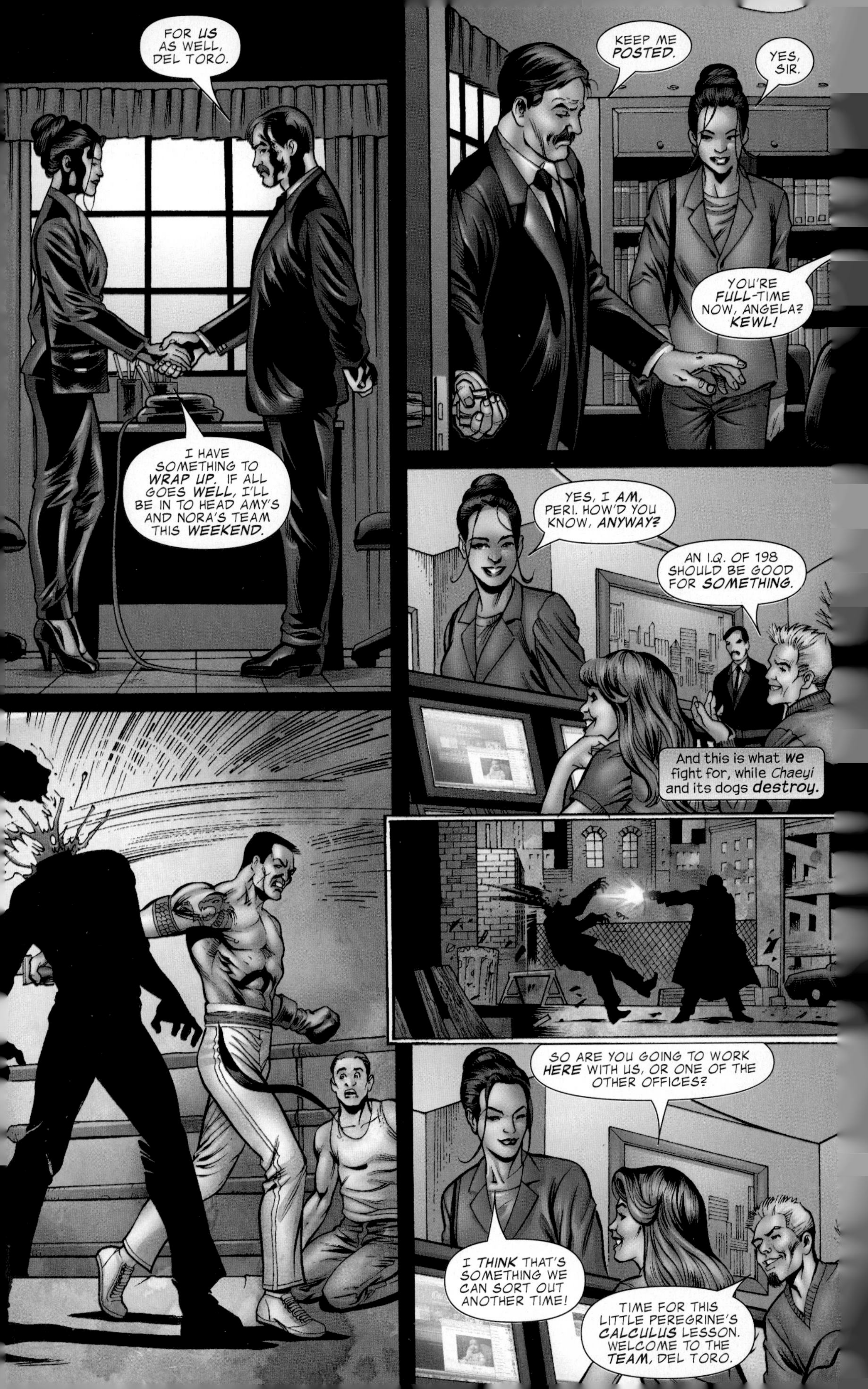

FOR US AS WELL, DEL TORO.
I HAVE SOMETHING TO WRAP UP. IF ALL GOES WELL, I'LL BE IN TO HEAD AMY'S AND NORA'S TEAM THIS WEEKEND.
KEEP ME POSTED.
YES, SIR.
YOU'RE FULL-TIME NOW, ANGELA? KEWL!
YES, I AM, PERI. HOW'D YOU KNOW, ANYWAY?
AN I.Q. OF 198 SHOULD BE GOOD FOR SOMETHING.
And this is what we fight for, while Chaeyi and its dogs destroy.
SO ARE YOU GOING TO WORK HERE WITH US, OR ONE OF THE OTHER OFFICES?
I THINK THAT'S SOMETHING WE CAN SORT OUT ANOTHER TIME!
TIME FOR THIS LITTLE PEREGRINE'S CALCULUS LESSON. WELCOME TO THE TEAM, DEL TORO.

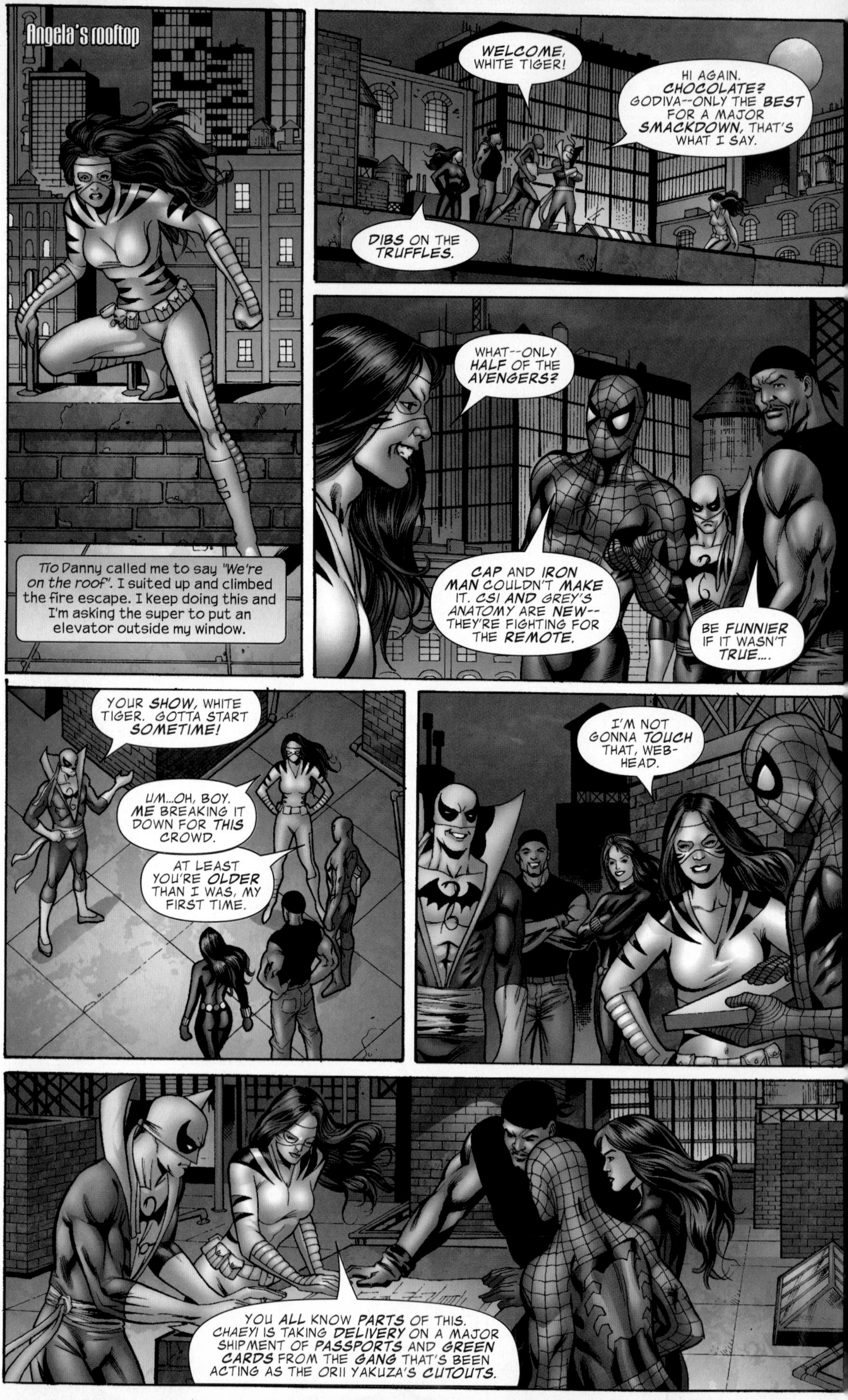
Angela's rooftop
Tío Danny called me to say "We're on the roof". I suited up and climbed the fire escape. I keep doing this and I'm asking the super to put an elevator outside my window.
WELCOME, WHITE TIGER!
HI AGAIN. CHOCOLATE? GODIVA--ONLY THE BEST FOR A MAJOR SMACKDOWN, THAT'S WHAT I SAY.
DIBS ON THE TRUFFLES.
WHAT--ONLY HALF OF THE AVENGERS?
CAP AND IRON MAN COULDN'T MAKE IT. CSI AND GREY'S ANATOMY ARE NEW--THEY'RE FIGHTING FOR THE REMOTE.
BE FUNNIER IF IT WASN'T TRUE....
YOUR SHOW, WHITE TIGER. GOTTA START SOMETIME!
UM...OH, BOY. ME BREAKING IT DOWN FOR THIS CROWD.
AT LEAST YOU'RE OLDER THAN I WAS, MY FIRST TIME.
I'M NOT GONNA TOUCH THAT, WEB-HEAD.
YOU ALL KNOW PARTS OF THIS. CHAEYI IS TAKING DELIVERY ON A MAJOR SHIPMENT OF PASSPORTS AND GREEN CARDS FROM THE GANG THAT'S BEEN ACTING AS THE ORII YAKUZA'S CUTOUTS.

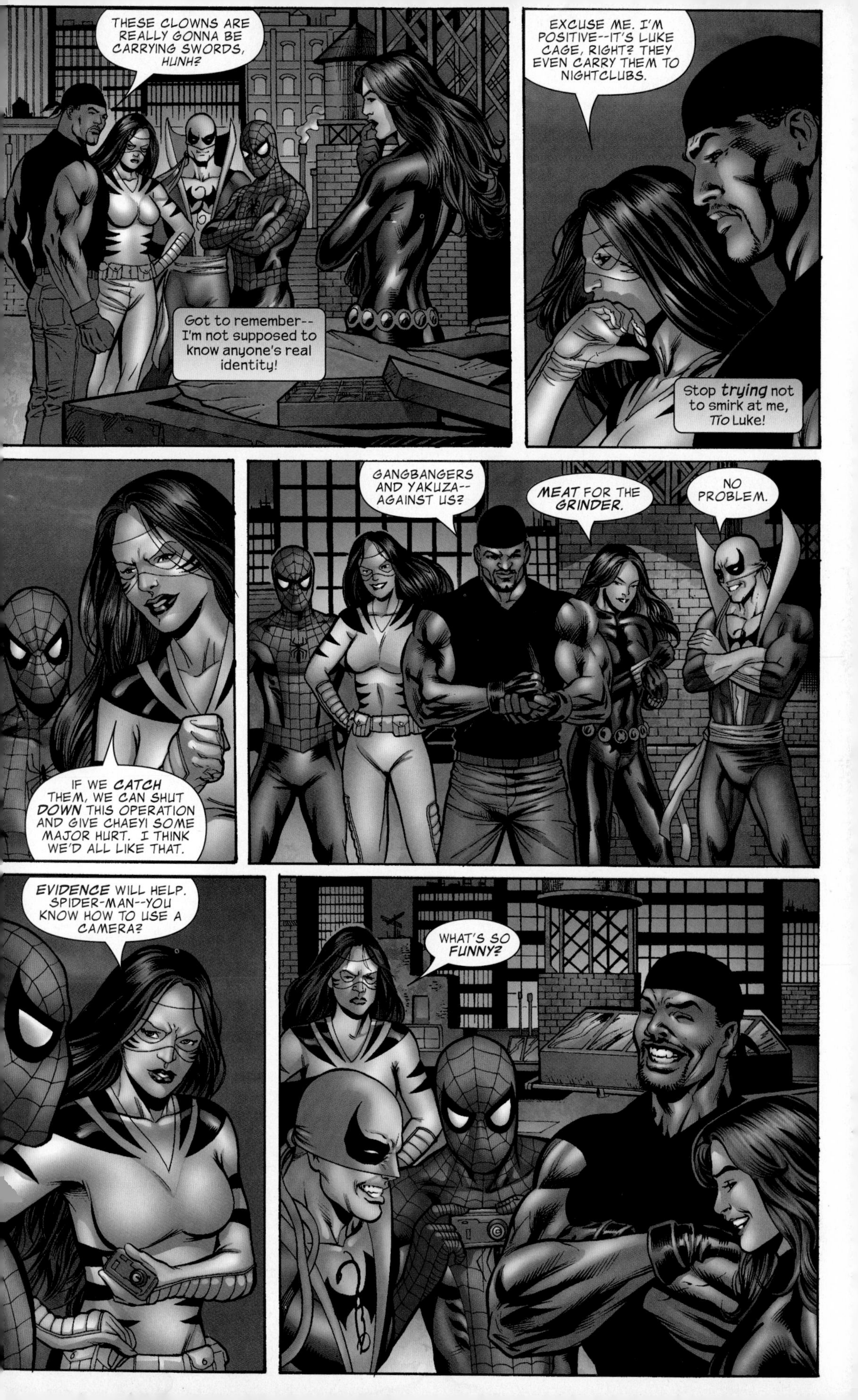
THESE CLOWNS ARE REALLY GONNA BE CARRYING SWORDS, HUNH?
Got to remember-- I'm not supposed to know anyone's real identity!
EXCUSE ME. I'M POSITIVE--IT'S LUKE CAGE, RIGHT? THEY EVEN CARRY THEM TO NIGHTCLUBS.
Stop trying not to smirk at me, Tío Luke!
IF WE CATCH THEM, WE CAN SHUT DOWN THIS OPERATION AND GIVE CHAEYI SOME MAJOR HURT. I THINK WE'D ALL LIKE THAT.
GANGBANGERS AND YAKUZA-- AGAINST US?
MEAT FOR THE GRINDER.
NO PROBLEM.
EVIDENCE WILL HELP. SPIDER-MAN--YOU KNOW HOW TO USE A CAMERA?
WHAT'S SO FUNNY?

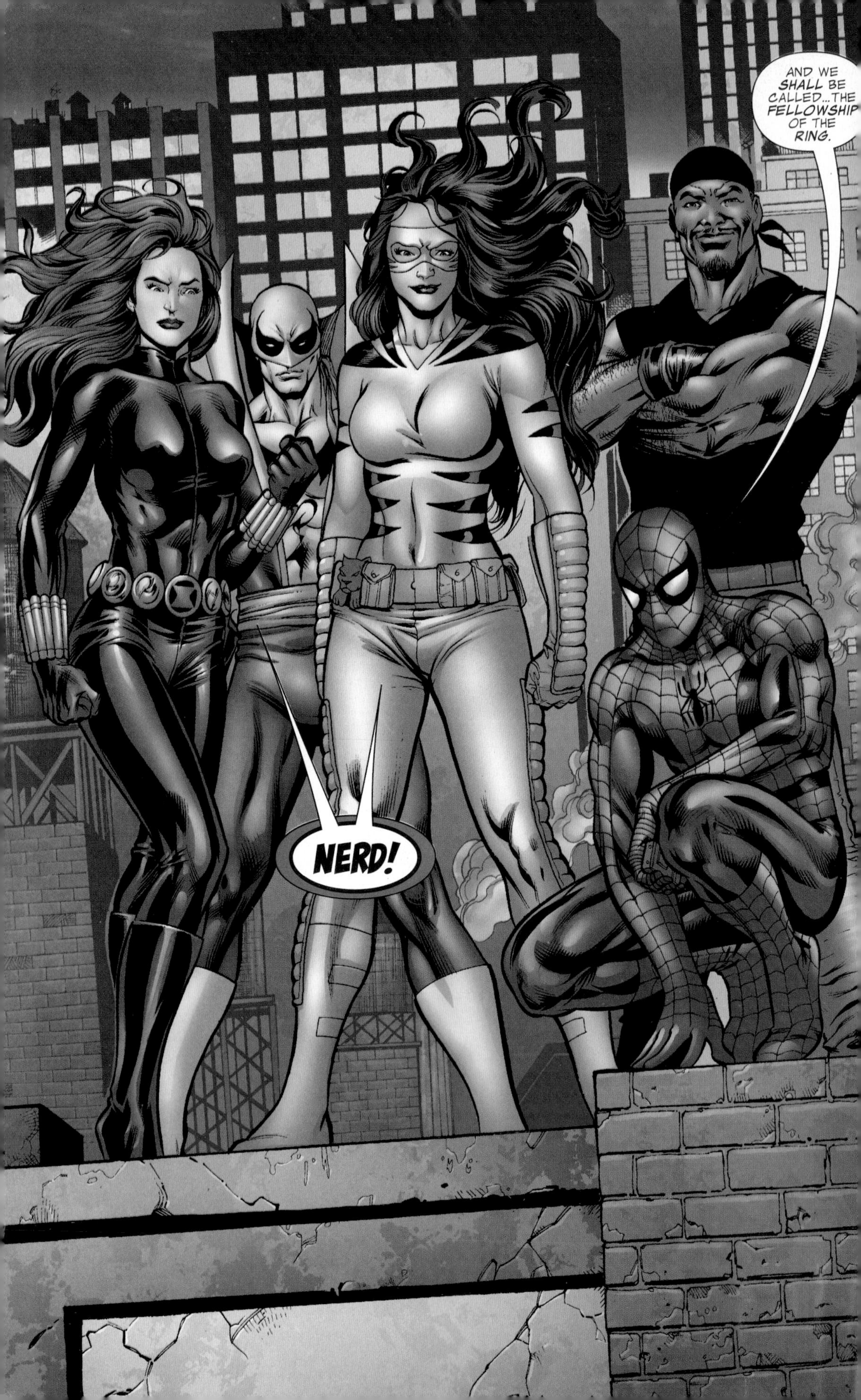
AND WE SHALL BE CALLED... THE FELLOWSHIP OF THE RING.
NERD!

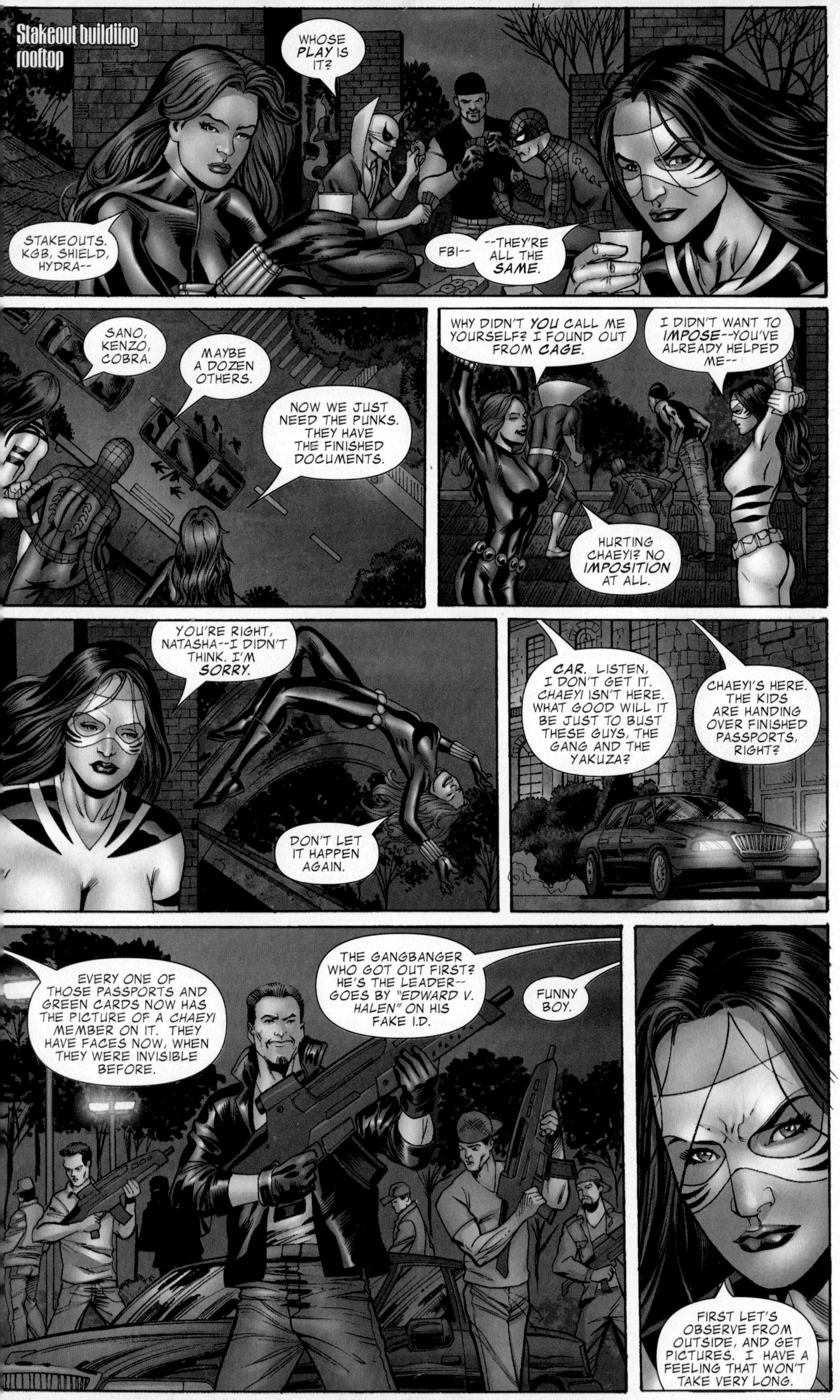
Stakeout building
rooftop
STAKEOUTS. KGB, SHIELD, HYDRA--
WHOSE PLAY IS IT?
FBI--
--THEY'RE ALL THE SAME.
SANO, KENZO, COBRA.
MAYBE A DOZEN OTHERS.
NOW WE JUST NEED THE PUNKS. THEY HAVE THE FINISHED DOCUMENTS.
WHY DIDN'T YOU CALL ME YOURSELF? I FOUND OUT FROM CAGE.
I DIDN'T WANT TO IMPOSE--YOU'VE ALREADY HELPED ME--
HURTING CHAEYI? NO IMPOSITION AT ALL.
YOU'RE RIGHT, NATASHA--I DIDN'T THINK. I'M SORRY.
DON'T LET IT HAPPEN AGAIN.
CAR. LISTEN, I DON'T GET IT. CHAEYI ISN'T HERE. WHAT GOOD WILL IT BE JUST TO BUST THESE GUYS, THE GANG AND THE YAKUZA?
CHAEYI'S HERE. THE KIDS ARE HANDING OVER FINISHED PASSPORTS, RIGHT?
EVERY ONE OF THOSE PASSPORTS AND GREEN CARDS NOW HAS THE PICTURE OF A CHAEYI MEMBER ON IT. THEY HAVE FACES NOW, WHEN THEY WERE INVISIBLE BEFORE.
THE GANGBANGER WHO GOT OUT FIRST? HE'S THE LEADER--GOES BY "EDWARD V. HALEN" ON HIS FAKE I.D.
FUNNY BOY.
FIRST LET'S OBSERVE FROM OUTSIDE, AND GET PICTURES. I HAVE A FEELING THAT WON'T TAKE VERY LONG.

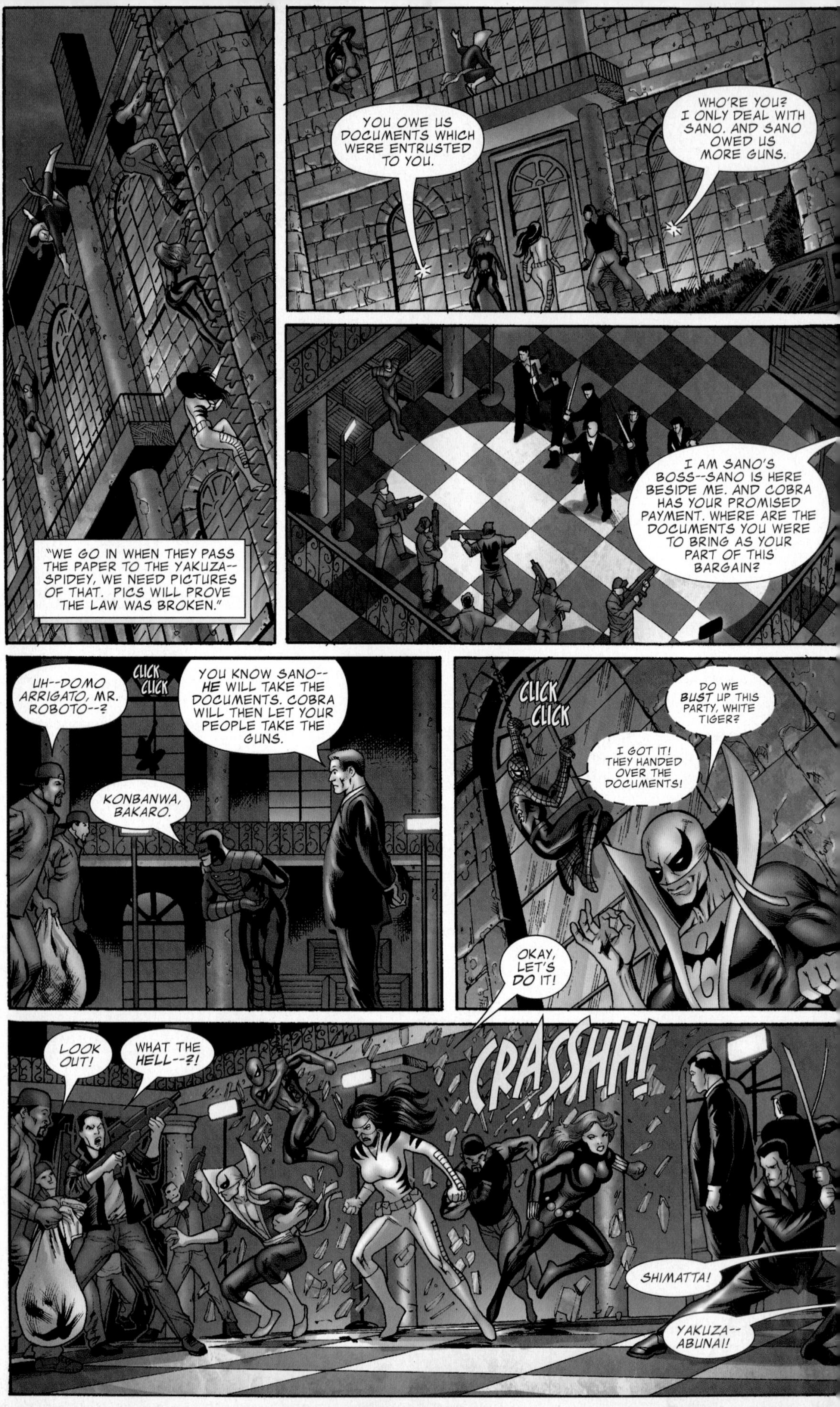
"WE GO IN WHEN THEY PASS THE PAPER TO THE YAKUZA--SPIDEY, WE NEED PICTURES OF THAT. PICS WILL PROVE THE LAW WAS BROKEN."
YOU OWE US DOCUMENTS WHICH WERE ENTRUSTED TO YOU.
WHO'RE YOU? I ONLY DEAL WITH SANO. AND SANO OWED US MORE GUNS.
I AM SANO'S BOSS--SANO IS HERE BESIDE ME. AND COBRA HAS YOUR PROMISED PAYMENT. WHERE ARE THE DOCUMENTS YOU WERE TO BRING AS YOUR PART OF THIS BARGAIN?
UH--DOMO ARRIGATO, MR. ROBOTO--?
CLICK CLICK
YOU KNOW SANO--HE WILL TAKE THE DOCUMENTS. COBRA WILL THEN LET YOUR PEOPLE TAKE THE GUNS.
KONBANWA, BAKARO.
CLICK CLICK
DO WE BUST UP THIS PARTY, WHITE TIGER?
I GOT IT! THEY HANDED OVER THE DOCUMENTS!
OKAY, LET'S DO IT!
LOOK OUT!
WHAT THE HELL--?!
CRASSHH!
SHIMATTA!
YAKUZA--ABUNAI!

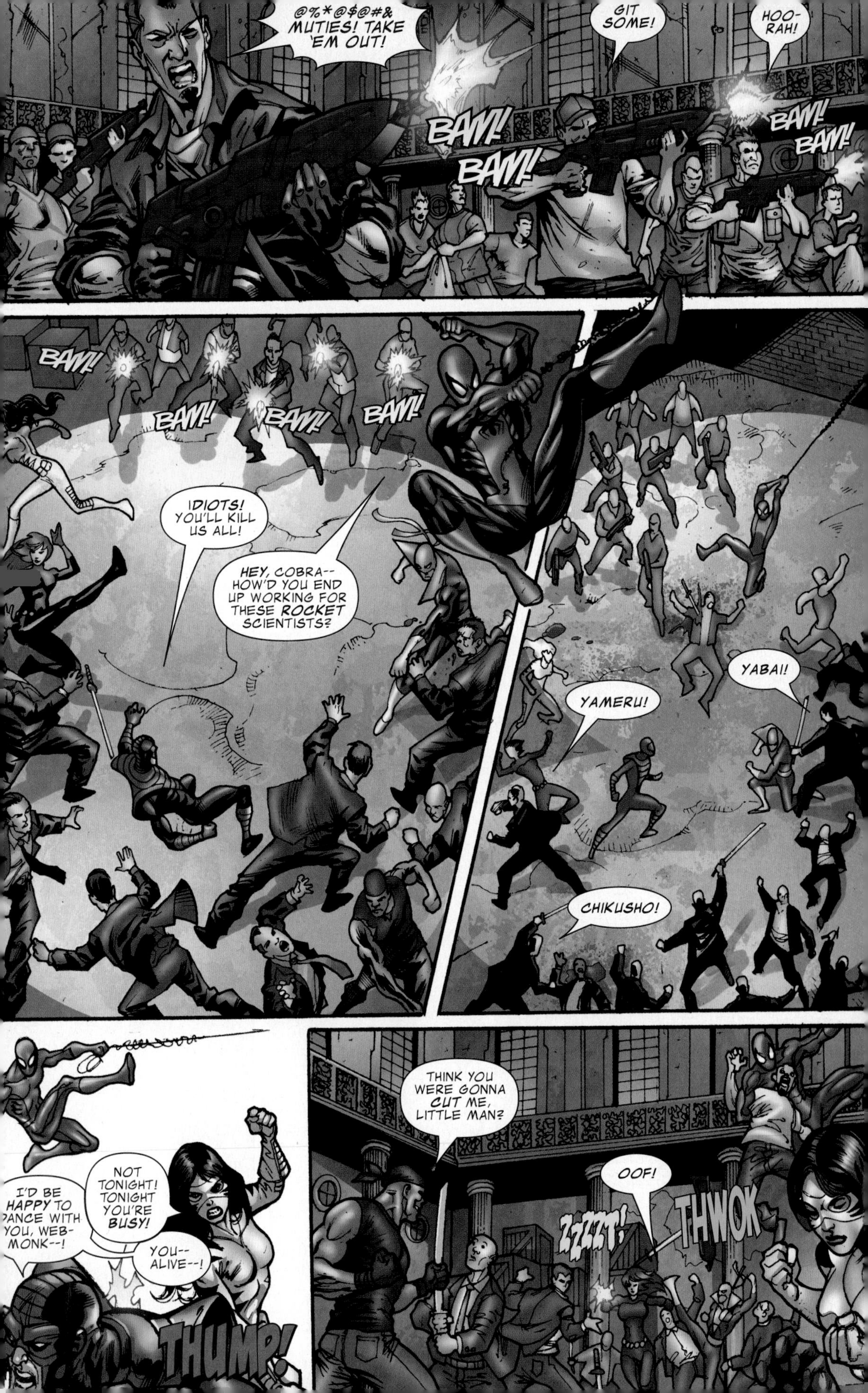
@%*@$@#& MUTIES! TAKE 'EM OUT!
GIT SOME!
HOO-RAH!
BAM!
BAM!
BAM!
BAM!
BAM!
BAM!
BAM!
BAM!
¡IDIOTS! YOU'LL KILL US ALL!
HEY, COBRA-- HOW'D YOU END UP WORKING FOR THESE ROCKET SCIENTISTS?
YAMERU!
YABAI!
CHIKUSHO!
I'D BE HAPPY TO DANCE WITH YOU, WEB-MONK--!
NOT TONIGHT! TONIGHT YOU'RE BUSY!
YOU-- ALIVE--!
THUMP!
THINK YOU WERE GONNA CUT ME, LITTLE MAN?
OOF!
ZZZZT!
THWOK

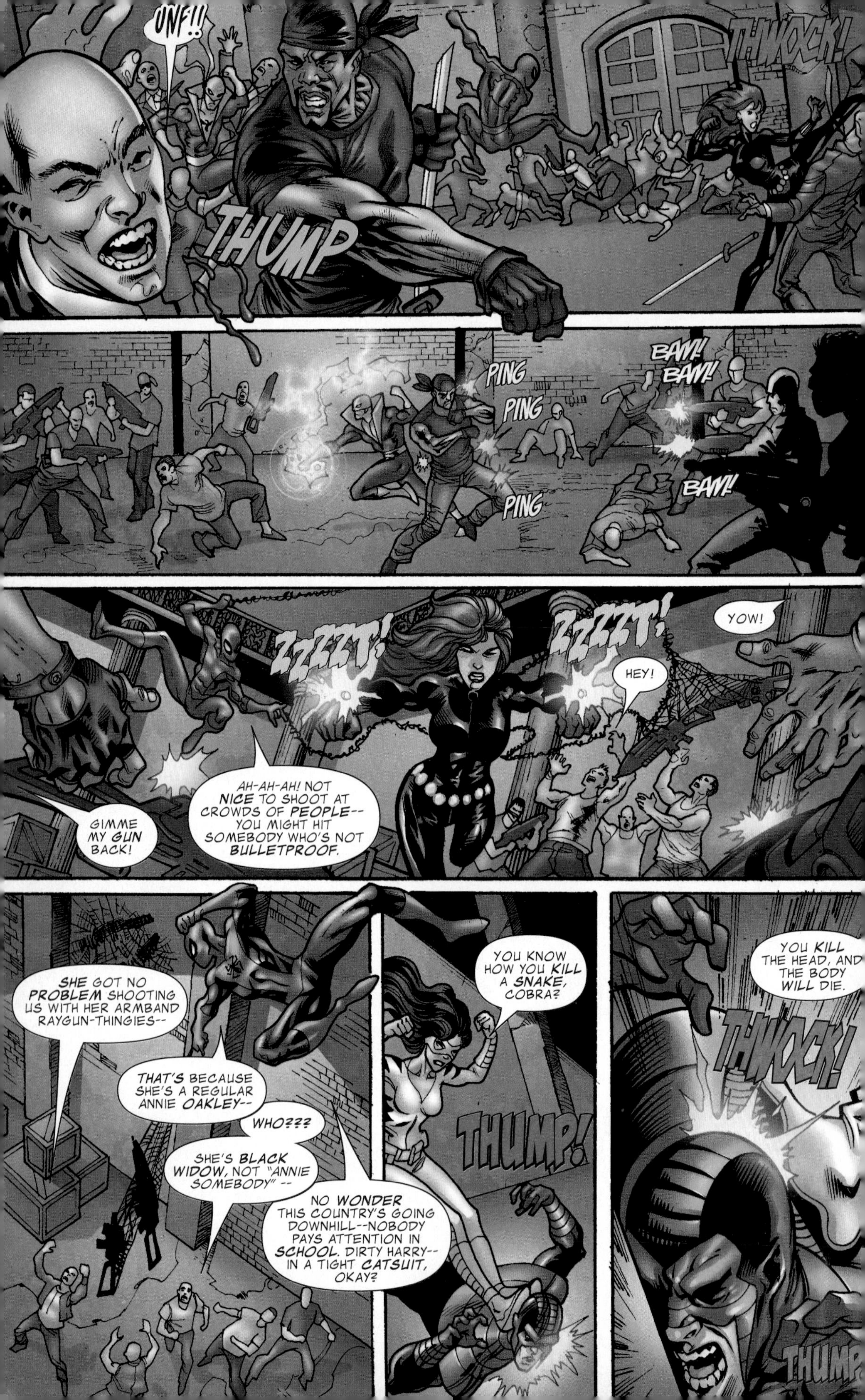
UNF!!
THWOCK!
THUMP
PING
PING
PING
BAM!
BAM!
BAM!
ZZZZT!
ZZZZT!
YOW!
HEY!
AH-AH-AH! NOT NICE TO SHOOT AT CROWDS OF PEOPLE-- YOU MIGHT HIT SOMEBODY WHO'S NOT BULLETPROOF.
GIMME MY GUN BACK!
SHE GOT NO PROBLEM SHOOTING US WITH HER ARMBAND RAYGUN-THINGIES--
THAT'S BECAUSE SHE'S A REGULAR ANNIE OAKLEY--
WHO???
SHE'S BLACK WIDOW, NOT "ANNIE SOMEBODY" --
NO WONDER THIS COUNTRY'S GOING DOWNHILL--NOBODY PAYS ATTENTION IN SCHOOL. DIRTY HARRY-- IN A TIGHT CATSUIT, OKAY?
YOU KNOW HOW YOU KILL A SNAKE, COBRA?
THUMP!
YOU KILL THE HEAD, AND THE BODY WILL DIE.
THWOCK!
THUMP

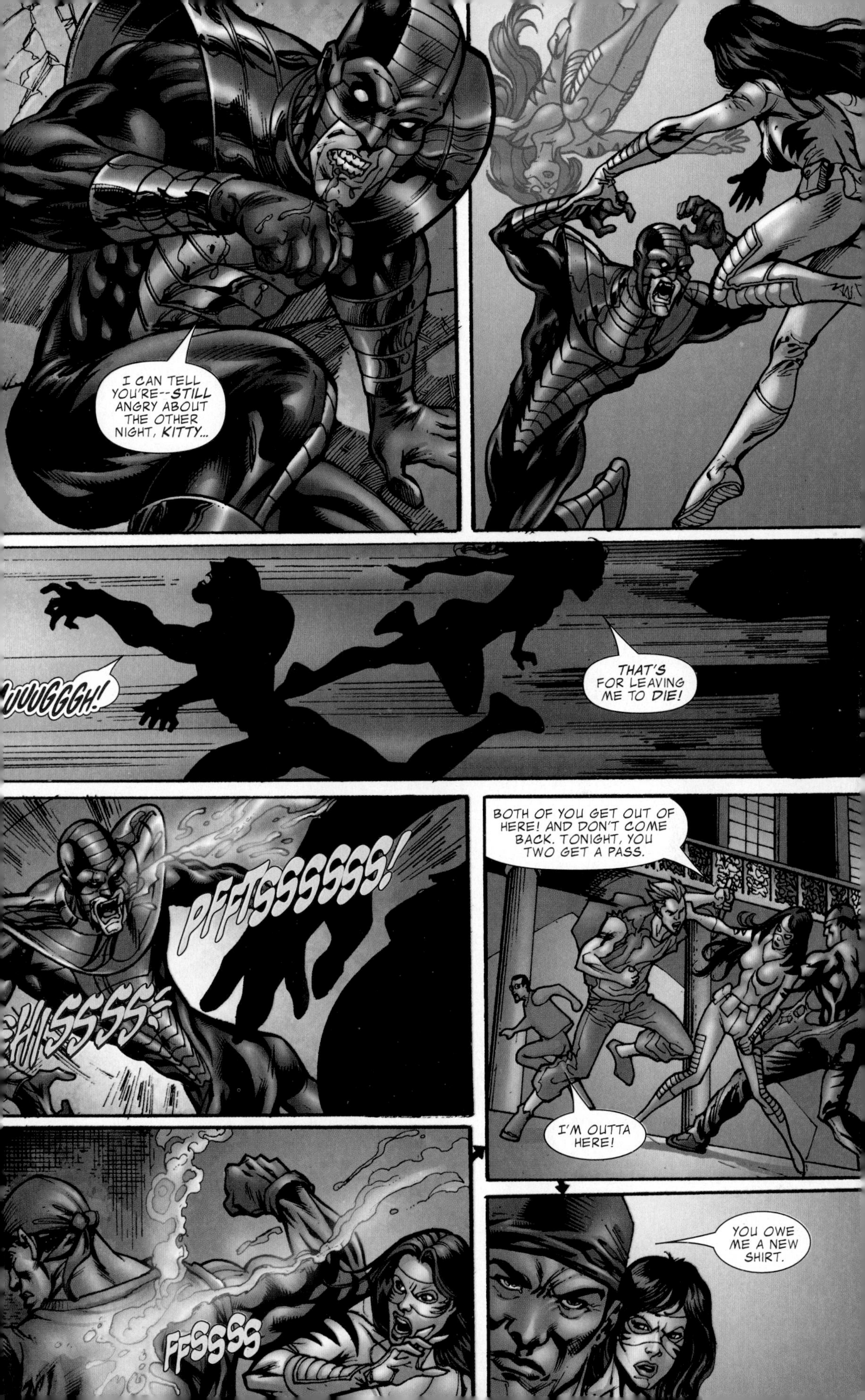
I CAN TELL YOU'RE--STILL ANGRY ABOUT THE OTHER NIGHT, KITTY...
UUUGGGH!
THAT'S FOR LEAVING ME TO DIE!
PFFTSSSSSS!
HISSSS
BOTH OF YOU GET OUT OF HERE! AND DON'T COME BACK. TONIGHT, YOU TWO GET A PASS.
I'M OUTTA HERE!
FFSSSS
YOU OWE ME A NEW SHIRT.

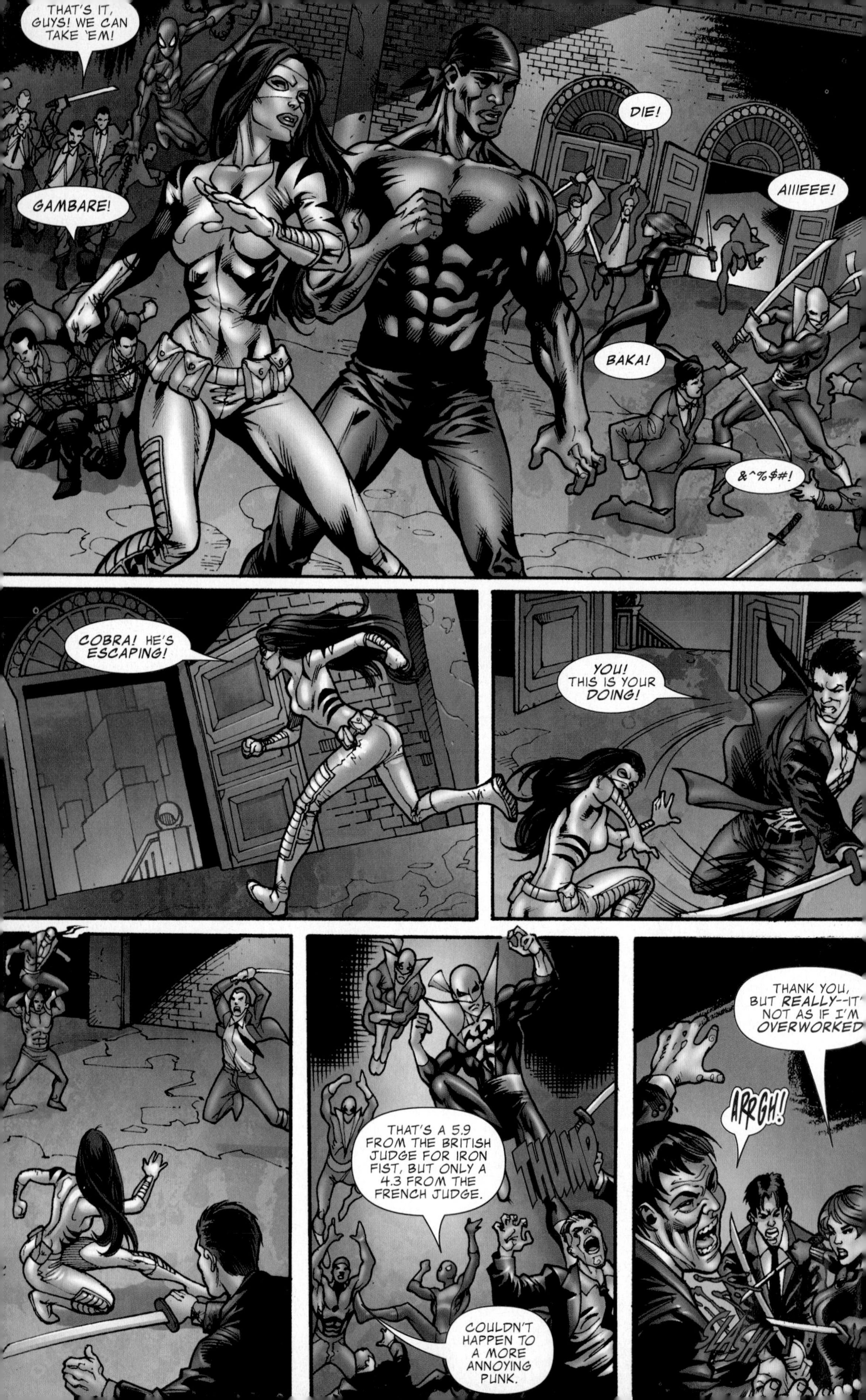

THAT'S IT, GUYS! WE CAN TAKE 'EM!
GAMBARE!
DIE!
AIIIEEE!
BAKA!
&^%$#!
COBRA! HE'S ESCAPING!
YOU! THIS IS YOUR DOING!
THAT'S A 5.9 FROM THE BRITISH JUDGE FOR IRON FIST, BUT ONLY A 4.3 FROM THE FRENCH JUDGE.
THUMP
COULDN'T HAPPEN TO A MORE ANNOYING PUNK.
THANK YOU, BUT REALLY--IT' NOT AS IF I'M OVERWORKED
ARRGH!

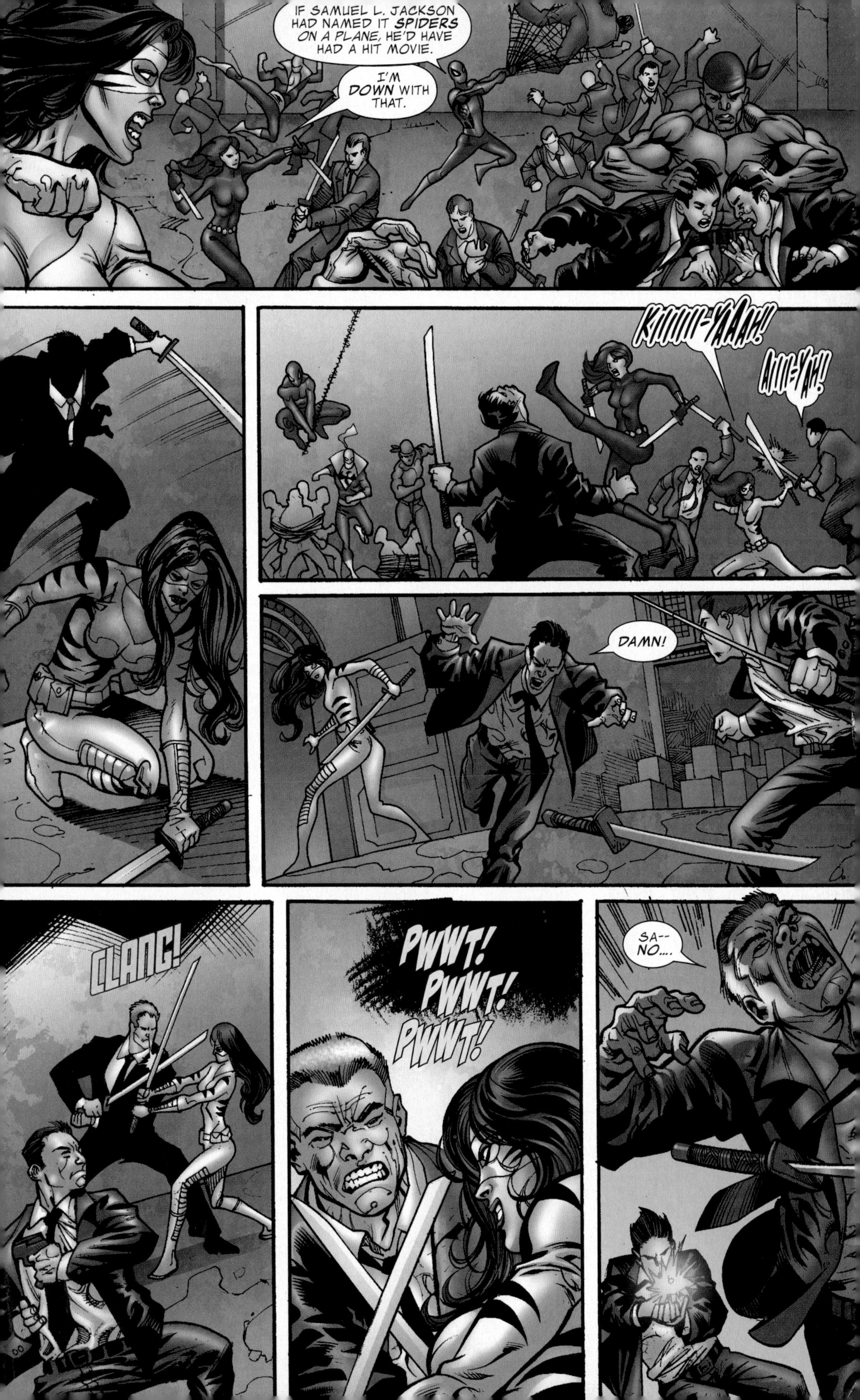
IF SAMUEL L. JACKSON HAD NAMED IT SPIDERS ON A PLANE, HE'D HAVE HAD A HIT MOVIE.
I'M DOWN WITH THAT.
KIIIIII-YAAAH!
AIII-YAH!
DAMN!
CLANG!
PWWT! PWWT! PWWT!
SA-- NO....

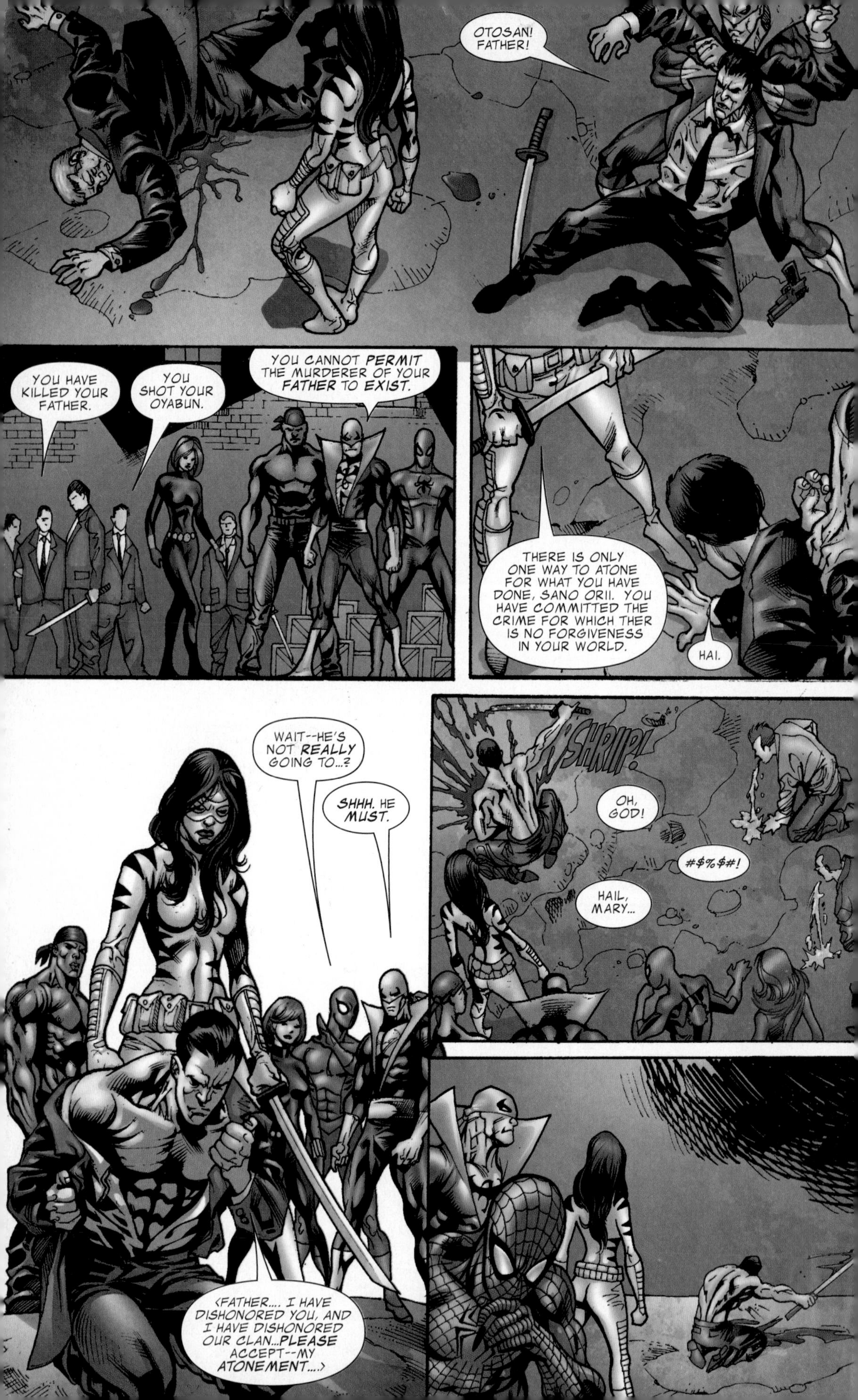
OTOSAN! FATHER!
YOU HAVE KILLED YOUR FATHER.
YOU SHOT YOUR OYABUN.
YOU CANNOT PERMIT THE MURDERER OF YOUR FATHER TO EXIST.
THERE IS ONLY ONE WAY TO ATONE FOR WHAT YOU HAVE DONE, SANO ORII. YOU HAVE COMMITTED THE CRIME FOR WHICH THER IS NO FORGIVENESS IN YOUR WORLD.
HAI.
WAIT--HE'S NOT REALLY GOING TO...?
SHHH. HE MUST.
<FATHER.... I HAVE DISHONORED YOU, AND I HAVE DISHONORED OUR CLAN...PLEASE ACCEPT--MY ATONEMENT....>
SHRIIP!
OH, GOD!
#$%$#!
HAIL, MARY...

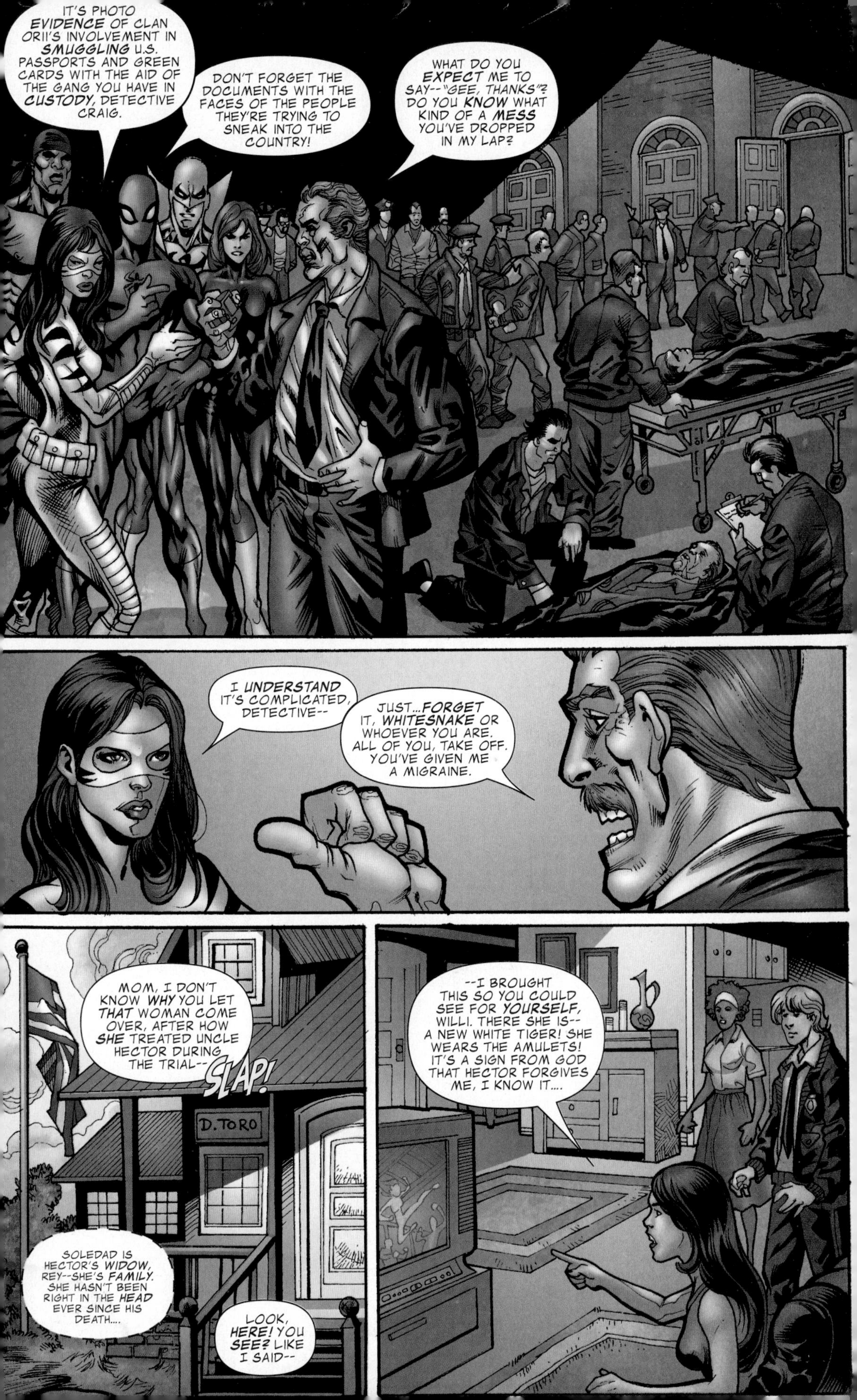
IT'S PHOTO EVIDENCE OF CLAN ORII'S INVOLVEMENT IN SMUGGLING U.S. PASSPORTS AND GREEN CARDS WITH THE AID OF THE GANG YOU HAVE IN CUSTODY, DETECTIVE CRAIG.
DON'T FORGET THE DOCUMENTS WITH THE FACES OF THE PEOPLE THEY'RE TRYING TO SNEAK INTO THE COUNTRY!
WHAT DO YOU EXPECT ME TO SAY--"GEE, THANKS"? DO YOU KNOW WHAT KIND OF A MESS YOU'VE DROPPED IN MY LAP?
I UNDERSTAND IT'S COMPLICATED, DETECTIVE--
JUST...FORGET IT, WHITESNAKE OR WHOEVER YOU ARE. ALL OF YOU, TAKE OFF. YOU'VE GIVEN ME A MIGRAINE.
MOM, I DON'T KNOW WHY YOU LET THAT WOMAN COME OVER, AFTER HOW SHE TREATED UNCLE HECTOR DURING THE TRIAL--
SLAP!
D. TORO
SOLEDAD IS HECTOR'S WIDOW, REY--SHE'S FAMILY. SHE HASN'T BEEN RIGHT IN THE HEAD EVER SINCE HIS DEATH....
LOOK, HERE! YOU SEE? LIKE I SAID--
--I BROUGHT THIS SO YOU COULD SEE FOR YOURSELF, WILLI. THERE SHE IS--A NEW WHITE TIGER! SHE WEARS THE AMULETS! IT'S A SIGN FROM GOD THAT HECTOR FORGIVES ME, I KNOW IT....

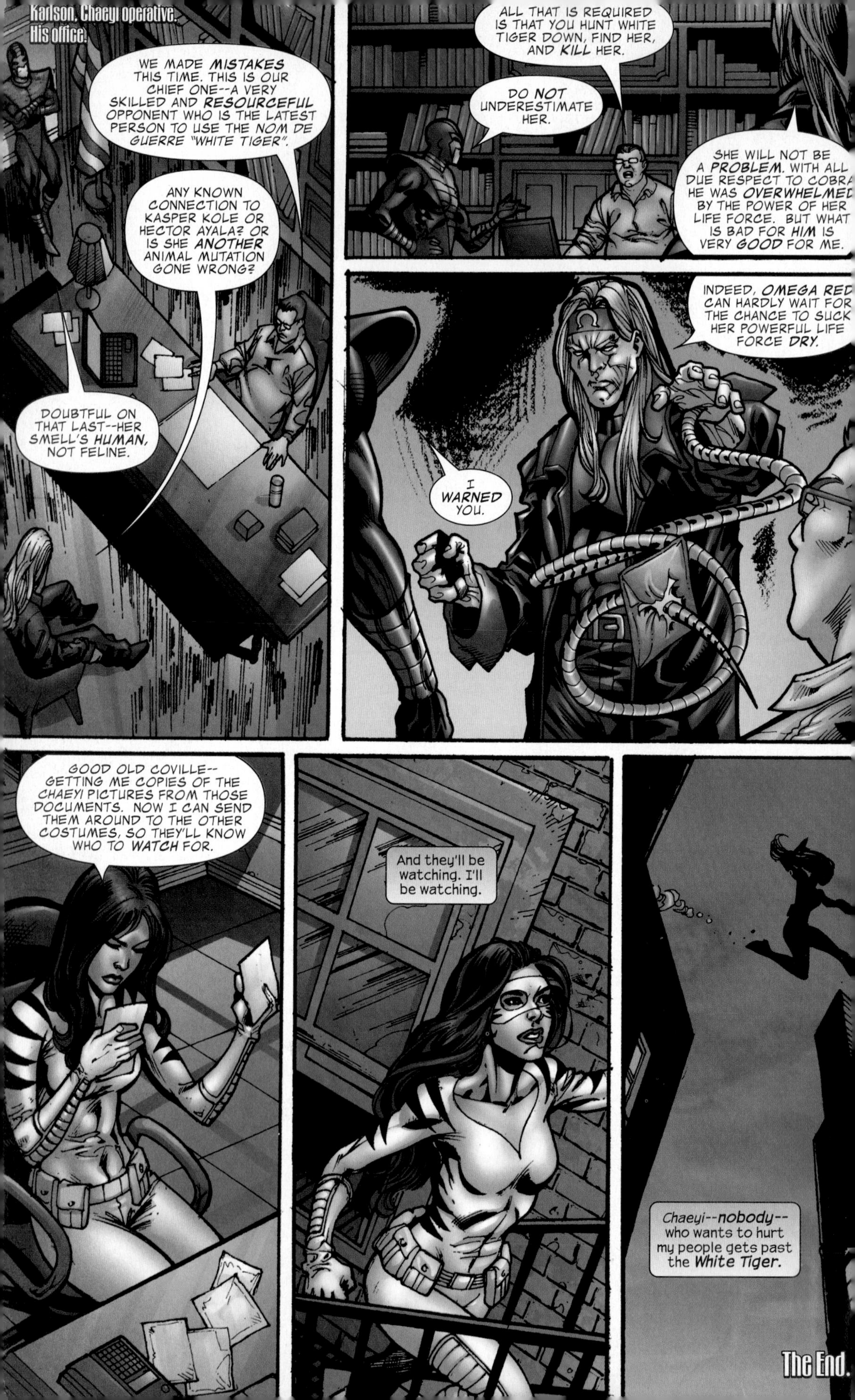
Karlson, Chaeyi operative.
His office.
WE MADE MISTAKES THIS TIME. THIS IS OUR CHIEF ONE--A VERY SKILLED AND RESOURCEFUL OPPONENT WHO IS THE LATEST PERSON TO USE THE NOM DE GUERRE "WHITE TIGER".
ANY KNOWN CONNECTION TO KASPER KOLE OR HECTOR AYALA? OR IS SHE ANOTHER ANIMAL MUTATION GONE WRONG?
DOUBTFUL ON THAT LAST--HER SMELL'S HUMAN, NOT FELINE.
ALL THAT IS REQUIRED IS THAT YOU HUNT WHITE TIGER DOWN, FIND HER, AND KILL HER.
DO NOT UNDERESTIMATE HER.
SHE WILL NOT BE A PROBLEM. WITH ALL DUE RESPECT TO COBRA HE WAS OVERWHELMED BY THE POWER OF HER LIFE FORCE. BUT WHAT IS BAD FOR HIM IS VERY GOOD FOR ME.
INDEED, OMEGA RED CAN HARDLY WAIT FOR THE CHANCE TO SUCK HER POWERFUL LIFE FORCE DRY.
I WARNED YOU.
GOOD OLD COVILLE--GETTING ME COPIES OF THE CHAEYI PICTURES FROM THOSE DOCUMENTS. NOW I CAN SEND THEM AROUND TO THE OTHER COSTUMES, SO THEY'LL KNOW WHO TO WATCH FOR.
And they'll be watching. I'll be watching.
Chaeyi--nobody--who wants to hurt my people gets past the White Tiger.
The End.

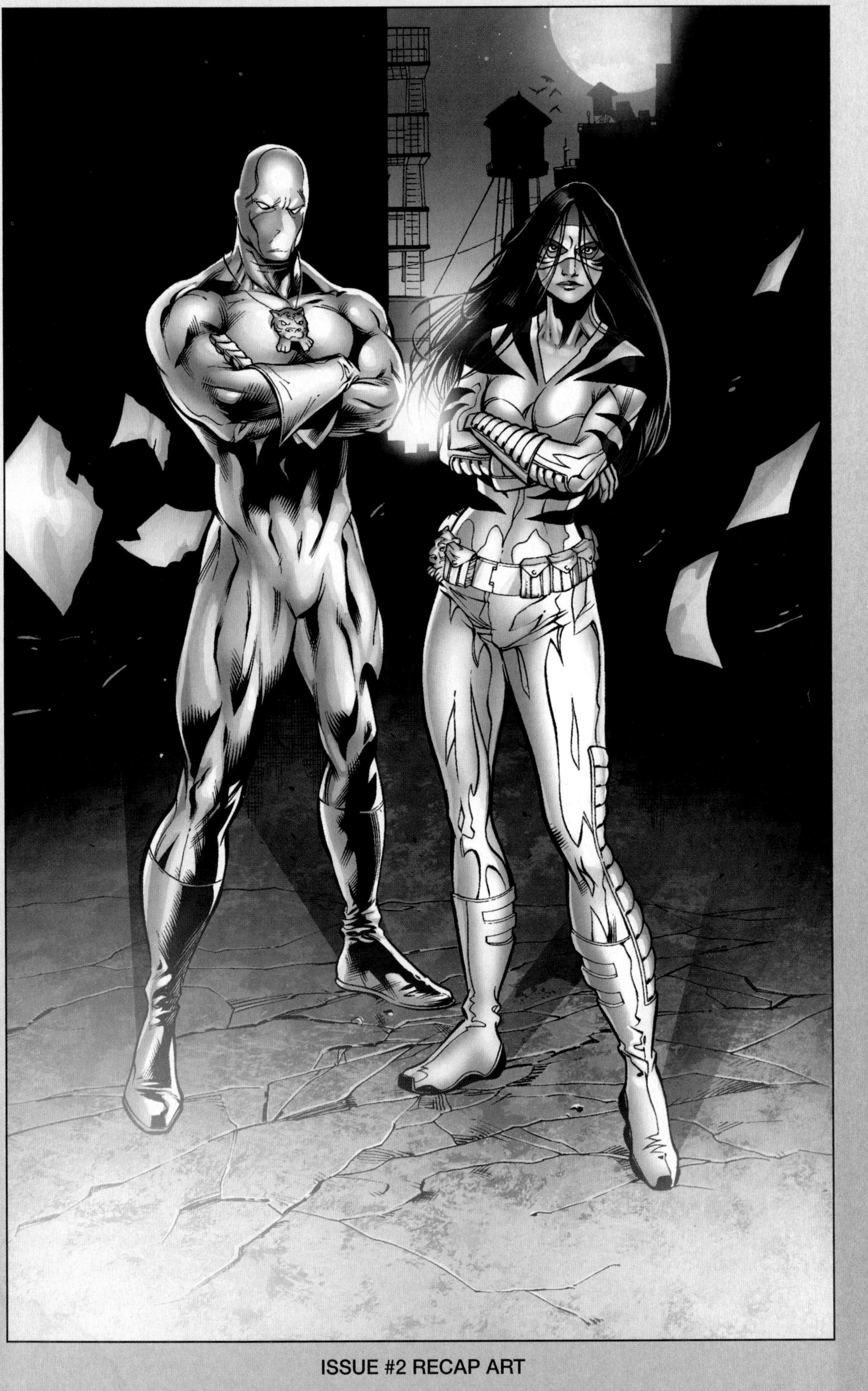

ISSUE #2 RECAP ART

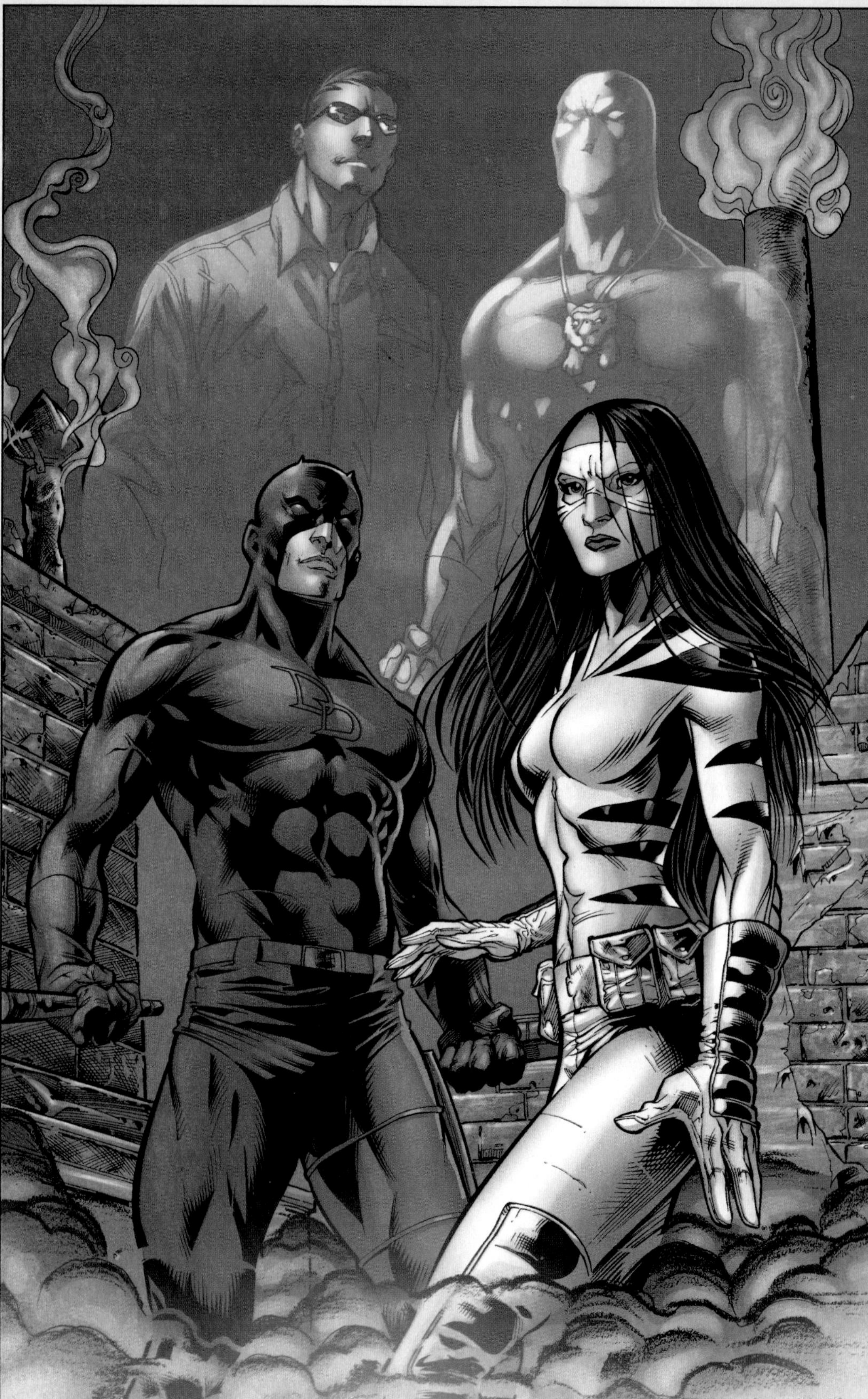

ISSUE #3 RECAP ART

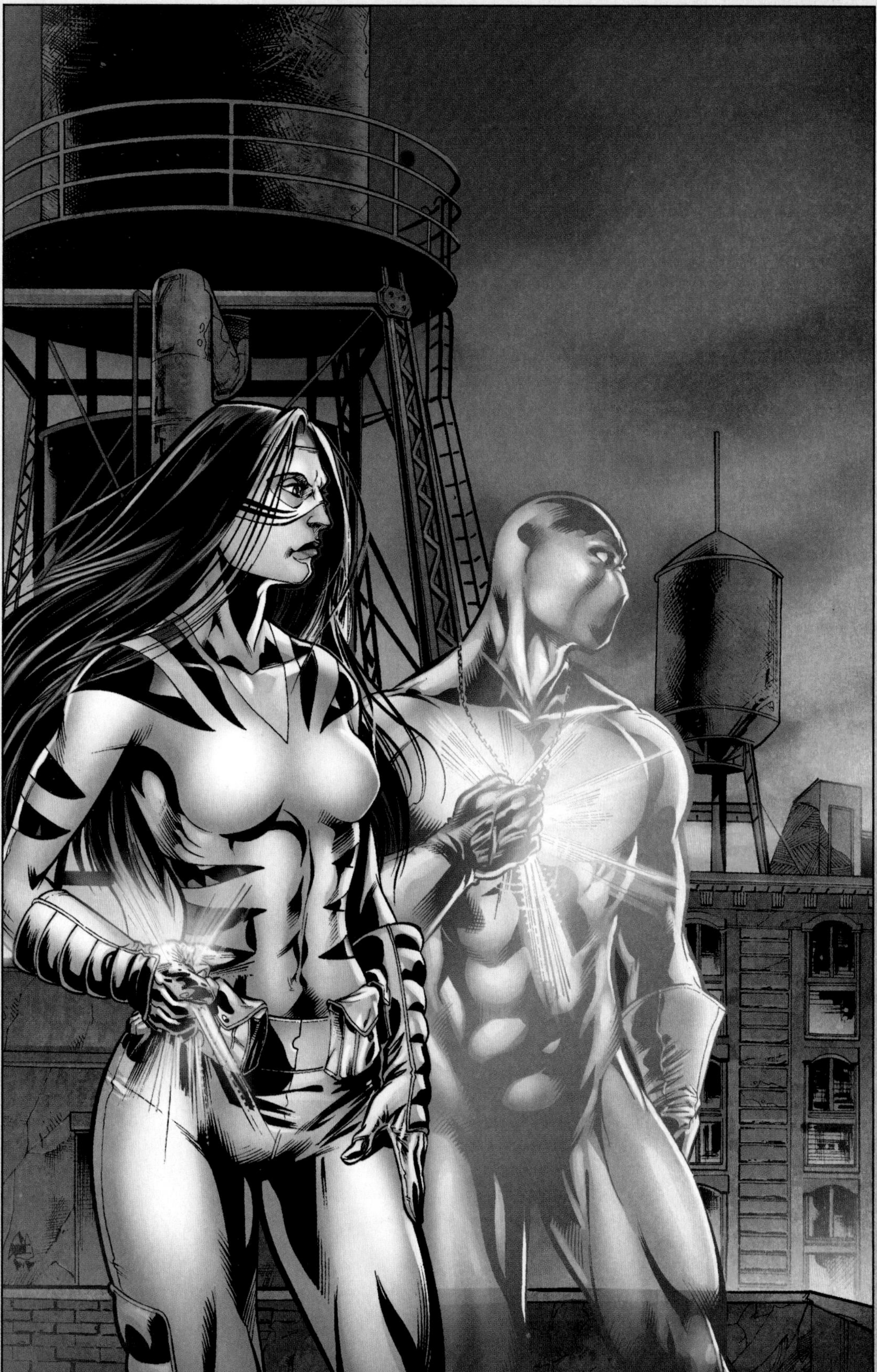

ISSUE #4 RECAP ART

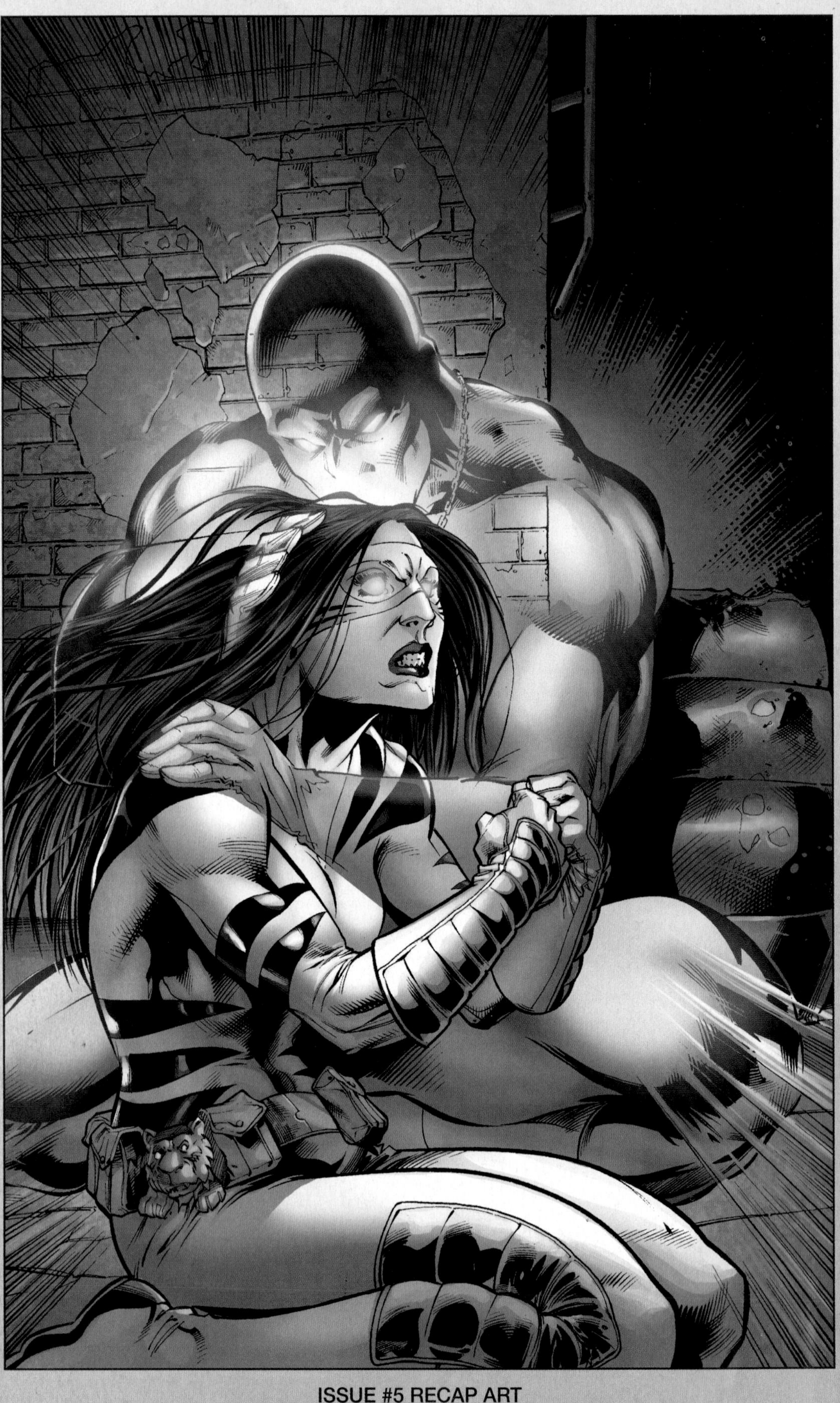

ISSUE #5 RECAP ART

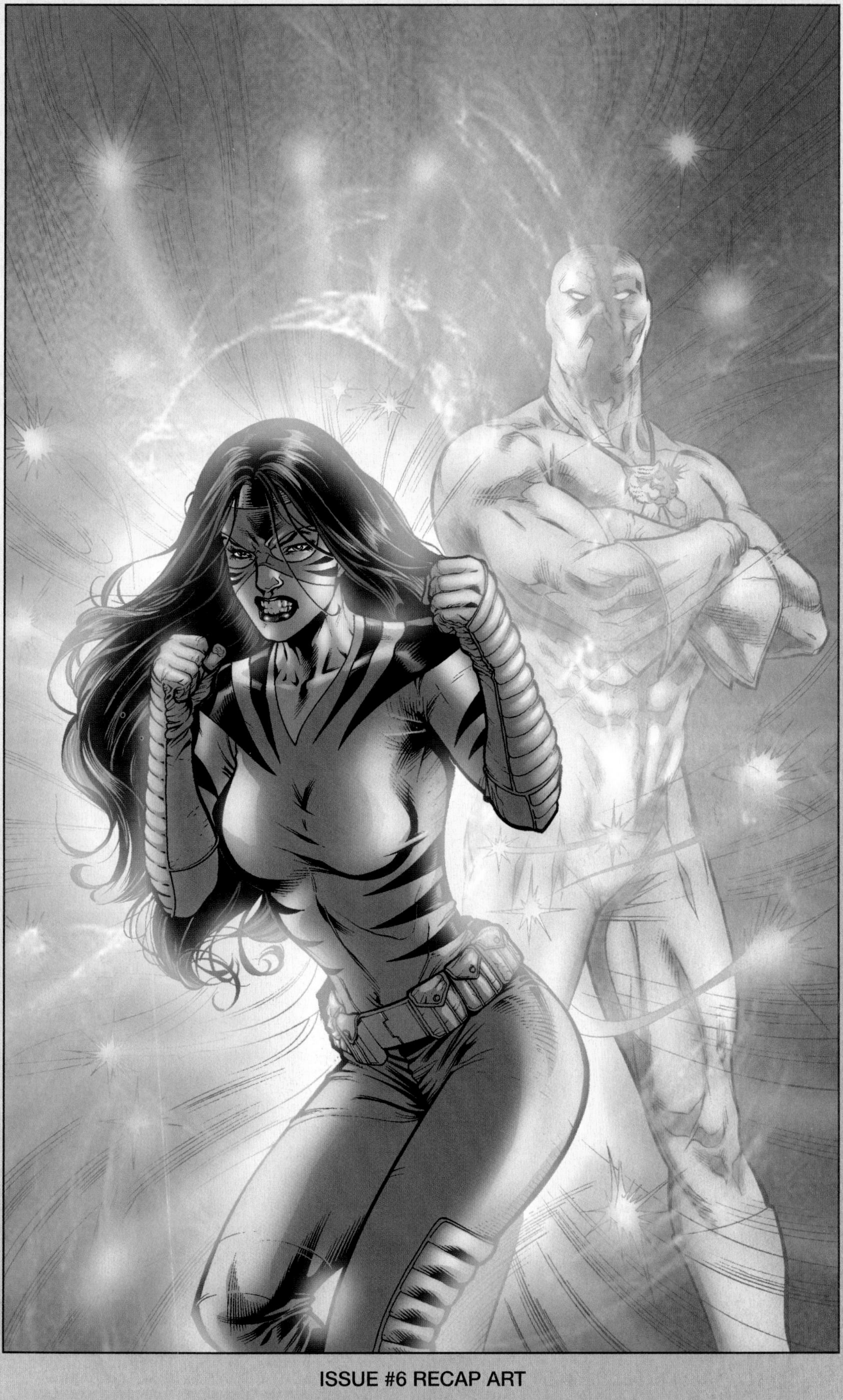

ISSUE #6 RECAP ART

WHITE TIGER

REAL NAME: Angela Del Toro
KNOWN ALIASES: La Tigresa Blanca
IDENTITY: Secret
OCCUPATION: Adventurer, former FBI agent
CITIZENSHIP: U.S.A.
PLACE OF BIRTH: Unrevealed
KNOWN RELATIVES: Awilda Ayala-Del Toro (mother), Filippo Ayala (uncle, deceased), Hector Ayala (White Tiger, uncle, deceased), Mrs. Ayala (aunt), Maria Ayala (grandmother, deceased), Nestor Ayala (grandfather, deceased)
GROUP AFFILIATION: Formerly FBI
EDUCATION: FBI training, police academy graduate
FIRST APPEARANCE: Daredevil Vol. 2 # 58 (2004)

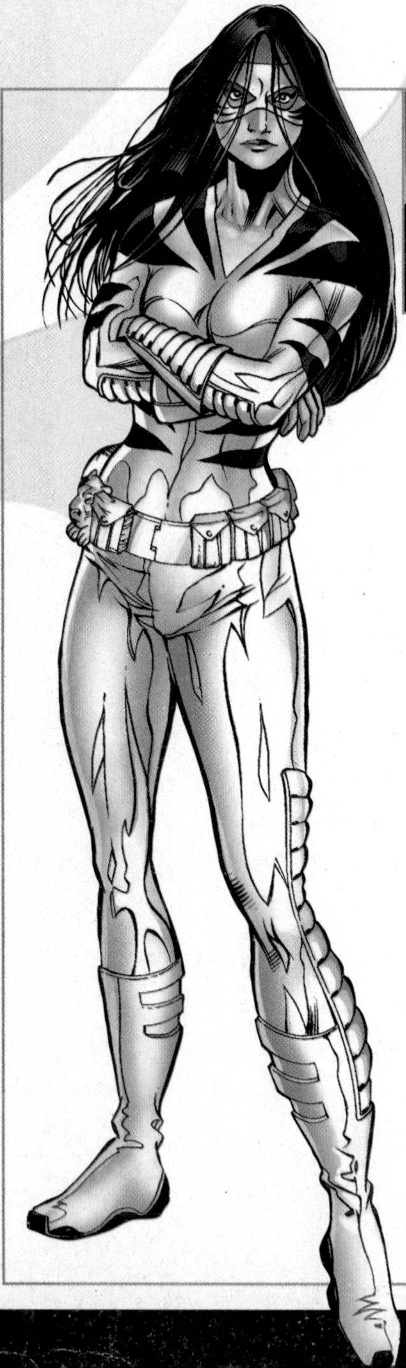

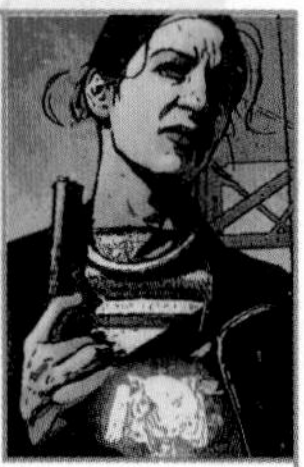

HISTORY: Angela Del Toro is the heir to a heroic legacy that began with the Jade Tiger, a long-lost enchanted statue from the fabled kingdom of K'un-Lun. The statue's paws and head resurfaced in America, where the Sons of the Tiger wore them as amulets that enhanced their martial arts prowess. When the Sons disbanded, their discarded amulets were discovered by Angela's uncle, the young Hector Ayala, who transformed into the superhuman White Tiger through their power. In this guise, Ayala fought foes such as the Corporation crime cartel and teamed with heroes such as Daredevil and Spider-Man. After the Tiger's secret identity was exposed, megalomaniac Gideon Mace slaughtered the Ayala family and nearly killed Hector, who decided to retire. His amulets passed through other hands over the years, but eventually found their way back to him. Going back into action as the White Tiger, Hector was framed for murder and convicted despite the efforts of his lawyer, Matt Murdock. Ayala was shot dead trying to escape, shortly before evidence emerged that belatedly proved his innocence.

Murdock himself had recently been "outed" as the masked crimefighter Daredevil. Trying to understand super heroes in general and her late uncle in particular, Angela – now a Federal Agent—volunteered to participate in the ongoing FBI investigation of Murdock; however, when Hector's amulets were handed down to her, an overwhelmed Angela asked Murdock to help her decide what to do with them. Knowing the terrible cost of the vigilante lifestyle – and having seen her own partner, Agent Harold Driver, killed during the Daredevil investigation – Angela wanted to know why anyone would ever play super hero. She told Murdock she was willing to quit the FBI and abandon her case if he could answer her questions. Murdock challenged her to scale St. Catherine's Cathedral, then engaged her in rooftop combat as Daredevil. Convinced of her ability, Murdock presented Angela with a final lesson by leading her to a robbery in progress. Subduing the robbers single-handedly, a proud Angela was touched by the awestruck gratitude of the shopkeeper she had rescued, and she finally began to understand her new calling. Shortly thereafter, Del Toro rescued Murdock from ex-crimelord Alexander Bont and his reluctant henchman Gladiator (Melvin Potter), making her mark as the new White Tiger.

HEIGHT: 5'8"
WEIGHT: 157 lbs.
EYES: Brown
HAIR: Brown

SUPERHUMAN POWERS: The White Tiger amulets augment Angela's strength, speed, stamina, durability, agility and reflexes to slightly superhuman levels, and also endow her with formidable martial arts skills.

PARAPHERNALIA: The White Tiger wears three mystical, glowing jade amulets shaped like a tiger's head and paws, which enhance her physical abilities and endow her with phenomenal martial arts skills.

POWER GRID	1 2 3 4 5 6 7
INTELLIGENCE	2
STRENGTH	3
SPEED	3
DURABILITY	3
ENERGY PROJECTION	1
FIGHTING SKILLS	5

Art by Phil Briones with Alex Maleev (inset); Text by Sean McQuaid